MORAL AUTHORITARIANISM

HAWAI'I STUDIES ON KOREA

Moral Authoritarianism

Neighborhood Associations in the Three Koreas, 1931–1972

SHINYOUNG KWON

University of Hawai'i Press, Honolulu
and
Center for Korean Studies, University of Hawai'i

First printed 2024

Library of Congress Cataloging-in-Publication Data

Names: Kwon, Shinyoung, author.
Title: Moral authoritarianism : neighborhood associations in the three
  Koreas, 1931–1972 / Shinyoung Kwon.
Other titles: Hawai'i studies on Korea.
Description: Honolulu : University of Hawai'i Press, [2023] | Series:
  Hawai'i studies on Korea | Includes bibliographical references and
  index.
Identifiers: LCCN 2023029708 (print) | LCCN 2023029709 (ebook) | ISBN
  9780824895105 (hardback) | ISBN 9780824896232 (trade paperback) | ISBN
  9780824896218 (epub) | ISBN 9780824896225 (kindle edition) | ISBN
  9780824896201 (pdf)
Subjects: LCSH: Neighborhood government—Korea—History—20th century. |
  Citizens' associations—Korea—History—20th century. | State-local
  relations—Korea—History—20th century. |
  Authoritarianism—Korea—History—20th century. | Korea—History—20th
  century.
Classification: LCC JS7392 .K88 2023 (print) | LCC JS7392 (ebook) | DDC
  307.3/362095190904—dc23/eng/20230703
LC record available at https://lccn.loc.gov/2023029708
LC ebook record available at https://lccn.loc.gov/2023029709

 The Center for Korean Studies was established in 1972 to coordinate and develop resources for the study of Korea at the University of Hawai'i. Reflecting the diversity of the academic disciplines represented by affiliated members of the university faculty, the Center seeks especially to promote interdisciplinary and intercultural studies. Hawai'i Studies on Korea, published jointly by the Center and the University of Hawai'i Press, offers a forum for research in the social sciences and humanities pertaining to Korea and its people.

Cover illustrations: (Left) The South Korean leaflet against North Korea, describing North Korea as a puppet of the Soviets and socialist policies. (Right) The North Korean leaflet again South Korea, describing that South Korea failed to eliminate the colonial remnants and depended on the U.S. Courtesy of The U.S. National Archives and Records Administration

Cover design by Aaron Lee

For Adam and Luke

CONTENTS

TABLES AND ILLUSTRATIONS

TABLES

ILLUSTRATIONS

ACKNOWLEDGMENTS

Writing an acknowledgment made me think about the history of this book, which took over a decade, while giving a sense that the completion is near. This project originates from my childhood experience that elementary school students were mobilized for weeding work, saving programs, and street cleaning in the mid-1980s of South Korea. In transforming my curiosity into academic subjects, I am tremendously indebted to my demanding academic adviser Bruce Cumings. When I had almost made up my mind about focusing on wartime colonial Korea, he urged me to do a periodical extension to postcolonial South Korea. His demand did not stop there. At the dissertation defense, he insisted that socialist North Korean sections should be included in a future book manuscript. This book would never be in its current form without his step-by-step advice under his rigorous scholarship.

I have relied on the academic guidance of many scholars to build up ideas at various stages and shape this book. Susan Burns taught me modern Japanese history and welcomed my questions. Kyeong-Hee Choi expanded my intellectual horizons to gender studies. Pranjit Duara inspired me to think of the East Asian context. Comments of the late Pang Ki-jung were valuable guides to war and colonialism. Kim Sŏng-bo permitted me to attend his seminar on North Korea at Yonsei University.

I have benefited from discussions with my intellectual companions. Hyun Suk Park always found time to read my chapters and to talk about my questions through the years. Tomoko Seto and Fei-Hsien Wang added Japanese and Chinese contexts, which helped me to bear comparative perspectives in mind. I am also grateful to Suzy Kim, Yoon Sun

Yang, and Ingu Hwang for their insightful comments. The meetings with anthropologist Poornima Paidipty were always fruitful.

The course of researching and writing this book owes much to financial support. Let me begin by thanking the generous scholarship of the University of Chicago, which gave me room to study without distraction. The travel grant of the Center for East Asian Studies of the University of Chicago provided initial research support. The Korea Foundation Graduate Studies Fellowship and the Korea Foundation Postdoctoral Fellowship at the University of Cambridge made dissertation writing and further research possible.

In addition, my special thanks go to those who helped with my archival research. Staff in the National Archives of South Korea kindly gave instructions every time I visited. Librarians in the Center on North Korea, an institution under the Ministry of Unification, helped me to photocopy North Korean newspapers. The staff of the Yonsei University library provided access to rare periodicals. Kim Jiyoung, a librarian at the University of Chicago, secured all books I requested. I also appreciate Cheehyung Harrison Kim and Masako Ikeda of the University of Hawai'i Press for their professionalism in the publication process.

I also would like to extend my thanks to my friends in Cambridge in the United Kingdom, Wai Tchang, Miriam Nathoo, Rachael Fenner, Begum Yazicioglu, Rita Vanharanta, and Uma Phillips. Their friendship and encouragement gave me huge comfort throughout the solitary writing process.

Finally, I thank my family for their love and patience. My husband Michael Shin gave me productive comments. My sons, Adam and Luke, frequently asked about my progress, which was a pleasant stimulus to me. There is no way to express my gratitude to my parents, Youngun Kwon and Junghee Kim. They not only sustained my spirits but also spent considerable time taking care of the boys. Their dedication deserves all credit in this book.

ABBREVIATIONS

CPKI	Committee for the Preparation of Korean Independence
DNUF	Democratic National United Front
IRAA	Imperial Rule Assistance Association
KPG	Korean Provisional Government
NA	Neighborhood Association
NCU	National Conference for Unification
NKPC	North Korean People's Committee
NKPPC	North Korean Provisional People's Committee
NSA	National Security Act
NSRRKI	National Society for the Rapid Realization of Korean Independence
PC	People's Committee
SCA	Soviet Civil Administration
SCI	Special Committee for Investigation
SPA	Supreme People's Assembly
UNTCOK	United Nations Temporary Commission on Korea
USAFIK	United States Armed Forces in Korea
USAMGIK	US Army Military Government in Korea

INTRODUCTION

On October 12, 1950, one year before being killed during a political skirmish, Kim Sŏng-ch'il, a young historian residing on the outskirts of Seoul, wrote an entry in his diary reflecting on the country's recent tumultuous history. At the time, only five years had elapsed since the end of the Second World War, in which Korea, being a Japanese colony, had participated. Merely two years had passed since the Korean Peninsula had been divided at the thirty-eighth parallel, four months since the Korean War had broken out, and two weeks since South Korea had recaptured the capital city of Seoul. Despite his relief that the city was back under South Korean control, Kim noted: "After the liberation, people restlessly denounced and spat at Hitler and Mussolini by pen or by tongue. Yet, I felt as if everything around me became like Hitler and Mussolini. This time, the outcry was over the group of puppets [North Korea], the sworn enemy; yet much of what it [South Korea] has done is cookie-cutter replicas of the North, as if cutting from a pattern."[1]

For a historian with many painful experiences of war, seeing the two sides as bipolar extremes would have only been natural. Instead, what he observed were the similarities between the wartime colonial order under imperial Japan and postcolonial Korea and those between the democratic South and the socialist North. The break with the colonial past that postcolonial Korea had touted, in his view, had failed to materialize.

The primary point of convergence that Kim identified between colonial Korea and the two postcolonial Korean states was the neighborhood association (NA). NAs dated back to the premodern Chosŏn period (1392–1910), when they had been used to assist local governance. In

1

the late nineteenth century, they had been in name only in the process of modernizing the local order, and in the 1910s, when the colonial government adopted the Japanese administrative order, they ceased to exist.[2] In 1938, one year after the outbreak of the second Sino-Japanese War, the colonial government reintroduced a modified version of this premodern practice for the nationwide state-led mass movement—Movement for General Mobilization of the National Spirit. Patriotic neighborhood associations (*aegukpan*) were formed throughout the country, with each NA made up of ten to twenty households, so that the entirety of Korea was organized into about 350,000 Patriotic NAs. Their total number was constantly changing due to population growth, demographic changes, and urban planning. With their direct and coercive links to the colonial government, Patriotic NAs became the basic unit for the collection of demographic information, ideological indoctrination, and the production and distribution of resources, including food. In short, it was the de facto center of the home front until the end of World War II.

With the war's end and the liberation of Korea, the colossal colonial mechanism that had facilitated the war effort should have outlived its usefulness. But instead of abolishing it, each of the two Koreas established revised versions. The democratic South introduced the "Citizens' NA" (*kungminban*). In 1961, following Park Chung Hee's coup, the Citizens' NA was renamed the "Reconstruction NA" (*chaegŏnban*). In socialist North Korea, the government replaced the colonial NA with the "People's NA" (*inminban*). As with the Patriotic NAs, all three postcolonial forms were committed to state-led mass campaigns. This book examines the NAs created by each of three states from the 1930s to the 1960s.

TIMES OF CONFRONTATION: 1930S TO 1960S

The four decades from the 1930s to the 1960s, which I label "the war decades," began with the Manchurian Incident on September 18, 1931. It marked the beginning of a highly militarized fourteen-year campaign of the Japanese empire that was aimed at building the Greater East Asian

Co-Prosperity Sphere against the West. The Japanese surrender to Allied forces on August 15, 1945, ended thirty-five years of Japanese colonialism, but it did not bring unity or peace; instead, colonialism was replaced by the Cold War. The growing tensions between the United States and the Soviet Union, as manifested in their separate occupations of Korea, were a prelude to the Korean War (1950–1953). In 1948, two separate Korean nations were established. With each claiming to be the "true" Korea, it was not long until minor military skirmishes between the two Koreas triggered a full-scale international war, in which Chinese forces and United Nations forces led by the United States became embroiled. In 1953, a cease-fire marked the end of hostilities. Thus, the two Koreas remain at war to this day, and any deterioration in relations threatens to reignite military hostilities.

To date, few studies have brought together the three warfare states, that is, wartime colonial Korea, South Korea, and North Korea. This oversight largely stems from two distinct political landmarks: independence in 1945 and division in 1948. Liberation was a historical turning point in that it transformed Korea from a colonial society into a postcolonial society. The sudden advent of the US's and the USSR's military governments after the Second World War and the establishment of two Korean governments, however, prompted historians to focus on the peninsula's division rather than interrogating the transition from the colonial to the postcolonial order. Owing to escalating Cold War ideological antagonisms after the Korean War, scholars concentrated on the deepening differences between the two Koreas, such as in their political structures and in their approaches to economic modernization. The relationship between the two Koreas was described as one of "antagonistic inter-dependence,"[3] meaning that while each nation marked opposite ends of multiple yardsticks—democracy versus socialism, development versus backwardness, and open society versus hermit kingdom—this bipolar identity was also critical to maintaining domestic cohesiveness in each Korean state.

This bipolar narrative was reinforced by how historians interpreted the impact of colonialism on each state. In the case of South Korea, although historians differed on individual points of interpretation, few disagreed that traces of colonialism were embedded in the new state's postcolonial order. Because Korean historians and journalists viewed

Korea's loss of autonomy to Japan as a national failure and any remnants of colonialism as undermining the political legitimacy of liberated South Korea, the question of collaboration and the failed purge of collaborators were volatile topics on which countless pages were written.[4] Some political scientists attributed South Korea's delayed democratic development to an overdeveloped state and an underdeveloped civil society—a product of the centralized bureaucracy and suppressive state apparatus of the colonial government.[5] Others looked to South Korea's colonial past to explain South Korea's postwar economic development and its system of capitalism,[6] while a third group cited elements of colonial culture, such as its militaristic education system and its hierarchical political and personal relationships, as impediments to South Korea moving beyond its authoritarian past.[7]

In contrast, the radical reforms introduced during North Korea's first five years of existence, combined with the anticapitalist and anti-imperialist rhetoric of North Korean leaders, led historians to assume that North Korea largely had succeeded in eradicating its colonial past. This conclusion is startling, given that there are separate scholarly works that approach both wartime colonial Korea and North Korea utilizing the concept of corporatism.[8] Similarly, historians have noted for both colonial Korea and North Korea that each sought a common collective identity based on antiliberalism and anti-individualism.[9] Despite such feasible links, historians have highlighted, instead, the social changes brought about by land reform that ended the tenancy system that had underpinned colonialism; the nationalization of enemy property; and the introduction of compulsory education, equal rights for men and women, and legal protection of workers' rights.

The marginalization of Japanese colonization's influence on North Korea was also propelled by Cold War ideology and competition. Early studies of North Korea emphasized the anticolonial, antifeudal, and Stalinist roots of North Korean state formation. More recently, scholars such as Kim Sŏng-bo and Suzy Kim have demonstrated the limits of Soviet influence on North Korea's development by shifting the focus from the USSR to the state-building efforts of Kim Il Sung and his band of anti-Japanese Manchuria guerillas. Specifically they highlight how Kim and his cohort combined precolonial traditions, reform ideas, and nationalist sentiments with socialism to create an indigenized socialism.[10] Although these revisionist histories broach the subject of colonial legacies, such as similarities between the security structures and everyday reforms of colonial Korea and North Korea, these subjects remain subsumed within the historiographical debate on the "Koreanization" of Soviet communism.

The different versions of NAs advanced during the war decades provide an opportunity to revisit the antagonistic triangular split with an eye to the historical transition from a colonial political order laden with anti-Western sentiment to two postcolonial political orders, both of Western origin—democracy and socialism. Against this backdrop, both states introduced modifications to their newly adopted political orders, claiming that local conditions—that is, the populace's political immaturity and the peninsula's geographic and ideological division—necessitated change. Both argued that they needed total mobilization of the populace and resources to establish their status as the "true Korea" and to overcome the colonial legacy of economic and political backwardness. Both states established an emergency political order that aimed at totalizing society by creating direct links to the masses that bypassed intermediary groups. The preponderance of the centralized state apparatus over civil society in both states facilitated wartime planning and hindered social resistance.

Through the lens of the different NAs created during the war decades, this book revisits mid-twentieth-century Korean history, moving beyond the two political landmarks and the triangular segregation that has defined the history of colonial Korea, South Korea, and North Korea. In this study, I make two broad interconnected claims. The first is that colonial NAs, tasked with the national mobilization of local Koreans, advanced programs of mass enlightenment that privileged state interests over individual rights, in the process blurring the line between morality and state authority and superimposing patriarchal familial relations on state–local society relations. The second is that the NAs of the two postliberation Koreas, despite their different ideological orientations, shared the same enlightenment mission with their earlier forms, and that this commonality is critical to understanding the authoritarian direction taken by South and North Korea.

MORAL AUTHORITARIANISM: STATE-LED MASS MOVEMENTS IN THE NEIGHBORHOOD SPACE

This book perceives the neighborhood space as a moral space. Since the Neolithic Age, when human settlement began, the space formed by residential proximity has been conceptualized as a unity, that is, a meaningful arrangement of people and objects synthesized by a moral idea of community. Spontaneously emerging from face-to-face interactions and mutual aid, the neighborhood has a communal image and is associated with egalitarian values. The nongeographic, emotional dimension of the neighborhood space means that its boundaries are not static; instead, they are often dynamic and contested. Residents may embrace some of the surrounding space and persons and disavow others. Relative position in the social structure, such as that dictated by age, occupation, and ethnicity, may affect how a resident evaluates belonging, thereby creating tensions and challenging the cohesiveness and coherence of the community. The fragile equilibrium of the community is preserved through moral expectations based on social norms and through social exclusions in cases when these moral expectations are violated.[11]

In East Asian history, this moral space has taken the form of NAs. Premodern Korea had the five-household mutual guarantee system (*ogajakt'ong*); in China, a community-based system of law enforcement and civil control (*baojia*) was formalized around the tenth century and extended to Taiwan in the eighteenth century.[12] Japan had several forerunners of the neighborhood association, including the five-family-unit system (*gonin-gumi*) that lasted from the seventeenth to the nineteenth century.[13] NAs maintained local order by demanding adherence to moral norms, assisted in tax collection, and organized civil projects like festivals, ritual ceremonies, and colabor.

By the early twentieth century, the NA substantially lost its administrative functions in Korea as the local administrative space should be adopted to a modern world order. The moral space was at odds with the core features of the modern space, that is, urbanization, compressed space, and the spatial split between the domestic sphere and the workspace. The geographic and social changes introduced by urbanization challenged spatial durability in traditional space of neighborhood and weakened the mutual bonds neighbors had fostered. Against the backdrop of increased social mobility and weaker social cohesion, associational groups based on impersonal relationships mushroomed in the urban context. The compression of space—the product of the introduction of a network of railroads nationwide and the rise of the print industry—allowed the state to extend its power over local communities. The state's political intervention at the local level disturbed the fragile equilibrium of the moral neighborhood space. The moral, psychological, and emotional features of the neighborhood did not align with the modern state, which sought to rationalize its administration more visibly and to measure its resources quantitatively. The neighborhood space's informality, its reliance on irregular personal relationships, and its small size were ill suited for a formal administrative district, in which the state contacted and exercised control over each person directly through tax collection, census taking, military conscription, and compulsory education. Finally, the spatial split reduced social contacts between neighbors, undermining the cohesiveness and moral authority in the neighborhood space. The moral space was gradually displaced by the features of modernity—rationalization, nationalized space, and impersonal relations.

Yet, in the 1930s, the Japanese colonial government reintroduced NAs to Korea in a revised form. The immediate cause for this move was to facilitate the war effort. Its reintroduction also reflected widespread concern about the atomization of the individual and skepticism about the market-oriented economy. This concern extended across Asia and beyond. Increasingly, an idealized image of the neighborhood, as a homogenous and egalitarian space characterized by harmonious communal bonds, was juxtaposed with the rampant individualism and profit-oriented practices of modern society. Reminiscent of the romantic allure of bygone days, this ahistorical image of the neighborhood space inspired numerous thinkers and politicians across the political spectrum to promote the neighborhood as the fundamental building block of society. While in communist countries, such as the Soviet Union and Cuba, the government attempted to utilize the neighborhood to shrink the private realm and revive a communal social sense, this revival in East Asia was inspired by growing anti-West sentiment.[14] Ruthless capitalism, selfish individualism, and party politics dominated by a handful of elites were depicted as alien Western norms. Thus, Japan's reintroduction of NAs in Korea also reflected the rise of an East Asianism that sought to free Asia from the shackles of Western modernity by restoring a sense of moral collective identity.

In East Asia, the link between the state and neighborhood associations has a long history. Their raison d'être was to help the state govern, not simply to provide a focal point for conviviality. As Benjamin Read notes, NAs in East Asia occupy a unique space between civil society associations and mass organizations or manifestations of state corporatism. Through a comparative analysis of China and Taiwan, he shows that administrative grassroots engagement simultaneously functioned to support the repressive state and to empower civil society.[15] The contemporary Japanese case shows a looser relation to public authority, because in 1947 the US military government in Japan forcibly disbanded NAs as part of its campaign to eradicate the wartime Japanese order. When NAs reemerged in postwar Japan, they were no longer under the direct command of government authorities. As Robert Pekkanen observes, contemporary NAs worked closely with the government, but on a voluntary and negotiated basis. They maintained control over their budgets, leadership selection, and operations and determined which government messages they would disseminate. This productive tension in the NA–government relationship in Japan, Pekkanen argues, is an essential feature that increases the social capital of the NA, allowing for the reinforcement of the social norm of participation and increasing the visibility of deviance.[16]

Interest in neighborhood associations as a means of encouraging civic participation and countering the objectification and depersonalization of modern social arrangements was not limited to East Asia or to the communist bloc. In many Western nations, the formation of neighborhood associations emerged spontaneously and/or with government support. Due to the unrivalled advantage of dense coverage, easy access to households, and quick responses, they became the loci of grassroots campaigns for urban reform and community improvement. Yet, here too, there was a discrepancy between its potential for participatory democracy and its reality. A study on Neighborhood-Representing Organizations (NROs) in the United States showed that NROs often devolved into instruments of social control by local governments and other authorities. NROs, the study concluded, "are worthwhile and democratic only when there is a real threat or common problem strong enough to unite and excite the residents." In the absence of a shared crisis, "NROs tend to become more closed, less democratic, and weaker."[17]

In each of the three Korean states, the central government sought a balance between NAs as self-governing voluntary associations and NAs as instruments of local administration. In pursuing this hybrid format, each state envisioned NAs as the basic unit for catalyzing voluntary mass participation in government programs. But the fusion of state authority, grassroots movement, and the neighborhood space cannot occur without exposing some inherent contradictions. A state-led movement cannot be spontaneous, and the neighborhood unit with its amorphous boundaries and moral dimension is ill suited for the realization of political ends. In rural neighborhoods, defined by tradition and social cohesion, political goals that contradicted existing values and norms were unlikely to generate popular enthusiasm. Conversely, in urban neighborhoods, defined only by residential proximity, the state found it difficult to inspire a sense of common cause.

Yet because each of the three states lacked political legitimacy, they needed to tap into the moral authority of the neighborhood so that they would not have to rely exclusively on bureaucratic force to mobilize the populace. The main advantage for the state's public relations was that once NAs became, in essence, a mouthpiece for the state, they reframed arguably political policies as unquestionable moral imperatives. The state could now demand obedience in the name of the united moral community, represented by the NA, rather than in the name of this or that political approach with which a substantial portion of the population disagreed. This pattern of relying on moral authoritarianism to ensure compliance with state policies was an essential feature of Japanese wartime colonialism, South Korea's "Korean-style democracy," and North Korea's "our own style of socialism."

PREFIXES: PATRIOTIC, CITIZEN, RECONSTRUCTION, AND PEOPLE

This book directs attention to the four NA prefixes—"patriotic" (colonial Korea), "citizen" and "reconstruction" (South Korea), and "people" (North Korea)—that made the amorphous space of neighborhood purposeful and turned this quintessential local space into a national space. In examining the prefixes, my analysis takes as its point of departure German historian Reinhard Koselleck's emphasis on the reciprocal relationship between continuities, changes, and innovations in the meanings and applications of social concepts on the one hand and large-scale structural transformations in government, society, and economy on the other.[18] The semantic choices of the three war states were not random. Conceptually, the prefixes reflected the interests, goals, and fields of political action of the respective states—overcoming the West, independence, division, and economic modernization. Yet, these designations did not simply mirror the social reality. They were also a means for the state to attempt to transform that reality. For example, prior to the creation of Patriotic NAs, the colonial state had never attempted to inculcate loyalty to Japan in Koreans, and Koreans had rarely sought inclusion in the Japanese polity. By labeling neighborhood associations as patriotic associations, Japan linguistically endeavored to create unity where none existed and direct the masses in the service of its cause. Stressing patriotism and the moral righteousness of the cause also obscured from view the centralized bureaucracy's reliance on coercion to ensure compliance.

The Japanese government's usage of the prefix "patriotic," as a sense of politically consented loyalty to a polity to which one belonged, left unmentioned the fact that it was the antithesis of Korean nationalism. Following Korea's territorial annexation in 1910, Korean nationalists had separated the spiritual realm from the tangible territory to construct a vision of Korean nationalism that highlighted culture, language, ethnicity, and ancient myths. This growing nationalist consciousness among the populace had given rise to the first mass movement in Korean history. The March First Movement in 1919, in which an estimated half a million to two million Koreans participated, began with the reading of a declaration of independence in Seoul and led to the establishment of the

Korean Provisional Government in Shanghai. Although this movement did not result in Korean independence, it transformed both Japanese occupation policy and South Korean nationalism. As Michael Shin argues, the cultural space, which nationalists had claimed as their domain, became a site of contestation between the colonized and the colonizer.[19]

In response to the uprising, the colonial government announced the new "Cultural Policy" (J. *Bunka seiji*), which aimed to cultivate ideological state apparatuses capable of actively penetrating Korean society through more subtle forms of power. The goal was to subsume Korean national identity to Japanese imperial interests. While the cultural history advanced by Japanese imperialists posited the inherent inferiority of the Koreans, Korean nationalists offered a different view of their culture that reflected forces at work within Korean society, such as economic change and the infusion of cultural currents from the West. For example, one of the keywords of 1920s Korean nationalism was "reconstruction." Not all nationalists, however, interpreted the meaning of "reconstruction" the same way. For most nationalists, the goal of reconstruction was the establishment of institutions to promote Korean culture. But for socialists, reconstruction became another term for class revolution. A struggle emerged between cultural nationalists and socialist nationalists for leadership over the masses. The limited freedom of the press introduced by the Cultural Policy allowed newspapers and journals to become sites of both the struggle within the nationalist movement and struggles between the nationalist movement and the colonial government.[20]

The onset of the Sino-Japanese War transformed colonial ruling policy yet again. Needing to mobilize both human and material resources in Korea for the war effort, the colonial government tried to encourage Koreans to think of themselves as Japanese imperial subjects and espouse its goals and values. To this end, it utilized the slogan "Japan and Korea are one entity" (J. *naisen ittai*), introduced the "patriotic" NAs, and imposed on Koreans the same obligations as the Japanese. Though the Cultural Policy of the 1920s and early 1930s made some progress in alleviating anti-Japanese emotion, its condescending overtones undermined its appeal for most Koreans. Living in a territory that was politically subordinate to Japan but institutionally and culturally separate from Japan meant that most Koreans had not developed a sense of loyalty to the Japanese imperial state. By using the prefix "patriotic," the colonial state thus linguistically tried to reconfigure the core-periphery relationship for the purpose of war mobilization.

While the colonial prefix "patriotic" stressed duty to the state, the two postcolonial prefixes "citizen" and "people," used by South and North Korea respectively, stressed the new political subjectivity of Koreans and the changed political topography. Linguistically, the new prefixes sought to distance the colonial past from the nation's future. In addition to negating the colonial past, the prefixes also stressed the ideological divide between the two Korean states. Although popular sovereignty at the moment of liberation had widespread support among the populace, no consensus existed on what form popular sovereignty should take. As in the 1920s, the two ideological camps within Korean nationalism vied for the support of the masses. Within the framework of this struggle emerged the descriptive prefixes "citizen" (*kungmin*) and "people" (*inmin*) to describe their respective political orientations.

For roughly six hundred years, these two words in Korea had been used to refer to general groups in society or to subjects of a dynasty. Their semantic change can be traced to the nineteenth century, when contact with the West brought about an epistemological transformation as Western political concepts were translated and incorporated into East Asian cultures. Because of their adaptability, missionaries and East Asian intellectuals settled on Chinese characters as the medium for translating and disseminating Western concepts in East Asia. When the Japanese embraced modernization and colonization in the late nineteenth and early twentieth centuries, Japanese scholars, educators, and imperial officials at home and abroad continued the practice of using Chinese characters to create new compound words to describe modern political concepts such as sovereignty, equality, freedom, and political rights.[21] But the actual conceptual divergence of *kungmin* and *inmin* emerged in the context of Japanese wartime colonial rule. To encourage a sense of territorial belonging and devotion to the Japanese cause, the Japanese included Koreans in the category of *kungmin*. Frequently attached to wartime propaganda, the term was intended to strengthen the image of the Korean people as subject to Japanese state power. In contrast, the term *inmin* was used during this period by East Asian socialists to build a united front against Japanese imperialism. The idea was to juxtapose the interests of the common people with those of Japanese collaborators and landlords to encourage ordinary Koreans to take up arms against Japanese imperial forces.[22]

The transformation of these two terms accelerated in the context of liberation and the emerging global Cold War. The wartime association of *inmin* with resistance to the Japanese and rejection of imperial state power made it the ideal term to advance a vision of an independent Korean social order. Unlike *kungmin,* its usage did not invoke memories of Japan's coercive wartime mobilization or of the hypocrisy of imperial Japan's policy of assimilation. In the brief space between liberation and the arrival of foreign occupation forces, local people of all political persuasions spontaneously organized "people's committees" (*inmin wiwŏnhoe*) to facilitate the transition from colonial rule to independence. However, increasingly these committees were dominated by socialists, and so the term *inmin* quickly became associated with socialism. Unwilling to share the term and wanting to distinguish their political orientation from that of socialists, conservatives for lack of a better choice chose *kungmin* to describe their vision of a liberal capitalist democracy; at the same time, they expressed resentment at their loss of control over the ideal word *inmin.*[23]

With the founding of two separate Korean states in 1948, these two words became the focal point of debates over which Korea was the "true" Korea. This debate became more acrimonious with the onset of the Korean War. Prior to the Korean War, the territorial boundary between the two Korean states had remained porous, with goods and people crossing it on a regular basis. But prosecution of the war and increasing global Cold War hostilities put an end to this blurring of the line of demarcation. The sharp territorial divide was accompanied by a pronounced ideological separation. In South Korea, the word *inmin* ceased to be used in any formal writings; conversely *kungmin* was no longer employed in North Korea. Just as NAs had been mobilized by the Japanese for war, the Citizens' NAs and People's NAs were mobilized to advance the Cold War objectives of their respective states.

While North Korea has retained the prefix "people" up to now, the military coup of Park Chung Hee on May 16, 1961, resulted in the prefix "citizen" (*kungmin*) being replaced with the prefix "reconstruction" (*chaegŏn*) in South Korea. Maintenance of the prefix "citizen" would have called attention to the new government's lack of political legitimacy; thus, Citizens' NAs became Reconstruction NAs. Unlike "citizen," which highlighted the agency of the populace, "reconstruction" both summarized the purpose of the military coup and served as its justification. The "revolution for national reconstruction" (*chaegŏn hyŏngmyŏng*), its leaders claimed, had been necessary to save the nation from collapse. Depicting previous Korean society as lacking in pioneering spirit and self-reliant will and as plagued by political incompetency and factionalism, South Korean leaders saw moral recovery and economic modernization as preconditions for liberal democracy. These preconditions required that the Korean people sacrifice individual rights and freedoms so that national self-reliance and self-sufficiency could be achieved.[24]

"KOREAN PARTICULARITIES": ANOTHER NAME FOR TRADITION

The bureaucracies of the three Korean war states expected NAs to volunteer their labor and to give their consent to government policies. Voluntarism, as historian Christopher Capozzola observes in the case of the United States in World War I, had multiple meanings in the context of war: "It denoted an expression of consent. It referred to organized activity outside state auspices. It was also an act of unpaid labor." Viewed from this angle, he contends that "winning the war meant capturing the hearts and minds" of the populace as well as "extracting significant amounts of unpaid labor."[25] The NAs were expected to galvanize popular passion for the cause and act as the hub for collecting all forms of unpaid labor from the civil sector. Recognizing that an individual should have a realm allegedly unpenetrated by the state, NAs seemingly were placed outside direct state control. Yet, in practice, the state exercised tight control over the NAs, claiming this was necessary for maintaining the integrity of the public and private sectors. This control revealed each of the three Korean states' fundamental concern that they could not harness popular passion for their cause.

This call for voluntarism has received little attention in the scholarly literature. Many scholars have dismissed it as meaningless and instead have focused on bureaucratic coercion.[26] Their exclusive focus on coercion reflects "the strong state and weak society model" that scholars mainly have used to describe state-society relations in Korea. As political scientist Melvin Gurtov has explained, "The 'strong state' or 'developmental state,' whether officially socialist or capitalist emphasized a one-party-dominant political system and a high degree of government intervention in economic planning and performance."[27] Within the framework of this model, the two questions for scholars became the following: Is authoritarianism necessary, if not sufficient, for the making of a strong or developmental state? Is democracy an impediment to economic development or an engine of development?[28] As a result, scholars largely ignored the significant difference between the three Korean states' regulatory capacity and their capacity to encourage participation. Yet, each of the three states worried about their inability to generate popular enthusiasm for their policies. This concern found expression in each state's consistent emphasis on morality and spirituality.

In times of war, states typically rely on appeals to nationalism and patriotism to rally the public for mass mobilization. However, for the three war states in Korea, appeals to nationalism and to patriotism were problematic for a variety of reasons. In the case of colonial Korea, a dissonance existed between patriotic fervor for the Japanese war effort and loyalty to the Korean nation. While in the immediate aftermath of World War II nationalism was a powerful motivating force for Koreans wanting to create a unified independent state, its effectiveness was seriously compromised when Korea was divided into two states. Neither state had an exclusive claim to Korean culture—the foundation of nationalism under colonial rule. Moreover, at the time of the Korean War, neither of the two Koreas had had sufficient time to create a political identity distinct from that of its counterpart. Thus, rather than inspiring unity, appeals to patriotism and to nationalism only exacerbated internal fissures within Korean society.

This book sees tradition as a complementary mechanism of dysfunctional nationalism and ineffective patriotism. As in other parts of the world, traditions in Korea that were claimed by their proponents to be of ancient origin were in fact modern inventions aimed at enhancing social cohesion and/or legitimating authority.[29] The invention of Korean tradition developed during two competitive historical waves at the turn of the twentieth century—social reform and colonization. At this politically critical moment, tradition became associated with backwardness and with Korea's loss of independence. The Japanese used this invented tradition to claim that Koreans were incapable of self-rule and required Japanese protection. While some Korean nationalists during this era insisted that political and economic modernization was the antidote to colonization, others saw in tradition a resource for creating a unique Korean national identity that would defend against imperialism and an alien modernity. Whether assessed positively or negatively, tradition was framed as the antithesis of modernity and figured prominently in conflicts between imperialism and nationalism and between the West and the East.

During the war decades, debates on tradition centered on the alleged particularities of Korean history. This focus first appeared in the 1930s when the threat of imminent war coincided with open skepticism about Western modernity. Prior to the 1930s, the urban space as receptive to modernization was contrasted with the rural space that seemingly remained unchanged despite the influx of modern elements and the state's coercive remapping of traditional space.[30] But war and skepticism about Western modernity led the colonial state to accept Korean traditions as part of a strategic reconciliation of Japanese and Korean cultures. Alleged cultural similarities between Koreans and the Japanese were utilized to frame the war as a struggle between East Asia and the West. To this end, Japan changed its self-representation from that of a modernized East Asian state that closely approximated Western modernity to that of the protector of East Asia from Western modernity. The so-called particularities of Korean history were reconfigured in South Korea into differences from Western democratic societies and in North Korea from other socialist nations.

Domestically, "Korean particularities" most often referred to the political incompetence and backwardness of the Korean people. The three states manipulated this idea in three ways. First, this notion justified denying the Korean people autonomy. The Koreans, the Japanese explained, lacked sufficient political maturity for self-rule and had not yet fully assimilated into the superior Japanese polity. In a similar vein, South Korean officials argued that the masses were too politically inexperienced to participate in a Western-style democracy; if the South Korean government acquiesced too soon to the demand for greater civil liberties, it would lead to civil disorder and economic ruin. Socialist leaders in North Korea also insisted that the Korean working class had not yet developed sufficient class consciousness for the socialist revolution. Thus, the alleged political incompetence and inexperience of the masses provided the rationalization for delaying political reform and for maintaining an aberrant and oppressive form of normative political systems.

Second, the states instrumentalized political immaturity and backwardness to stimulate voluntarism. Prior to the 1930s, Japanese colonizers saw Korea as a supplier of agrarian products and as a market for Japanese products; thus, most Koreans remained illiterate and uneducated. With the onset of war, the Japanese realized that a Korean populace unindoctrinated in state ideologies could obstruct the war effort. The colonial government thus stressed education and economic reform as a path from political immaturity to mass enlightenment. The promise of a higher standard of living was expected to awaken the dormant desires of the Korean masses for assimilation into the Japanese polity. In South and North Korea, democratic and socialist enlightenment respectively superseded colonial enlightenment.

Lastly, the three Korean war states manipulated the populace's alleged political immaturity to lead a program of enlightenment that aimed at creating material prosperity while maintaining tradition-based morality. Self-reliance in the context of striving for material prosperity was encouraged, while deviation from a morality based on community and tradition was not tolerated. Situating the state at the zenith of the community, this model of enlightenment saw individual subjectivity as meaningful only when it aligned with state interests. When individual interests diverged from state interests, the supreme goal of social prosperity was sidelined by self-aggrandizement. The level of enlightenment, each state posited, was proportional with the degree to which the populace complied with state demands. The resoluteness of the collective will, created by enlightenment, would determine the future of the state and of the individual. The mass was objectified in the enlightenment, with their right to use reason given over to the states; conversely the states had ultimate subjectivity in supervising them. NAs were the basic unit of this community-based statist system.

At the core of the NAs' community-centric morality was family-based morality. Weighed against a Western moral identity that stressed an individually oriented morality, Korea's community-based, family-oriented morality was regarded as a social virtue because of its effectiveness in reinforcing state structures and authority. Within the familial structure of the NAs, the state assumed the role of family patriarch, thereby enhancing its moral authority and compensating for its lack of political legitimacy. It also deluded the politically fickle masses into thinking that participation in the state-led enlightenment was a moral imperative, thereby curtailing the right to reject the state-led enlightenment. The fusion of morality, politics, and enlightenment, intersecting with war mobilization, was a constitutive feature of modernity in the three Korean states. This dynamic, which first found expression under authoritarian colonial rule, culminated with the emergence of two authoritarian Korean states in the 1970s: one under the guise of "Korean-style democracy" and the other dubbed "our own style of socialism."

CHANGING GENDER AND POLITICAL DYNAMICS: MEN, WOMEN, AND THE MORAL STATES

Taking as its starting point Joan Scott's contention that politics constructs gender and gender constructs politics, this book sees changing power dynamics between men and women in the neighborhood space as political turning points.[31] In all three Koreas, participation in NAs was gendered. When women were proactive in NAs, men tended to become passive. Conversely, when male leadership and participation increased, women retreated into the shadows. This gendered divide in NA participation was the product both of traditional Korean patriarchal social norms that prohibited men and women from working together and prescribed separate male and female spaces and of a new modern gender ideology that entered Korea via Protestant missionaries and Japanese colonizers in the early twentieth century. According to this new Western-influenced gender ideology, Korean women's lack of education was an impediment to Korea's modernization and enlightenment. Thus, Korea needed to cultivate a new ideal woman, who could manage a modern household and raise well-informed children capable of leading a modern state. This new gender ideology was captured in the phrase "wise mother and good wife" (*hyŏnmo yangch'ŏ*), which adopted the Japanese phrase "good wife and wise mother" (*ryōsai-kenbo*), coined in 1875.[32] This ideology remained a hot topic for years to come.

Whether NAs leaned more toward male or female participation depended on which sphere—domestic or work—they were seen as belonging to. This was open to interpretation because the tasks NAs were assigned as part of mobilizing the population for the war effort straddled the female-male labor divide. On the one hand, NAs were responsible for rationalizing consumption, which included introducing reform in hygiene and diet as well as improved trash collection. Traditionally associated with the domestic sphere, these tasks were regarded as the responsibility of women. On the other hand, administrative functions such as handling wartime rationing, census taking, roadwork, and grain collection were considered men's work. For that reason, both men and women could claim rightful leadership over NAs or refuse to participate on the grounds that NA jobs fell within the sphere of the opposite sex.

Japanese colonial officials believed that men should take the leading role in NAs. With the conceptualization of NAs as an apolitical familial community, they framed NAs as part of the Japanese patriarchal family, at the apex of which was the Japanese emperor. They argued that the household, its properties, and its labor were the responsibility of a male patriarch, and that the collective of households organized into NAs should be led by a male patriarch who would answer to a superior male patriarch, that is, the Japanese colonizer. This proposed hierarchical system of patriarchal hegemony mirrored the Japanese family system (the *ie* system) that was codified in the Meiji Civic Code (1898–1947).[33] In short, the Japanese colonizer dreamed of a moral patriarchal Japanese empire that linked patriotism to familial ties and loyalties.

Unlike what the colonial scheme proposed, Korean men avoided participation in NA activities, arguing that the jobs of NAs belonged to women. The patriarchal vision of an apolitical familial community meshed well with contemporary notions in Korea of male dominance over women. However, it contradicted the notion of "nationalized masculinity" that many upper- and middle-class Korean men had embraced, which merged traditional neo-Confucian ideas about manhood with a new European militarized discourse of manhood. Whereas in premodern

Korean society, fighting prowess was only an acceptable masculine virtue among commoners, masculinized modernity recognized the need for aristocratic and middle-class men to develop their physical strength and fighting skills.[34] Given that the Japanese government refused to recognize the political subjectivity of Korean men, serving as NA heads under the Japanese colonizer would have contradicted this nationalized vision of manhood.

Men's indifference to NAs accelerated women's assumption of leadership roles in the NAs. Female intellectuals and local women with some education in Korea saw NAs as an opportunity to expand on the limited opportunities that the "wise mother and good wife" ideology had opened to some of them. The ambiguous positioning of NAs between the public and private spheres facilitated women's advancement to leadership positions. By claiming that the neighborhood space was an extension of the familial domestic space, local women could assume leadership roles without transgressing traditional gender norms while at the same time acquiring modern knowledge, leadership skills, and experience. Although at one level the NAs liberated women, the NAs' underlying patriarchal tenets subsumed women under state ideology. By supporting the state-directed NAs, women inadvertently undermined the autonomy of local society and acted as a bulwark of wartime colonial rule.

Following liberation in 1945, Japanese imperial family ideology lost ground in Korea. The conflict between state and local patriarchs, a main factor in frustrating the patriarchal project of the colonial government, thereby giving room for women to advance in NAs, no longer existed. Against the backdrop of the US and Soviet occupation of Korea and the rise of the Cold War, NAs became the vehicle through which each Korean state attempted to create fervor for its respective system of governance and to remake Koreans as political subjects within those systems. Beyond this ideological purpose, NAs also allowed the respective Korean states to carry out necessary administrative functions, such as census taking and the distribution of rationed goods. Since these political and administrative duties fell within the purview of traditional men's work, men now embraced leadership roles in NAs and women retreated from playing a leading role in NAs.

By the early 1960s, when the North had completed the socialist transition from a people's democracy, however, women had once again replaced men as the dominant force in NAs in North Korea. Initially, it seemed that North Korea would overcome this pattern of either one sex or the other acting as the driving force behind NAs based on a gendered division of labor. Shortly after the liberation, North Korean leaders legally liberated women from the "triple subordination" of family, society, and politics and abolished the patriarchal family registry (*hojŏk*) that had underpinned patriarchal hegemony under Japanese rule. But these measures did not result in the complete dissolution of social norms about appropriate gender relations and the division of labor. Although women were no longer confined to the domestic sphere, the home remained a women's space.[35] In the 1960s, when the North Korean government made NAs responsible for the management of residential areas and childcare for post–Korean War recovery and the transition to socialism, men began to retreat from participating in NA activities. The rise of the Great Red Family ideology to introduce an indigenized form of socialism in North Korea propelled women into leadership positions in the 1960s. Kim Il Sung was represented as the supreme patriarch of the Great Red Family that encompassed all Koreans, and North Korean women were designated the primary leaders of the domestic sphere, responsible for educating children in socialist values and revolutionizing the family.

In contrast, South Korean men continued to be the dominant force in NAs until the early 1970s. South Korean leaders conceptualized the nation as an extended form of family in the early 1950s, through the One-Nation Ideology. It understood that South Koreans shared a single bloodline, one that could be traced back to ancient times, and placed South Korean president Syngman Rhee as the political and moral leader and father of this nation.[36] When the South Korean government framed political policies as moral imperatives, NAs, as the smallest unit of nation-building, were tasked with implementing government policy and with promoting patriotism through moral amity. As the moral function of NAs was linked to their administrative and political functions seen as acceptable male jobs, men remained committed to NA leadership and women found it difficult to challenge male leadership. This situation did not change until the early 1970s, when rapid industrialization and economic development resulted in a massive influx of Korean families into urban centers. Over time, as the government came to recognize that many men no longer had time to spend on NA duties and that women spent more time at home and had more knowledge of their neighbors, the government began to urge women to assume leadership of NAs. As a result, rather than the sudden and clear shift to female NA leadership in 1960s North Korea, the number of women in leadership positions in South Korean NAs slowly increased over the course of the 1970s. But as in colonial Korea and North Korea, the gendered political ideology of the state, combined with the perception of NA tasks as either belonging to the public or domestic sphere, determined whether men or women led.

ORGANIZATION

The book is divided into three parts, each having three chapters. Part I focuses on wartime colonial Korea. Chapter 1 examines Japanese colonial rule in the 1930s and the introduction of patriotic NAs for the purposes of wartime mobilization and social indoctrination. Chapter 2 differentiates Patriotic NAs in Korea from NAs in Japan (*tonarigumi*) to highlight the colonial dimension of wartime assimilation policy. Chapter 3 focuses on NA practices aimed at the family such as the gathering of demographic information and the rationalization of everyday life; it details how within the framework of NAs, conflicts between state and local society turned into gendered conflicts.

Part II shifts the focus to postcolonial South Korea. Chapter 4 details the transition from colonial patriotic NAs to citizen NAs; it focuses on two factors that explain the continuance of NAs in South Korea: the postliberation food crisis triggered by the sudden end of economic controls and the demographic upheaval and ideological hostilities spurred by the division of Korea. Chapter 5 looks at South Korean Citizens' NAs under North Korean occupation during the Korean War. On occupying Seoul, South Korea's capital, the North renamed them North Korean People's NAs and used them for their census taking, propaganda, and labor mobilization. Chapter 6 looks at NAs in postwar South Korea. Blaming the slow postwar recovery on the decentralized administration and national disunity caused by party politics, the state legalized the NAs under the auspices of realizing participatory democracy. This move sparked a backlash from critics who claimed that the compulsory activities of NAs were totalitarian practices found only in colonial and socialist regimes.

Part III addresses People's NAs in the socialist North. Chapter 7 explores the transformation of colonial Patriotic NAs into People's NAs and analyzes the claim that the North successfully expunged the colonial legacy. Chapter 8 examines People's NAs in relation to post–Korean War socialist reforms. When North Korea embarked on its own style of socialism, the North assigned them the task of managing residential areas. This decision exponentially increased women's leadership, due to the social norm that women were responsible for home management and childcare. Chapter 9 examines the Ch'ŏllima campaign in which the NAs played a pivotal role. Under the slogan of unifying politics and everyday morality, this campaign sought to build a socialist mode of living, the final embodiment of which was the Great Red Home.

PART I

Patriotic Neighborhood Associations in Colonial Korea

CHAPTER 1

The Birth of Patriotic Neighborhood Associations

Patriotic Neighborhood Associations [hereafter Patriotic NAs] are *something characteristic of Korea* in the Movement for General Mobilization of National Spirit.

—Shiobara Tokisaburō[1]

With the outbreak of the Sino-Japanese War in July 1937, Japanese colonial rule in Korea entered its final stage. During that first year, Koreans experienced no significant changes in their daily routines; no battles were fought on Korean soil, and the Japanese had not yet imposed military conscription or mobilized labor in Korea for the war effort. Only with the enactment of the General Mobilization Law in April 1938 that led to the creation of the Korean League for the General Mobilization of the National Spirit (*Kungmin chŏngsin ch'ongdong'wŏn Chosŏn yŏnmaeng*) in July 1938 did Koreans see tangible changes. Within a few months, the league partitioned the Korean territory and created over 350,000 Patriotic NAs, each consisting of approximately ten to twenty families. Suddenly, all Koreans and Japanese settlers were inducted into Patriotic NAs. Until the collapse of the Japanese empire in 1945, the activities of Patriotic NAs, in which the entire populace participated, were geared toward the war effort.

The establishment of Patriotic NAs introduced two noteworthy changes in Japanese colonialism. First, unlike earlier changes to colonial policy that had been made in Japan, the colonial government independently made the decision to reintroduce NAs in Korea, thereby reversing the normative flow from core to periphery. Proud of its newfound body, the colonial government insisted that Japan needed an organization analogous to the Patriotic NAs.[2] "Something characteristic of Korea"—to use the expression prevalent at that time—was for the first time being urged upon the colonizer. At the end of 1940, Japan formally involved its neighborhood associations (*tonarigumi*) in the war effort. Second, by reimposing a modified form of NAs on neighborhood spaces across the nation, the colonial government broke with conventional colonial practice of relying on the Korean landlord class and local nobles to handle local affairs. With the establishment of Patriotic NAs, the colonial government signaled its intention to make use of the knowledge it had gained of Korean society under the 1920s Cultural Policy (*Bunka seiji*) to dominate Korean society directly by penetrating the moral space of the neighborhood.

In fact, both developments owed their origins to the 1920s Cultural Policy. As noted in the Introduction, the Cultural Policy was the Government-General's response to the 1919 March First Movement. Recognizing that its repressive military rule had contributed to this nationwide uprising, the Government-General had replaced the military police with civilian police and allowed for freedom of speech, press, and association. Also, it sponsored broad ethnographic research on local customs, folklore, and local conditions. Although this cultural project at first glance appeared apolitical, it was an essential step for developing a more sophisticated form of colonial rule, which tightened the colonial government's grip over Korean society by introducing more subtle forms of control. As Michael Shin notes, "Ethnographic research by the colonial state constituted 'Chosŏn [Korean] culture' as a distinct object of knowledge, its aim was not simply to justify Japan's occupation" by labeling Korean culture as inferior "but also to define new targets for colonial power."[3] The knowledge that the colonial government gained of Korean culture during the 1920s empowered it to act independently of the Japanese government, as it could now claim an expertise in Korean culture that the Japanese government did not have. It used its knowledge of so-called Korean particularities—that is, features its ethnographic researchers claimed were unique to Korean culture and the Korean people, such as backwardness, servility, and political incompetence—to penetrate more deeply into local Korean society. Without the ethnographic research, the colonial government would not have had the confidence or knowledge base required to infiltrate the neighborhood space. In short, the 1920s Cultural Policy was a necessary precursor of the Patriotic NAs.

Yet, the inclusion of the prefix "patriotic" in neighborhood associations signaled the demise of the Cultural Policy and the decline of its concomitant concept of "Korean particularities." The 1920s policy had reflected Japan's guiding principle for that era: "Imperialism externally, constitutionalism internally."[4] Designating itself as the homeland and its colonies as external lands, Japan placed Korea and Taiwan outside its constitutional boundary and created a separate colonial legal space in which all political activities were banned. Against the backdrop of imminent war, however, maintaining this dual system of rule no longer seemed advantageous. As the prefix "patriotic" suggests, the empire needed the colonized to identify with the colonizer to ensure loyalty. The 1920s cultural policy that positioned Korea outside the Japanese polity created an atmosphere in which anti-Japanese Korean nationalism and anti-imperialist socialism had thrived. The line of demarcation between Japan and Korea would need to be redefined if Japan hoped to win the loyalty of the Korean people. By the late 1930s, this redrawing of colonial relations had solidified into an assimilation policy that de-emphasized earlier Japanese claims of "Korean particularities." At the center of the new wartime assimilation strategy was the patriotic NA, a revitalized tradition that was born of the cultural language of the 1920s and the mounting rhetoric of war in the early 1930s.

GOVERNOR GENERAL UGAKI KAZUSHIGE AND SOCIAL INDOCTRINATION

Former minister of war Ugaki Kazushige (1868–1956) arrived in Kyŏngsŏng (the colonial name for Seoul), the capital of South Korea, on July 14, 1931, as the sixth governor general; he succeeded Saitō Makoto (1858–1936), who left the position to serve as prime minister of Japan from 1932 to 1934.[5] He was not unfamiliar with Korea or with the posting. From April 1927 to October 1927, he had served as the temporary governor general of Korea. During his short tenure in Korea, he had gained some familiarity with Korean culture and society and understood the Cultural Policy designed by his predecessor Saitō Makoto. However, the Manchurian Incident that erupted two months after he assumed office in 1931 pushed Ugaki to advance policies more in keeping with the incoming era of military expansion than the Cultural Policy of the previous decade.

A heated issue in the early 1930s was the formation of a regional economic-political bloc in East Asia in response to protectionist measures introduced by Great Britain and the United States to combat the effects of the Great Depression. The general idea behind the bloc was to enhance economic independence by constructing firm economic connections in East Asia; the focus for this bloc was Japan and Manchuria. However, the Kwantung Army, a security force in the Kwantung Leased Territory and South Manchurian Railway zone after the Russo-Japanese War (1904–1905), and Japanese business leaders differed on the extent to which the state should control Manchuria's economic development. Business leaders argued that state planning and government economic controls should only be used to discourage the growth of Japanese industries that would undermine existing domestic production. They should not be used to restrict the freedom of capital, to interfere in the management of industry, or to restrict business profits. In contrast, radical reformists in the Kwantung Army wanted to build a state-controlled economy that "exclude[d] financial capital and political parties from Manchuria." They blamed the *zaibatsu*, vertically organized business conglomerates, for the current economic crisis, claiming that these Japanese businesses had pursued their private interests at the expense of public interests. The radical reformers in the military wanted to develop heavy industries in Manchuria under state control. The Japan-Manchuria Business Council, a representative body of the business sector, objected, arguing that a policy of complete economic control would act as a check on the flow of urgently needed capital from Japan required to fund the economic development of Manchuria. Economic development in Manchuria, they believed, should focus on creating markets for Japanese consumer goods and facilitating the transfer of raw materials to Japan.[6]

Against the backdrop of this intense dispute over the role of private capital in Manchuria, Ugaki advanced a third perspective that challenged the assumption that the bloc economy should focus solely on Japan and Manchuria. He inserted the Korean Peninsula as an economic connector between the Japanese metropole and the Manchurian hinterland and envisioned the East Sea, surrounded by four countries—Japan, the Soviet Union, Manchuria, and Korea—as the center of the East Asian bloc economy.[7] Given its extensive industrial development, Japan would provide leadership for the bloc and concentrate on industries that required more sophisticated facilities and equipment, such as automobiles and machinery. Korea would focus on light industries, such as textile manufacturing, rubber, and consumer goods, while Manchuria would supply food and natural resources. He believed that by assigning each region a specific economic role, tensions within and between regions would be minimized. Moreover, by bolstering regional economic interdependence, the Japanese empire could achieve autarky or economic self-sufficiency.[8] Achieving autarky, he believed, required the industrialization of Korea. If Korean light industries were developed, he opined, it would "have enormous impacts on the [economic] ups and downs of Japan in the future."[9]

The big picture behind this hierarchical bloc economy brought the idea of development to the fore. In pursuing the development of both agriculture and industry, Ugaki partitioned Korea into a southern part and a northern part. For the southern part of Korea, he wanted to improve productivity, while maintaining its existing roles as producer of rice for the metropole and as supplier of cotton for the Japanese textile industry. For the northern part of Korea, which remained underdeveloped but which was rich in minerals and other natural resources, he intended to develop it as a site for the iron, steel, and electric industries.[10] To ensure efficient transportation across Korea and between Korea, Japan, and Manchuria, he promoted civil engineering projects such as railroads, canals, and road construction.[11]

Transmigration policies soon followed that promoted the envisioned economic restructuring. Ugaki relocated the extra labor force from the southern part to the northern part, which lacked sufficient human resources for the envisioned industrial projects. In addition to the redistribution of the Korean population, Ugaki planned to relocate three hundred thousand Korean households to Manchuria. To this end, the Korean-Manchuria Development Company was established, and colonial government officers were dispatched to Manchuria under the guise of preventing Koreans from being discriminated against by Japanese peasants who had been sent by Japanese organizations.[12] Ugaki also provided financial support to Korean businesspersons willing to develop enterprises in Manchuria.[13] Ostensibly aimed at alleviating poverty in Korea, the plan allowed the colonial government to be involved in Manchurian development projects, thereby giving it greater leverage in the bloc economy.

The capital investment for development projects in Korea was provided by Japanese *zaibatsu* and Korean landlords willing to convert their property into industrial capital.[14] They were the only available sources of capital, given the Japanese government's lopsided interest in Manchuria.[15] Needing to attract capital investment in Korea through promises of cheap labor, Ugaki refused to enforce Japan's Factory Law and the Important Industries Control Law in Korea; the former afforded workers in Japan some protection from abusive labor practices, including the employment of children, and the latter imposed restrictions on industrial competition.[16] However, creating the circumstances favorable to potential investors would likely inflame social antipathy against colonial rule and aggravate class tensions. As it happened, both had already reached alarming levels. As policies in favor of landlords pushed the majority of peasants into debt, collective actions against landlords and capitalists became ubiquitous, and socialism intertwined with anti-imperialism spread rapidly.[17] These developments placed pressure on Ugaki to mitigate poverty, to relieve conflicts between landlords and peasants, and to reduce the formidable force of socialism fused with mass nationalism.

Faced with the choice to continue giving favors to potential investors or to restrain the class conflicts aggravated by ethnic antagonisms, Ugaki chose to attribute the origins of widespread poverty in Korea to individual indolence and inherent Korean national tendencies. Because Korea had never developed past a premodern mode of existence, Ugaki contended, the concepts of hard work, frugality, and self-sufficiency had disappeared from the Korean vocabulary. As a result, Korea had slipped into a stagnant limbo that had solidified into a national characteristic, which accounted for widespread poverty in Korea. By attributing Korean poverty to inherent national characteristics, he countered the socialist emphasis on the structural origins of poverty and rejected the idea that Japanese colonial policy had contributed to Korean poverty. He also sent the message that his plan for modernizing the Korean economy provided a path of redemption that would allow Koreans to overcome past missed opportunities and solve the mounting poverty problem.[18]

Ugaki approached the issue of poverty utilizing the concept of social indoctrination that had gradually taken root since the Cultural Policy of the 1920s and that reflected a new wave in social work at that time. Instead of providing economic aid to poverty-stricken people as had been the custom in the past, social workers argued that they should concentrate their efforts on poverty prevention. To this end, they believed that the poor must be educated in new habits: savings, self-discipline, abstinence from alcohol and tobacco, and the avoidance of excessive formalities and vanity. The idea was that by transforming the habits and daily life of the poor, economic changes would follow. The new approach also put an emphasis on spatial reform. As in the social settlement movement that began in the 1880s and peaked in the 1920s in Europe and the United States, reformers in Korea sponsored communal activities and established facilities for orphans and prostitutes, as well as social and cultural facilities like libraries and public markets.[19] This educational and cultural approach to poverty prevention fit well with Ugaki's desire to avoid introducing any legal or institutional reforms.

Unlike social work that targeted the needy, colonial social indoctrination was aimed at the entire colonized population. This approach reflected widespread awareness that "Koreans lacked knowledge, techniques and public consciousness, due to the lack of education and the primitive level of social life."[20] Prior to the 1930s, the colonial government had shown little interest in developing human resources, as evidenced by the fact that as late as 1931, elementary school attendance hovered around 17 percent.[21] From its perspective, enlightening the colonized risked undermining its political monopoly. However, in the early 1930s, the colonial government realized that the shortage of skilled workers and the lack of loyalty to the Japanese empire in Korea had the potential to undermine the envisioned economic development scheme.

Social indoctrination put equal emphasis on teaching "state consciousness" (J. *kokutai*) and providing practical training. Ugaki stressed the importance of the former, noting his shock when he observed that schools in Korea had not raised the Japanese flag for his inauguration or on Japanese national holidays.[22] He understood that a Korean society without state consciousness reinforced the popularity of socialism and of deep-seated anti-Japan nationalism—both of which he argued stemmed from "a groundless prejudice against Japan." According to Ugaki, Korea prior to Japanese annexation had been ill equipped to survive the harsh reality of international politics in East Asia. However, because Koreans failed to recognize the inevitability of their colonization, they did not appreciate the goodwill that Japan had extended to Korea by placing it under its protection. Ugaki also expressed regret that the principle of self-determination promoted by US president Woodrow Wilson during and after the First World War, as well as the anti-imperialist rhetoric of socialists, had intensified Koreans' bias against Japan.[23] He believed that eradicating Korean prejudice against Japan would germinate friendly relations between the two societies and eventually subdue Korean nationalism and socialism. To this end, he suggested the slogan "Harmony between Japan and Korea" (J. *naisenyuwa*)—a slogan that betokened the transition from the separation of the colonized from the colonizer to the assimilation of Korea.

THE EDUCATION BUREAU, "KOREAN PARTICULARITIES," AND STATE-LED MASS MOVEMENTS

Ugaki transferred the Social Section from the Bureau of Home Affairs to the Education Bureau in 1932 and made it responsible for the management of social indoctrination movements. The reshuffle was unusual, because the Social Section's focus until that time had had no direct bearing on education. Established in 1921, the section provided economic relief to those hit by natural disasters, addressed homelessness, and provided aid to orphans.[24] Conversely, the Education Bureau's responsibilities had not included dealing with unemployment, social conflicts, or the management of job research centers, orphanages, and public housing. Unusual as the move may have seemed, it aligned well with Ugaki's emphasis on spiritual development as necessary for economic development and social stability and with the cultural and educational approach to social work that had gained currency in Korea. Once the transfer was completed, the Education Bureau increasingly advanced social indoctrination as an integral part of economic restructuring.[25]

The shift to social indoctrination also resulted in a major shake-up in personnel within the Education Bureau. During his six-year tenure in Korea, Ugaki had three Education Bureau directors: Hayashi Shigeki from 1931 to 1933, Watanabe Yutahiro from 1933 to 1935, and Tominaga Fumikazu from 1935 to 1937. None of these men had any previous experience in education or social work.[26] Instead the three directors shared a reputation of being knowledgeable about Korean society. Each had come to Korea shortly after graduating from Tokyo Imperial University, and at the time of their appointment as Education Bureau director each had already served for fifteen years in Korea. As provincial governors in the early 1930s, they had promoted local development projects, and their success in these endeavors had given them some fame. Hayashi was well known for the project to pave local roads in North Chŏlla Province; Watanabe was one of the pivotal planners of the Self-Revitalization Campaign; and Tominaga had sufficient expertise in Korean traditions to publish several articles and a book on Chosŏn Korea's community compact system—a form of village covenants whose main goal was to promote social improvement through moral regeneration in the countryside.[27]

In collaboration with Korean Social Section chiefs, the three Japanese directors readily agreed that the existing social indoctrination program needed to be modified to reflect the differences between Korean and Japanese society.[28] In an address, Director Watanabe explained that "we need to make a correction quickly. The social policies *inappropriate* to Korea under the *wrong prejudice* will invite critical *difficulties* in several years."[29] For Watanabe, it was *inappropriate* that social work in Korean centered on urban areas when 80 percent of the population lived and worked on farms. This error, he contended, resulted from the *wrong prejudice* of earlier Japanese colonial officers, who had falsely assumed that Japanese and Korean society were identical, when in fact Japan was much more urbanized than Korea. Watanabe believed that it was critical for social policy in Korea to reflect Korean realities; if the focus of social indoctrination was not shifted from urban to rural areas, it would not be well received by Koreans, leading to critical *difficulties*.

The colonial government's inattention to rural areas had allowed nationalist and socialist groups to establish roots in local farming communities. Under the Cultural Policy of the 1920s that had allowed Koreans to establish nonpolitical movements, nationalists had established social enlightenment programs in villages and farming communities. Because these education and local improvement programs had been well received by Korean farmers, nationalist networks succeeded in establishing significant local community ties.[30] Similarly, socialist groups, in concert with labor unions and peasant unions, took an active role in peasant labor movements in the 1920s. Their involvement in the peasant labor movement reflected a shift in strategy from programs aimed at developing an elite cadre to a new campaign called "Into the Masses" that recognized the importance of mass agitation.[31]

To make inroads in rural Korean society, the bureau would have to compete with these two well-established movements. Although the colonial government shared with these movements a rejection of profit-oriented individualism, its objective of inspiring loyalty to the Japanese empire placed it at odds with both these movements. While nationalists and socialists held different attitudes toward capitalism, they both rejected imperialism and championed independence. The Education Bureau had to create a campaign attractive to Koreans that would displace the two established movements.[32]

To contend with these established movements, the bureau needed a cause that would be persuasive to Koreans and that would utilize an organizational network familiar to them. With reference to the cause, it placed equal emphasis on moral regeneration and economic improvement. Morality, the bureau believed, would act as a check on socialism and on excessive profit-oriented capitalism while still allowing for the pursuit of a form of capitalist economic development that fostered self-reliance, communal sensibility, and mutual prosperity.[33] According to Director Hayashi, Koreans across the economic spectrum lacked morals. The inhumane selfishness of the wealthy had resulted in widespread economic hardship, while the loss of a spirit of self-reliance among the poor had worsened these conditions. Moral deterioration, rather than structural inequities, accounted for Korean poverty. Koreans must be made to realize that they had been deceived by socialists who attributed poverty to the structures of ownership and production. Only through economic activities grounded in a spirit of self-reliance and restrained selfishness, Hayashi asserted, could class conflict be overcome, and material prosperity and social harmony be guaranteed.[34]

As for the local organization through which the bureau reached the masses, a growing number of officials within the bureau argued that the social indoctrination campaigns must reflect Korean traditional practices. Yi Kak-chong, a Korean advisor to the bureau, numbered among these voices. Citing the powerful influence of naturally formed villages in rural areas, he repeatedly highlighted the importance of local administrations collaborating with local leaders. He found that the numerous clan villages—that is, villages that had evolved from an extended family and its accumulated communal property and that had developed a communal *lieu de memoire* at which regular gatherings were held—held greater influence over local society than the formal local administration.[35] Based on consanguinity, intimate economic relationships, and cultural authority rooted in rituals, clan villages coped collectively with economic hardship and promoted social edification. The solidarity that they advanced convinced him that the organizations for the movements by the bureau should not lose touch with traditional villages.[36]

In 1932, Director Hayashi ordered a nationwide survey of existing community compacts.[37] Tominaga, then the provincial governor of North Hamgyŏng, was one of those who responded quickly to the nationwide survey. As noted earlier, he was well versed in these local covenants that regulated social relationships in rural communities, having researched the topic in the 1920s. His research had helped him to understand the premodern Korean social order based on two overlapping sites of power—that of the centralized government and that of local nobles. From his perspective, local nobles were the conduits for the centralized government to exercise sociopolitical leverage over local society. The local aristocratic class created their own system of morality, which through the community compact they disseminated to the villagers. At the same time, they acted as liaisons for bureaucrats from the central government in need of administrative assistance in dealing with tax collection and census taking. This arrangement was mutually beneficial to local nobles and the centralized state.[38] Having reached the conclusion that in premodern Korea there was almost no line of demarcation between the official administration and the private community compact,[39] Tominaga applied this model to contemporary local administration. While he was provincial governor of North Hamgyŏng, 436 community compacts were created and placed at the service of the Campaign for Improving the Rural Area that succeeded in checking North Hamgyŏng's peasant movement.[40]

When Tominaga became Education Bureau director, he continued to promote community compacts. By May 1937, the number of organizations in Korea based on the community compact system nationwide had reached a record high of 35,679, and this number did not include statistics from five provinces.[41] Slowly, the incorporation of Korean traditional practices allowed the colonial state-led social indoctrination movements, along with youth groups, wives' groups, cooperatives, and lecture series, to transform Korean society.[42]

GOVERNOR GENERAL MINAMI JIRŌ AND EDUCATION BUREAU DIRECTOR SHIOBARA TOKISABURŌ

In August 1936, roughly one year prior to the outbreak of the Sino-Japanese War, Ugaki returned to Japan and the new governor general, Minami Jirō, arrived by ship in Korea. Although a known close associate of Ugaki, he was on good terms with the army. In 1931, Minami had succeeded Ugaki as minister of war. In 1934, he became commander of the Kwantung Army and concurrently served as Japanese ambassador of Manchukuo. Despite having been forced to resign in the wake of the 1936 February 26 Incident, an attempted coup led by radical young military officers in which leading politicians, including two former prime ministers, were assassinated, he was appointed Korea's governor general on Ugaki's recommendation. Making use of his previous experience in Manchuria and his good relations with the Kwantung Army, he advanced the slogan "Chosŏn and Manchuria are like one" to defuse conflicts between Ugaki and the Kwantung Army and between Korea and Manchuria.[43]

Having inherited Ugaki's industrial development plan, Minami concentrated on channeling funds to military-related industries.[44] Under his leadership, Ugaki's message of "Harmony between Japan and Korea" shifted to a more homogenizing message, "Japan and Korea are one body" (K. *naesŏnilch'e* or J. *naisenittai*), and Koreans were identified as Japanese imperial subjects. Shifting to a more war-related agenda, Minami appointed Shiobara Tokisaburō, well known as an extreme Japanese nationalist, as the new Education Bureau director. Compared with Ugaki's three directors, who had lengthy experience in Korea, Shiobara had almost no experience in Korea. After graduating from law school at Tokyo Imperial University, he worked at the Ministry of Transportation in Japan and moved to Taiwan and then Manchuria, where he met Minami, who at that time was commander of the Kwantung Army. In 1937, Shiobara accepted Minami's offer to come to Korea to work in the Office of Secretaries. On July 3, 1937, four days before the outbreak of the Sino-Japanese War, Minami appointed him director of the Education Bureau. To offset his rudimentary understanding of Korea, he was teamed with Kim Tae-u, the new Korean chief of the Social Education Section, and Yi Kak-chong of the advisory committee. Both men were knowledgeable of Korean "particularities," and both were strong supporters of incorporating Korean customs into local programs. Nicknamed "the peninsula's Hitler," Shiobara was the de facto master designer of all ideological mobilization efforts until March 1940 when he returned to Japan.[45]

For Shiobara, the end goal of social indoctrination was to turn Koreans into Japanese imperial subjects—that is, people who unconditionally revered the Japanese emperor. They would see in the emperor the path to prosperity and to the reclamation of the beauty of Asian culture that had been contaminated by individualism and by materialist Western culture.[46] Shiobara wanted the twenty-three million Korean imperial subjects to embrace all government guidelines with unconditional trust. But he realized the existing social indoctrination program could not produce the results he sought. Frustrated, he wrote, "The total population of Korea is twenty-three million. Those who have had any education are only about between one million twenty thousand and one million thirty thousand. That is less than one-twentieth [of Koreans]. All members of the youth group, of the women's organizations, and of the institutions covered by the Movement for Improving Rural Areas total only five million. Seventeen million people are still outside the reach of social indoctrination."[47] These comments reveal his frank concern that less than one-quarter of Koreans were being reached by social indoctrination

institutions. The frustration was readily confirmed when an officer con-
fessed that social indoctrination movements were beset by a shortage
of social institutions, making it difficult to orchestrate movements on a
national scale.[48]

Neither the lecture program nor existing campaigns impressed
Shiobara. Lectures, he asserted, did not require Koreans' active participation and thus did not signal Koreans' dedication to Japan.[49] As for
written propaganda, he had serious doubts about its efficacy, given
that 67.33 percent of men and 88.98 percent of women had had no formal education.[50] Radio communication, a potential alternative to written
materials, was seriously hampered, because few villages and rural communities had radios. The radio distribution program had reached only
1,273 villages, while 70,792 villages remained without a single radio.[51]
As for campaign practices, he concerned that the practices might be
advantageous for building group leadership, but the groups were a mere
collection of independent bodies that could not work together.[52] The
ideal organization, he argued, would be monolithic, so that from top to
bottom it could work as a singular organic unit for the realization of national goals. It should also be durable so that once goals were fulfilled,
the organization would remain intact.[53] In short, he envisioned a state
in which all Korean groups and individuals fell under the umbrella of
one giant organization over which the government had total control,
and in which there were no intermediary agents. Rather than restructure existing networks, Shiobara wanted to create an entirely new
organization.[54]

To realize the organic state, Shiobara and the Education Bureau
turned their attention to the family for three reasons. First, there was
no institution other than the family that encompassed women. Women
were seen as uninterested in the state, outside state consciousness, and
thus mostly beyond the reach of social indoctrination.[55] Reaching women
mattered to the colonial state, because with the war, rationalizing
private consumption—an activity that fell within women's domain in
traditional and contemporary discourse in Korea—had taken on great
significance.[56] With Japan absorbing more private capital to offset the
cost of war and regulating its outflow to prevent inflation, the colonial
state could no longer rely on Japanese private capital, as Ugaki had, to
fund its campaigns.[57] To make matters worse, Korea, which had been a

market for Japanese commodities, was now expected to be self-sufficient and even to supply Japan with commodities that it lacked.[58] For this reason, Shiobara felt it was urgent that social indoctrination reach women, who to date had displayed no interest in the wartime mobilization effort.[59]

Second, the notion of family had the cultural power to distinguish the moral East from the legal West and to differentiate "Japanese totalitarianism"—a term, tantamount to Japanism, used by colonial officers at that time—from Nazism. It was argued, unlike Western countries based on rights, true Japanese imperial subjects make up one extended family. The true prosperity of the family lies in harmony, not in claims made against the patriarch for rights. "What seven-year-old children claim their rights is not a custom of the Japanese family."[60] This idea was applied to imperial politics: Righteousness mediates between the Japanese emperor and his subjects whereas affection mediates between father and son.[61] In other words, just as family members heed the moral authority of family patriarchs, to preserve harmony, imperial subjects should obey the Japanese emperor who, as the supreme patriarch, acts to restore balance in the East.

Similarly, Japanese totalitarianism was viewed as a sort of familial totalitarianism, while Nazism, it was argued, originated from class struggle and from the notion of German racial superiority. While Nazi imperialism sought living space (*Lebensraum*) for Germans, Japanese imperialism sought to unite the various branches of the Asian family and the world into one extended family (J. *hakkōichiu*). The inclusiveness of Japanese imperialism was contrasted with the exclusiveness of Nazism to argue that Japanese totalitarianism was "the sincere totalitarianism."[62] This concept of the global family, in which Japan was the moral center of power and Korea was one of its branches, provided the foundation for the colonial government's drive to transcend individualism and selfish nationalism, which they defined as Korean nationalism, to preserve the virtues of the East.

Lastly, Shiobara and the bureau viewed the home as a hotbed of individualism, family egoism, and Korean nationalism, because it was where individual habits and cultural practices were learned. Yet they also saw in the home a potential seedbed for assimilating Koreans into the extended family of Japanese totalitarianism. But first, they had to find a way to tap into this traditionally private sphere so that they could remake Koreans as imperial subjects. To this end, the Standard for the Reform of Daily Life under Emergency Conditions, in which the Government General overtly expressed its disapproval of Korean national customs, individual habits, and patterns of private consumption, was issued in 1938. It encouraged Koreans to adopt a new way of life, in which they, as part of the Greater East Asia Co-Prosperity Sphere, an outgrowth of the Japan-Manchuria economic bloc discussed earlier in this chapter, committed themselves wholeheartedly to the war cause. This commitment included an obligation for Koreans to pay regular homage to the Japanese emperor at state Shinto shrines, utter daily oaths of loyalty to the Japanese sovereign each morning while bowing to the east, speak only Japanese in the home and in public, and practice frugality.[63] To naturalize this way of life, Shiobara wanted every waking moment of Koreans' lives to be shaped by social indoctrination.[64] He believed that the survival of Japanese totalitarianism depended on the reform of private family life.

The neighborhood space was once and for all chosen as the new organizational base for mass movements led by the state. Suited to local communal practices and congruous with the values of the East sought by the colonial state, the neighborhood's proximity to the family would provide the colonial state with an effective entry point into family life so they could reform this private sphere in accordance with state goals.

Once the decision was made, Shiobara made fast headway to build a new organization for general mobilization. Accompanied by Social Indoctrination Section Chief Kim Tae-u, Shiobara held a private meeting on June 12, 1938, with ten representatives of civil society. Five of those in attendance were Koreans; the remaining five were Japanese civilians, including the former director of the Education Bureau, Hayashi Shigeki. At the meeting, they resolved to establish the Korean League for the General Mobilization of the National Spirit.[65] Two days later, the steering committee drafted the league's platform and made a list of approximately seventy social groups that would become part of the league. The steering committee included several prominent Koreans: Kim Sŏng-su, Pak Hŭng-sik, and Han Sang-yong from the business sector; Kim Hwal-lan from the education sector; and Ch'oe Rin from the religious sector. On June 22, 1938, a general convention was held in

Kyŏngsŏng and the league was officially inaugurated on July 7, 1938.[66] Administrative Superintendent Ono Rokuichiro, the second most powerful figure in the colonial government, served as honorary president, while Director Shiobara was chair of the board.[67]

Following the administrative order on August 24, 1938, to establish local branches, the league began to establish local branches throughout the countryside. With the full support of board members who visited local provinces to give endorsement speeches, provincial governments established provincial associations.[68] Counties, towns, and local groups, such as the Red Cross, cooperatives, women's groups, and youth groups, were also advised to set up local branches.[69] By the end of September 1938, there were 13 provincial associations and by the end of June 1939, 239 county associations, 2,352 town associations, and 61,915 village associations were set up.[70]

The final step for the Korean League was to create Patriotic NAs, each made up of about ten households. The Korean League published cartoons, posters, and pamphlets, as well as enlisted prominent leaders to deliver special talks and lectures to generate enthusiasm among local Koreans. Meetings for Patriotic NA leaders were held so that they could learn about their duties and receive tips on managing Patriotic NAs, while heads of households were convened to procure assurances of their cooperation. A steady stream of newspaper articles about successful Patriotic NAs and about participating local youth groups nudged passive neighborhoods into action.[71] As a result, by the end of June 1939, 347,728 Patriotic NAs had been formed across Korea.[72] Each NA rallied its members to champion the Japanese spirit and to advance the wartime agenda. In theory, everyone in Korea from the governor general down to the smallest infant belonged to a Patriotic NA, a totalitarian body whose structures overlapped with those of the bureaucratic hierarchy.

ASSEMBLIES OF PATRIARCHAL PATRIOTIC NAs

The NAs allowed the Korean League to reach areas previously untouched by social indoctrination as Shiobara had planned. However, he found ineffective communication of the league with hundreds of thousands of

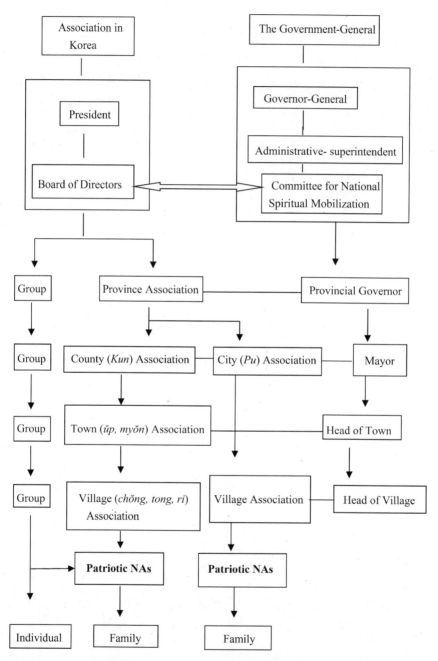

FIGURE 1.1.   The Korean League for the General Mobilization of National
Spirit in 1938. Chōsen sōtokufu, *Sōdōin* (General mobilization) 1, no. 1
(1939): 45.

Patriotic NAs that showed inconsistent responses to state-led campaigns.[73] There was a proposal that would have provided financial compensation to Patriotic NA heads who invested significant time in the organization, but insufficient funds for any additional expenditures made it unlikely for Shiobara to accept the proposal. Instead, he argued, NAs were intended to foster the spirit of voluntarism; members were expected to willingly abandon private interests to promote the public goals. If NA heads were paid, it would undermine the fundamental premise behind the organization.[74] At first glance, the above rationale seems to suggest that Shiobara advocated voluntarism over bureaucratic intervention, but in truth, he did not have complete faith in either. While he argued that a "forcible push, threat, or encouragement would not work in the everyday realm or in matters of consumption," he also recognized that voluntarism had limits, as it tended to wane once a campaign goal was achieved.[75] Wary of relying solely on either voluntarism or bureaucratic force, he wanted the management of Patriotic NAs to be voluntary, but subject to government supervision.

The problem, however, was still voluntarism. By considering geography and local customs in delineating neighborhood spaces, the league wanted to leave existing communal bonds intact to motivate collective participation. But it failed to draw sufficient attention to Patriotic NAs, let alone invoke passion for voluntary service.[76] The main reason was that from the outset the Patriotic NAs did not call upon Koreans to volunteer. Membership was automatically and mandatorily given to all heads of household without any advance notice or any meeting at which the league tried to persuade Koreans of the righteousness of its goals. As a result, Koreans did not even understand if membership was conferred upon an individual or upon a family.[77]

The chasm between planning and reality was especially pronounced in urban Patriotic NAs. People in the city were reproached for "spoiled spirits" and physical weakness, and urban Patriotic NAs were urged to emulate the rural Patriotic NAs that significantly outperformed those in urban areas.[78] This difference in performance owed to the government's decision in the early 1930s to under Governor General Ugaki shift its social indoctrination efforts from urban communities to rural ones, as discussed earlier. The reduced focus on urban areas in the early 1930s meant that urban residents had not been tamed by years of the state-led mass movements. In addition, Korean nationalism was more pronounced in the cities than in rural areas thanks to print culture, commerce, modern education, and anti-Japanese Christianity.[79] This made cities hubs for socialist and nationalist intellectuals and the epicenter of large-scale movements against Japan. Korean nationalism outweighed Japanese state patriotism in cities. The regional differences among Patriotic NAs reflected the political topography of urban-centered nationalism and rural-centered social indoctrination.

Patriotic NAs, which were based on agrarian traditions, had aspects incompatible with urban life. As noted at the time, "Patriotic NAs are more or less inadequate in cities owing to different occupations and frequent demographic moves." [80] There was almost nothing to glue residents together in cities except residential proximity. The more diversified a region became, the less communal solidarity there was. What solidarity did exist quickly dissipated owing to the high demographic mobility in cities; thus, compared to the countryside, urban neighborhood cohesion was fragile. Integrated Patriotic NAs in which Koreans and Japanese both belonged, which were commonplace in cities, seldom developed communal cohesion; instead, they were plagued by ethnic conflicts stemming from cultural differences.[81] Occupational diversity also made it hard to create bonds of mutuality between members of urban NAs. The situation in First Kyoku District highlights that different everyday livelihoods made cooperation unlikely. Most of its residents worked in the service sector. The rest were employed as office workers, government officials, and merchants. Mr. Kanzaki, who headed this district, complained about the challenge of arranging times for meetings due to clashing schedules.[82]

Neither men nor women found Patriotic NAs compelling. The societal expectation was that women's place was in the home. The pronounced division between home and workplace introduced by modernity reinforced this belief, thus intensifying the social practice of the two sexes avoiding working or socializing with one another. The colonial government ignored this reality, asking Patriotic NAs to facilitate teamwork on projects that did not distinguish between production and consumption or between physical labor and household management. Unwilling to have anything to do with tasks traditionally considered women's work, men often ignored NA guidelines that encouraged male leadership and

refused to actively participate, reasoning that NAs "belonged to women."
[83] The nine-to-five work schedule provided male "monthly-paid workers" with an excellent excuse to avoid participation in Patriotic NAs.

Looking to enhance social interactions between neighbors, Kyŏngsŏng's city league adopted as its model the monthly assemblies of rural
villages. They were not only a classic way of dealing with local affairs in
premodern agrarian Korean society but also instrumental in generating
rural economic development and promoting social indoctrination in
the early 1930s.[84] The routine interaction between neighbors was expected to reinforce communal bonds in NAs despite frequent demographic changes within urban spaces. In October 1939, the city announced that it would hold a mass assembly to celebrate Patriotic Day.
Previously, the observance of Patriotic Day, which fell on the first day
of each month, had only been required of schoolchildren. But for the
November 1939 observance, all nine thousand of the city's Patriotic NAs
were scheduled to gather in honor of the event.[85] On October 31, the
city announced that restaurants, cinemas, department stores, and cafés
would be closed on Patriotic Day, so that city residents could practice
wartime self-restraint.[86]

On November 1, 1939, a siren sounded throughout the city at 7:00
a.m. The siren signaled representatives from each household to gather
outside their homes. Under the direction of the head of the Patriotic
NAs, who carried the NA's flag, they were to march to a designated place.
Depending on the number of patriotic NAs in a district, the size of these
assemblies could number up to two thousand persons.[87] Even Governor
General Minami was not exempt from this directive. As an ordinary
member of a Patriotic NA that included his family and the families of
his driver, gardener, and secretaries, he was required to attend the
Kyŏngbok district assembly. Minami joined more than one thousand
other people at the required meeting, held at the playground of Ch'ŏng'un
Elementary School.[88] Once assembled, all participants bowed to the east
to acknowledge the emperor. This greeting to the emperor was followed
by a moment of silence in honor of the army troops fighting in the war.
The district league chair then gave a short speech outlining the war situation and advising them of the proper moral code of conduct for
Japanese imperial subjects. Afterwards, the people recited in unison the
Imperial Subject Oath (K. *Hwangguk sinmin sŏsa*): "First, we are subjects

of the imperial land. We repay sovereign and country with loyalty. Second, we, subjects of the imperial land, will cooperate in mutual faith and affection, and make stronger thereby the corpus of the state. Third, we, subjects of the imperial land, will cultivate our powers of discipline and sacrifice, and enhance the imperial way."[89] The ceremonial assembly ended with the lowering of the Japanese national flag.[90] From start to finish, the ceremony lasted thirty minutes so as not to disrupt people's daily lives.[91]

On May 8, 1940, mandated additional monthly assemblies by Kyŏng-sŏng linked Patriotic NAs to four types of monthly assemblies. The first was the general assembly hosted by the district league on each Patriotic Day. The second required assembly led by the heads of subdistricts took place on the third day of each month. The third assembly required only the presence of Patriotic NA heads and was held on the fifth day of each month. The fourth assembly, held on the seventh day of each month, was a gathering of the heads of households of each Patriotic NA.[92] In December 1940, the colonial government compelled all Korean Patriotic NAs to have multilayered monthly assemblies.[93] Reimagined as a national practice, the assemblies were expected to shorten the time it took to notify local Patriotic NAs of new policies.

Patriotic NA assemblies were significantly longer in duration, lasting up to two hours. Starting time for these assemblies was set at 8:00 to 10:00 p.m. in the summer and 7:00 to 9:00 p.m. in the winter.[94] However, NA heads could adjust these times in keeping with local exigencies.[95] The meeting place varied by Patriotic NA. Some had set locales for meetings, usually at the home of the headperson. In other NAs, households took turns hosting the meeting.[96] The meetings followed the same routine as the general assemblies. Each commenced with opening remarks, followed by the greeting to the Japanese emperor, and a moment of silence in honor of military troops. Afterwards, there was a discussion session that lasted roughly one hour.[97] The meeting closed with everyone reciting the Imperial Subject Oath. Attendees were encouraged to linger after meetings to listen to radio programming together or to take part in other recreational activities. Postmeeting activities, it was hoped, would foster amicable relations between neighbors.[98]

The hour-long discussion was the focal point of the Patriotic NA assembly. After a recitation of the previous month's accomplishments and shortfalls, the NA head announced a new agenda, which reflected the interests of the colonial government. Patriotic NAs could not modify or contest the basic agenda; they could, however, determine how agenda goals were realized. For example, rural Patriotic NAs had no say over the compulsory grain collection quota, but they could decide how much each family in the NA would contribute.[99] Similarly, urban Patriotic NAs decided how rations would be distributed, based on the economic realities of member families.[100] This limited control over the agenda was designed to give NA members a sense of being actively involved as loyal Japanese imperial subjects in the decision-making process. However, voluntarism without a right to contest or refuse to comply was reduced to active passivity.

The headperson ensured that heads of household would relay decisions made in the assembly to family members and supervise the implementation of those decisions for the rest of the month. In this way, responsibility for turning Koreans into Japanese imperial subjects became the responsibility of heads of household. Along with this spatial transfer to the private domestic sphere, this move also reflected a shift in the locus of power from state bureaucratic to patriarchal authority, in that male patriarchs determined the time and labor of women and the rest of the family members. The reliance of the colonial government on patriarchal authority was justified based on the belief that "family members can take a full rest and have affectionate family lives only when they are held together under the authority of the family head."[101]

By the same token, the Government-General envisioned Patriotic NAs as a quasi-extended family in which male family patriarchs answered to a higher-ranking male patriarch, that is, the head of the NA. As patriarch of this extended family, it was the responsibility of the NA head to bring order to the neighborhood and to solve disputes between neighbors. In keeping with this patriarchal hierarchy, loyalty was owed the Government-General, because only it could ensure prosperity and peace for the greater family of Koreans, which in turn was a branch of the Japanese family. Thus, at the apex of this patriarchal hierarchy was the Japanese emperor, who as the supreme father maintained public morality and safeguarded the economic and political interests of the East Asian bloc. NAs were the local manifestation of this hierarchically organized empire in which the moral space of the neighborhood was instrumentalized for the political interests of the state.

CONCLUSION

The birth of Patriotic NAs marked the institutional completion of Japanese wartime colonial policy. In the early 1930s, economic depression and the growing crisis of war led the colonial government to pursue direct dominance over the colonized Koreans and to claim the East as an alternative to Western modernity. The outcome was state-led mass movements that drew on Korean agrarian communal traditions to overcome traditional anti-Japanese sentiment and to counteract the encroachment of nationalist and socialist movements in rural areas. With the outbreak of the Sino-Japanese War, the colonial government heightened the state-led mass movement by placing the moral space of the neighborhood at the service of the Korean League for the General Mobilization of the National Spirit through the creation of Patriotic NAs. With their almost universal coverage, access to the private family sphere, community-centered morality, and voluntarism, NAs were able to penetrate a Korean society in which anti-Japanese sentiment was widespread. Owing to the centralized bureaucracy's direct intervention, these volunteer associations spread quickly across Korea. However, because of their vast coverage, budgetary deficiencies, and other social factors such as urbanization, class distinctions, and gender norms, the colonial government could not always control Patriotic NAs' response to the government agenda. To rectify this situation, it mandated Patriotic NA assemblies. In essence, NAs became a microcosm of Japan's family-centered imperial ideology.

CHAPTER 2

The Colonial Politics of Naming

Korea is neither a place to be absorbed into Japan, nor a place to be independent of Japan. It should flourish in subordination to Japan.
—Shiobara Tokisaburō[1]

In October 1942, after the wartime paper shortage and censorship rules had driven most newspapers and magazines out of business, *Kokumin sōryoku* (Concerted National Power), a magazine put out by the Government-General, published a brief, five-line article titled "*Aikokuhan* and *Tonarigumi.*" *Aikokuhan* was the Japanese name for Patriotic Neighborhood Associations (Patriotic NAs) in Korea, and *tonarigumi* was the name for the system of neighborhood associations in Japan. The article made clear that the Government-General did not approve of Koreans conflating the two: "There is no *tonarigumi* in Korea. Some Korean wives call it *tonarigumi,* even though they live in Korea and are talking about Patriotic NAs. Both are similar in function. However, Korea does not have *tonarigumi;* instead it has Patriotic NAs. Call them Patriotic NAs, not *tonarigumi.*"[2] Neither Korea's adoption of the term "*tonarigumi*" nor the Government-General's strong objection to it makes sense on initial inspection. Patriotic NAs had been established in Korea in 1938, two years before *tonarigumi* had been placed under the Imperial Rule Assistance Association (Taiseiyokusankai, hereafter IRAA) in Japan. During those two years, Koreans had regularly taken part in the everyday activities of Patriotic NAs; thus, the name "Patriotic NAs" already had a strong presence in Korea. Since no organizational change had been introduced to Patriotic NAs, Koreans' sudden preference for "*tonarigumi*" seems surprising.

Equally surprising was the Government-General's vehement reaction, as Patriotic NAs and *tonarigumi* were similar systems with similar functions. Both were based on the spatial unit of the neighborhood. Each unit had a selected headperson and held regular gatherings to mobilize residents in line with national campaigns. The units were responsible for allocating rationed goods and government bonds, distributing government propaganda, and carrying out street cleanings and everyday reforms. This, therefore, raises the question why the Government-General was concerned enough by the populace's use of the Japanese term *tonarigumi* for Patriotic NAs to make an official statement denouncing the use of the former term. What political price would the Government-General pay if Patriotic NAs in Korea were identified with the *tonarigumi* of Japan? This chapter examines the historical juncture at which the artificial change in linguistic practice occurred and the political implications for the Government-General under Japanese wartime imperial politics.

The tension perceived in the name of the two NAs reflected the instability of wartime colonialism. Colonial policies in the 1930s were defined by two conflicting terms: "Korean particularities" and assimilation. Before 1937, the Government-General placed greater emphasis on the distinctiveness of Korean society. It underscored the differences between Japanese and Korean society to spotlight its own roles in the bloc economy and established a certain degree of autonomy in implementing Japanese policy. The outbreak of war, however, destabilized this arrangement. The Government-General realized that it needed to place greater emphasis on assimilation to inspire Koreans to mobilize voluntarily for the Japanese war effort. At the same time, it wanted to preserve its limited autonomy vis-à-vis Japan as well as its dominance over Korean society. Thus, it did not completely abandon the discourse of Korean particularities; instead, it devised a bilayered political order: that is, it framed its relationship with Japan as political and defined the Korean space as nonpolitical. This strategy initially allowed the colonial government concomitantly to promote Korea's assimilation into Japan and the distinctiveness of Korean culture. However, as we shall see, when Koreans spontaneously began using the Japanese term "*tonarigumi*" in lieu of "Patriotic NAs," it exposed the fundamental contradiction in the wartime colonial order in Korea.

THE JAPANESE NEW ORDER AND
THE KOREAN NEW ORDER

In summer 1940, the phrase "New Order" (J. *Shintaisei*) dominated Japanese politics. The outbreak of World War II in Europe in September 1939, along with the United States' termination of the 1911 Treaty of Commerce and Navigation with Japan on January 1, 1940—a move that freed the way for imposing an economic embargo—led Japan to focus on Southeast Asia as a potential new source of defense-related raw materials.[3] This quest for raw materials prompted Japan to redefine the objective of the Sino-Japanese War to consider the expanded territorial frame. Whereas previously the war objective had been to establish a "New Order" in East Asia, the new objective was to establish a "New Order" in Greater East Asia. On September 27, 1940, Japan signed the Tripartite Pact with Germany and Italy, in which Germany and Italy recognized "the leadership of Japan in the establishment of a New Order in Greater East Asia" and Japan acknowledged the primacy of Germany and Italy in Europe.

Beyond providing Japan's war rationale, the concept of a "New Order" also found resonance in Japan owing to the repudiation of political parties in the 1930s. As Andrew Gordon notes, "In just three years, the multiple shocks of the depression, military expansion, assassination, and intense social conflict foreclosed Japan's liberal and democratic options."[4] Between 1936 and 1940, military leaders and bureaucrats increasingly replaced independent political parties, business associations, labor unions, and tenant unions as the primary shapers of Japanese policy. Viewing "domestic unrest" as an impediment to national defense, these leaders advocated political and economic reform at home and expansion abroad. To eliminate labor unrest and popular discontent, they called for policies to nationalize industry and to control private property and argued that war would strengthen the people and their nationalism. The "New Order" they envisioned as the solution to Japan's problems, eliminating all intermediaries between the emperor and the people, thereby creating a national body unified in a total war system.[5]

On July 26, 1940, the Second Konoe Cabinet released the Basic National Policy Outline (J. *Kihon kokusaku yōkō*) that identified establishing the "New Order" of Greater East Asia as Japan's primary mission. Likening the mission to "making the world one house" (J. *hakkō ichi*), the New Order called for integrating Japan, its colonies, and Manchukuo for the mutual prosperity of all. In the political realm, this meant eliminating the parliamentary system by merging the political parties into one national organization committed to realizing state interests—that is, the IRAA. In the economic realm, it entailed trying to overcome the pitfalls of the liberal capitalist system by replacing unrestricted competition between large business enterprises with state planning, guidance, and control. The State Planning Board (J. *Kikakuin*) took over the banking system, introduced price controls, and made businesses accountable to the state rather than to shareholders. The goal was to facilitate the war effort by creating the conditions for economic self-sufficiency. Morally, it meant abandoning the slavish adulation of the West that threatened to destroy Japanese culture and values. Rather than selfish individualism, the Japanese should dedicate themselves to advancing the interests of the nation. Thus purified, the Japanese would drive Western liberalism out of Asia, so that the Asian people could live in harmony under the Japanese emperor's benevolent rule.[6] The IRAA, the institutional body responsible for implementing the plan, mobilized the Japanese people toward this goal through neighborhood associations (*tonarigumi*).

The launching of the IRAA, however, was delayed by three months owing to disagreements about the direction that the organization should take. IRAA authorities, including Prime Minister Konoe Fumimaro, viewed the IRAA as a new national political party that would replace all existing parties, incorporate the military, and serve as the foundation for a mass national movement. The Home Ministry, however, wanted to place the IRAA under its control and use it to assist in the administration of the war mobilization at the local level. A third group argued that the IRAA should be neither a political party nor an instrument of local administration; it should be a separate public body focused on promoting Asian moral values in the populace.[7]

There was also disagreement over the economic reforms that should be pursued by the New Order. The Konoe Cabinet wanted the IRAA to impose strict regulations on large businesses and restructure small and mid-size businesses to reduce popular economic unrest.[8] However, the business sector and extreme-right political parties expressed strong opposition, arguing that the proposed controls on private enterprise amounted to communism. Supporters disputed this claim, pointing out that the reforms did not eliminate private interests or private ownership. Still, the idea that the reforms would amount to communism persisted, and no decision was reached on economic policy prior to the launch of the IRAA, with Prime Minister Konoe as chair, on October 12, 1940.[9]

On October 16, 1940, Governor General Minami Jirō held a provisional meeting of provincial governors at which he announced the establishment of a "Korean New Order" (K. *Chosŏn sinch'eje*) in response to the Japanese New Order. In keeping with the New Order movement in Japan, he ordered that all existing state-led movements be incorporated into the new Movement for Concerted National Power (K. *Kungmin ch'ongnyŏk undong*) for realizing the Korean New Order. Prior to this announcement, state-led movements had been divided according to social sector. The Movement for Improving Rural Areas focused on economic development, while the Movement for the General Mobilization of the National Spirit concentrated on the cultural and spiritual domain. The two movements were now combined and renamed the Movement for Concerted National Power. The League for Concerted National Power (K. *Kungmin ch'ongnyŏk yŏnmaeng*) was newly established to promote the movement. All subunits of the two previous movements, that is, the Korean League for the General Mobilization of National Spirit, community compacts, committees for improving rural areas, and economic cooperatives, were dissolved into the new league. In lieu of these units, roughly 350,000 Patriotic NAs were placed under the authority of the League for Concerted National Power.[10] As a result, Patriotic NAs became the primary unit of organization responsible for implementing wartime mobilization programs under the cause of concerted national power: everyday activities in Patriotic NAs were expected to eliminate the notion of private individual interests, thereby cultivating imperial subjects who were singularly committed to serving the interests of Japan.

With the organizational reshuffle, the wartime order in Japan and in Korea was established: the Japanese New Order under the IRAA and the Korean New Order under the League for Concerted National Power. The difference in the organizations' names attracted attention. When the Korean League for the General Mobilization of the National Spirit was established in 1938, the colonial government had taken its name from the Central League for the General Mobilization of the National Spirit in Japan, the national body which was organized in 1937 in order to lead the Movement for the General Mobilization of the National Spirit in Japan. This time, however, the Government-General did not opt to name both the movement and the new national body after its Japanese counterpart.

A remark made by Minami at a meeting of provincial governors suggested a reason for this divergence: "We did not name the League for Concerted National Power after the IRAA, the name for the new political system in Japan, so as to prevent Koreans from interpreting the movement in Korea as a *political* one."[11] Minami's comment indicated that he considered the IRAA to be a mass political body—a view shared by Prime Minister Konoe Fumimaro. Since Koreans did not have political rights under Japanese rule, adopting the Japanese name with its political connotations might encourage the aspirations of Koreans for political and economic reform—something that Minami clearly did not want to do.

Minami's desire to divorce the Korean movement from politics is also evidenced by his refusal to introduce domestic reforms comparable to those introduced in Japan. For example, the Japanese government initiated economic reforms that prioritized the general welfare of the public over big business. Instead, in explaining the Japanese New Order to Koreans, Minami focused on its international political goals. According to him, Japan had reached an agreement to bring international disputes to an end and to redesign the world order in concert with Germany and Italy. Under the agreement, Japan would take responsibility for establishing and leading a New Order in East Asia. This New Order, he asserted, would be free from non-Asian influences. Currently, he lamented, East Asia was a long way from achieving this goal; the economy of East Asia remained heavily dependent on the United States and Great Britain; and Western cultural norms, such as individualism and liberalism, had gained widespread acceptance across East Asia, while East Asian virtues were being forgotten. Overcoming the economic and cultural crisis, Minami explained, required developing an economically self-sufficient bloc of Asian nations, thereby shutting out the West and allowing the Japanese spirit once again to thrive: "Everything that has been tarnished by exposure to the West will be restored by the Japanese spirit."[12]

In identifying the Korean New Order with the economic and cultural recovery of the East, the colonial government made it clear that domestic political reform was not the goal of the New Korean Order. Once the New Order was divorced from political reform, the government introduced a new turn of phrase to explain differences between the Japanese New Order and the Korean New Order. At the October 1940 meeting of bureau directors, Minami noted that the League for Concerted National Power, the umbrella organization for the Movement for Concerted National Power to which Patriotic NAs belonged, assisted "politics by the governor general," while the IRAA, to which Japanese NAs (*tonarigumi*) belonged, assisted imperial rule.[13] In short, although similar in structure, the two NA systems supported different politics within the Japanese empire: "politics by the governor general" and imperial rule.

The phrase "politics by the governor general" simultaneously communicated that the governor general had considerable independence from the Japanese civilian government and that he held the preponderance of power in colonial Korea. Since the position was not subject to the supervision of the Japanese cabinet, the Japanese emperor, rather than the prime minister, made the appointment. The strategic military importance of Korea led to the Japanese Army's deep involvement in selecting the governor general of Korea. In the 1920s, during the Taishō Democracy, the Japanese civilian government attempted to check the military's power by claiming a role in selecting the governor general of Korea. In particular, Prime Minister Hara Takashi tried to place Korea under his authority by overturning the existing separation between mainland Japan and Korea.[14] However, this effort failed when the Japanese Diet vetoed the proposal to allow Koreans representation in the Diet; this move, it feared, would give Koreans too much power and endanger Japanese political control.[15] Thus, despite a weakening in the military's political power in the 1920s, all eight governors general of Korea were military officers and served as the Japanese emperor's proxy. So long as their actions were not at variance with those of the Japanese government, the governors general could exercise immense authority in Korea, including issuing laws, ordinances, and regulations; the only limits were that the governor general could not authorize military actions, make diplomatic decisions, or issue currency.[16] When the Japanese government wanted legal action in Korea, it contacted the governor general, who made modifications as appropriate based on the situation in Korea before issuing the action under his name.[17]

The governor general had a firm grip on the bureaucracy, as there was little interdepartmental strife and few serious internal challenges to his authority. From the beginning of colonial rule, the Government-General excluded Koreans from holding certain core positions in the bureaucracy. Although the Japanese could not avoid employing some Koreans in government posts, they relegated the few thousand Koreans in the bureaucracy to secondary positions at local branch offices, while the Japanese monopolized the high-ranking positions at central headquarters.[18] In the late 1920s, when the colonial government established local assemblies with the intent to nourish those who would collaborate with it and funnel policies down to local society, a few local elites were authorized to attend assembly meetings.[19] Local assemblies were a pivotal place to raise local issues, such as education, transportation, and electricity, but Koreans had neither the right to vote nor the right to propose policy.[20]

Japanese bureaucrats with long-term careers in Korea also relegated their short-term colleagues to less prestigious posts, justifying this maneuver by claiming that Korea was so different from Japan that short-term officers could not possibly govern effectively. Japanese officers who did spend extended periods in Korea were frequently transferred between bureaus, for example, moving to the Education Bureau from the Bureau of Agriculture. These frequent personnel reshuffles prevented strong factions from forming within the government. Despite some concern that this practice would hinder the development of specialized expertise, it continued because most believed that it would prevent interdepartmental competition and defuse tensions between bureaucrats—two chronic issues in Japan. "Integrated administration," as the practice was called, allowed administrators to implement the will of the governor general effectively.[21] The two features of "politics by the governor general"—relative independence from Japan and a highly centralized power structure in Korea—gave the governor general near-absolute power in how Japanese political and economic interests were represented and realized in Korea.

In the early 1930s, "politics by the governor general" was materialized in the claim of "Korean particularities" and the slogan "Harmony between Japan and Korea" (K. *naesŏnyunghwa*) As discussed in chapter 1, the economic depression had catalyzed the Japanese empire to concentrate its efforts on advancing a bloc economy. Responding to the new atmosphere, Governor General Ugaki Kazushige replaced the Cultural Policy of the 1920s with a new development policy. The aim of the new policy was to establish Korea as a significant partner in the empire's bloc economy while at the same time quelling Korean nationalism, which in the 1920s had intensified due to the economic crisis and the inroads that nationalist and socialist groups had made in rural areas. Before the new policy could be implemented, Ugaki needed Japan's approval and the support of Korean society. Ugaki's strategy entailed an appeal to "Korean particularities." With reference to Japan, this entailed claiming that Korea was so different from Japan that applying Japan's policy to Korea without any modifications would result in failure. Korea needed a separate policy, formulated by the Government-General since it best understood Korean society. Based on this claim, the Government-General retained significant control over economic development in Korea.

However, the outbreak of war in 1937 threatened to undermine the Government-General's ability to pursue an autonomous policy. To increase administrative efficiency, the Japanese government wanted to apply war-related laws directly to Korea. The Government-General objected since this would limit its authority vis-à-vis the Japanese government. To block this move, the Government-General once again appealed to Korean particularities, and the Japanese government acquiesced.[22] In the context of war, the colonial government also wanted to place more emphasis on the unity of the two nations to facilitate Korean's voluntary mobilization for the war effort. Thus, the slogan "Harmony between Japan and Korea" was replaced with a new slogan, "Japan and Korea are one body" (J. *naisenittai*). The new slogan, however, placed colonial officials in an awkward position; they needed to maintain the notion of difference to preserve the autonomy of the Government-General and to justify to Koreans postponing domestic political reforms. At the same time, to inspire Koreans to participate wholeheartedly in the Japanese war effort, they needed to emphasize to Koreans that the new policy of "Japan and Korea are one body" would bring about the total integration of Koreans into the Japanese empire and end discrimination. In fact, this strategy produced some success; the dissolution of the colonizer-colonized divide prompted some Koreans to embrace wartime collaboration with the Japanese. In fact, at his postwar trial on charges of collaborating with the enemy, Cho Pyŏng-sang, a Korean who served on the board of the League for General Mobilization of the National Spirit, dated his decision to collaborate with the Japanese to the introduction of *naisenittai*.[23]

The complicated wartime political interests of the Government-General became apparent during a discussion forum of the League for Concerted National Power held at the Chosŏn Hotel on October 28, 1940. Discussants included six leading figures from the league (General Secretary Kawagishi Bunzarō, Director of the Training Department Shiobara Tokisaburō, Director of the General Affairs Shimagawa Kyōgen, Director of the Social Indoctrination Department Mitsubashi Koichirō, Director of the Finance Department Mizuta Naomasa, and chief of the Concerted National Power Section Nobuhara Sato) and eight newspaper journalists.[24] The goal of the forum was to provide the Korean public with details about the restructuring of the League for the General Mobilization of the National Spirit, including how organizationally and functionally the new League for Concerted National Power differed from its predecessor.

The forum began by addressing the reasons for replacing the League for the General Mobilization of the National Spirit with the League for Concerted National Power. Shiobara acknowledged that the introduction of the New Order in Japan had been the immediate catalyst for the restructuring. However, he also highlighted practical and organizational problems with the original league. Specifically, he noted that its confinement to the "spiritual realm" prevented it from assisting with productivity, mandatory rice collection, and the purchase of government bonds. The new organization would combine the spiritual and economic realms, thus overcoming the shortcomings of its predecessor. He believed that the organizational stability of the League for the General Mobilization of the National Spirit, combined with the lack of competing groups in Korea, would allow the restructuring to proceed more quickly than in Japan, where the IRAA was having difficulty integrating existing interest groups.[25]

In explaining the transition to journalists at the forum, Shiobara opined that the movements promoted by the League for Concerted

National Power "should keep pace with the powerful driving force of 'politics by the Governor General.'"[26] This link between "politics by the governor general" and the new league was familiar to journalists. As noted earlier, the Government-General, to distinguish between the IRAA and the League for Concerted National Power, had released a statement in which it explained that the IRAA assisted with imperial rule and the new Korean League assisted with "politics by the governor general." However, the link between the two organizations confused journalists, as it appeared to contradict Governor General Minami's declaration that the league's activities were limited to the nonpolitical realm. To resolve the confusion, one journalist inquired if Concerted National Power movements, in accordance with Minami's position, were nonpolitical. In his reply, Shiobara affirmed Minami's definition, adding that Concerted National Power movements were action oriented, not politically motivated. Another journalist voiced his impression that Concerted National Power movements must have something to do with politics since they were directly linked to "politics by the governor general." This time Mitsuhashi, the director of the Social Indoctrination Department, answered, "I do not work with political movements."[27] Unlike the journalists, the apparent contradiction of having nonpolitical movements assisting with "politics by the governor general" did not disturb high-ranking bureaucrats on the panel.

The panel discussed two interrelated levels of political engagement—domestic politics in Korea and in Japan and imperial politics between Japan and the Government-General in Korea. With reference to domestic politics, General Secretary Kawagishi expressed disapproval of the Japanese Diet and of party politics in Japan:

> The IRAA movement in inland Japan aims at facilitating politics through a national organization. This objective, however, may take two years to five years. . . . At any rate, we [the Japanese empire] need to dissolve institutions based on liberal principles and replace them with a system that everyone can support. This is the fundamental idea of the IRAA movement. IRAA is the core as well as the driving force. . . . In my opinion, we should not extend parliamentary politics to Korea. If we do, considering their influence in the inland, it will be difficult to replace this system later. They [the Japanese] are struggling to prevent

conflicts among political parties and factions and to build a system subject to the interests of the state. By assisting or strengthening "politics
by the governor general," I believe that we, in Korea, can ensure the
people's commitment to a unified, authoritative movement.[28]

In his view, Japan's parliamentary system, marred by factionalism and
party politics, was the primary cause for the disintegration of Japanese
society and morale. Thus, he saw no need to introduce a comparable
system in Korea. Shiobara supported Kawagishi's assessment; he had
visited Tokyo in mid-September and thus witnessed firsthand how existing interest groups were undermining the efforts of the IRAA. He
disparaged liberal politics and described the Japanese system as a "rat-
tling hurly-burly."[29] Like Kawagishi, Shiobara believed that introducing
a parliamentary system in Korea would threaten the driving force of "politics by the governor-general."

Yet, high-ranking colonial officials did not unilaterally reject a representative system. At the level of imperial politics, they believed that
Korea needed representation in Japan. During discussions, one reporter
suggested that it might be helpful if Korea chose representatives from
different sectors of Korean society, such as business executives and educational authorities, to travel to Japan to speak about the situation in
Korea. Mitsuhashi acknowledged that the Government-General had not
given this issue adequate consideration in the past. However, he added,
the only person suitable for representing the interests of Korea to Japan
was the governor general.[30]

In addition to rejecting a representative system except at the
imperial level, Shiobara also idealized at the forum a charismatic
decision-maker at the helm of a highly centralized political order. Most
people, he noted, praise liberal politics, but "true politics is unilaterally
carrying out policy decisions."[31] Thus, his understanding of active participation by the masses did not extend to policymaking, only implementation. For Shiobara, the worldview of the individual was necessarily partial. Thus, a government should impose on the individual an
impartial view that encompassed the general interests of society. It
could only do so if totalitarian and led by one true leader. Individuals, all biased, should obey the impartial state and its leader with ab-
solute trust. The state and its leader, for their part, should constantly

discipline individuals to ensure they follow their impartially determined directions.[32]

The colonial claim of "Korean particularities" reinforced the notion of colonized individuals as ill suited for a life based on general, impartial principles. The term was utilized in several contexts. The colonial government, claiming different conditions, used it to sustain its autonomy from Japan. It also, based on the assumption that Koreans—unlike the Japanese—were politically immature, justified assimilation policies on the one hand and enforced the social and political deprecation of Koreans on the other.[33] Koreans, the colonial government claimed, owing to their political immaturity, were partial to their specific location and its interests. They, therefore, pursued local Korean interests without considering the greater outlook of the Japanese empire. The conclusion was that the governor general, the only one capable of an impartial and general view of the political matters at hand, should govern Koreans autocratically, ignoring the populace's views on government matters. While this understanding closed the door on Korean participation in the policymaking process, it committed them to obedience in implementing policy. Patriotic NAs were to facilitate this latter aim by assisting "politics by the governor general in the nonpolitical realm." Koreans, in the neighborhood space, were to learn the kind of patriotism for which they were supposedly culturally suited—unconditional loyalty and obedience to the governor general.

Despite these efforts to differentiate the Korean New Order from the New Order in Japan, the rumor that Korea would have a branch of the IRAA persisted. The rumor was fueled by reports that the Provisional Committee for the IRAA in Tokyo had plans to establish IRAA branches throughout the Japanese empire. Given the past practice of Korea and Japan having parallel organizations, most Koreans accepted the rumors as fact. To dispel these rumors, on December 23, 1940, Nobuhara Sato, chief of the Concerted National Power Section, issued a statement in which he stressed that the League for Concerted National Power would lead all national movements in Korea. He explained that since Korean society was different from Japanese society, there would be no branch of the IRAA in Korea.[34]

The separation of the two national institutions required official Japanese approval, prompting Kawagishi, the general secretary of the

League for Concerted National Power, to travel to Tokyo in January 1941 to present the Government-General's case for a distinct institution. During his two-week visit, he met with Japanese politicians, government bureaucrats, and officers of the IRAA. Among those with whom he met was Gotō Fumio, the former interim prime minister who now served on the Central Cooperative Council of the IRAA. On January 8, 1941, Kawagishi explained to Gotō the situation as follows: "Korea is so different from Japan that we named the Korean institution the League for Concerted National Power, rather replicating the name of Japan's institution. However, its goals are the same as the IRAA."[35] Kawagishi, thus, identified the league with the interests of the IRAA, while at the same time reasserting the autonomy of the Government-General to choose how IRAA campaigns were implemented in Korea. Although the historical record is silent on the details of the meeting, the IRAA gave a verbal commitment that the imperial government would not establish an IRAA branch in Korea; the Government-General, as before, was free to lead Korean movements in line with Japanese goals.[36]

On February 12 and 13, 1941, a meeting was held in Tokyo to discuss expediting the IRAA movement. At the meeting, Kawagishi expressed the firm will of the Government-General in Korea to serve as Japan's representative in Korea. As Kawagishi later reported, Japan's endorsement of this arrangement may have reflected its respect for the level of organization of the league under the Government-General's leadership. Alternatively, the decision to allow the Government-General to use its own organization to advance the New Order in East Asia may have been because Japan, owing to the intense battle over the political nature of the IRAA in Japan, was unable to establish branch offices of the IRAA in Korea or other parts of the empire. In any case, in the immediate wake of the February meeting, Japan announced that organizations in Japan's "overseas possessions" (J. gaichi) for promoting the war effort need not be established as branches of the IRAA; thus, they could have different names. However, a liaison office should be established to facilitate communication with the IRAA.[37] This announcement marked mainland Japan's official recognition of Patriotic NAs under the auspices of the league, as distinct from tonarigumi under the authority of the IRAA. "Politics by the governor general" had survived unscathed.

PATRIOTIC NAs AND PROMOTING THE
USE OF JAPANESE IN THE HOME

To strengthen Koreans' loyalty to Japan, the Government-General, beginning in 1941, imbued Korean Patriotic NAs with state-focused "Japanese" cultural traditions. One of these traditions, introduced to show that the core of society is the state, was *amanoya sugahara*, a prototype of the national assembly. The alleged Japanese communal moral values to be promoted in NAs, such as family-like neighborly relations, mutual aid, and community-based crime prevention, were identified with two Japanese traditions—*goningumi*, groups of five households collectively held responsible for the conduct of all members during the Edo period; and traditional religious associations such as Iseokō and Kannonkō.[38] Korea, and by extension Patriotic NAs, were perceived as part of the Greater East Asia Co-Prosperity Sphere. The sphere and Patriotic NAs were to embody an idealized traditional Asian culture before its pollution by the West. This was the culture for which the East, led by Japan, was supposedly fighting.

The colonial government's efforts to push cultural assimilation were also found in the expectation that Koreans master the Japanese language. Throughout the 1930s, it established Japanese language programs in Korea to improve communications between colonizer and colonized and to foster cultural harmony between the two societies. With the outbreak of war in 1937, cultivating a shared language took on added significance, as the future of the Japanese imperial state, many officials believed, depended on cementing a collective cultural identity.[39] As a result, Japanese language programs in Korea proliferated. Local villages, religious organizations, and social indoctrination institutions were encouraged to offer language classes. Beginning in 1938, the government distributed roughly one hundred thousand Japanese textbooks, and an estimated three hundred thousand Koreans took some type of Japanese language course in the 1930s.[40] Slowly the number of Koreans with Japanese language skills increased. While in 1923, only 4.08 percent of Koreans had Japanese language skills, this figure had risen to 7.8 percent in 1933 and to 13.89 percent by the end of 1939.[41]

Around 1942, the Government-General overhauled its approach to Japanese language learning to accelerate Koreans' mastery of Japanese.

The immediate cause for the change in approach was the massive influx of Koreans into Japan that followed the introduction of the 1938 General Mobilization Law. An estimated one million Koreans had relocated to Japan by the end of 1941.[42] As most had minimal or no knowledge of the Japanese language and were unfamiliar with Japanese social customs, they could not effectively participate in Japanese associational life. For example, in Hiroshima, where in July 1939 an estimated 34,000 Koreans lived, the heads of NAs complained that they had difficulties in organizing units with Korean members owing to the absence of shared cultural practices, that is, language and social customs. In some areas dominated by Koreans, no NAs could be formed owing to cultural barriers.[43]

The Japanese government had recognized the seriousness of the language issue, making it one of the core topics for discussion at the meeting of the Central Association for Concord (*Chūō kyōwakai*) on December 4, 1940, at which Prime Minister Konoe Fumimaro, the minister of internal affairs, the education minister, the welfare minister, the mayor of Tokyo, and Governor-General Minami were in attendance. At the meeting Konoe reiterated his position that Japanese victory at war hinged on creating one nation through cultural assimilation; Minami pledged his commitment to reducing cultural differences through his policy of *naisenittai* that encouraged Koreans to embrace Japanese identity and discard Koreanness.[44]

The upcoming plan to draft Koreans into the Japanese military also made the Government-General feel it urgent to accelerate Japanese language learning. Koreans would need to speak the same language as their commanders if they were to serve effectively in the army. Colonial officials also argued that once the Japanese military controlled South Asia, Japanese would become the official language of Greater Asia. To function in this Greater Asian society, Koreans would need to know Japanese.[45] At a regularly scheduled meeting with provincial governors on April 21–23, 1942, the provincial governor of South Hamgyŏng noted a disconnect between Korea's lackluster language program and the importance assigned to Japanese proficiency for Koreans becoming full-fledged Japanese imperial subjects. He proposed that the colonial state launch a nationwide campaign to promote conversational proficiency in the Japanese language. The proposal garnered strong support from the Education Bureau and was approved.[46]

On May 21, 1942, followed by the announcement of Governor General Minami on May 11 that military conscript would be introduced in Korea, the colonial government published "Essentials of the Movement to Disseminate the National Language." It identified the objective of the movement as "comprehension of Japanese by all Koreans" (J. *zenkai*) and "everyday use of Japanese" (J. *jōyō*). According to the document, the movement would target every Korean who did not understand Japanese.[47] At the time of its release, the Government-General estimated that about nineteen million out of twenty-two million Koreans needed to learn Japanese.[48]

One of the principal targets of the campaign was the home, as evidenced by the government's insistence on using the slogan "Let's speak Japanese at home."[49] The use of Japanese in the most private sphere and everyday life realm likely to resist sudden external pressure would be a crucial mark that Koreans were entirely accustomed to communicating in Japanese. Yet Koreans rarely spoke Japanese at home, regardless of their level of proficiency. In the case of Kyŏngsŏng, an estimated 20 percent of the populace understood Japanese, yet in only 0.13 percent of Korean homes (190 out of 150,000) did family members use Japanese in the home.[50] The most obvious explanation for this low rate was the gender gap in Japanese language proficiency, in which men were three to four times more likely to be proficient in Japanese than women. The national figures showed a trend with 22.05 percent of men understanding Japanese versus 5.55 percent of women.[51] By designating the home as a target site for Japanese usage, the campaign sought to ensure that all Koreans, including housewives, used Japanese in their daily life.

Shortly after "Essentials of the Movement to Disseminate the National Language" was released, publications began using Japanese characters instead of Korean ones. The articles in the periodical brochure *Aikokuhan* (Patriotic NAs), written in Korean and distributed to all Patriotic NAs, were translated into Japanese.[52] Christian churches were told to use the Bible in Japanese translation.[53] Korean newspapers and magazines printed articles in Korean and Japanese, and radio broadcasts used Japanese.[54] Even consumer product labels were changed from Korean to Japanese.[55] The flood of Japanese literature did not stop here. Posters on Japanese language learning filled streets, buses, theaters, shops, trains, and trams, and schools did craftwork to urge people to communicate in Japanese at home.[56] The use of Japanese became mandatory for meetings at banks, post offices, and large shops, thus encouraging the employment of translators for those who did not yet understand Japanese.[57] All of these were visible signals informing Koreans of the Movement for the Dissemination of the National Language.

The starting point of the campaign was schools. Schools were asked to create charts on which students' progress in Japanese could be recorded. They held monthly Japanese language competitions and at the end of July submitted a report on each student's level of Japanese proficiency. To motivate teachers, those who made substantial contributions to the campaign were prioritized for promotion. Similarly, teachers prioritized students who demonstrated fluency in Japanese when writing letters of recommendation.[58] Some schools operated an honors club in which membership required fluency in Japanese; a student's membership in such clubs was canceled if the student ever used Korean, rather than Japanese, to communicate.[59] Older students were strongly advised to teach Japanese to students in lower grades.[60]

As students became acclimated to using Japanese in the classroom, they were expected to teach the language to other family members at home. In keeping with the slogan "One word each day," schoolteachers assigned students one Japanese vocabulary word each day to teach their family members.[61] In addition to assigning the daily vocabulary words, schools held monthly meetings at which parents studied and practiced speaking in Japanese. Some also offered special Japanese language courses for parents every Sunday night; housewives received articles in Japanese on practical topics, such as alternative diet and recycling.[62] Across Korea, licensed language schools, night schools, Sunday schools, and temporary Japanese language centers offered countless Japanese language courses to accommodate different schedules and populations.[63] These included three-month intensive Japanese courses, short-term courses (one to two months in length), summer vacation courses, and courses for farmers during the off-peak farming season.[64]

However, the campaign by educational institutions was hampered by the low prioritization that Japan had given education in Korea since annexation in 1910. The colonial government had ignored the demands of Korean society for the state to build more elementary schools. As a result, only 17 percent of Korean children attended elementary school in 1931.[65] This attitude changed in the 1930s, when the colonial government recognized the value of schools as vehicles for social indoctrination. In 1934, the colonial government announced that every town (*myŏn*) should have one primary school. By 1941, elementary school attendance had risen to 45.6 percent.[66] Although this had been a steep increase, over 50 percent of school-age children remained beyond the reach of educational institutions. Acutely aware of this issue, local governments suggested that introducing compulsory education would solve the problem of insufficient proficiency in Japanese.[67] Others argued that continuing to increase the number of schools was the most effective way of bringing more children into the educational system.[68] Neither of these suggestions, however, was feasible, as the wartime Government-General did not have the financial means to build more schools or to hire enough teachers for a compulsory elementary education system.

Even with the current number of schools, there were not enough teachers to provide language training for over nineteen million Koreans. Consequently, the Government-General mobilized as instructors anyone with Japanese language skills. Schoolteachers and staff were required to teach evening language classes in addition to their regular teaching schedule.[69] Middle school students were expected to work as volunteer Japanese teachers during summer vacations.[70] Public officials were also enlisted to teach Japanese every Wednesday evening and for one hour every Saturday.[71] Finance cooperatives required their staff to teach language courses at night schools as well as dispatched them to villages twice a year to teach three-month intensive courses.[72] Retired female schoolteachers and Korean housewives with a high school education taught language courses.[73] So desperate was the need for teachers that even those with only an elementary school diploma were tapped as potential language teachers.[74]

Against the backdrop of the limited scope of the program and work force shortages, the Government-General took advantage of Patriotic NA assemblies to advance the campaign. Given their national coverage and the regularity of their meetings, they had substantial potential to compensate for the shortage of educational facilities. On April 14, 1942, Minami, as an experiment, directed that Patriotic NA assemblies be conducted in Japanese as a preparatory step to making Japanese the official language.[75] This experiment was readily accepted by the residents of Ch'ŏnggye town in Kyŏngsŏng, the majority of whom were Japanese. Even before the directive, Japanese was the language used at NA assemblies there. To accommodate the few Koreans who lived in the area, announcements were provided in Korean translation. Upon receiving the governor general's directive, the town stopped translating announcements and required the Korean minority to learn Japanese.[76] However, the situation in Ch'ŏnggye town was unusual; in rural areas and on the outskirts of urban centers, most Patriotic NA leaders and members did not have sufficient Japanese language skills to conduct NA assemblies in Japanese. The Government-General realized that enforcing the directive would lead to antipathy toward NAs. Nevertheless, there was no other institution with comparable nationwide coverage. Rather than hold Patriotic NA assemblies in Japanese, it returned to its original plan to mobilize NA assemblies for language training sessions.[77]

Before the plan could begin in earnest, Patriotic NA heads needed to be taught Japanese language skills. Contrary to the expectations of the Government-General, the proficiency of NA heads was not dramatically higher than that of the general population. Take, for example, Kyŏnggi Province, which had roughly three million residents and 33,027 Patriotic NAs, with 30,754 Korean leaders and 2,273 Japanese leaders. Of these leaders, approximately 38 percent (11,637) were able to speak and read Japanese, compared with roughly 23 percent of all residents.[78] This low figure meant that 62 percent of NA heads required remedial Japanese language lessons before the NA program could be implemented for members. Patriotic NA leaders were warned that if they did not develop fluency quickly, they would no longer be allowed to serve as NA heads.[79] Wanting to move quickly to the next stage, provincial governments prioritized their enrollment in specialized two-hour daily courses at schools or village halls.[80] Using the textbook *Kokugo Kyōhon* (National Language Handbook), the focus was on teaching NA heads basic vocabulary used in everyday life and practical phrases needed for conducting air raid drills.[81]

Once NA heads gained basic proficiency, Japanese language sessions at NA assemblies were introduced. These sessions took various forms. At some NA assemblies, members read together the Japanese edition of *Aikokuhan,* the official periodical for Patriotic NAs.[82] Other NA leaders had each member bring two Japanese phrases that they wanted to learn; they would then spend thirty minutes practicing these phrases before the start of the regular meeting.[83] Still other heads required members to learn one vocabulary word each day.[84] During the actual meetings, members would practice reading the monthly action lists in Japanese.[85] Some NA leaders administered Japanese language tests at each monthly assembly, awarding special ration stamps to those who scored the highest.[86] Beyond these monthly language sessions during NA assemblies, some Patriotic NAs established their own Japanese language courses. For example, 530 NAs in Chongsŏng County of North Hamgyŏng Province planned to offer Japanese courses from 7:00 p.m. to 9:00 p.m. each evening from October 1942 to March 1943.[87] Patriotic NA heads regularly wrote reports summarizing how many member households used Japanese in the home. Once or twice a year, some towns asked residents to give presentations in Japanese to assess how much residents' Japanese language skills had improved.[88]

To incentivize the campaign, Patriotic NAs in which over 80 percent of members (excluding the elderly and toddlers) used Japanese in their daily life were awarded an honorific title, "Patriotic NA with Everyday Use of Japanese."[89] In addition, each family where Japanese was the language in the home received a special door placard titled "Home with Everyday Use of Japanese" and was entitled to receive additional rations such as rice or fertilizer, while the rations of low-performing Patriotic NAs were reduced.[90] It was also common knowledge that children who spoke Japanese at home would receive preferential treatment in the elementary school admission process.[91]

Assessing the effectiveness of the Japanese learning campaign is difficult. On the one hand, the economic benefits of participation, such as increased rations and educational opportunities for children, may have encouraged Koreans to participate in the campaign. On the other hand, the difficulty of overcoming deeply ingrained linguistic habits, combined with irregular access to Japanese language programs, makes it unlikely that the roughly 20 million Koreans without conversational Japanese skills at the start of the program suddenly began speaking Japanese fluently. Yet it is highly probable in the context of the campaign that most Koreans heard and learned some basic Japanese vocabulary, such as words commonly used in everyday life. "*Tonarigumi*" was most likely one of these words, given that Patriotic NAs, a core institution of the campaign, utilized translations of their leaflets and announcements to teach Japanese. Thus, most Koreans would have been repeatedly exposed to the Japanese word for "neighborhood association" as part of NA language training sessions. Given their familiarity with the word and the government's insistence on using Japanese, it is not surprising that over time the Japanese term *tonarigumi* replaced the Korean term for Patriotic NAs in everyday parlance.

The use of *tonarigumi* for Patriotic NAs was further reinforced by the official newspaper of the Government-General, *Maeil sinbo*. The paper described *tonarigumi* as a Japanese organization similar to a Patriotic NA and published articles praising its models. The two terms "Patriotic NAs" and "*tonarigumi*" increasingly became conflated. For example, in an article on an exemplary Patriotic NA, *Maeil sinbo* described it as "a flower of *tonarigumi* spirit."[92] In July 1942, when the colonial government introduced a campaign calling on Koreans to show kindness to others in various public settings, the newspaper called it a "*tonarigumi* movement," rather than a Patriotic NA movement.[93]

The Government-General should have been pleased that Koreans were adopting Japanese vocabulary, given the amount of time and money it had invested in teaching Japanese to Koreans. However, this linguistic assimilation could not be tolerated, because it threatened to upset the delicate balance that colonial officials sought to maintain between Korean particularities and Korean unity with Japan. Although colonial officials wanted to integrate Koreans into the Japanese war effort, they also wanted to maintain their dominance over Korean society and their autonomy from the Japanese inland.

WAR, IMPERIALISM, AND PATRIOTIC NAs

The epigraph of this chapter—"Korea is neither a place to be absorbed into Japan, nor a place to be independent of Japan. It should flourish in subordination to Japan"—demonstrates that the relationship between the colonizer and the colonized periphery was not fixed. As a territory of the Japanese empire, Korea occupied a liminal space somewhere between independence from Japan and dissolution into Japan through assimilation. It was essential that neither be realized, since ending this indeterminate relationship would mean the termination of colonial rule. Instead, flexibility in defining the term "subordination" allowed for an infinite narrowing of the distance between the two extremes while at the same time preserving the tension between the two. In the same vein, the similarity could be significantly amplified but not to the magnitude that they became identical.

The Government-General had been authorized to prevent the extremes of independence and dissolution and to pursue subordinated prosperity. In the early and mid-1930s, when the Government-General asserted Korea's importance for the Asian bloc economy, it had nudged Korea toward independence. The outbreak of war in 1937, however, led the Government-General to swing back toward assimilation. Subordinated prosperity was indicative of Korea's economic contribution to the imperial war economy, and mobilization took the form of state-led mass movements. Patriotic NAs, therefore, carried both the wartime language of assimilation and the colonial language of "Korean particularities."

Amid the growing wartime crisis, Japan introduced in 1940 the "New Order," pushing colonized Korea further in the direction of dissolution. At that moment, Japan wanted to reform the existing political order as well as the economic structure to establish a singular wartime order in the name of the national defense state. It was a tangible sign that colonialism in which there was a clear line of demarcation between the colonizer and the colonized would be at variance with war aims. Thanks to the cultural assimilation policy, the conflicting forces had room for coexistence, but the contradiction could not be concealed indefinitely. The political challenge that the New Order posed to the Government-General emanated from the Japanese government wanting to increase administrative efficiency and from Korean society wanting to ameliorate unequal political relations.

Prioritizing "Korean particularities" and "politics by the governor general," the Government-General devised a bilayered political order.

The first layer consisted of a *political* realm—the core-periphery relation-ship between Japan and Korea, in which it had sole responsibility for representing the interests of Koreans to Japan and for implementing Japanese policy in Korea. The second layer was a nonpolitical realm—the relationship of the colonial government to Korean society. Korea's dissolution into Japan was held at bay by a politics that juxtaposed Pa-triotic NAs under the Korean New Order with the *tonarigumi* under the Japanese New Order. Whereas the *tonarigumi* system was under the aus-pices of a political IRAA that was loyal to the Japanese emperor, Patri-otic NAs were under the auspices of a nonpolitical League for Concerted National Power. Patriotic NAs demonstrated their loyalty to the Japanese emperor by obeying the governor general who represented Japan in Korea and Korea in Japan. This arrangement enabled the governor gen-eral, who straddled Japan and Korea, to exercise political agency in pol-icymaking and implementation. Conversely, it locked Patriotic NAs and Koreans into a nonpolitical realm that denied them access to decision making but required their obedience in policy implementation.

The bilayered political order faithfully reflected the Government-General's intention of subordinating Korea to Japan while at the same time warding off dissolution and independence by framing Korea as a nonpolitical space. Patriotic NAs, as nonpolitical, were a strategic sphere used to demarcate the Government-General's autonomy from Japan as well as to preclude the diffusion of political power in Korea. The latter, if not circumvented, would have undermined the Government-General's power monopoly. Thus, Patriotic NAs signified that colonized Korea would support rule by the governor general in the nonpolitical realm so that the governor general could participate in imperial politics as a rep-resentative of Korea. It gave the Government-General room to preserve its interests in the bilayered political structure.

However, the wartime colonial order could not maintain this deli-cate balance indefinitely. The Japanese-language learning campaign, as evidenced by Koreans electing to use the Japanese word "*tonarigumi*" in lieu of Patriotic NAs, failed to maintain the distinction between the two signifiers—"*tonarigumi*"and "Patriotic NAs." The Government-General's statement remonstrating against Koreans for using "*tonarigumi*" tacitly disclosed that Patriotic NAs' assimilation policies meant neither political nor institutional equality for Korea vis-à-vis Japan. Moreover, the interpretation of *tonarigumi* as belonging to the political realm did not remain valid for long. The economic and political reforms of the Japanese New Order, designed to protect the masses and give them access to the political sphere, gave way to authoritarian measures. This transformation ultimately led *tonarigumi*, like its Korean counterpart, to be defined as a nonpolitical national organization. The signifier had been divorced from the signified.[94]

In 1942, administrative unification between mainland Japan and its peripheries undermined the Government-General's position in wartime imperial politics. Once the Imperial Rule Assistance Diet (*Taisei yokusan*) in April 1942 approved Tōjō Hideki to hold concurrently multiple positions—prime minister, home minister, minister of commerce and industry, foreign minister, minister of education, and minister of munitions—Japan's colonies were no longer immune to centralization. To integrate the colonial administrations into the cabinet, Japan not only planned to establish the Great East Asia Ministry to specialize in Korea and Taiwan but also proposed a bill to transfer the colonial administration to the Home Ministry.[95] In June 1945, the League for Concerted National Power was incorporated into the National Voluntary Army. Immediately prior to Japan's surrender, Japan passed a bill that gave Koreans and Taiwanese the right to vote and to send representatives to the Japanese Diet.[96]

The above events reveal that Korea during the last stages of the war moved significantly toward dissolution into the colonizer. How did different Koreans with their various relationships with the colonial power respond to this situation? How did the Government-General that had worked so hard to preserve the precarious balance between independence and dissolution react? These questions remain unanswered because the surrender of Japan in August 1945 rendered them moot. However, the case of Algeria, a colony in the French empire, raises an interesting possibility. In the aftermath of the World War II and in the 1950s, Algerian social movements employed the political and cultural language of France to challenge the fundamental basis of colonial rule.[97] Perhaps, if war had not brought liberation, the pendulum in the relationship between the colonizer Japan and Korea would have swung again in the direction of independence as it had in the early 1930s. It is possible under these circumstances that assimilation policies would have led Patriotic NAs to appropriate and adapt the political and cultural language of the colonizer as a basis for independence in much the way Algerians had.

CHAPTER 3

At the Intersection of Family Indoctrination and Opportunities for Women

The notion that individuals can get membership in Patriotic NAs is incorrect. They should be made up of families.

—Shiobara Tokisaburō[1]

Patriotic NAs are the soul of movements by the League for Concerted National Power.

—Minami Jirō[2]

On a 5.3-by-8-centimeter wooden name tag, given to a Patriotic NA member, the following information was engraved:

Address in Family Registry (*Hojŏk*): Pusan City, Sujŏng District 243.
Address in Residential Household Registry (*Kiryu*): Pusan, Chwach'ŏn District 52.
Patriotic NA: Chwach'ŏn town, 4th *ku,* 7th *cho,* 2nd Patriotic NA.
Household head: Owŏn Kŭmsuk, born September 8, Meiji year 42.[3]

As was common practice, the tag did not include the identity of the carrier or the names of those eligible to carry it. Only the name of the head of household appeared on the card. Anyone listed under Owŏn Kŭmsuk on the family registry or the residential household registry (hereafter residential registry) could carry the name tag. The interests of the card bearer, in turn, were represented by the head of household at Patriotic NA assemblies.

The card mirrored the family-based system of collective identity used in Patriotic NA records. Through this system, Patriotic NAs acted as the intermediary between families (and by extension individuals) and the wartime colonial state. As go-between, Patriotic NAs provided the opening through which state-led movements penetrated the private domestic sphere. Through their participation in Patriotic NAs, housewives, who had largely been beyond the reaches of state programming, became intimately entangled in the war effort. Already unpopular among Korean males, NAs became sites of women's empowerment as they assumed leading roles in implementing the state-controlled system of data collection, rationing, and savings. They also allowed women to break free of traditions and customs that had confined women to the house and denied them access to the education and skill sets needed to take their first steps toward independence.

THE CENSUS: FAMILY REGISTRY AND RESIDENTIAL HOUSEHOLD REGISTRY

Across Korea on July 10, 1943, at 8:00 p.m., Patriotic NA assemblies simultaneously commenced. Every assembly opened with participants listening to the radio programming that the colonial state had mandated in March 1941, and for which NAs had been required to buy a radio receiver. The programming began with the airing of the Concerted National Power anthem and the Patriotic NA song, after which a monthly address by a ranking colonial official was broadcast.[4] The speaker for July 1943 was Director Sōda Fukuzō of the Justice Bureau. He delivered a fifteen-minute speech, "Let's Carry Out the Family Registry and Residential Registry Schemes," in which he linked the necessity of the two registries being accurate with the scheduled introduction of the military draft in 1944:

> As members of Patriotic NAs well know, the war has intensified. Military conscripts and ration stamps can only be run properly with accurate statistics on demographic mobility. You should recognize that

the accuracy of those two registries is not only of great importance to the military draft but also greatly impacts consumption. . . . From an individual perspective, those who are not on both registries will be excluded from honorary military conscription and compulsory education. Even though he/she was registered on them [the registries], errors, such as in the date of birth, will create problems for being drafted or going to school. . . . Since the military draft, for which Koreans have wished, is on the verge of being enacted, it is time to embrace the family registry and the residential registry.[5]

In announcing the upcoming draft, Director Sōda indirectly revealed that the colonial government to date had placed inadequate emphasis on the collection of accurate demographic information. He called on Patriotic NAs to play an active role in rectifying these oversights.

However, garnering cooperation was not as straightforward a proposition as his speech suggested. Despite his claim that Koreans eagerly awaited the draft's imposition, Sōda knew its unpopularity among Koreans. To ensure cooperation with data collection, he claimed that noncooperation with the census would negatively impact education and the distribution of food rations. He instructed NA heads to check that all families in their NAs appeared in the family registry and to verify that the residential registry was up to date by comparing the ration stamp allotment with the list of residents in the NA. Director Sōda ended his speech by asking the assembled members who were literate to fill out forms for illiterate members prior to leaving the assembly. He was eager to utilize the Patriotic NAs to acquire the missing demographic information that the colonial government saw as essential for the war effort.

Collecting reliable demographic information began with the introduction of the surname-change policy (K. *Ch'angssi kaemyŏng*), a part of the new Civil Ordinances Reform for Korea that took effect on February 1, 1940. The policy required the 4.2 million Korean family heads listed in the family registry to create Japanese surnames and to report them to the local government responsible for the family registry. The new surnames, officials emphasized, were signifiers for the Japanese-style household rather than for patrilineage, as had been Korean custom. Each family was encouraged to choose a name that preferably was different from that of the main branch of the traditional Korean family.

The name-change policy, thus, was about more than names; it aimed at transforming the Korean family system into a Japanese one. It was also intended to facilitate the incorporation of Korean soldiers into the Japanese military unit by eliminating a visible mark of distinction between the two cultures.[6]

On unveiling the mass movement to adopt Japanese surnames, the Government-General billed the policy as a path for Koreans to complete the process of becoming full Japanese imperial subjects. The official period for registering the new surname was from February 11 to August 10, 1940. Despite its enthusiastic promotion, few Koreans responded. By the end of February, only 0.4 percent of Koreans had answered the call to adopt a Japanese surname; by March that figure had risen only to 1.5 percent, and by the end of April, the figure was 3.9 percent. Embarrassed by the low participation rate, the colonial government announced a special name-change event in May and mobilized the Patriotic NAs.[7] NA heads were advised to remind their members at the monthly assembly and in one-on-one meetings of the disadvantages of neglecting or defying the policy. For example, schools would not accept children who did not have a Japanese surname; employment would be denied to those who did not change their names; and government institutions, such as the postal service, would not provide services to Koreans who did not adopt Japanese surnames. In addition, Koreans who refused the name change would be subject to political surveillance and would be ineligible to receive ration cards.[8] The warnings issued by NA heads at the behest of the colonial government had the desired effect; by the end of August, 80 percent of Korean family heads had changed their surnames, and a new family registry had been created.[9]

The new family registry, however, failed to overcome the shortcomings of its predecessor. Despite most Koreans having now complied with the name-change policy, the registry still contained countless errors and gaps in information and excluded the 20 percent of Koreans who had not complied. As the civil section chief of the Justice Bureau lamented, "Most family registries, it can be assumed, contain errors in gender and age," and while "on average 47,000 Koreans have registered their names on family registries in the last three years, it is still estimated that hundreds of thousands are not on the family registry."[10] His apprehension about the accuracy of the information in the new family registry was confirmed in a sample survey at an elementary school that showed that about 60 percent of family registries had errors.[11]

The Justice Bureau director attributed omissions and errors to "the low civility of Koreans," "the incompetence of Korean officials," and the "disinterest of Koreans."[12] However, he failed to mention that the errors reflected three decades of colonial rule, in which little effort had been made to promote social modernization in Korea. Because most Koreans had little or no access to public education or medical services—the typical means through which modern states developed a personal data collection system—they had little motivation to correct errors in the family registry or even to maintain one. The high infant mortality rate in colonial Korea also meant that families often delayed registering newborn babies until the likelihood of their survival seemed more assured.[13]

The numerous errors and omissions were exacerbated by the antiquated legal definition of family and the rules governing the family registry that undermined its effectiveness in tracking the movements of families and individuals. First, the address that appeared for a family in the registry by law could not be changed. Second, the law specified that there could only be one registry per family. If for any reason other than divorce or legal termination of family relations between parent and child—the two exceptions recognized by law—a family member(s) left the household, their official place of residence remained unchanged in the family registry. This system of recording, which dated to premodern Korea, had posed no major issues so long as Korea remained a traditional agriculture-based society in which people seldom moved. However, the upsurge in immigration to Japan and China, the development of modern transportation systems, and rapid growth in urbanization in the 1930s had made the registry system obsolete. More than four million Koreans, it was estimated, lived at addresses other than that which appeared in the family registry.[14]

The growing discrepancy between the legal addresses and the actual residential addresses was a wake-up call for the Government-General, which without accurate addresses could not guarantee that every male eligible for conscription would receive the letter notifying them of the date and time they should report for the required physical examination.

Moreover, without accurate data, the government could not prevent Koreans from creating fictive family members or registering at more than one location to receive a larger food ration.[15]

To rectify this situation, the Government-General enacted the Residential Household Registry Law on October 15, 1942. Under the law, the residential registry was created. The new residential registry was a modified version of the 1911 residential registries, which the Police Bureau had used to maintain public order. Unlike the family registry, the 1911 residential registries were less concerned with family relations, and more interested in families and individuals as economic units. Thus, family members who belonged to different households appeared in different residential registries. Also, if residents living in the same house had separate financial accounts, they also appeared separately in the residential registries. The advantage that the 1911 residential registries had over the traditional family registry was that it included individuals that fell outside the normative family, such as orphans, vagrants, illegitimate children, or children of concubines whose fathers refused to include their names on the family registry. However, because the 1911 registries had been primarily used by police to track criminals and political dissidents, the accuracy of their information for noncriminal elements of Korean society remained in question. With the 1942 Residential Household Registry Law, the Government-General expanded the administrative scope of the 1911 registry system and made the Justice Bureau, rather than the Police Bureau, responsible for its administration.[16] Through this transfer, the colonial government hoped to change the negative image associated with the registry as an instrument of policing, obtain more accurate information on the actual residential addresses of Koreans, and acquire a means of verifying the accuracy of information in the family registry.

Under the 1942 Residential Household Registry Law, anyone who resided in a location that did not correspond with his or her address in the family registry or who did not appear in the family registry, including Japanese residents and other foreigners, had to fill out and submit the residential registry form with local authorities. The form asked applicants to provide their address as listed in the family registry and the name of the family head. Applicants were also asked to provide information on cohabitants at their place of residence, including the cohabitants' date of birth and their relationship to the household head. Lastly, it required that all such forms be signed by the head of household. Upon receipt of the document, government officials were required to compare the information provided with that which appeared in the family registry and to verify its accuracy.[17] Through this system of checks and balances, the residential registry and the family registry together managed wartime demographic information.

Under the slogan "Let's accomplish the goal through the force of Patriotic NAs," the colonial government placed the submission of the residential registry on the October 1942 action list for Patriotic NAs.[18] The small size of NAs suited the registry campaign, as it facilitated the identification of demographic movements of individuals, such as when a child of a member family left home to pursue studies or a new baby was born into a family. Moreover, because the NAs were responsible for the distribution of rations, the NA head could exert significant pressure on members to report address changes and changes in family numbers. Given that ration stamps were handed out at the monthly NA meetings, newcomers to the neighborhood needed to attend. Thus, NA heads had the means to check regularly whether members' registrations were accurate.[19]

NA heads were placed in charge of dispensing the various forms used to track the movements of Koreans and the composition of families. For example, there were specific forms for households that included servants and their families, for households in which multiple families resided under the same roof, and for households in which the head of household lived apart from other family members.[20] Because the Government-General had no way of knowing which forms each of the roughly 350,000 NAs might need or how many of each form, NA heads were also responsible for retrieving the necessary forms from their towns.[21] After collecting the forms from each household, NA heads were required to review the forms prior to submitting them to the local town office.

To help people understand the family registry and the residential registry, the government developed a simple question-and-answer format to instruct Koreans on the importance of keeping their information up to date.[22] Despite such campaign materials, there were a gamut of issues that could arise due to complex family dynamics. For example, one man did not know if he should include the woman with whom he lived out of wedlock in his family registry. When he inquired at the monthly NA meeting, a colonial officer who was in attendance answered that the woman should submit a separate residential registry form, and the man should list her as an affiliated person. In other words, this relationship should be documented as two independent households living in one house. At the same assembly, there was another man who had both a legal wife and a concubine. Although he mainly resided with the concubine, he sometimes stayed with his legal wife and children and provided financial support for both households. He asked the colonial officer which woman should submit a separate residential registry. The response was that the man should register as the head of household for the residence in which his legal wife resided, and the concubine should submit her registration independent of his.[23]

In early 1943, as Patriotic NAs were busily helping members complete residential registration forms, the colonial government sent NAs a flyer titled "Let's drive out these people from our Patriotic NAs" that clearly detailed who should be ostracized from the neighborhood space:

Those who did not have a family registry.
Those who did not submit a residential registry.
Those who failed to register a child born into the family.
Those who did not register the death of a family member.
Those who did not register a marriage.
Those who appeared on neither a family registry nor a residential registry, especially if they were supposed to be drafted into the army the next year, that is, all males born between December 2, 1923 and December 1, 1924.
Hurry up![24]

With its emphasis on securing information on males eligible for the draft, the flyer presaged the Family Registry and Residential Registry Comprehensive Inspection (K. *Hojŏk mit kiryu ilje chosa*, hereafter, the Inspection). Scheduled for March 1, 1943, the Inspection collected personal information on all men under twenty years of age, excluding Korean men living abroad.[25] The campaign to gather demographic information that had started with the creation of surnames in 1940 was approaching its final stage, that is, the implementation of the military draft.

The Government-General decided to use NA heads as surveyors for the Inspection. Although being an NA head was normally an honorary position for which no financial compensation was provided, the NA heads received financial compensation for Inspection duties. During the last week of January 1943, they were required to complete a two-day training course for the upcoming Inspection. NA heads were responsible for doing a preliminary survey on February 10, 1943, and a main inspection on March 1, 1943. The questionnaires used for the two events were identical. NA heads asked each person his Japanese surname, his traditional Korean surname, the individual's date of birth as it appeared on the family registry, the actual date of birth if different from that which appeared on the registry, whether the person had a family registry, the address on the family registry, whether the person had submitted a residential registry, the address on the residential registry, the Japanese surname of the family head, and the individual's relationship to the family head. During the preliminary survey, each NA head interviewed all men listed in the NA's ration book and in the Patriotic NA registry, thereby ascertaining the exact number of males under twenty years of age in the NA.[26]

To ensure that no one went uncounted due to errors in the family registry or failure to complete the residential registry, NA members were told that they must update their registries prior to the main inspection on March 1, 1943. Once both surveys were completed, NA heads submitted the results to their local government's town office. Working with the Family Registry Department, local government offices confirmed the information and notified NA heads of any errors or ambiguous answers. NA heads, in turn, pressured household heads to correct the errors. By eliminating errors and ensuring that Koreans were registered in the census system, local authorities were able to assemble a nearly complete list of Korean males under twenty years of age who were eligible for conscription.[27]

The decision to enlist Patriotic NAs to collect wartime demographic information was highly successful. Describing the campaign's success as an "unexpected harvest," the colonial government was cheered by the fact that it no longer needed to rely on the antiquated family registry for data. Thanks to the residential registry, it learned that 10,630,473 people, or 41.2 percent of the total population, resided at an address different from their legal address in the family registry. The Government-General also discovered that 9.5 percent of the population, approximately 630,000 people, were not listed on any family registry.[28] The inspection resulted in 2,253,052 errors in the family registry being corrected.[29] Through their participation in this campaign, Patriotic NAs facilitated Koreans' assimilation into the Japanese family system and their integration into the Japanese military. They also provided the data used by the colonial government to control Korean consumption.

CONSUMPTION REGULATION

Yi Okpun, a housewife living in Kyŏnggi, recounted years later her forced weekly visits to a Shinto shrine as a part of the assimilation policy in the 1940s. Because the head of her NA was Japanese, she explained, he insisted that the "whole neighborhood cell" make the weekly trek together to the shrine on South Mountain. Even though this trip required her to take a tram and walk up the hill to the shrine with her small infant in tow, she could not skip the pilgrimage, because the NA head distributed food ration cards at an impromptu assembly immediately after the ceremony was complete. As she noted years later, "I didn't care [about the shrine]. Just get the food ration card!"[30] Her story reveals the role that rationing would play in ensuring Koreans' submission to the colonial government's war mobilization strategy and to the authority of Patriotic NAs.

The legal ground of food rationing was the Law for the Control of Resources (K. *Mulja t'ongjeryŏng*) on December 15, 1941. It created a two-channel system for managing and distributing limited resources to the populace. To manage the flow and distribution of commodities and consumer goods, the colonial government dissolved all private wholesale companies and replaced them with a single nationwide wholesale company under government control. The new nationwide wholesale company had exclusive rights to purchase from producers and to distribute goods to government-licensed retailers. Licensed retailers could only sell products to those who had ration cards, and they were required to keep detailed records of sales and to return used ration cards to the local government. If a retailer was found guilty of illegal activities, such as trading on the black market, its license was revoked.[31]

The 1941 law also established a separate government-controlled channel for rationing. Based on patterns of consumption and on supply, guidelines were created for each item subject to rationing. Although the supply and rationing channels were distinct, the two worked closely together, as it was critical that the number of ration stamps issued did not exceed available inventory. Once ration stamps for an item had been printed, they were sent to the offices of the provincial governors, which apportioned the cards to town officials, who in turn gave them to NA heads for distribution among their members. Upon receipt of the ration stamps, NA heads called an assembly to discuss the needs of each household and divide the ration cards among its members. Patriotic NAs were forbidden from directly handling goods or money.[32] The ration stamps could only be used on the date specified on the ration stamps and only at the designated retail shop.[33]

The Government-General justified its use of Patriotic NAs for distributing rations on the grounds that NA leaders had intimate knowledge of the needs of the NAs' members and thus would be able to ensure a fair distribution of the cards. Fairness, the colonial government reasoned, would ensure the success of rationing programs.[34] By fair, it did not mean uniform rationing, whereby each bearer of a ration stamp was entitled to the same quantity of a particular commodity regardless of class, social status, or need. For example, in Japan, all ration card holders were entitled to two bottles of beer; it did not matter whether the person actually drank beer or not. Isaka Keiichirō, the chief of the First Section of Commerce in Korea, railed against this practice, declaring that truly fair rationing must take into consideration the use value of a commodity rather than indiscriminately distributing items for which some consumers had no need.[35] NA heads, he asserted, were in a position to scrutinize each household's patterns of consumption and determine the use value of each commodity to that household.

The rationed items for which Patriotic NA leaders were responsible were rice, salt, rubber shoes, gasoline, and cotton.[36] The nationwide rationing of rice began in 1942. At that time, free trading of rice was banned, and the Korean Food Management Company (*Chosŏn singnyang yŏngdan*) was assigned exclusive control over the collection, delivery, storage, and distribution of rice. Except for their annual consumption allowance, farming households were required to hand over all rice that they produced to the Government-General, and consumers were only allowed to buy a fixed amount of rice from designated merchants. The goal was to increase rice exports to Japan by curtailing Koreans' consumption of rice.

To prevent farming families from engaging in illegal hoarding or diverting rice supplies to the black market, the Government-General imposed collection quotas on NAs rather than on individual households. The government asserted that NAs should work together to increase rice production; increased production would allow each household to have more rice for personal consumption. Conversely, the government warned that decreased production would result in less rice for personal consumption.[37]

Collective responsibility for rice collection quotas turned rural NA assemblies into discussion forums on how best to meet the collective quota. In North P'yŏng'an, the provincial government advised NAs that the quota for each household should be based on land size and on the number of families per household. When collection day arrived, farmers brought their share of the quota to the front of the house in which the NA head lived. Under the watchful eye of provincial government officials and policemen and in view of all NA members, the grain was weighed. Once the grain was collected, NA members took turns guarding it until it was delivered to the local collection hub. Once the rice collection process was completed, Patriotic NAs that met their quota were rewarded with special ration stamps with which members could purchase items such as towels or shoes.[38]

Nonproducers in urban areas could obtain rice rations with the ration account books, which were sent to each town to be distributed by the NA heads to the households in their NA. Each account book included the address of the rice retailer where the purchase could be made and the name and address of the household head. To receive a ration account book, each head of household had to complete a form that asked the number of household members and their ages. Once this was completed, the head of the Patriotic NA would sign the form, thereby attesting to the accuracy of the information. Only then would the local office specify the amount of rice the head of household could purchase and at what price.[39]

The ration system included procedures for reporting any changes in address or in the composition of the family. For example, in Kyŏngsŏng, the city with the largest nonproducer population, ration accounts for households that relocated to the city were only issued after the head of household had reported to the new NA head and completed the residential registry. If a household left the city, the head of its Patriotic NA was required to report the relocation so that the household's ration account could be terminated. Similarly, if there were any changes in family composition, such as a death or birth in the family, the head of household was required to revise the information in the rice account book. The revised information then had to be verified by the NA head.[40]

For nonfoodstuffs, such as rubber shoes, cotton products, and towels, NA heads periodically issued ration stamps with which members could purchase these items. Because these items were in short supply and often were the source of conflict, receipt of these stamps was at the discretion of the NA head, who was advised to consider group dynamics and the living standards of households in determining who should receive stamps for these coveted items. However, receipt of the stamps did not necessarily guarantee that a family would be able to acquire exactly what its members needed. For example, in the case of rubber shoes, the size one needed was an important factor, given that the Cooperative of Rubber Shoe Retailers, the central institution in charge of distributing rubber shoes, could not predict exactly who would require new shoes and in what sizes. Consequently, the most popular sizes ran out quickly, leaving many stamp recipients unable to find shoes that fit their feet.[41] To avoid this issue, stamp recipients often told their NA head in advance their shoe sizes, so that the NA could request the appropriate sizes. These requests were then taken under advisement by the cooperative in distributing rubber shoes to retail shops. If the size issue remained unresolved despite the advance order, the recipients could trade the stamps with other members of their NA for something else they needed or try to exchange the shoes with a neighboring NA for a pair that did fit.[42]

Towels, a consumer good traditionally imported from Japan, were in such short supply that a household of four was only allotted one towel per year.[43] As Japan diverted resources to wartime industries, the production of consumer goods such as towels decreased dramatically. As a result, Japan struggled to meet domestic demand and drastically reduced exports to Korea. Unable to find an alternative source, the Government-General charged NA heads with determining which of its members were in most desperate need of this scarce consumer good.[44] If this method failed, it recommended that at the NA assembly, household heads should draw straws to determine who received a ration stamp for this item.[45]

Rationing provoked tensions between NA members and frequently embroiled NAs in scandals.[46] However, Koreans no longer afforded to claim disinterest in Patriotic NAs. Failure to attend NA assemblies meant that households could not make known their needs for scarce items such as shoes or towels. In some cases, failure to attend NA assemblies meant forfeiting one's rations, as some NA leaders—such as Kim Kǔn-suk, a NA headwoman in Kyŏngsŏng—used ration stamps to guarantee their members' active participation. At a meeting of NA heads, she related that she had told her members that if they did not come to assemblies, they would receive "no ration stamps." Many of the other NA heads in attendance expressed their support, noting that members learned "beneficial lessons and created bonds with neighbors" through participation in the assemblies. If members did not attend, it was tantamount to ignoring one's familial obligations.[47] Similarly, headman Kim Chae-gil reported that he promoted attendance by only approving ration stamp requests made at the assembly. He bragged that this policy had led to such remarkable solidarity among members, that each week members gathered to clean the neighborhood.[48] Communal economic activities and exchanges such as a communal garden and collective purchase of vegetables were commonplace in Patriotic NAs.[49]

The Government-General linked Patriotic NAs to the government-mandated savings program. Its exhortation to save more and spend less was a familiar one for Koreans. Since the early 1930s, it had organized saving cooperatives to accumulate capital for economic development and to reduce household debt in rural areas.[50] But unlike these earlier programs, the colonial government framed participation in wartime savings as patriotic voluntarism and introduced a barrage of special saving events. For example, on Patriotic Day, Koreans were encouraged to abstain from smoking and to save the money that they would have spent on cigarettes. To commemorate personal milestones, such as birthdays and wedding anniversaries, the government recommended that Koreans save money rather than spend it on parties or gifts. Koreans were also asked to forgo lunch on a regular basis and to create patriotic savings accounts, for which ideally each day they would set aside some money.[51]

The savings targets set by the Government-General increased exponentially each year as Japan sought additional monies to fund the Pacific War. In 1938, it set a savings target of 1.8 billion *wŏn*; in 1939, the target rose to 10 billion *wŏn*, and by 1941, it had reached 12 billion *wŏn*. These dramatic increases necessitated that the Government-General abandon its call for voluntary participation and impose a compulsory savings program. In October 1941, it enacted the Korean Savings Cooperatives Law (*Chosŏn kungminjŏch'uk chohamnyŏng*), which stipulated the creation of three new types of saving cooperatives nationwide: regionally based cooperatives, occupational cooperatives, and social group cooperatives. The law also provided for the continuation of the existing commercial-industrial cooperatives.[52] As a part of the regionally based cooperatives, Patriotic NA heads were told to set a savings target for each household and to raise funds through colabor projects.[53]

Central to the local saving efforts were heads of Patriotic NAs, whose status and power in the community were greatly enhanced by the introduction of rationing. Although no official penalty existed, ordinary Koreans were concerned that noncompliance with the savings initiatives would cause a disadvantage in receiving essential rationing items such as soap, shoes, salt, and gas. Conversely, NA heads did not want to risk losing their newfound authority by failing to meet the government's goals. This dynamic pushed Patriotic NAs to create new types of savings in an effort to meet the increasingly unrealistic targets. For example, in the Second Patriotic NA in the Sixth District of Nusang in Kyŏngsŏng, a savings account was created for each household. Every twenty-fifth day, the headperson collected the money that each household had saved and deposited it on its behalf in the Saving Cooperatives in Kwanghwamun. Upon his return, he presented each household with its updated savings account book in which the deposit had been recorded.[54] The headperson of the Thirteenth Patriotic NA of Sogyŏk in Kyŏngsŏng prohibited members from throwing a lavish party in honor of a child's first birthday. In lieu of the customary large banquet and gift giving, the

NA head would collect money from members to establish a savings account in the baby's honor.[55]

At the end of 1942, the heads of Patriotic NAs were assigned yet another wartime task: pushing each household to buy a certain number of government bonds. This new demand was prompted by Japan having drastically increased Korea's bond quota. Prior to 1942, finance cooperatives, business enterprises, banks, and other institutions had been required to fulfill the quota, but with the increase in the quota from 3,200,000 *wŏn* in 1941 to 9,000,000 *wŏn* in 1942, it was obvious that the existing method would not suffice. The solution was to have Patriotic NA heads pressure each household head to buy a certain number of government bonds based on that household's tax tier.[56] Already pushed to their limits by rationing and by government savings targets, Koreans refused to buy bonds, claiming that they had no money or that the tax tier assigned to them was too high. The Government-General was not blind to the issue; however, it had no other option, if it was to meet Korea's quota. As one government officer noted, "People listen to heads whereas they ignore officers."[57]

"BUSINESS FOR WOMEN": HOME LIFE REFORM

Two short novels, *The Night of February 15* by Ch'oe Chŏng-hŭi, published in 1942, and *Ch'ŏngnyangni, an Outskirt of Kyŏngsŏng* by Chŏng In-t'aek, published in 1941, recount the lives of women who served as heads of Patriotic NAs. In both novels, the female protagonists were excited when appointed. Their husbands, however, had very different reactions. In *The Night of February 15,* the husband reacted angrily and demanded that his wife turn down the appointment, claiming that "home is the woman's workplace."[58] In contrast, the husband in the second novel congratulated his wife and promised to support her in her role as NA head. From the privacy of their home, he listened carefully to her concerns and offered his advice on NA affairs. However, he avoided participating in NA activities led by his wife, as he believed that Patriotic NAs were an extension of the domestic sphere and thus not a suitable sphere for male participation.[59] In short, both men believed that the domestic sphere was women's domain; the difference was that the second husband saw the NA as an extension of the domestic sphere and so did not object to his wife playing a leading role.

Unlike the two Korean men depicted above, whose yardstick for measuring Patriotic NAs was the domestic sphere, the Government-General viewed Patriotic NAs as communities based on a traditional patriarchal family relationship. As discussed in chapter 1, the colonial state expected NAs to mirror the extended family ideology of the Japanese empire. It organized the NAs hierarchically whereby a male patriarch, that is, the NA head, ruled over the households within his NA, which in turn were led by male patriarchs.[60] Although the NA's organizational structure reinforced traditional male authority, the colonial state's goal of extending state indoctrination to women by unshackling them from the confines of the home meant that NAs also opened a new space outside the home for women. Although initially denied leadership roles, some women began to see Patriotic NAs as a first step toward asserting women's agency in society.

The patriarchal structure imposed by the government proved difficult to realize in practice, as men quickly labeled the work of Patriotic NAs as "women's work" and avoided participating in NA activities. The catalyst for this gender-biased reaction was the government's decision to charge Patriotic NAs with implementing the home life reforms stipulated by the 1938 Standard for the Reform of Daily Life under Emergency Conditions. Targeting behaviors such as personal and domestic hygiene, diet, dress, frugality, and recycling, the home life reforms demanded by the government overlapped with the duties outlined for women in the Weekly Schedule of Housewives.[61] The government, in fact, unwisely framed the reforms as belonging to women's sphere when it proclaimed, "The reform of everyday life starts in the home."[62] This proclamation alienated men even as it failed to attract women, who were reluctant to work with a male NA head because they were accustomed to gender segregation at work and at home. A child or servant was often sent to represent the household at Patriotic NA assemblies, which were shunned by both household heads and housewives.[63] The government's envisioned penetration of the neighborhood space (and by extension the family space) appeared in shambles, stymied by traditional notions of gender relations and labor.

Against the backdrop of these gendered tensions, the Government-General decided to integrate the Home Airstrike Defense Cooperatives (*Kajŏng pangho chohap*) into Patriotic NAs in November 1940. The cooperatives, established as part of the Air Strike Defense Law (*Panggongbŏp*) enacted in November 1937, had been placed under the jurisdiction of the local police and were intended as a defense against possible aerial bombardments. Made up of five to twenty households, the cooperatives were initially established only in cities, where the risk of enemy air attacks was the greatest. In 1939, following the creation of the Police and Air Strike Defense Association (*kyŏngbangdan*), cooperatives were established throughout Korea. One year later, the Government-General announced that all cooperatives should be dissolved by the end of March 1941, and that Patriotic NAs should assume responsibility for air defense. It explained the merger as follows: "Home Airstrike Defense Cooperatives were organized by housewives in the vicinity with the goal of defending our territory. Given the cooperatives were almost equal in size to Patriotic NAs, incorporating the cooperatives into the League for Concerted National Power seemed highly promising."[64] The decision was in line with the establishment of the Korean New Order, which subsumed all state-led movements under the league and Patriotic NAs.

The merger fundamentally altered the gender balance of Patriotic NAs, because the cooperatives had been dominated by women. Given that women were the most likely persons to be "at home at all times," and thus were in the best position to counter air strikes, the Government-General realized the practicality of training women in air defense rather than men, who might be at work at the time of an aerial bombardment.[65] In fact, air defense became so synonymous with women's work that when asked when the next air defense exercise would be held, men often responded, "That is women's business. I have no idea."[66] Moreover, during scheduled air defense exercises, some men intentionally left home to do errands or go to the cinema to avoid association with this feminine activity.[67]

Once Patriotic NAs took over air defense training, which already had a strong gender bias, Patriotic NAs' association with women's work became more pronounced. By the end of 1942, an estimated 70 percent of Patriotic NA heads in Kyŏngsŏng were women.[68] This upsurge in the number of headwomen cemented the notion that Patriotic NAs were part of the domain of women. The notion of Patriotic NA assemblies as gatherings of male patriarchs under the leadership of a superior male patriarch quickly eroded. As Hiramoto Naozō, an NA headman in Okjŏng in Kyŏngsŏng, observed disdainfully, his monthly assemblies had devolved into women's chat sessions.[69] Yet, women were awakening to the opportunities that NAs afforded them. Hwang Ch'o-rim, a headwoman of Chongno in Kyŏngsŏng, noted that only after the dissolution of the air defense cooperatives, which led to women assuming leadership in NAs, did the door open for housewives to acquire new skills outside the home.[70]

Women donned *mompei* (baggy working pants for women) and trained as firefighters. They regularly practiced passing buckets of water and sand as well as how to use ladders, shovels, and hoses to prevent the spread of fires to adjoining buildings. They were also taught first aid so that they could tend to those injured during the bombings or while fighting the fires.[71] These regular training sessions, which were intended to ensure that the women did not panic during a real emergency, were often joint sessions involving multiple NAs. Hundreds of women, each lined up behind their respective NA head, would gather at a public square or sports field. Prior to commencing practice, they would swear their eternal loyalty to the Japanese emperor and promise to defend their neighborhood from enemy attacks. Then, each line would practice bucket passing, donning masks, and giving first aid.[72]

Not long after women began training for air defense in the NAs, local authorities voiced their objections to women's increased role in Patriotic NAs. In some cases, NA heads tried to force male heads of household to attend NA assemblies by linking their attendance to a household's receipt of the rice ration. Male household heads who did not show up to assemblies, some NA heads declared, would only receive ration cards for nonrice foodstuffs.[73] Such tensions prompted the general secretary of the league to hold a roundtable discussion in Kyŏngsŏng on May 10, 1941, to address women's growing presence in NAs. In attendance were four local government representatives and eleven NA heads from districts across the city. During discussions, Mr. Miyahara, the representative of the Fifth District of Pon in Kyŏngsŏng, lamented that since NAs had taken over air defense, men's numbers at NA assemblies had dwindled. He noted that in his district, there were only one or two men serving as heads of Patriotic NAs; the rest were women. He argued that it was critical that men take back leadership of NAs, because once the military draft was imposed, the task of air defense would become more complicated. Women, he asserted, had neither the physical strength nor the intellectual aptitude required to perform these duties as well as their male counterparts. While Patriotic NAs needed women's assistance to implement hygienic and sanitary reforms, women should not be allowed to replace men as the primary force behind NAs. For this reason, Mr. Miyahara had advised NAs in his district to hold a separate women's monthly assembly one day after the men's monthly assembly.[74] From his perspective, this compromise solution would maintain the traditional spatial separation of the sexes, thus allowing men to reclaim NAs as a masculine space, while still allowing a role for women.

The Government-General apparently found Mr. Miyahara's proposed solution appealing. Since conscription had not yet been imposed in Korea, there was no manpower shortage, as was the case in Japan.[75] Railing against the disappearance of men from monthly NA gatherings and the shift of responsibility to women, it unveiled the following guidelines for Patriotic NAs in June 1941 that echoed Miyahara's proposal:

1. Hold a monthly assembly regardless of what happens.
2. Hold a temporary assembly if necessary.
3. Have a headman when possible.
4. Hold an assembly on the seventh day of every month that uses the national radio programming.
5. Hold a separate women's assembly in urban areas to promote lifestyle reform.[76]

Yet, this proposed return to male dominance of NAs did not go unchallenged. On July 3, 1941, at a second roundtable discussion held in Kyŏngsŏng, eight headwomen contested the gendered assumptions of the Government-General and the four local male leaders in attendance. Hwang Ch'o-rim, a headwoman in Chongno in Kyŏngsŏng, asserted, "I think women are more appropriate for the Patriotic NA leadership than men. Since housewives took over leadership, Patriotic NAs have worked much better."[77]

Her statement received the support of the other headwomen in attendance, who highlighted how much more had been accomplished under women's leadership than under men's. They noted that as women, they were able to develop more intimate relationships with the housewives whose job it was to manage household affairs. These more personal relationships also made them more effective at facilitating communication between housewives in different households. Thus, headwomen were more suited to the task of dissolving boundaries between households and collecting the detailed information about member households that was needed for rationing. Having this exact information also allowed headwomen to identify those families still practicing extravagant rituals and pressure them for change. As Ch'oe Chŏng-hŭi, another headwoman in Chongno, explained, "Only headwomen can build Patriotic NAs, whose basic unit is the home, by unleashing homes to take only that which is necessary and to discard the unnecessary."[78] In short, the women presented Patriotic NAs as an extension of the domestic sphere. Women could work with women in the service of the state to rationalize home life without upsetting existing gender norms.

Unlike the headwomen who insisted on the appropriateness of female leadership in Patriotic NAs, male local authorities voiced reservations. Although none of them denied that the headwomen had made significant contributions to actuating Patriotic NAs, and they even recognized that women were more suitable for doing some tasks, they remained unconvinced that women had the skill sets necessary to lead NAs. Mr. Matsumoto, a representative from the First District of Chongno, explained that he planned to "gradually replace headwomen with headmen," as only a few headwomen possessed the necessary qualifications to lead. He noted, "While in some Patriotic NAs all women are qualified to assume leadership, in others there is not even one woman capable of leading." Mr. Matsuhara from the Chungbu District and Mr. Kim from the Chunghak District argued not only that headmen were better qualified to manage rationing than women but that rationing had spurred men's interest in NAs. As proof, Mr. Kim, whose district had more headmen than headwomen, asserted that in his district, the policy was to give attendance stamps to household heads who showed up for the village assembly and to allocate ration stamps to those household heads who came to the Patriotic NA assemblies. As for home-related issues, male Patriotic NA heads in his district appointed qualified housewives to serve as vice-headwomen to handle NA tasks that fell within women's sphere of influence.[79] This compromise solution was the best way to preserve NAs as a patriarchal family system in which women also could play an active role.

The roundtable had produced two options: accept female leadership of Patriotic NAs or create a two-tiered system of leadership in which women leaders were subordinate to their male counterparts and exercised authority only over tasks labeled as women's work. The colonial government was unlikely to accept the former solution, since the traditional practice of gender-segregated households and workplaces meant that men would refuse to participate in any organization led by women. Given the colonial government's decision to integrate most mobilization programs into Patriotic NAs, risking men's nonparticipation was not an option. Moreover, a women's group already existed; thus, transforming Patriotic NAs into women-centered communities would be redundant. For these reasons, the colonial government preferred the latter alternative, believing that rationing could be used to force male involvement in Patriotic NAs if women's role in home life reform was subordinated under male leadership. In August 1941, officials in Kyŏngsŏng ordered the city's roughly ten thousand Patriotic NAs to appoint vice-headwomen. This partial retreat from the originally envisioned patriarchal system of NAs, the government rationalized as follows: "Without the full cooperation of housewives, a frugal lifestyle, savings, and recycling cannot be accomplished."[80] Needing women's engagement in home life reform, the Government-General accepted a limited leadership role for women in the Patriotic NAs.

Reuse and recycling were subjects crucial to home life reform. Women in some Patriotic NAs separated paper waste from food waste, so that the latter could be used for animal feed or fertilizer; others made boxes and bags from old magazines for additional income or salvaged materials to make rubber bags.[81] More than that, the colonial government called on Patriotic NAs to launch the Trash Reduction-Collection Movement. By 1941, the trash collection issue had reached crisis proportions in Kyŏngsŏng. Due to the government's financial retrenchment and the labor shortage, the city's Cleaning Department lacked the means to hire more workers, secure more carts, and acquire sufficient fuel for collection trucks. The city's rapid growth between 1940 and 1941 also exacerbated the problem as the quantity of trash increased from 640,000 kilograms per day to 800,000 kilograms per day. The city's NAs were enlisted to reduce trash and to assist the city government in collecting and disposing of trash.[82]

The garbage collection campaign initially encompassed approximately 30 percent of the city—thirty-nine out of the ninety-eight districts, about forty thousand households or two hundred thousand people. Each district designated two days a week for garbage collection—Monday and Thursday or Tuesday and Friday. Apart from three districts, the collection time was in the morning.[83] There were two means of garbage collection. Twenty-nine districts carried garbage to a collection point while ten districts put their garbage in front of their houses. East Kongdŏk, a district made up of 2,833 households, opted for the former collection method. On the chosen days, members of each Patriotic NA were required to carry their garbage to one of the eleven designated collection points prior to 11:00 a.m. Once all the garbage bags had been transported to the collection point, a representative for the NA head contacted the city to take the garbage away.[84]

Pyŏngmok, a district with 877 households, chose the second collection method. Every Tuesday and Friday morning at 8:00 a.m., NA heads knocked on the gates of each household to remind residents that they should put their garbage out in front of the gate before 11:00 a.m. Moving from west to east, city garbage collectors picked the garbage up. The city announced that it had reduced the number of carts needed from thirteen to three and the number of workers needed from twenty-two to six, thereby saving substantial resources and money.[85] Pleased with the outcome, the city issued a celebratory statement that the new program resulted in cleaner homes and districts and contributed to the prevention of the spread of infectious diseases.[86]

Patriotic NAs were also committed to reducing rice consumption as a means of home life reform. Since the 1910 annexation, Korea had been a major supplier of rice to Japan; rice imports from Korea had allowed the Japanese government to stabilize rice prices at home. With the onset of war, Korea's role as a rice supplier to Japan increased in importance. The Government-General prioritized exporting rice to Japan, out of the fear that a sharp reduction in supplies of rice from Korea would provoke a food crisis in Japan and negatively impact the war effort. It imported cheaper grains such as millet, soy, and pearl barley from Manchuria for Korean consumption.[87] The campaign to reduce rice consumption began with the misleading proclamation that saving rice had the same effect as increasing rice production. According to the colonial government, 720 tons of rice could be saved per day, and 259,200 tons per year, if five million Korean households saved two-thirds of a cup of rice per day.[88]

As part of the campaign, housewives in Patriotic NAs were bombarded with patriotic propaganda proclaiming the benefits of dietary reform. Those over the age of forty were urged to eat only two meals a day, with a tacit warning that three meals might cause disease. The campaign also extolled the nutritional benefits of brown rice and promoted "patriotic bread" as a dietary alternative to rice.[89] In a series of lectures sponsored by local governments in conjunction with patriotic wives' groups, women were taught that supplementary grains such as barley, wheat, rye, potato, sweet potato, and corn had nutritional values equal to those of rice. With a multitude of recipes provided by nutrition research institutions, women's groups offered cooking demonstrations for housewives and female students.[90] Three times per month, Koreans were asked to celebrate "A Day Free from Rice"; as the day for these events drew near, Patriotic NAs would remind housewives to cook rice-free meals.[91] In tandem with the rice-saving campaign, the women of the Fifth Patriotic NA in the ninth district of Mokpo city in South Chŏlla Province ran cooking classes that provided instruction in the preparation of dishes to replace rice, such as bread, dumplings, and noodles. In recognition of the contribution its cooking classes made to the campaign, this Patriotic NA was selected as one of forty-two exemplary Patriotic NAs in 1942.[92]

Home life reform, a critical point of intersection between war mobilization and programs of enlightenment, had far-reaching repercussions for the patriarchal leadership of Patriotic NAs. The focus on home life reform, combined with the introduction of male conscription and labor service, inevitably led to women assuming responsibility for NA leadership. Forced to accept this new reality, the Government-General reversed its earlier guidelines calling for male NA heads only and instead advised NA headwomen to seek their husband's counsel before making decisions about NA activities.[93] Open debate about the appropriate gender composition of NA leadership ceased, and officials turned their attention to urging male heads of household to attend NA assemblies whenever possible.[94]

The shift to women-led NAs pleased female intellectuals who endorsed the war effort because of the ways in which it had transformed women's lives. Ko Hwang-kyŏng, a committee member in charge of housewives in the League for Concerted National Power, noted how the war mobilization had finally awakened women to the need to abandon irrational traditions and habits: "The reform of eating habits, dress, and household management practices, which had made no significant headway among women, gained impetus from the war."[95] Similarly, headwoman Ch'oe Chŏng-hŭi argued that the war effort had opened women's eyes to the advantages of managing their households in a "scientific" manner.[96] Headwoman Hwang Ch'o-rim noted positively the organizational activities that war mobilization had opened to women and the bonds that had formed between women as they worked together to solve communal problems. Owing to these new responsibilities outside the home, she asserted, women had broken free of the repressive customs that confined them to serving husband, in-laws, and children within the home space.[97] For these women, the price of war and submission to colonial authorities was outweighed by women's enlightenment.

CONCLUSION

Patriotic NAs opened the family space to state intervention. Once rationing was imposed, Koreans were virtually unable to resist the state's intrusion via NAs into the intimate domestic sphere. Although cooperation largely was based on coercion and fear that noncompliance would jeopardize lives under wartime economic control and lead to ostracism from the neighborhood community, there was also an element of collaboration, particularly once women assumed substantial responsibility for NA operations. Recognizing that NAs created a space in which women could exercise agency outside the home, some Korean women became enthusiastic supporters of war mobilization. Female activists, who for years had sought to awaken Korean women to the advantages of modernization, work outside the home, and rationalization, believed war mobilization had awoken women from their slumber and allowed them to transcend traditional roles and boundaries. Thus, many women were willing to collaborate in imposing the state's agenda—a pattern that would continue after World War II in South and North Korea.

PART II

Citizens' Neighborhood Associations in South Korea

CHAPTER 4

Reborn into Citizens' Neighborhood Associations

It does not matter who established Patriotic NAs in the past or what the political intent was. . . . It would be worthwhile to make use of Patriotic NAs after adjusting them to suit our [South Korea's] purposes.[1]

On August 15, 1945, Emperor Hirohito announced Japan's surrender to Allied forces; that same day, spontaneous mass celebrations erupted in the streets of Korea. The Korean people removed Japanese judges, town officials, and police officers from their positions, burned the Imperial Edict on Education, and destroyed Shinto altars.[2] Confronted by this eruption of unbridled rage, Endō Ryūsaku, secretary of political affairs for Governor General Abe Nobuyuki, approached Yŏ Un-hyŏng, a center-left Korean leader. He demanded the creation of a peacekeeping administration that would guarantee Japanese citizens' safe passage to Japan. In return, he would agree to release Korean political activists from prison, to continue the distribution of food rations for three months, and to refrain from interfering in Korean nation-building efforts. Shortly after the meeting, Yŏ met with other influential Koreans who had not supported the colonial government to discuss the creation of an interim administrative authority. This meeting led to the creation of the Committee for the Preparation of Korean Independence (CPKI), a broad left-right coalition.[3] It initiated a three-week interregnum period in which the once-formidable Government-General awaited the arrival of US forces to which officially it would surrender authority.

The rapid rise of Korean authority in the wake of the demise of colonial authority also affected Patriotic NAs, which had tightly bound Koreans' daily life to Japanese war efforts and assimilation policies. Monthly radio programs tailored for NA assemblies stopped, and Koreans no longer had to attend mandated NA activities such as Japanese lessons, visits to Shinto shrines, air strike and firefighting training, and the purchasing of government bonds. The neighborhood space returned to its erstwhile condition of being free from political links, thereby making Patriotic NAs a thing of the past.

However, in August 1949, four years after liberation, Patriotic NAs reappeared under a new name: Citizens' NAs (*kungminban*). The four-year period between liberation and the reemergence of NAs witnessed neither the development of national consensus nor a single sovereign Korean state. Instead, Korea had been divided into two zones of military occupation along the thirty-eighth parallel line by the United States and the Soviet Union (1945–1948). As the Cold War divide between the two superpowers solidified, so too did the ideological divide within occupied Korea. In the South, the US military government, intent on creating a nonsocialist government, took steps to ensure that socialists were excluded from power. Similarly, in the North, nonsocialists were increasingly marginalized. This territorial and ideological division culminated with the creation of two polities in 1948. This process was accompanied by the repoliticization of the neighborhood space, as both Koreas chose to resurrect their defunct neighborhood associations despite their association with the colonial past.

This chapter explores how and why Patriotic NAs reemerged as Citizens' NAs in the postcolonial South. At first glance, the despised Patriotic NAs, the primary conduit through which Japanese assimilation policies and coercive wartime mobilization had been imposed on Koreans, seemed an unlikely institution for US occupation authorities and South Korean officials, who wanted to establish their legitimacy with the Korean people, to relaunch. Yet, NAs proved practically and politically useful. US occupation authorities, after a disastrous decision to reintroduce a free rice market, needed an institution through which to administer an equitable rice rationing program. The NAs' previous experience with rice rationing and with collecting the demographic information needed for rationing made them the logical alternative. As rationing came to an end under the new South Korean government, Patriotic NAs appeared to be disbanded. Against the backdrop of challenges to the South Korean government's legitimacy and growing Cold War tensions, however, NAs tracked the movements of the populace and identified potential subversives. It was not long before the Cold War rhetoric restored NAs' mass campaign function under a new nomenclature, Citizens' NAs, and set the stage for the return to moral authoritarianism in the South.

RICE RATIONING AND THE "GHOST" POPULATION

The demise of colonial rule did not mean the immediate end of the wartime rice rationing program. Instead, the CPKI had taken over the management of the wartime program from Japanese officials. Although aware of the program's unpopularity, the CPKI understood that with rice being the backbone of the Korean economy and the most important food in the Korean diet, careful planning was needed before any change in the method of distributing rice could be made. As Bruce Cumings noted, "Korea's economy essentially functioned on a rice standard rather than a gold or other monetary standard."[4] Without exact information about the current level of supply, the status of transportation, and distribution facilities, any change could lead to an unprecedented economic and social disaster. Given the chaotic postwar situation, the CPKI opted to maintain the status quo.

This cautious approach ended shortly after the arrival of US Army Corps XXIV under the command of Lieutenant General John R. Hodge, whom on September 8, 1945, General Douglas MacArthur, supreme allied commander, Southwest Pacific Area, had appointed as the commanding general of the United States Army in Korea (USAFIK). Less than one month after replacing the colonial government as the controlling authority over the Korean Peninsula south of the thirty-eighth parallel, the US Army Military Government in Korea (hereafter USAMGIK) issued General Order No. 5 on October 5, 1945, which introduced a free rice market. The decision reflected American economic assumptions that failed to factor in local realities as well as political considerations.

Although US officials had received reports from the CPKI on nationwide severe food shortages, they believed that the rice deficit was a temporary problem. In addition to thinking that the upcoming October crop would alleviate the rice shortage, they predicted that the introduction of free market trade would lead to an influx into the market of hoarded and recently harvested rice, thereby lowering prices, and would boost rice production. In fact, they estimated that there would be an oversupply of rice, since there would be no further deliveries to Japan and the repatriation of Japanese people would reduce the number of rice consumers. While some warned that sudden removal of restrictions would cause runaway inflation, US officials clung to the optimistic view that prices would be quickly stabilized after a brief increase.[5]

There were also political reasons for introducing a free rice market. First, US authorities feared that the continuation of the hated Japanese restrictions would adversely affect the Americans' popularity among Koreans and thus damage Korean cooperation with occupying forces. Second, the USAMGIK worried that maintaining the program would solidify the political influence of left-oriented people's committees.[6] Since the USAMGIK lacked sufficient personnel to assume control, the administration of rice rationing inevitably would have fallen to people's committees. By deregulating rice, the USAMGIK curbed people's committees from solidifying their grip on local society, thereby setting the stage to outlaw them in December 1945.[7]

But the deregulation of the rice market turned out to be an imprudent decision. Although prices did fall as American officials had predicted—dropping from 63 wŏn per kilogram in August to 9.4 wŏn by the end of October 1945—they quickly rebounded.[8] At first, this rebound sparked few concerns among officials, who assumed that rising prices would entice farmers and rice brokers into releasing more rice, which in turn would prevent prices from continuing to rise. Contrary to the prediction, prices continued to soar.[9] Stunned by the unexpected deterioration of the grain market and the accompanying social unrest in urban areas, the USAMGIK realized that it had to stabilize rice prices if it hoped to regain control over the economy and quell public unrest.[10] If it failed, the socialist political and economic system in place in North Korea might appear the superior option to Koreans in the South.

One variable that Americans had not carefully considered in predicting the course of rice prices was the massive demographic influx into the cities. After liberation, ports and train stations were crowded with thousands of Japanese settlers going back to Japan and with Koreans returning from Manchuria and Japan. Just two years after liberation, South Korea's population had increased by roughly three million.[11] By July 30, 1947, an estimated 2.5 million Koreans had returned to Korea and roughly 470,000 Koreans had relocated from the North to the South.[12] Needing to find employment, most repatriates opted for the city. As a result, between 1945 and 1950, Seoul's population increased by 75 percent, and Taejŏn experienced a 92 percent increase.[13] Most of these repatriates lacked financial resources. Concerned about inflation in Japan and Korea, the US military government in Japan placed strict limits on currency exchange; Koreans leaving Japan could not exchange yen worth more than 1,000 *wŏn*. In Manchuria, the situation was even worse; Chinese officials, hostile to Koreans, often confiscated land owned by Koreans without providing any financial compensation.[14] Given the existing shortage of food and housing in urban areas in the South, this massive influx of destitute repatriates created an unprecedented food and housing crisis that fueled popular discontent.[15]

The introduction of a free rice market was an unmitigated disaster that left the USAMGIK with no choice other than to reverse course. Major General Archer L. Lerch, the military governor of Korea, signed Ordinance No. 45, National Rice Collection on January 25, 1946; based on this ordinance, rationing was reintroduced in February 1946. Aimed at collecting rice from producers for distribution among nonproducers, the ordinance stipulated that producers could only retain rice needed for self-consumption for one year, which was set at roughly sixty-seven and one-half kilograms per household member. Any rice over that amount, producers were required to sell to the government.[16] However, unlike under Japanese rule, the USAMGIK did not unilaterally eliminate the free market; producers were allowed to sell rice designated for self-consumption on the free market.

Commensurate with the ordinance, the USAMGIK revived the Japanese apparatus for rice control—the apex of which was the Central Office of Foodstuffs in tandem with the Central Office of Price in

May 1946.[17] To recover shipping capacity, which was only one-tenth of what it had been in 1944, the USAMGIK nationalized the railroad companies in May 1946.[18] The railroad companies, which largely had been owned by the Japanese, were in a state of poor repair. Repairing the railroads became a top priority of the military government as it was the fastest way to transport rice to the cities where it was most needed. Also, by securing control of the railroads, it denied profiteers access to the primary means of getting rice to the cities.

The US rice control policy had support across the political spectrum, although the reasons for supporting it varied greatly. The Korean Democratic Party (*Han'guk minjudang,* hereafter KDP), which represented the interests of landlords, preferred a free market economy, but it begrudgingly accepted the reinstitution of a controlled economy as a necessary short-term measure to quell popular unrest.[19] The landlords resented the compulsory collection of rice, because it deprived them of the opportunity to commercialize rice. The promise of preferential treatment in receiving other goods in short supply, such as towels and soaps, in their estimation was inadequate compensation for the losses they incurred owing to the low price the government paid for rice, which was 30 percent below market value.[20] By contrast, leftists wholeheartedly supported the reintroduction of rice control. They perceived it as a promising first step toward more extensive reforms of the market and of landlordism. The Korean People's Party (*Chosŏn inmindang*) advocated for an even stronger intervention in the collection and distribution of rice, asserting that the free market system disproportionately victimized the urban working class.[21] Taking it a step further, the Democratic National Front (*Minjujuŭi minjok chŏnsŏn*), a wide alliance of leftists led by the Korean Communist Party (*Chosŏn kongsandang*), insisted that the resolution of the rice crisis required immediate land reform, that is, the redistribution of land to peasants. They attributed the current crisis to hoarding by landlords and profiteers.[22]

Reintroducing rice control posed a political dilemma for the US-AMGIK, as it did not want to empower the left-oriented people's committees and it lacked the resources and manpower to administer the program itself. The most obvious alternative to using the people's committees was to revive Patriotic NAs. However, this meant resurrecting collective memories of Koreans' forced mobilization for the Japanese war effort. For Korean nationalists, who wanted to expunge all remnants of the authoritarian colonial system, Patriotic NAs' recent history of close collaboration with Japanese authorities made this solution unacceptable. They warned that if NAs were placed in charge of administering the current program, Koreans would equate it with the unpopular wartime rice rationing program, thereby undermining the likelihood of the populace's cooperation. As an alternative, they proposed that local cooperatives or civil committees without any ties to state bureaucracy be placed for collecting and confiscating rice hoarded by landlords and profiteers.[23]

However, not all Koreans believed that Patriotic NAs were incompatible with the creation of an independent postcolonial nation-state in Korea. For example, the editorial staff of *Seoul sinmun* highlighted the usefulness of Patriotic NAs, even as it acknowledged that under colonial rule, NAs had been the primary institution through which the Japanese had carried out its "bureaucratic practices" and perpetuated "national discrimination." Such abuses, the paper argued, were unlikely to continue in the future, since Koreans, rather than Japanese officials, would be responsible for the management of Patriotic NAs and could operate them as they chose. The paper reminded its readers that prior to colonization, there had been traditional Korean institutions that had been very similar to Patriotic NAs, and that these institutions had fostered mutual aid—a value deeply embedded in Korean culture. Having Patriotic NAs take over the new rationing programs, the paper contended, would deprive middlemen of opportunities to accumulate enormous profits in the course of rice circulation and eventually empower Koreans to assume responsibility for self-government.[24]

The above argument received strong support from urban residents, who as the hardest hit by the food crisis, desperately wanted to expedite the introduction of rice rationing. At 11:00 a.m., on February 11, 1946, public authorities in Seoul held an emergency meeting on the rice crisis at which about five hundred people, including US military authorities, the Police Bureau's director, the city's mayor, landlords, and district representatives, were in attendance. Military authorities asked local officials for their voluntary cooperation in implementing the Rice Collection Ordinance; the director of the Police Bureau seconded this request, adding that district representatives should make it clear to residents that it was their patriotic duty to sell to the government any stockpiles of rice they might have and to consume rice frugally.[25] In response, district representatives demanded immediate implementation of rice rationing. They warned that unless the government guaranteed a minimum subsistence level of rice, calls for voluntary compliance in the name of patriotism and communal morality would fall on deaf ears. In lieu of urging voluntary cooperation, they recommended that more drastic measures be taken to overcome the food crisis in Seoul. Specifically, to end the profiteering of middlemen, they suggested that the government institute a program of search and seizure as well as the immediate reintroduction of rice rationing via existing administrative institutions, including Patriotic NAs.[26]

Creating an equitable system of rationing required reliable demographic information, and Patriotic NAs were the most efficient means for acquiring that information. Under colonial rule, as discussed in the chapter 3, the residential registry, the mechanism through which the government tracked the movements of the population, had been linked to Patriotic NAs responsible for administering rationing. Thus, when the USAMGIK reintroduced a free rice market, it undermined the ability of the registry to provide accurate information about the whereabouts of Koreans. Since updating one's address was no longer associated with receiving one's rice rations, Koreans had little motivation to report their movements to the residential registry, especially given that many Koreans assumed that the American occupiers, like their previous occupiers, would use the registry to implement a system of forced labor. Against the backdrop of massive demographic shifts in the aftermath of the war, the registry became useless as a tool for rationing. Reestablishing the link between the registry and Patriotic NAs was the quickest way to ensure the reliability of the census and administer rice rationing effectively. The USAMGIK and Korean leaders concurred; Patriotic NAs should resume their wartime responsibility for rationing and for providing accurate demographic data.[27]

Korea's "ghost population" (yuryŏng in'gu), which had disappeared when rationing ended, now reappeared as news spread of US plans to reimplement rationing. As during the war, Koreans began creating "ghosts," that is, fictitious persons to secure extra rations. For example, a person living alone in the city might falsely claim that various family members resided with him or her. Similarly, married children might claim that their parents lived in their household, while their parents claimed that those same children resided in their household.[28] In November 1948 alone, government officials verified that 209,147 persons listed on the residential registry for Seoul did not exist.[29]

The escalation of "ghost populations" undermined efforts to ensure an equitable distribution of rice rations and contributed to the eruption of the 1946 Autumn Harvest Uprising. From September to December, over 250,000 Koreans across the South, including workers, students, and peasants, marched to demand an increase in the rice ration as well as rice for unemployed workers. They expressed their outrage at the wealthy who hoarded rice, the police force that utilized violence to enforce the rice control policy, and the US military government.[30] As Mark Gayn, a foreign correspondent for the *Toronto Star*, noted in his eyewitness account, "it was a full-scale revolution" that placed the USAMGIK on the defensive.[31] Accusing leftists and agitators from the North of having instigated the uprising, the USAMGIK, with the assistance of the Korean police and rightist student organizations, crushed the demonstrations and uprisings.[32] However, the uprising made clear that Koreans had strong reservations about liberal capitalism. US occupiers came to see eliminating "ghost populations" and meeting rice collection quotas as equally important barometers for measuring the successful arrival of the postcolonial order and for assessing the populace's acceptance of liberal capitalism over North Korean socialism.

Upon reestablishing the colonial relationship between Patriotic NAs, the census, and rationing, officials concerned instructed the heads of NAs to visit every household to ascertain the actual number of residents. This data was then used to administer the rice rationing program. To prevent abuses of the system by Patriotic NA heads, the USAMGIK instituted a dual system of reporting, whereby the responsibility for confirming the legitimacy of new arrivals was shared by NA heads and by all households in an NA. If a member of a household was discovered to be a "ghost," the rice account book of that household was confiscated until such time that all members of the Patriotic NA signed a form attesting to the accuracy of that household's demographic information.[33]

By 1949, rice rationing through the Patriotic NAs was winding down. With the end of occupation, the Korean government began considering changes to the USAMGIK's rice control policy. Although a consensus existed among Korean government officials that it was too soon to eliminate the rationing program completely, they no longer believed that circumstances warranted including all nonproducers in the program. However, Korean officials disagreed about which nonproducers should be excluded from the program. Some argued that inclusion in the program should be based on income; eliminating nonproducers with the means to purchase rice on the free market would ensure that those in need could receive a larger share of the available rice supply. Allowing wealthy nonproducers to participate in the rice rationing program, they argued, served only to widen the class divide and increase popular discontent. Other officials contended that the right to receive rice rations should be limited to major population centers with high concentrations of nonproducers. This latter proposal was soon discarded on the grounds that it was too urbancentric and did not consider nonproducers in rural areas. On April 9, 1949, a decision was finally reached; Prime Minister Yi Pŏm-sŏk announced that only low-income nonproducers would be eligible to receive rice rations.[34]

Patriotic NAs now faced the difficult task of deciding which of their members qualified to receive the rice ration. In April 1949, Patriotic NAs across the South held a special assembly to decide which members were eligible to participate in the new program. Once a decision was reached, Patriotic NA heads were to distribute cards to beneficiaries and submit a new ration list to the town office.[35] However, most families were unwilling to relinquish their ration rights. As Ch'oi Chŏng-hŭi, a writer and former Patriotic NA head, noted: "As soon as the headman said that he would survey who needed the rice ration immediately following the opening remarks, everyone yelled at the same time, 'I cannot live without it.'"[36] With everyone clamoring for inclusion on the new list, tensions between neighbors and delays in submitting the list, especially in poverty-stricken areas, inevitably occurred as NA heads tried to mediate between the interests of various members. Frustrated by the delays in reporting, the Agriculture Ministry warned that if the new ration lists were not submitted immediately, it would arbitrarily decide on recipients.[37] The warning led some Patriotic NAs to divide their quotas equally among all member households, rather than selecting beneficiaries based on need. Displeased with this solution, the ministry issued a reminder that Patriotic NAs should select beneficiaries, not discuss distribution.[38]

Although the transition to a need-based system of rationing was chaotic, it was a critical step toward ending the decades-long link between Patriotic NAs and the rationing system. This separation had been postponed by USAMGIK's initial mismanagement of the postwar food crisis and its unwillingness to utilize leftist people's committees to administer the rationing program. Instead, US authorities opted to revive the previous colonial mechanism—Patriotic NAs. However, Patriotic NAs under the USAMGIK no longer served as the site of state-led movements. Instead, their role was limited to the administering of rations, which allowed Koreans to disassociate Patriotic NAs from the colonial past to some extent.

GROWING VIGILANCE AGAINST COMMUNISM

Not long after Patriotic NAs were detached from rice rationing, the Transitory Resident Registration (*yusukgye*, hereafter the Registration) was issued on July 25, 1949. It required civilians to report any guests between the ages of sixteen and sixty staying in their homes to the head of their Patriotic NA; it also required them to inform their NA heads of any stays away from home, including vacations, visits to relatives' homes, and business trips. To gain civilian support for the measure, the Police Bureau sponsored a slogan contest. On August 25, 1949, the winning slogans were announced. First prize went to the slogan "Let's ferret out hidden enemies through the Registration."[39] As this choice indicates, the South Korean government had assigned Patriotic NAs a new responsibility—to expose enemies hiding amid the population. Against the backdrop of a peninsula divided along Cold War ideological lines, "enemies" in the South became synonymous with leftists. The postcolonial neighborhood space became the front line of defense against these potentially subversive forces.

Yet, in 1945, no Korean would have predicted the division of the Korean Peninsula. Having been liberated from Japanese colonial rule,

Koreans had as their primary goal creating a united, independent nation-state. But under occupation, this goal proved illusory. Socialists found themselves marginalized in the US occupation zone, and nonsocialists suffered the same fate in the Soviet occupation zone. The US–USSR Joint Commission, established in 1945, met in March 1946 and adjourned in May 1946 without having reached any agreement on Korean unification. A year later the commission reconvened, but once again the meeting ended in failure. Convinced of the futility of any further meetings, the US decided to bring the question of Korea before the UN General Assembly. When the UN agreed to consider the problem in September 1947, the Soviets proposed that both sides immediately withdraw their troops from the peninsula, leaving Koreans to form their own government. The United States recommended that troop withdrawal be postponed until after elections under UN supervision were held in both zones. Once elections were held, the new Korean government could decide on the withdrawal of occupation forces. In October 1947, the US proposed the creation of a temporary UN commission that would observe the elections and act as advisors to the new Korean government in setting up governmental machinery and in the troop withdrawal process.[40]

When the UN General Assembly passed the US resolution, the Soviet Union gave notice that it would not cooperate with the United Nations Temporary Commission on Korea (UNTCOK). In January 1948, the North, skeptical of the commission's neutrality, refused entry to the UNTCOK. Instead of abandoning its mission, the UNTCOK decided in February 1948 that it would observe elections in the South, where it had been allowed entry. On May 10, 1948, voters in the South went to the polls to vote for representatives for the National Assembly. On May 21, the newly elected representatives met in Seoul. By July, they had devised a constitution that called for a president elected by the National Assembly. Eight days later, on July 20, the assembly chose Syngman Rhee as president. On August 15, 1948, Rhee's formal inauguration took place, and the Republic of Korea (ROK) was officially established.

The formation of the Republic of Korea, which claimed legitimacy for the entire Korean peninsula, triggered parallel action in the North. On August 25, 1948, elections for delegations for the Supreme People's Assembly (SPA) were held. On September 2, the SPA convened, and on

September 8, it adopted a constitution. The following day, the Democratic People's Republic of Korea (DPRK) was established. Like its South Korean counterpart, it claimed sovereignty over the entire Korean Peninsula.[41]

The division of Korea at the state level did not immediately result in a rupture in Korean civil society. The territorial boundary at the thirty-eighth parallel, arbitrarily agreed upon by the United States and the Soviet Union, remained relatively porous. Although North Korea stopped supplying electricity to the South in May 1948 and South Korea announced in March 1949 that it would no longer trade with the North, people and goods, subject to stringent inspections, continued to cross the border on a daily basis.[42] Moreover, despite two separate legal systems based on different political and economic ideologies, ordinary Koreans on one side of the border still saw themselves as sharing a common national identity with Koreans on the opposite side. For a variety of personal and political reasons, many South Koreans opposed the division. Despite efforts by the USAMGIK and the newly formed government to ostracize socialists, there remained in the South some committed socialist activists who wanted to see a united, socialist Korea. In short, substantial segments of the population rejected the legitimacy of the newly formed South Korean government.

The Yŏsun Incident, on October 19, 1948, underscored the unpopularity of the South Korean government. Ordered to suppress a popular armed uprising on Cheju Island, the Fourteenth Regiment of the ROK Army, responsible for border patrol (*Kukpang kyŏngbidae*), refused. The Cheju Committee of the Workers' Party of South Korea (*Namjosŏn rodongdang*) had launched an armed struggle against the May 1948 elections, thus making Cheju Island the only place in the South where the UN-supervised elections did not occur. When Rhee assumed the presidency, he mobilized troops to suppress the rebellion. However, left-leaning soldiers in the Fourteenth Regiment disobeyed orders, lending their support to the people of Cheju. The rebellion quickly gained momentum. By October 21, rebel forces occupied a substantial portion of eastern South Chŏlla Province and rebuked the South Korean government for failing to punish collaborators and for instigating the division of Korea. They also called for the immediate withdrawal of the US military from Korea. The Rhee government responded by declaring martial law, and US and South Korean military forces were dispatched to suppress the rebellion. By the time the dust settled, an estimated ten thousand civilians had been killed.[43]

Stunned by the discovery that leftists had substantial networks within the army, the National Assembly held emergency hearings from October 27 to the end of October. Following a briefing on the losses inflicted by insurgent forces, legislators inquired after the belated reaction of the government to the protests and its ineffective suppression of leftists. Defense Minister Yi Pŏm-sŏk explained that the army was trying to ascertain the whereabouts of leftists, but the operation had been impeded by the close relationship between leftists and civilians. The defense minister also claimed, "Only a small number of persons in the army had been involved in the incident. However, because of the leftist networks among the masses and among students, the revolting army members had been able to take over Yŏsu."[44] The local people, he continued, had provided the insurgents with food and shelter, rather than reporting them to the police.

Interior Minister Yun Ch'i-yŏng admitted government responsibility for the incident, citing its failure to provide the masses with adequate political education about democracy. He attributed this error in judgment to overconfidence: having established a constitutional democracy that guaranteed the freedom of citizens, officials had incorrectly assumed that the masses were prepared to take part in a democratic system. This failure to educate the masses, he claimed, had made communities in the South vulnerable to communist infiltration. Thus, he contended that the future of South Korea depended on the government taking sweeping actions to drive out communists in the South: "Whether democracy is appropriate does not matter now. . . . In order to survive, we must strengthen our security. . . . I hope that you will support my future policies."[45]

In calling on the National Assembly to support the promotion of security over that of democracy, Minister Yun cited the populace's "political immaturity" as justification. Yun's discursive strategy was highly reminiscent of that used by the Japanese when they had spoken of the "low civility" of the Korean masses to advance the notion of Japanese superiority and to justify state-led movements that combined mobilization and programs of mass enlightenment. This similarity in argument is not surprising, given that many in Rhee's administration, including Interior Minister Yun, had supported the Japanese imperial state during the Pacific War. Yet, the two discourses were not identical. Within colonial discourse, Koreans had been apolitical beings. In contrast, the constitution of South Korea endowed Koreans with certain political rights, including freedom of speech, media, and assembly. However, for government officials, the Yŏsun Incident had exposed the need to place limits on those rights, lest their exercise jeopardize national security.

The solution was the enactment of the National Security Act (NSA) on December 1, 1948—the stated purpose of which was to "suppress anti-State acts that endanger national security and to ensure [the] nation's security, people's life and freedom."[46] The NSA, in effect, outlawed communism, socialism, and supporting North Korea. By the end of 1949, 118,621 alleged leftists had been arrested. The National Guidance League (*Kungmin podoyŏnmaeng*) was established to rehabilitate these alleged leftists on June 5, 1949.[47]

At roughly the same time that the Rhee government rolled out its campaign against leftists, the National Assembly abandoned its prosecution of Japanese collaborators. In September 1948, roughly one month prior to the Yŏsun Incident, the National Assembly had passed the Act for Punishing Anti-National Conduct (*Panminjok haeng'wi ch'ŏbŏlbŏp*); under the act, the Special Committee for Investigation (SCI) was created to investigate and prosecute Japanese collaborators. If found guilty, the accused could be subject to forfeiture of their political rights, confiscation of property, and even the death penalty.[48] However, the SCI encountered resistance from those who accused SCI members of being communist sympathizers. In fact, the Rhee administration used the NSA to strike back at national assembly members who pursued Japanese collaborators, called for the withdrawal of US troops, and demanded negotiations on the unification of Korea. By autumn 1949, eighteen national assembly members, including National Assembly Vice-Chairman Kim Yak-su, had been arrested under the NSA. Their imprisonment drastically weakened the SCI, which disbanded in October 1949. The search for wartime collaborators had been replaced by the pursuit of Cold War enemies.

Amid this shift in the political topography, in April 1949, the Interior Ministry first charged Patriotic NAs with monitoring the movements of neighbors. To this end, it provided NA heads with two types of forms: one form to document absences for two weeks or more and another form to record absences for less than two weeks. NA members were also encouraged to volunteer such information to their NA heads. NA heads were told to provide the local police station with an accurate list of residents and up-to-date information on the movement of residents, as well as report any suspicious individuals or activities. In addition, policemen should attend the meetings of the Patriotic NA to which they belonged and report any irregularities or instances of noncompliance. Based on these reports, the local police had the authority to call for the election of a new NA head.[49]

The Interior Ministry's use of the police to enforce NA compliance with the Registration quickly drew harsh criticism, resulting in a temporary halt in the Registration. Opponents argued that the program was ripe for abuse. Innocent civilians could easily find themselves on a government watchlist as potential subversives simply because they failed to report movements when going on a business trip or vacation. Moreover, it destroyed traditional neighborhood bonds, as it called on neighbors to police one another. The program, they claimed, was "antidemocratic" and "fascist."[50] As such, it violated the South Korean constitution, which guaranteed all citizens "freedom of residence and the right to move at will" as well as protected citizens from arbitrary arrest. On April 29, 1949, ninety-three national legislators signed a statement calling for the abolition of the Registration.[51] On May 11, 1949, in response to the public outcry, the interior minister acknowledged that the national government had no legal authority to enforce the Registration: "Its objective is to hunt down rebellious people. . . . It does not have any legal grounds, but we ask for the moral cooperation of the people."[52]

By reframing the Registration as a moral obligation rather than a legal one, the government hoped to avoid any further legal confrontations as well as widespread defiance. The Interior Ministry also loosened the restrictions it had put in place. NA members no longer had to provide their NA heads with written statements about their travels; oral reports sufficed. In addition, those who traveled regularly were no longer required to report each trip to their NA head; and prosecutions for violating the Registration were limited to repeat offenders and to cases in which someone knowingly provided shelter to antigovernmental actors.[53]

On June 4, 1949, the Interior Ministry reintroduced the Registration and on July 25, 1949, it went back into effect. On the first day of its implementation, police stations were bustling with NA heads, but the submitted forms gave little indication that the Registration would be effective in tracking down subversives. Instead, police stations found themselves inundated with forms documenting the mundane movements of ordinary citizens. For instance, the police station in Hoehyŏn town in Seoul received twenty-eight reports from NA heads between 10:00 p.m. on July 25 and 9:00 a.m. the next day. They covered irrelevant activities such as a student returning home for vacation, a mother visiting her daughter who had given birth, and a man going on a business trip. Additionally, the head of the First NA in the town said few people seemed willing to volunteer information about the movements of household members or guests.[54] This reluctance was confirmed when police uncovered 36,786 violations for the month of August 1949 alone.[55]

The Registration did not appear to be a success for the Interior Ministry. The ministry lacked the authority to enforce it, the level of compliance by NAs was uneven, and few subversives were captured. However, this assessment fails to take into consideration the way in which the Registration shifted the populace's antipathy from collaboration with the Japanese to potential communist infiltration. By reframing the Registration as a moral obligation and mobilizing the moral space of the neighborhood for its implementation, the ministry overcame a legal impasse and successfully introduced a new normative code of conduct based on Cold War values. In short, the ministry successfully repeated the strategy employed by Japanese colonizers; it turned anti-Communism into the clarion call that East Asian values had been under wartime colonial rule. Having discovered a formula for success, the ministry was primed to play a leading role in creating the political discourse for a nation that remained deeply divided over issues of national security, division of power, and the appropriate parameters of political freedom.

CITIZENS' NAs FOR APOLITICAL
PAN-NATIONAL MOVEMENTS

On August 24, 1949, one month after the Registration went into effect, the government announced that Patriotic NAs would be reorganized as Citizens' NAs and that the new NAs would be used for joint government-civilian mass campaigns. To emphasize the dual nature of this venture, the announcement was made simultaneously at a government meeting attended by President Syngman Rhee, the ministerial heads, and the local provincial governors and at a convention of the National Society (*Kungminhoe*), a nongovernmental organization established in February 1946 under Rhee's leadership to promote apolitical pan-national Korean movements.[56]

The structural reorganization of NAs under the umbrella of the government and the National Society was a postcolonial adaptation of a colonial practice. The change in prefix from "patriotic" to "citizens" created the impression of a break from the colonial past, as it emphasized the newly gained political subjectivity of South Koreans. The Cold War language that underpinned the promotional campaigns also differentiated Citizens' NAs from their predecessors. However, like their predecessors, Citizens' NAs were nongovernmental bodies in name only, as Rhee was the leader of the South Korean government and of the National Society. Rhee's authority over the national government and over the ostensibly nongovernmental organization under which Citizens' NAs operated meant that the South Korean government had secured the same access to the moral space of the neighborhood as had the colonial government when it placed Patriotic NAs under the dual control of the Government-General and of the "independent" League for Concerted National Power.

The decision to recreate this colonial power structure most likely stemmed from the fact that Rhee had no mass political base due to his years abroad. At the time of Korea's liberation, Rhee had been living in the United States for over two decades. Born in 1875 to an impoverished aristocratic Korean family, Rhee first traveled to the United States in 1904; in 1907, he received a bachelor of arts from George Washington University, then in 1908 a master of arts from Harvard University, and finally a doctor of philosophy in government in 1910 from Princeton

University. His return to Korea in 1910 coincided with Japan's annexation of his homeland. Rhee was a committed nationalist, whose political views and activities soon placed him at odds with Japanese authorities, and in 1912, he left Korea again for Hawaii. In 1919, he was elected in absentia president of the Korean Provisional Government (KPG) in Shanghai. The following year, he relocated to Shanghai but returned to the United States in 1925 after an internal dispute resulted in his being ousted from the KPG. Upon returning to the United States, Rhee still called himself the "Minister Plenipotentiary and Envoy Extraordinary" (of the KPG) and continued to fight for international recognition of the KPG as the legitimate government of Korea.[57]

When Rhee arrived in Korea on October 16, 1945, a host of political parties had already begun to emerge. The Korean Communist Party (*Chosŏn kongsandang*), dissolved by the colonial regime in 1928, was reestablished in August 1945. The KDP, which represented the interests of the landlord class, developed in September 1945, and major figures of the KPG such as Kim Ku and Kim Kyu-sik started the Korean Independence Party (*Han'guk tongniptang*). By 1948, there were an additional forty-eight registered political parties. Most of these nascent political parties, however, had no specific political platform or underlying ideology; their identity was synonymous with the prominent Korean personality associated with them. Moreover, few of these parties had the time or the financial means to build local chapters or networks.[58] Thus, to gain a political foothold among the populace, they relied on local organizations such as labor unions, peasant unions, women's groups, and youth groups to mobilize the populace. Youth groups, in particular, were drawn to these personality-centered parties. At rallies, they would stand in front of speakers and prompt attendees to applaud and shout in support of their chosen leader. They also attempted to disrupt the rallies of other political parties. Eruptions of violence, and even political assassinations, were not uncommon.[59]

The mushrooming of political parties and the accompanying violence convinced Rhee that Korea was not ready for party politics. He believed that having "more than three parties was bad for the country," because it led to overheated competition, confused the people, and fostered factionalism at the expense of national interests.[60] In addition, Rhee saw Korea as a natural entity characterized by a shared bloodline and ancestry. There should be one Korean nation "occupied by one united people" and social inequalities, factionalism, and disparities in wealth should be eliminated in national unity.[61]

The chaotic political atmosphere with its plethora of personality-centered political parties also made Rhee realize that his long stay in the United States placed him at a distinct disadvantage in this crowded field of political parties. Although the US occupiers felt that Rhee had major name recognition and a wide following, most Koreans did not, making it unlikely that he could garner sufficient popular support to establish a viable political party. Thus, instead of trying to create his own political party or joining an existing one, Rhee maneuvered to position himself as a mediator between the various party leaders. Arguing that achieving independence required Koreans to speak with a unified voice, he rallied leaders from various political parties to launch the Central Council for the Rapid Realization of Korean Independence (*Taehan tongnip ch'oksŏng chung'ang hyŏbŭihoe*) in October 1945. Because Rhee embraced pro-Japanese Koreans while excluding left-leaning anti-Japanese activists, leftists and some nationalists refused to embrace his concept of unity, resulting in the coalition's demise.[62]

A decisive political opportunity arose for Rhee in December 1945 when the foreign ministers of the United States, Great Britain, and the Soviet Union met in Moscow to discuss issues concerning the Far East, including Korea. At the conference, a decision was reached to establish a US–USSR Joint Commission to make recommendations for the creation of a single Korean government. In the meanwhile, Korea would be placed under a four-power trusteeship (the United States, Great Britain, the Soviet Union, and China) for a period of up to five years. This decision angered many Koreans, who wanted immediate independence and who feared that escalating Cold War tensions would result in the arbitrary boundary at the thirty-eighth parallel becoming irreversible and lead to the permanent military occupation of Korea by the two superpowers. The decision of the Moscow Conference instantly simplified Korea's complex political landscape, splitting Korean politicians into two camps—leftists who accepted the trusteeship as a practical interim step toward a united, independent Korea and rightists who opposed it on the grounds that it represented the recolonization of Korea. The consolidation of the various factions into two camps allowed Rhee to convince rightist political parties, social organizations, and individuals to establish the National Society for the Rapid Realization of Korean Independence (*Taehan tongnip ch'oksŏng kungminhoe*, or NSRRKI) on February 8, 1946. The NSRRKI held its first general convention on June 10–11, 1946, at which it pledged to prioritize the creation of a self-reliant and independent Korea. To this end, it committed to promoting a national movement that transcended party politics.[63]

The NSRRKI became the vehicle through which Rhee became a household name. The idea of an apolitical national movement dedicated to the creation of a unified independent state was extremely appealing to Koreans for whom the traumatic memory of colonial rule was still fresh. As a result, by June 1946, the NSRRKI had an estimated eight million members and a network of offices in every province in the South.[64] Bolstered by its rising popularity, the NSSRKI reaffirmed its commitment to resisting the establishment of a trusteeship in Korea.[65] Following Rhee's election as NSRRKI chair, he was depicted as a national savior—a leader who could unite Koreans and transcend petty party politics. With the help of local elites, lawyers, and doctors who staffed the local offices of the NSRRKI, Rhee's political star rose rapidly.[66]

When in August 1947 the second meeting of the US–USSR Joint Commission ended in failure, it paved the way for Rhee to assume the office of the presidency in the South. As noted earlier, the breakdown of these negotiations prompted the United States to bring the issue before the United Nations. When the UN rejected the Soviet proposal for immediate independence in favor of the US proposal to hold elections under UN supervision, the North refused to take part and the UN decided to proceed with elections in the South. The decision to hold elections without the North split the NSRRKI into two factions—one faction, led by Kim Ku, that opposed holding elections confined to the South and the other, led by Rhee, that supported immediate elections and promised unification later. After some internal conflicts, Rhee's faction emerged victorious, elections for the first National Assembly were held on May 10, 1948, and on July 20, 1948, Rhee was named the first president of South Korea.[67]

The National Assembly elections demonstrated that none of Korea's countless political parties had sufficient popular support to dominate the elections. Eighty-five of the two hundred seats (40.3 percent) were won by candidates with no party affiliation. Fifty-five assemblymen (26.1 percent) were associated with the NSRRKI.[68] But the establishment of an independent South Korean government deprived it of its reason for existing. Admittedly, a unified Korea, the other half of its stated goal, had not been realized, but achieving half its goal sufficed to undermine the political coalition. Infighting between the various political parties that made up the NSRRKI quickly erupted. Rhee's supporters wanted to turn it into the ruling party to buttress Rhee in the National Assembly. Those who did not support Rhee wanted to make it into an opposition party. Still others wanted it to remain unaffiliated with any political party. Amid these mounting internal tensions, it held a meeting in September 1948 to define its relationship with the political parties and with the Rhee administration. It resolved to remain independent from the political parties and to promote pan-national movements.[69]

The ambiguity of the term "pan-national movement" (*kungmin undong*) was key. The term allowed the NSRRKI to maintain its estimated eight million members, who belonged to various political parties or had joined without any party affiliation. If it shifted its identity to that of a political party, it risked many members withdrawing from the organization. But the distinction that the NSRRKI drew between itself and the political parties was not always as clear cut as the organization's rhetoric suggested. Members who belonged to political parties could use their affiliation with the NSRRKI to advance their causes on the national stage. It needed to clearly delineate which national movements were acceptable for the organization to promote. To avoid conflict, it chose to support only "pure" or "apolitical" movements, that is, movements that advanced national and ideological causes which no one would contest. In its estimation, this meant movements that promoted anticommunism and national strength through military and economic development as well as mass enlightenment. Ideological division and dependence upon foreign aid, the NSRRKI opined, were the two greatest threats to Korean independence and national security.[70]

The NSRRKI proposed that it be allowed to mobilize NAs to promote its "apolitical" pan-national movements. Since neighborhood associations were not affiliated with any political party and encompassed the entire population, they were the ideal structure for advancing the NSRRKI's "pure" campaigns. However, the colonial prefix "patriotic" would need to be changed to something that reflected the NSRRKI's emphasis on "pure" campaigns dedicated to promoting independence—Citizens' NAs. On November 17, 1948, Vice-Chair Myŏng Che-se and five high-ranking NSRRKI staff members asked Rhee to approve the use of neighborhood associations as a mass base for their campaigns. Furthermore, they proposed the creation of a Government-Civilian Commission made up of the executive members of the NSRRKI, ministerial ministers, and provincial governors as well as the creation of local commissions made up of local leaders and local officers in provinces, counties, towns, and villages.[71] This hierarchal institutional structure would resume the wartime role of NAs as the loci of nationwide movements.

Despite redefining neighborhood associations as citizens' gatherings, the NSRRKI's proposal largely recreated the organizational structures and relationships of colonial Patriotic NAs. As discussed in chapter 1, Patriotic NAs fell under the jurisdiction of the League for Concerted National Power, an ostensibly nongovernmental body. However, the bureaucratic hierarchy of the league overlapped with that of the government, thereby allowing the Government-General to advance its agenda while maintaining the illusion that the campaigns promoted in Patriotic NAs were voluntary rather than mandated. Similarly, under the NSRRKI's proposal, Citizens' NAs would fall under the NSRRKI, a nongovernmental body. Like the league, the NSRRKI was independent in name only, as Rhee served as its head while also serving as the head of the South Korean government. The proposal strengthened the connection between NAs under the NSRRKI and the government by creating the government-civilian commissions that once again required NAs to answer to local town authorities. The so-called apolitical mass campaigns sponsored by the NSRRKI would in fact be closely coordinated with the government. Thus, like its predecessor, these campaigns extolled and encouraged voluntary participation while in fact being involuntary and bureaucratic.

The superimposition of the wartime colonial structure onto the democratic order provided Rhee with a unique opportunity to remake himself as a populist presidential leader. As chair of the NSRRKI, he could cultivate his direct relationship with the masses through its control over the NAs. This new leadership role was instrumental in Rhee maintaining his presidential authority, which was being challenged by the National Assembly. No sooner had the National Assembly elected him as president than tensions developed between Rhee and the KDP, because he failed to follow through on his promise to appoint a significant number of its members to important positions within his government.[72] While Rhee's lack of a party affiliation in 1948 had given him an advantage with the independent legislators who made up 42 percent of the National Assembly, it now worked against him. Angered by Rhee's betrayal, the KDP built an alliance with various anti-Rhee factions within the National Assembly. Out of this coalition, on February 10, 1949, a new, stronger political party emerged, the Democratic People's Party (*Minju kungmindang*). It proposed a constitutional amendment to replace the presidential system with a parliamentary system. If Rhee was to survive this challenge to his authority, he needed to be able to counter the proposed amendment by claiming that his presidency represented the will of the people.

The conflict between Rhee and the National Assembly was exacerbated by debates on the appropriate level of autonomy that should be given to local governments. The South Korean constitution guaranteed the establishment of local elective bodies. "The organization and power of local councils, and the election of members; election procedures for heads of local governments; and other matters pertaining to the organization and operation of local governments" were to be set by law.[73] There were three models of local autonomy under consideration. Under the first model, the central government would be responsible for appointing all local officials; this option would severely limit residents' access to the decision-making process. At the other extreme was the option to give residents the right to elect all local government officials, who, in turn, would have total authority over local affairs. The third option, a compromise between the two extremes, would allow the state bureaucracy to appoint some local officials and residents to vote for others.[74] While heated debates on Local Autonomy Act were predicted, the Interior Ministry tendered a temporary bill for local administration.[75] Accepting the temporary condition, the National Assembly passed the Temporary Local Administration Law (*Chibanghaengjŏng'e kwanhan imsijoch'ibŏp*) on November 17, 1948. The law gave the national government the authority to appoint all provincial governors and mayors. Moreover, once appointed, they would be placed under the direct supervision of the ministry.[76] However, the National Assembly countered with the Local Autonomy Act (*Chibang chach'ibŏp*), which provided for the election of local government officials by the people and placed restrictions on the national government's supervisory authority over local affairs.[77]

After a series of intense debates, a compromise Local Autonomy Act was passed on July 4, 1949, which slightly favored the National Assembly's emphasis on providing for greater local autonomy. After defining the administrative units of local governance—that is, provinces, counties (cities), and towns—the act provided for the direct election of representatives for provincial, city, and town councils by the people. The mayor of Seoul and provincial governors were to be appointed by the central government; the mayors of other cities and chiefs of towns were to be elected by the respective assemblies. The law also provided for a system of checks and balances at the local level. The local assemblies, if dissatisfied with the local administration, had the right to audit the local administration and pass a vote of no confidence. The local administrator, with the approval of the provincial governor, had the right to dissolve the assembly if dissatisfied with its performance. Strict limitations also were placed on the Interior Ministry's authority to intervene in local affairs. It had the right to audit local finances, and it could nullify a local law only when it contradicted a national law.[78]

The act fell short of Rhee's expectations and so to prevent it going into effect, he chose not to set a date for local elections. The vice-interior minister, Chang Kyŏng-kŭn, accounted for the delay as follows: "In this time of crisis that requires national integrity, we must prevent the Act from creating many disorderly countries within one country. For a local society to have independent authority from the central government, it must demonstrate the necessary prerequisites: the moral foundations as members of that society, politic conscience, the training, and the financial means, thus before implementation, the government must lead an enlightenment campaign and secure finance sufficient to give local governments financial support."[79] Central to his explanation for postponing the local elections was the reference to "national integrity." For Koreans, this word had strong connotations, as its absence was associated with Korea's inability to resist colonization and its recent occupation by US military forces, which also was viewed by many as a national humiliation. Consequently, "national integrity" had become a Korean obsession, and now with Korea's division and the accompanying political turmoil, Chang's allusion to "national integrity" provoked extreme trepidation about the nation's future. This apocalyptic future Chang emphasized by likening local elections to the creation of many countries. However, he did not dare use the appeal to national integrity as an excuse for permanently canceling local elections, since South Koreans also associated "national integrity" with achieving an independent democratic order—a milestone that differentiated present-day South Korea from the colonial past and from life under US military occupation. Thus, he framed the failure to schedule local elections as a temporary postponement until such time the Korean people had achieved enlightenment and the South Korean economy had been modernized.

The needed enlightenment campaign, referenced by Chang, was none other than the joint government-civilian venture first proposed to Rhee by the NSRRKI in November 1948. Under the updated plan, both Patriotic NAs and the NSRRKI were given new names: Citizens' NAs and the National Society (*Kungminhoe*) respectively. The details of the plan were officially unveiled at a meeting on August 24, 1949, attended by Rhee, the ministers, and the provincial governors:

I. The National Society, the hub of the voluntary patriotic passion of citizens, is tasked with completing missions set by the government and aimed at defeating communism.
II. The National Society is authorized to collect membership fees from all households.
III. Both the government and the National Society are authorized to supervise national movements.
IV. Patriotic NAs are converted into Citizens' NAs and placed under jurisdiction of the National Society.[80]

The cooperative relationship between the government and the National Society, as well as their dual access to Citizens' NAs for national movements, was approved.

The use of the phrase "the hub of the voluntary patriotic passion of citizens" to describe the National Society contrasted sharply with the compulsory features of the plan. All households, through their membership in neighborhood associations, were inducted into the National

Society. Compulsory membership meant that South Korean households had no choice other than to pay the tax mandated in the second clause. The first and third clauses established the government's relationship to Citizens' NAs. The first clause specified government control over campaigns to be carried out by Citizen's NAs, and the third clause established the government's power to enforce "voluntarism." As under Japanese colonial rule, the South Korean government had co-opted the moral space of the neighborhood for state-led campaigns.

The problematic nature of this cooptation did not go unnoticed. When at a press conference, reporters raised concerns that NAs would be abused by the government for political ends, the interior minister countered, "The fundamental idea behind the national movement is to combine voluntary passions with governmental policy. Thus, it is better for the government to avoid taking a primary role in its supervision."[81] His assertion, however, that the government's desire to promote voluntarism was best served by the government playing only a limited advisory role did little to quell concerns, given that the line between national interests and political interests had never been clearly defined. This lack of clarity was compounded by Rhee's authority over Citizens' NAs as president of South Korea and as chair of the National Society. If Rhee chose to conflate his political interests with those of the nation, there was nothing to prevent him from mobilizing Citizens' NAs to secure his reelection. It remained to be seen if the nebulous line between political and national interests would survive the 1952 elections, or if the manipulation of Citizens' NAs would result in the reintroduction of moral authoritarianism.

CONCLUSION

The US military's temporary resurrection of Patriotic NAs as a practical and politically expedient solution to Korea's postwar food shortage and economic crisis became permanent under the new South Korean polity. Once their administrative usefulness in administering rice rationing had been demonstrated, South Koreans considerably ceased to associate NAs with the colonial past; instead, they highlighted NAs' centuries-long role in Korean communal culture. Although initially the South

Korean government continued the American practice of limiting NAs to fulfilling administrative tasks, popular challenges to the South Korean government's legitimacy and Cold War competition with North Korea led South Korean leaders to resurrect NAs' campaign function, which the Japanese had used to promote assimilation policies and wartime mobilization. Under South Korean auspices, Citizens' NAs, under the leadership of the National Society, were tasked with carrying out "apolitical" or "pure" national movements, which the government determined. The movements that the National Society believed met this criterion were those that promoted anticommunism and national strength through military and economic modernization. This already-blurred boundary between national interests and political interests was exacerbated by the dual power structure that placed Rhee at the top of the hierarchy of the National Society and of the government. There was no institutional barrier to prevent Rhee from mobilizing Citizens' NAs to secure his future election. In placing people's "passions" at the service of the government, officials had repeated the Japanese strategy of disguising moral authoritarianism as voluntarism.

CHAPTER 5

The Summer of 1950

The Two Faces of NAs

At a time like this, it is lamentable that I did not learn a skill that would have promptly and thoroughly transformed me, much like how a cicada casts off its shell.

—Kim Sŏng-ch'il.[1]

Despite the creation of two distinct governments in 1948, neither Korean state believed the division was permanent. Unwilling to compromise with the other, however, each challenged the legitimacy of its counterpart. A South Korean propaganda poster (see figure 5.1) depicted Kim Il Sung as a monster with two horns and a body covered with hair, sitting at a table on which the nameplate read "Puppet prime minister."[2] North Korea countered by claiming that the South lacked legitimacy since it maintained colonial vestiges, failed to punish Koreans who collaborated with the Japanese, and had been recolonized by the United States. A North Korean political cartoon (see figure 5.2) showed the emblematic figure of Uncle Sam with an anvil on which is written "By order of the United States"; he is preceded by a group of UN delegates struggling under the weight of a large stake on which is written "Colonization of Korea." A large hand blocks their path. The message of the cartoon is clear: All that stands between Korea and its subjugation by a new colonizer is North Korea.[3] For the two Korean states, the outbreak of the Korean War on June 25, 1950, following a series of small-scale military engagements, signaled a clash between two political and economic visions for Korea: liberal democracy versus people's democracy.

FIGURE 5.1.   Image of North Korea (from the South). RG 242, SA 2011, box 1059, item 2–76, Chŏndanji (Pamphlet). Courtesy of the National Archives and Records Administration (NARA).

Shortly after the war commenced on June 25, 1950, North Korea captured Seoul and quickly began the process of reshaping South Korean institutions in accord with the North Korean order. At the local level, this endeavor entailed the co-optation of existing Citizens' NAs. Renamed People's NAs, NAs became the primary institution through which political reeducation, labor mobilization, and military recruitment of South Koreans took place. When in September 1950, South Korean forces recovered the capital city, People's NAs returned to being Citizens' NAs. But everything was not as before; the once-porous geographical and ideological divide between the two states became opaque and inflexible in the wake of Seoul's recapture and the 1953 armistice. Through the lens of the diary of Kim Sŏng-ch'il, a young historian residing in occupied Seoul, this chapter traces the political, ideological, and psychological upheavals that defined the first year of the Korean War, remade the relationship between the two Koreas, and gave rise to a form of patriotism in the South that prioritized anticommunism at the expense of liberal democracy.

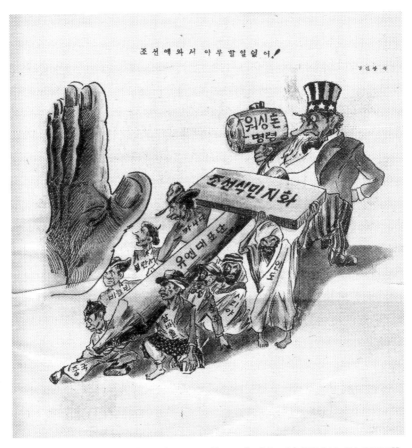

FIGURE 5.2.   Image of South Korea (from the North) RG 242, SA 2007 II, box 623, *Horang'i* 5 (Pyongyang: Rodong sinmunsa, 1947): 5. Courtesy of the National Archives and Records Administration (NARA).

THE DIARY: AUTHOR AND VENUE

Born in 1913, Kim Sŏng-ch'il grew up in Yŏngch'ŏn in North Kyŏngsang Province. In 1927, he moved to Taegu to pursue a postsecondary degree. One year later, he was involved in a student political protest against colonial rule that resulted in his imprisonment for one year. Upon his release, he returned home, where he remained for three years before traveling to Kyŏngsŏng (Seoul) and to Japan to resume his studies. In 1937, he received an undergraduate degree from the Kyŏngsŏng Imperial

College of Law. Shortly thereafter, he found employment at the Finance Cooperatives, but in 1941 he quit to study history at Kyŏngsŏng Imperial College. In 1943, he was arrested for defying the Government-General's labor mobilization but was released owing to a health issue. He worked at the Finance Cooperatives in North Ch'ungch'ŏng Province from 1944 until liberation. In 1945, Kim was transferred to its Seoul office.

Kim's diary opens in December 1945 against the backdrop of the establishment of the US military government in Seoul, intensifying tensions between the United States and the Soviet Union, and growing political polarization. Upon returning to Seoul, Kim discovers that his three best friends—Kim Tŭk-chung, Yi Ch'ŏl, and Ch'oe Pong-rae—are fighting for the socialist cause. While it did not surprise Kim, who was aware of their political beliefs, he harbored doubts about "whether the path my sincere friends are pursuing is the best way to rebuild Korea."[4] From time to time, Kim and his friends engaged in debates on political issues, including relations between the South and the US and between the North and the USSR. Kim maintained a critical stance toward the North and disagreed with his friends who insisted that Korea was being recolonized by US financial capital.[5] Nonetheless, he did not support the South Korean government, contrasting the seeming lack of corruption in the North with the political cronyism that plagued the South.[6] At odds with both the political right and left, Kim was enraged by both sides' efforts to gain control of the Finance Cooperatives for which he worked. When in March 1946 it became clear that the cooperatives were no longer neutral and had taken a turn to the political right, he resigned.[7]

In 1947, upon completing his degree in history, Kim gained employment in the History Department at Seoul National University. He and his family settled in Son'gajang village of the Chŏngnŭng in north Seoul.[8] Kim's neighborhood was made up of approximately twenty households, and the Citizens' NA to which he belonged was both occupationally and politically diverse.[9] Numbering among its members were an elderly woman who lived with her grandchildren, day workers, a medical doctor, and a university professor, as well as several small-business operators. Despite the political division and the NAs' responsibility for monitoring the daily movements of Koreans through the Transitory

Resident Registration, there was still no ideological hostility between neighbors. Kim and his leftist neighbor Hong regularly engaged in fiery political debates while remaining good friends. Similarly, Dr. Cho, a rightist medical doctor, enjoyed intense political discussions with his neighbor, a leftist beekeeper. But the war would redefine the contours of acceptable political beliefs and create ideological barriers between former good friends.

THE OUTBREAK OF THE KOREAN WAR

Between June 25 and June 27, 1950, rumors about troop movements traveled quickly among neighbors, rumors that were often more accurate than the officially sanctioned South Korean media reports on developments. While working in his vegetable garden on June 25, Kim encountered a neighbor returning home from downtown who told him that war had broken out early that morning. The previous night, Kim recalled, the cannon sounds in the distance had seemed different from those on other nights. The next day, on his way to the university, he heard that North Korean troops were already marching toward Ŭijŏngbu, a city roughly twelve miles north of Seoul. On June 27, his neighbors fled the village, and a soldier warned him that the village might soon become a battleground.[10]

In contrast to these rumors, the newspapers reported that the ROK Army was pushing back North Korean troops. On the radio, Kim heard that the government planned to relocate to Suwŏn, but he later learned that South Korean officials, including President Rhee, remained in Seoul. The Bureau of Public Information urged residents to remain calm, as the North Korean Army was in retreat. The Defense Ministry told people to hold their positions as the US Air Force would join the war soon.[11]

Unsure if he should trust village rumors or public announcements, Kim decided that he would remain at home but sent his wife and children to stay at a relative's house in the city. However, as pressure in the village mounted to evacuate, he decided to join his family. On the morning of June 28, he returned home with his family only to discover that the South Korean government had abandoned the city and that as part of the retreat, South Korean forces had destroyed all the major bridges over the Han River.[12]

Although Kim's diary gives no reason for his return, it seems that Kim did not take the war too seriously. After passing some North Korean troops on his way back to Seoul on June 28, he wrote, "I don't feel they are my enemy. I feel as if my siblings, who have been away for a long time, have returned home. This feeling is not because I lack loyalty to the South. What is the difference between them [the North Korean troops] and the South Korean troops I saw yesterday?"[13] But having returned, Kim's family was now trapped in occupied Seoul. As advised by a neighbor who operated a grocery store, Kim hid rice, clothes, and blankets and stockpiled eggs, noodles, and cigarettes. Preparation for life under North Korean rule also entailed burning South Korean government bonds and any documents that might be viewed by North Koreans as politically suspect.[14]

Beyond erasing his personal political identity, Kim soon realized that survival also meant redefining the boundaries of acceptable neighborhood discussions: "People who left the villages are coming back. Everyone celebrates each other's safe return, but no one talks about politics and the current situation."[15] The animated political discussions of the past quickly gave way to suspicion and mutual wariness. His neighbor Mr. Sŏ, who belonged to the Workers' Party of South Korea (*Namjosŏn rodongdang*), worked actively for the village's people's committee (PC), while Dr. Cho, his rightist neighbor, disappeared. According to rumors, he had been shot and killed at the hospital.[16] "It was obvious," Kim wrote, "that the world had been turned upside down."[17]

Kim's leftist college friends soon returned to the neighborhood. Hong, with whom Kim had regularly debated politics, was released from prison. Since Korea's liberation from Japan, Hong's political orientation had made him subject to police surveillance and multiple arrests for suspected involvement in leftist political actions. Under North Korean rule, the former South Korean political prisoner assumed a high-level position in the Seoul judicial system.[18] Kim also saw Ch'oe Pong-rae, a leftist friend from his college days who had moved to the North before the war and now came back as a North Korean officer. Although their earlier friendship had been based on mutual respect for their differing political views and Ch'oe still showed unchanged friendship, Kim now exercised caution when speaking with Ch'oe in a conversation about North Korea. He noted in his diary, "Being unable to trust anyone was certainly a tragedy."[19]

ELECTION: A HEAD OF A NEIGHBORHOOD ASSOCIATION

During the first three months of the war, the North continued to seize territory from the South. North Korea justified its conquests by claiming that it was liberating the South from US imperialism and from the collaborationist regime of Syngman Rhee. Increasingly concerned that the United States would intervene directly in the war, the North felt it was urgent that it move quickly to transform South Korean economic and political institutions in line with the North Korean order.

Central to North Korean efforts to reshape the local order in South Korea were Citizens' NAs. Upon seizing power, North Korean officials ordered that "all officials and heads of NAs" be sent to the People's Court.[20] However, unlike commissioned officers, judges, and prosecution officers, the North had no intention of unilaterally eliminating NA heads. Recognizing how useful NAs had been in the state-building process in North Korea, the plan was to use the People's Court to determine which Citizens' NA heads were "qualified" to lead in concert with the occupying authorities. The verdict depended on one's political orientation, meaning those found to harbor anti-North sentiments would not be returning home. Only those NA heads whom the court deemed capable of assisting the occupiers in overturning the current political order would resume their duties; the rest would be replaced by new heads who either genuinely supported the North's agenda or were politically astute enough to feign support.

Lee Yun-ki, the head of the Citizens' NA to which Kim belonged, enthusiastically supported the North's agenda. Born to a poor family, he had quit elementary school and made a living by running a small convenience store. On July 2, four days into the occupation, Kim heard that Lee had been assigned to manage two hundred households. The North Korean government had also bestowed upon his family the honorific title "Democratic Family," indicating that the North Korean government believed other families should emulate his family.[21] Lee's meteoric rise reflected the North's urgent need to enlist the cooperation of Koreans well versed in local affairs to handle local administration. Prioritizing loyalty over experience or skill, the North filled local posts based on recommendations from known leftists or from individuals who after converting to the cause submitted statements of confession.[22] Since Lee had no previous record of leftist political activism, Kim guessed that his recommendation came from his siblings, who had been political prisoners under Rhee's regime.[23]

Three weeks after his first unexpected promotion, Lee's career took another surprising turn when on July 26, 1950, he ran for a position on the Chŏngnŭng village people's committee. For a month prior to the election, the North invested significant time and energy into restoring the people's committees that the US military government had made illegal. During the first week of July, North Korean minister of justice Li Sŭng-yŏp was named as chair of the Seoul Provisional People's Committee. Under his leadership, nine county-level people's committees were reestablished in Seoul.[24] The next step was to prepare for the election of village-level people's committees. Facing the imminent engagement of US and UN forces in the war, North Korean officials viewed the election as a strategic means of uniting the two Koreas under a single state apparatus, thereby validating its occupation. Since Rhee had delayed the implementation of the Local Autonomy Act, it was the first local election for South Koreans.

The elections for village-level people's committees were carried out largely in the same way as those in North Korea. Anyone over the age of twenty, regardless of social status, property holdings, sex, or duration of residence, was eligible to vote and run for office; the two exceptions were Japanese collaborators and the insane. Depending on the number of residents, each village needed to elect five or seven representatives. Residents were authorized to nominate candidates, to have open discussions on each candidate, and to vote. To maximize participation, an electorate could nominate as many candidates as it wanted and had the right to express the pros and cons of each candidate. The top five or seven candidates who received the most votes assumed office.[25] Being pressed for time, the decision was made to proceed with a one-day election, using a show of hands, rather than the two-day process used in the North that culminated with a secret ballot.

The North Korean authorities had advertised in newspapers, on radio, and at mass rallies that the election would take place on July 27. Hence Kim was surprised when on July 26, "before dawn, the headman knocked on the door, asking us to come out quickly. Waking up the children, we all went out. Everyone headed to a secluded place on a small mountain in the village, leaving the village almost empty. Before 5:00 a.m., more than ten thousand people eligible to vote had gathered in the square in front of a tomb."[26] The North attributed the departure from the advertised time and location for the election to wartime security concerns (e.g., possible air raids) and to the summer heat wave.[27] As the North had not had time to make a proper list of eligible voters, NA heads were responsible for confirming the identities of those eligible to vote. The NA head to which Kim belonged handed a small piece of paper on which Kim's name was written and Kim submitted it to an official as evidence he participated in the voting.

The makeshift elections, Kim noted, favored candidates such as Lee who had leftist ties. Unfamiliar with the North Korean electoral process, most South Koreans remained passive while North Korean supporters established procedures organized an election committee, and chose a chair to preside over the election. In fact, Kim had the impression that the list of candidates was predetermined, given that when one participant barely spoke up, the chair had no difficulty recording the name of the nominee. Of the nine candidates, eight, including Lee, came from peasant or working-class families affiliated with the Workers' Party of South Korea. One candidate, named Kong, was a member of the Korean Independence Party. His party affiliation sparked an intense debate about whether it was appropriate for him to serve on the village committee. Rather than protest, Kong withdrew from the election, leaving eight candidates vying for seven positions. When Lee's name was called, no one objected, and so the chair declared that Lee had been unanimously elected to the village people's committee.

Lee's political star continued to rise. In September, elections for the position of provincial judge for the province of Kyŏnggi were to be in the town of Sung'in. The town, on which North Korea had bestowed the honorific title "Democratic Town," gave the right to hold the election to the village of Chŏngnŭng, which similarly bore the title "Democratic Village." Lee was one of two candidates for whom villagers could vote. On September 12, the election was held. Because Kim was in hiding to avoid "volunteer" conscription into the army, his wife represented the family at the election. Upon returning home after Lee's victory, she told Kim that like the village committee elections, the results of this election seemed predetermined. The chair, she explained, "seemed to advocate for Mr. Lee," which confused those in attendance because they believed that the other candidate had more experience and a "nobler character" than Lee.[28]

Skeptical of the North's obsession with elections and the feverish haste with which they were carried out, Kim wrote derisively of Lee's stunning elevation from NA head to provisional judge in three months: "My surprise at having such a great figure as my neighbor knew no end." For Kim, the flurry of elections seemed to be driven more by mob mentality than fairness. He noted in his diary that those who "innocently raised their hands" for the candidate of their choice, quickly lowered them "after being chastised by the person next to them." Kim also objected to the method of counting, pointing out that tens of thousands of votes could not be accurately tabulated through a show of hands. His suspicions about election integrity were further confirmed when a person described how polling staff easily recorded candidates' names despite the cacophony of noises that drowned out the voices of those making nominations. Of this phenomenon, he cryptically wrote, "It is indeed a mystery."[29] For its part, the North Korean government touted the elections as an unparalleled success, issuing lofty statements such as "The historic democratic election witnessed 100 percent turnout" and "With thunderous applause, candidates possessing glorious experiences with class conflict were chosen to represent the people."[30]

RELOCATION AND THE VOLUNTEER ARMY: A HEAD OF THE PEOPLE'S NA

On July 14, two weeks after the occupation began, Kim noted in his journal that Kim Ik-hyŏn, a relative who worked as an NA head in central Seoul, visited him seeking advice about a job offer he had received from the village people's committee. Although Kim includes no entry in his diary explaining how his relative came to be an NA head, Kim's relative, unlike Lee Yun-ki, clearly did not support the regime and was unhappy with the assignments to NA heads. Kim described his relative's predicament as follows:

> At present, he is a head of a neighborhood association. What agonizes him about his job is not only that he must maintain the Volunteer Army (*Ŭiyonggun*) recruitment list and deliver relocation notices to his neighbors, but he must also manage labor mobilizations and attendance at daily mass rallies. He sees that his neighbors are suffering from hunger and illness, and he is overcome with guilt for carrying out orders. Thus, he wants to quit the position but has hesitated to resign, because it would place him under pressure to join the Volunteer Army. Now, he has a chance to work for the people's committee; this would guarantee his status and to some extent improve his living conditions. However, it would also be proof that he supported the People's Republic [the North] with enthusiasm. Given the uncertainty of the war's outcome, he does not know what to do.[31]

Kim's diary entry makes clear that the position of NA head was a potentially attractive option for young men who were not committed to the socialist cause and wanted to ward off a clash with North Korean authorities over military service. However, it came at the price of potentially alienating one's neighbors by enforcing the orders of North Korean authorities.

Since North Korea did not have any legal grounds to conscript South Koreans into the People's Army, its authorities mobilized South Koreans via the so-called Volunteer Army. NA heads were required to provide local authorities with a list of those eligible to serve in the Volunteer Army, that is, all men between the ages of seventeen and thirty-nine. However, because the North hoped to win the populace's cooperation, Workers' Party members, NA heads, and the staff of people's committees were moved to the back of the recruitment line, while youths who had belonged to rightist youth groups were moved to the front of the line.[32]

The East Town of Sihŭng County in Kyŏnggi Province illustrates how this system worked. Roughly 20.1 percent of East Town's total male population (1,332 out of 6,635), or 10.2 percent of the total population, was listed as eligible for service in the Volunteer Army. This equated to one person out of every two households in the town.[33] By early September, approximately 16 percent of youths on the list (210 out of 1,332) had been recruited into the Volunteer Army. It included only three headmen: thirty-one-year-old Pak Pok-pong, twenty-three-year-old Yu Kwang-un, and thirty-year-old Cho Kwang-yŏp. Pak Pok-pong and Yu Kwang-un were drafted into the army, but both were discharged after only three days of service.[34]

In lieu of serving in the Volunteer Army, the three NA heads joined either the Self-Defense Force or Fire Brigade, the two primary entities responsible for local security.[35] The Self-Defense Force was responsible for guarding bridges, railways, and other public facilities of strategic military significance. Members also staffed guard posts, kept an eye out for enemy paratroopers, reported on the movements of strangers, and surveilled the activities of those branded as reactionaries.[36] The Fire Brigade was made up of twenty people from each village; members were on call twenty-four hours per day and were responsible for extinguishing fires ignited during air raids. Additionally, the Fire Brigade maintained an inventory of available fire extinguishers, buckets, sandbags, and hoses as well as kept records on the locations of flammables that might be vulnerable in the event of an air attack.[37] As airstrikes grew in number, the North increasingly relied on NA heads to act as their liaisons with local communities, communicating orders to the populace and providing them with information about the local situation.

By fulfilling this essential function for the North, NA heads, like Kim's relative, were able to delay their conscription into the Volunteer Army. Although Kim's relative appreciated the safety being an NA head afforded him, the position exacted a high psychological price on NA heads who did not support the North's cause. Their feelings of guilt were amplified by their role in mobilizing labor and in ensuring attendance at mass rallies. The North announced an intensive mobilization effort including labor force and vehicles, for the purpose of repairing roads and bridges; the announcement was accompanied by the warning that those who did not comply would face punishment. This mobilization reflected the North's decision to apply the North Korean Act of Labor Mobilization to the "liberated" territory. In accordance with the act's terms, local authorities in Seoul and the surrounding areas established committees for labor mobilization (*Roryŏk tong'wŏn wiwŏnhoe*), which had authority over People's NAs.

A labor mobilization in Kŭmch'on village in Kyŏnggi is illustrative of the role that NA heads played in such mobilizations. The village, made up of 627 households, had nine NAs, the size of which varied from twenty-three households to 160 households. Whenever the town notified the village of its labor quota, the village PC chair, who was also chair of the committee for labor mobilization, called a meeting of NA heads to determine how much of that quota each NA would be responsible for fulfilling. The village PC chair placed the heads of the second and third NAs in charge of producing propaganda materials for the labor campaign, such as posters, slogans, and banners. Although the division of labor was ultimately at the discretion of NA heads, the village chair reminded heads that the decision-making process should be impartial, so as to ensure compliance. NAs should neither favor friends and family nor penalize those with whom they had no relationship or with whom they did not get along.[38]

The notices announcing additional labor and/or rallies seldom came with much warning, and typically the expectation was that the additional labor requirement would be finished within one or two days from receipt of the notice. This placed NA heads, already overwhelmed by their regular responsibilities, under increased pressure. For example, on September 8, 1950, the nine NA heads in Kŭmch'on village received notification from village authorities that they were responsible for producing 350 straw-woven bags that would be used for packaging rice. The deadline was 10:00 a.m. on September 10.[39] The weaving process was extremely time-consuming and required the labor of two or three persons to complete. Despite the short notice, the labor-intensive process, and the fact that NA heads were already busy with the summer grain harvest, all NAs met their quota.

On September 15, the same nine NA heads were notified that a meeting of NA heads would take place that evening at 5:00 p.m. At the meeting, they were informed that there would be a rally the next day. The NA heads had to scramble to notify members to ensure that attendance met the expectations of North Korean authorities.[40] Given the unpopularity of these rallies with South Koreans, who had little interest in North Korean propaganda and who were exhausted from the constant demands for additional labor, NA heads sometimes had to cajole members to participate by reminding them that nonattendance could result in them being labeled as reactionaries (*pandong*).

Calls for war-related work placed additional pressure on NA heads. These jobs, which included transportation of weapons, military construction projects, and airstrike repair work, were carried out under cover of darkness to ensure secrecy. Misan village of Sorae town in Puch'ŏn County offers a case in point. The village, composed of 134 households and 842 residents, had twelve People's NAs. There were 361 people eligible for labor mobilization (194 men and 167 women). At 11:30 a.m. on September 8, the village received a notice to mobilize ninety-eight people to build a defensive position in Inchon, the place where the UN army executed Operation Chromite (the Battle of Inchon) on September 15. Those mobilized from the village for the nine-day project were expected to gather in front of the police station by 3:00 p.m. that same day. Thus, each of the twelve NA heads had roughly three hours to find eight people from their respective NAs for the project.[41] Given that all village staff signed an oath to make labor quotas at any cost and were held accountable for any failure, it is not difficult to imagine hard-pressed NA heads using persuasion and threats to enlist NA members.[42]

Kim's relative found this pressure to fulfill labor quotas agonizing, as he knew many of his neighbors were hungry and struggling to survive. The offer to work for the village people's committee seemed the ideal solution. It would relieve him of the burden of mobilizing neighbors for hard labor and still allow him to avoid service in the Volunteer Army. The job also came with increased food rations. Despite these potential benefits, Kim's relative worried that if the tide of the war turned, working for the people's committee would make him vulnerable to charges of collaborating with the enemy. If he remained an NA head, he believed that he would be safe from such allegations, since NAs, unlike the people's committees, were not officially part of the state apparatus.

Kim's diary does not tell us if his relative decided to take the job or continue in his position as NA head. But the angst that Kim's relative related and that Kim documented highlights the liminal space that neighborhood associations occupied between official state apparatus and community self-help organization. On the one hand, NAs allowed the state to exert political pressure directly on the neighborhood. On the other hand, they created loopholes for evading state actions and there was a shared sense of community.

POTENTIAL REACTIONARIES: WOMEN ON THE FRONT LINES OF LABOR MOBILIZATION

Wartime chaos, the stream of refugees into Seoul, and fires caused by airstrikes made existing data on population and personal property obsolete. In addition to ordering NA heads not to destroy the demographic records, the North placed NA heads in charge of gathering up-to-date demographic information such as household size and the name of the household head, as well as the ages, educational background, and occupations of those living in the household and their relationship to the household head.[43] This raw data was used to calculate the available labor force of a household.

For those residents who did not support the North, but whose NA heads did, the common complaint was that "people don't even have an inch to maneuver."[44] By contrast, an NA head who was less than enthusiastic about the North often shouted loudly, "Open the door!" This announcement gave time for young men on the eligibility list for the Volunteer Army and for alleged political reactionaries in the household to hide under the floor or up on the roof.[45] Aware that the survey information most likely was inaccurate, the North conducted late-night raids and warned NAs that if it was discovered that they were harboring political reactionaries or misrepresenting their household's composition, the entire NA would be punished.[46]

To calculate the labor force of a household, the North rated household members based on their age and sex on a scale from 0 to 1. As seen in the form in figure 5.3 for the Chang Su-hwan household, there were fourteen people in the household, thirteen of whom were family members along with one employee. The form gives the full name of the employee but identifies family members only by their relationship to the household head. Thus, rather than individual names, one sees the following notations: wife, two sons, two daughters-in-law, and seven

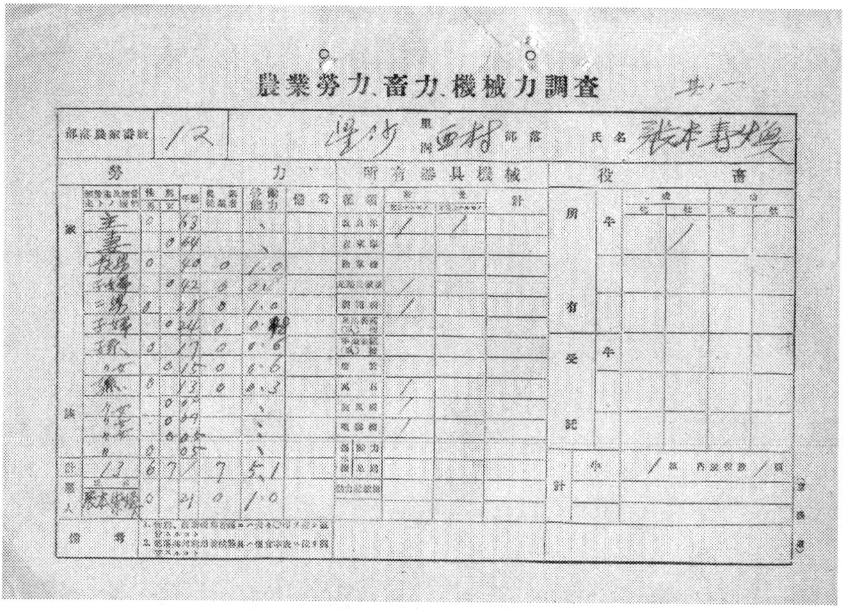

FIGURE 5.3.   Form of "Survey of labor force, machinery power and livestock,"
RG 242, SA 2009 II, box 770, item 111. Courtesy of the NARA.

grandchildren. Only the head of household's name, Chang Su-hwan, appears on the form. The next three columns note the age, sex, and work status of household members. Those over the age of sixty in the household (the household head and his wife), and those under the age of ten (four of the grandchildren) were given a score of zero. The remaining household members' scores ranged from 0.3 to 1.0. The head of household's two sons, who were forty and twenty-eight years of age, each received a score of 1.0. His two daughters-in law, ages forty-two and twenty-four, were each rated 0.8. The two grandchildren who were in their mid-teens were both listed as 0.6, with no distinction in their scores based on sex. The thirteen-year-old granddaughter was listed as 0.3. Adding their scores together, the household labor force score was 6.1, including that of the employee.[47]

The form indicates a mobilization scheme based on the patriarchal family. Although it was generated by household, only the employee was listed by name, thus distinguishing him from the family members.

Moreover, the fact that family members were identified only in relationship to the family head is suggestive of a communication hierarchy, whereby the male family head is the point of contact with the NA head. In other words, when an NA head delivered a public notice, such as the family's labor quota for a project, the family head was responsible for making sure the quota was met. The North's system of quantifying individual labor was intended to safeguard against NA heads imposing indiscriminate or excessive quotas on a family. [48]

The plan also aligned with existing gender norms. Those jobs that required less physical labor or traditionally were considered women's work were filled by the elderly and women. The Women's Alliance, in general, was responsible for organizing women's labor projects, such as sewing military uniforms, doing laundry, preparing medical dressings, and writing letters to soldiers on the battlefield. Assigned to do the women's political enlightenment program, the alliance also offered literacy classes as well as political lectures on North Korean reforms, the North Korean constitution, and international politics. For more labor-intensive jobs, such as bridge construction, road repair, and the transportation of munitions and food for the army, women were advised to be prepared to take the place of men on these jobs in the event the men were needed in the military.[49]

Still, North Korean authorities preferred to use men and wanted to create the impression that able-bodied South Korean men were voluntarily showing up to labor for the North. However, this patriarchal plan for labor mobilization did not go as planned, due to the widespread disappearance of men with the highest labor rankings. An entry in Kim's diary from July 15, 1950, hints at the reasons for men's absence as well its consequences for women:

> These days, it is quite common for women to participate in the mass rallies. When people noticed that the rallies were turned into political rallies to draft people for the Volunteer Army, the rallies became crowded with women and old people. Some young men are there, but all of them are exempt due to their position of employment, party affiliation, or service for the government.... Housewives are overworked by having to attend all of them. In addition, it is a pity that they are responsible for getting food for the family. The only way men

can make a living is through supporting the communist party. No longer is it commonplace to see men trading jewelry and clothes for food. Thus, women must find something to eat. In every household, men have been reduced to taking care of children in a nook of the house or slothfully taking a nap. Yet, they cannot rest easy, as they tremble with trepidation knowing at any time they may be struck by lightning.[50]

The lightning of which Kim spoke, of course, referred to being caught and forcibly enlisted in the Volunteer Army. Like most other men in the village, the day that Kim wrote this, he did not attend the first general assembly of the Peasant Association. His wife assumed this responsibility as well as the job of procuring food, as Kim and other men from the village hid in the shadows.

At thirty-seven years of age, Kim fell within the bracket eligible for military conscription. His likelihood of being drafted increased when due to his lack of commitment to the North Korean cause, he lost his teaching position at Seoul National University—a position that had exempted him from military service. From the outset of the occupation, Kim had been displeased by the political overtones that the university had taken on: university buildings were shared with the Seoul People's Committee (later, shared with the US–UN army); socialist intellectuals established the University Self-Rule Committee and assumed key university positions; professors and staff were mobilized to repair buildings in the Yong'san District that had been destroyed by US airstrikes; and there were open discussions about the Volunteer Army that included a tacit push to join. Moreover, every time he went to the university, he was annoyed to find that he needed to rewrite or revise his autobiography.[51] As he distanced himself from university politics, he received a letter notifying him that he had been sacked, on August 9, 1950.[52]

Kim knew that his layoff placed him in a precarious position. If his neighbors discovered that he had been fired, his lackluster enthusiasm for the North Korean regime made him vulnerable to being labeled a reactionary, forcibly recruited into the Volunteer Army, or even brought before the People's Court. Although Lee, an ardent supporter of the North, was no longer the NA head to which Kim belonged, his subsequent rapid political rise had given him more authority, not less, over the neighborhood space. In this scenario, Kim realized his prospects were bleak: "If I were labeled a reactionary, any type of punishment is possible and could happen at any time."[53] Confronted with this bleak picture, Kim withheld information about his layoff, even from Hong, one of his closest socialist friends.

Strictly speaking, Kim did not meet the criteria for being branded either a political or economic reactionary—the two primary categories identified by the North. The category of political reactionary applied to South Korean politicians, public officers, police officers, military officers, and political party members. The property of those branded as such was subject to confiscation as "enemy property."[54] Given that Kim was an academic and had no party affiliation, the likelihood of his being labeled a political reactionary was fairly low.

The category of economic reactionary covered the landlord class and those reluctant to comply with the North's economic measures. On July 4, 1950, North Korea introduced in the occupied South the same radical land redistribution measures that it had introduced in North Korea in early 1946: the confiscation of lands from landlords, followed by free distribution to farmers.[55] Kim's orchards, however, were not subject to the land reform, and he maintained control over this property.

The North also ordered NAs to inventory farming machinery, livestock, seed, warehouses, vehicles, and even furniture for the purposes of transitioning items in urgent demand from private ownership to communal ownership.[56] Any vehicle that was not registered, North Korean authorities warned, would be subject to confiscation. They also banned the private slaughtering of livestock. In this way, the North gained control over the right to private property. However, before forcibly confiscating livestock or vehicles, such as bikes, handcarts, and wagons, the North asked South Koreans to turn these items over voluntarily when requested by authorities.[57] Given the risks that came with noncompliance, such requests were seldom denied. Like other South Koreans in the occupied zone, Kim submitted an inventory of his livestock and obediently "donated" chickens, ducks, goats, and rabbits when requested.[58]

Even though he did not fall within the parameters of either the political or economic reactionary category, Kim's worries were not assuaged, owing to the third catchall category—cultural reactionary. The *damanegi* (onion) incident illustrates how anyone might suddenly be deemed a cultural reactionary. On July 25, 1950, a woman, presumably Kim's housekeeper, went to the grocery store owned by the former NA head, Lee. Out of habit, owing to the Japanese colonial language policy, the woman asked Lee's wife for an onion using the Japanese word for onion, *damanegi,* rather than the Korean word *yangp'a.* Mrs. Lee found fault with the housekeeper's choice of word: "Did you say *damanegi?* If you want to speak in Japanese, go to Japan. No doubt you are from a re-actionary family." On hearing about the incident, Kim's wife swiftly came to the woman's defense, calling on Lee's wife to apologize for mak-ing such an unfounded accusation. However, her call for an apology escalated into a verbal brawl, in which Mrs. Lee insinuated that the en-tire Kim family was reactionary because the family had "not put slogans in front of the house gate."[59] The indiscriminate use of the term suggests how commonplace it had become to denounce one's neighbor as reac-tionary. Similarly, Mrs. Kim's knee-jerk reaction to the term's use high-lights the villagers' omnipresent dread that the label might stick.

Disconcerted by the incident, Kim noted in his journal, "Life is farcical. I have no memory of committing a crime. No one is pursuing me. Yet I have become so frightened that I evade people. Everything is ambiguous: Who will be labeled a reactionary, what process will be taken, and how one will be punished. Depending on political necessity or the mood of the many stool pigeons, anyone can be a reactionary."[60] This emotional pressure led Kim to avoid going outside. His family be-came accustomed to keeping the house gate locked. That way, if anyone came looking for him, he would have time to remove his shoes and hide somewhere in the house, while his wife went to the gate to explain his absence.[61]

Representing the family became a significant part of Mrs. Kim's daily schedule. For example, on August 17, 1950, the following notice was is-sued: "One adult male from each household should gather in front of the people's committee office at eight o'clock at night."[62] As was her custom, she showed up in lieu of her husband, claiming that he was out of town for a lecture.[63] After the roll call, she was excused from service because she said that there was her infant at home. Kim later learned that the women who were not excused did not return from the mobilization until early the following morning. The project, it was said, involved transporting war materials, presumably bullets, over substantial distances. Although his wife escaped this mobilization, later entries in his diary note several mobilizations in which she did participate, such as in the construction of bomb shelters and in collective farming projects.[64] Beyond these labor mobilizations, Kim's wife also represented the family at early morning assemblies and rallies and at political and cultural lectures. Wherever she went, she observed that the few men one saw wore an armband designating them as supervisors, while most workers were women.[65]

The overwhelming number of women at mass rallies and engaging in labor projects did not please North Korean authorities, especially once the United States committed significant resources and personnel to the war effort. They blamed the slow progress made on construction projects, such as bomb shelters, on the need to rely on female laborers.[66] They interrogated women about the whereabouts of male family members, and mothers were instructed to leave babies at home as they would be expected to work.[67] As the lack of progress became a more pressing concern, authorities placed additional pressure on NA heads to find adult males for these projects. However, the unpredictability of airstrikes and the need to keep military operations under wraps meant that NA heads did not receive the notices for labor mobilization until the last minute. The time factor meant that they had no choice but to accept the excuses that women made for the men in the household, as they did not have time to track down the missing male workers. It seemed more prudent to accept women workers for these last-minute projects than risk not making quota.

PROPAGANDA AND RUMORS

The scarcer food became in occupied South Korea, the more desperate Kim became for accurate war-related news. However, he was surrounded by conflicting narratives. Newspapers in the occupied South printed only North Korean propaganda—the headlines of which consistently boasted about the North's advances into the South's territory and about Kim Il Sung's resolution to win the war by August 1950. In sharp contrast to these optimistic assessments of North Korean progress, the reports of

shortwave radio operators, to which Kim clandestinely listened, referenced foreign news media stories claiming that US general MacArthur
had given North Korea a two-week deadline to surrender.[68]

These competing narratives frustrated Kim. They began with the
outbreak of the war, and conflicting news reports between rumor and
the South Korean government announcement had resulted in Kim
and his family being trapped in Seoul. Soon, there were visual clues of
the North's impending capture of Seoul. The movement of North Korean troops into Seoul was accompanied by the appearance of its propaganda. Slogans such as "Welcome the Democratic People's Republic of
Korea," "Hooray for a highly gifted leader, General Kim Il Sung!" and
"Hooray for Stalin, a friend of the underdogs!" popped up on streetlamps
and fences.[69]

South Korean flags also disappeared from house gates, replaced by
North Korean ones. While South Korean socialists saw in the appearance of North Korean flags the promise of the revolution that had never
been realized in the South, conservatives viewed this development with
outrage. For Kim, who prioritized unity over any ideology, the North Korean flag was a visual symbol of a nation's tragic division.[70] But what
disturbed Kim the most were the numerous images of Stalin plastered
around the city, as he believed that the North, like the South, was overly
dependent on a foreign power. He wanted an independent Korea, not
one that was a satellite state of either the United States or the Soviet
Union. When he asked his friend Ch'oe Pong-rae, now a North Korean
officer, if perhaps the images were excessive, Ch'oe replied, "There is no
need to consider the feelings of South Koreans whose political awareness lags behind. We must show the right things from the beginning and
push the masses to follow us."[71] Ch'oe's dismissive reply portended the
impatience and inflexibility that would characterize the North's efforts
to impose its political order on the South.

The North Koreans did not take time to bridge the political rifts that
had developed between South and North Koreans in the five years since
liberation. Instead, they belittled the South Korean state as a mixture of
US imperialism, Japanese colonialism, and feudal remnants from premodern Korea. Given this assessment, they saw no need for compromise:
the plan was to replace the South Korean order with the North Korean
order, and North Korean developments since liberation were to be

imposed immediately in the South. To prepare the South for the new order, the Culture and Propaganda Ministry (*Munhwa sŏnjŏnsŏng*) devised an extensive propaganda campaign that included posters, slogans, cartoons, radio broadcasts, newspapers stories, mass rallies, political lectures, and cultural performances.[72] Beyond a visual display of North Korean power, the campaign's objective was to convince South Koreans of the superiority of the North Korean system.

Kim's diary highlighted two roles that People's NAs played in the North's propaganda campaign. The first was to remake South Koreans' behavior so that it conformed to North Korean norms. For example, through People's NAs, the order was issued that all households should display a North Korean flag and a minimum of three slogans on their front gates.[73] NA heads were charged with checking that member households complied with the order. No one dared disobey, since failure to comply meant risking being labeled a reactionary. Second, People's NAs became the exclusive channel for information distribution. All South Korean newspapers that were critical of the North were shut down. The only three remaining papers—*Haebang ilbo* (Liberation), *Rodong sinmun* (Workers' paper), and *Chosŏn inminbo* (People's report)—were published by the North Korean government. In conjunction with the ban, the North also eliminated all private news distribution channels; instead, the People's NAs distributed the approved papers once a week or every ten days.[74] Nothing critical of the North appeared in print, so that all South Koreans saw was the visual propaganda produced by the North.

The North's monopoly on information, as well as the pressure to conform exerted through the NAs, seemed at least outwardly to produce the desired result. South Koreans quickly conformed to the North's demands for labor and for the display of flags and slogans. To what degree South Koreans experienced a change of heart remained unclear. Although Kim lamented the requirement to switch flags, he was willing to entertain the North Korean order if it would bring unity to Korea. However, he remained uncomfortable with what he saw as mindless slogans. Ignoring the requirement that all slogans must be derived from the words of Kim Il Sung or *Rodong sinmun,* he made up his own slogans: "I am pleased to create unification through our own efforts" and "I hope for a world where no one suffers from hunger as long as people work hard."[75] For Kim, unification and equitable reward for one's labor were two possible positive outcomes for a Korea unified under the North's control. Yet even these imagined favorable outcomes did not convince him that the North Korean cause was necessarily the right way forward. Although he was disillusioned by the South Korean government's failure to provide the residents of Seoul with accurate information and its decision to blow up the bridges, leaving most residents trapped in the city, he still could not commit to North Korean people's democracy. He posted neither his slogans nor the official ones on his house's gate.[76]

The control that North Korea exercised over printed materials disturbed Kim, because it resurrected memories of the measures taken by the wartime colonial government. At that time, Patriotic NAs had been responsible for the distribution of the only sanctioned news source, the newspaper *Maeil sinbo.* This similarity, along with others such as the requisite mass mobilization of labor and coercive conscription policies, made Kim wary of the accuracy of official news sources and skeptical of North Korean claims that they, unlike the South, had rid the nation of vestiges of colonialism.[77] If one believed the newspapers, Kim noted in his journal on August 29, 1950, then everything was "always going well," since all one read were "endless complements, laudatory addresses, and fervent responses from the people" to the North's reforms.[78]

Having no other source of information, Kim began critically analyzing what was and what was not included in the approved news sources. For example, after reading in the official media that the US president, Harry S. Truman, had decided not to intervene in Korea, he expressed his doubts in his diary: "The 38th parallel was the result of WWII which marked the boundary between the spheres of influence of the US and USSR. If the US withdrew, it would be like abandoning its wartime accomplishments. Is that likely?"[79] On August 21, after belatedly receiving a copy of the *Chosŏn inminbo* from August 15, 1950, that included an address by Kim Il Sung in which he declared that August would be the month that saw the liberation of South Korea, Kim reinterpreted the North Korean ruler's boastful words to mean, "If the war does not end by August, we will miss our opportunity for victory," because North Korea lacked the resources to continue the fight beyond then.[80] Similarly, on August 25, when the official newspapers heralded victory at Taegu, Kim doubted their accuracy, noting the difference in how this alleged victory was communicated from previous victories. Earlier reports of victory, he highlighted, had included concrete details, such as names of places taken. Comparatively, this news account of victory was much more abstract. At best, Kim concluded, the battle was a stalemate.[81]

As Kim became increasingly savvy in interpreting North Korean propaganda, his prose became interlaced with sarcasm. On August 28, 1950, he saw a news story about a group of women, children, and the elderly, who according to the paper had "volunteered" to walk eighty kilometers to deliver food to the army in Seoul. The article described the volunteers as avid supporters of the North, who had undertaken the mission. He found this story preposterous, as he knew that women and children from a remote rural village most likely were indifferent to politics. Given this lie, it was equally unlikely that they had "volunteered" for the journey. The airstrikes and illness that the newspaper article claimed that these "volunteers" endured, Kim believed, exposed the cruelty of North Korean actions: "It [the article] confused me because I cannot understand its intended message. I am unsure if the writer is a fanatic supporter who wants to brag or a closet reactionary who wants to disclose the harsh reality of the People's Republic. Who could possibly believe in its political greatness after reading this article?"[82]

Such stories made skeptics of many, and the trade in rumors continued to escalate. Ironically, the People's NAs, which were supposed to control information distribution, became the breeding ground for the exchange and transmission of unofficial news. Each time people gathered for labor mobilizations, rallies, or enlightenment programs, they communicated with one another about what they had heard from relatives, friends, and illicit shortwave radio operators. Despite the North's desire to limit people's information to its propaganda, they never succeeded completely in eliminating outside sources of information.

The United States contributed to the local rumor mill through its psychological warfare campaign. Shortly after President Truman decided to send US troops to aid UN and South Korean forces, the United States began bombarding Korea with propaganda leaflets. Between July and August of 1950, over five million propaganda leaflets, called *ppira,* were dropped from aircraft.[83] In early August, the US aircraft dropped a leaflet advising South Koreans living within a fifteen-kilometer radius of Seoul to evacuate. This advisory gave credence to a rumor already in circulation that the US planned to drop an atomic bomb on the city.

Although Kim thought this course of action unlikely, many believed the rumor and evacuated.[84]

When in September 1950 injured youths from the Volunteer Army began returning to the village, rumors and reality collided, as the former conscripts recounted the experience of US aerial attacks. The implication of these firsthand accounts was that the South was rolling back the battlefield gains of the North.[85] Shortly before hearing these reports, Kim heard a rumor that US–UN forces had succeeded in landing at Inchon; this rumor contradicted the North's announcement that the People's Army had successfully repelled the enemy's landing attempt. Upon hearing that residents from Wŏlmi Island near Inchon had been evacuated to his village, Kim dismissed the official account as false.[86]

In mid-September, after hearing rumors that North Korean military convoys with high-profile political prisoners in tow were in retreat, Kim heard from his wife that several of his socialist neighbors were headed north as well. Mr. Lee, Kim's neighbor whose political star had risen under the North's leadership, joined the Volunteer Army. His wife was headed with him to the North. Similarly, Hong, Kim's trusted socialist friend who resided in Kim's orchard hut, was also headed for North Korea. Despite these signs that Seoul would not be under North Korean control for much longer, Kim remained in hiding, as there were also rumors that North Korean soldiers were indiscriminately murdering South Koreans as they retreated.[87]

Kim remained in his home, deeply saddened by the exodus of friends and neighbors, most of whom left without saying good-bye. On September 26, 1950, Kim Ch'un-dŭk, a former college roommate and actor, stopped by Kim's house to say good-bye. Seeing his friend's many bags of luggage, Kim worried that his friend, who had contracted tuberculosis a few years before, lacked the strength to complete the arduous trek. But beyond concern for his friend's personal welfare, Kim also felt frustrated that so many intellectuals, professionals, artists, and actors had chosen the North over the South, despite many of them not being committed socialists. This talent drain, he believed, could have been prevented. If the South had introduced significant land reform and prosecuted Japanese collaborators, the moderates would have stayed.[88]

On September 28, 1950, after months of hiding, Kim left the safety of his house. In his diary, he wrote of the experience: "I felt as if I had been revived after dying." The North Korean troops were gone, and their departure also brought the end to the labor mobilizations and rallies that had been forced upon the neighborhood space.

PATRIOTS OR COLLABORATORS: THE RETURN TO CITIZENS' NAs

Kim's feelings of relief were soon replaced by feelings of disappointment and shame, when the neighborhood space was touched by violent acts of revenge and transformed again into a political battleground. On September 30, 1950, two days after the South recovered Seoul, a police report noted that People's NA Head Pyŏn Chu-sŏk had been murdered by some South Korean soldiers on a small mountain in Yŏnhŭi town in Seoul.[89] On October 10, 1950, two weeks after the South recaptured Seoul, Kim heard that the new head of his NA planned to update the members' list, which was no longer accurate. Many families that had overtly supported North Korea had left, while other supporters had been captured or forcibly conscripted into the military. The request to gather updated demographic information, however, was about more than collecting the necessary data to normalize the local administration of government. When the neighbors gathered to get the new forms, the new NA head instructed, "Names should be written in Chinese characters."[90] It made clear that the South wanted to draw a clear distinction between the two states by overturning the North Korean policy of using Korean letters and symbols. Kim had supported this North Korean policy for two reasons. First, most ordinary Koreans were not fluent in Chinese characters; thus, their reintroduction undermined the ability of the lower classes to communicate in writing. Second, the use of the Korean language had become an important symbol of independence and equality in the Korean independence movements. Consequently, Kim saw the decision to return to Chinese characters as petty and spiteful. Worse yet, he worried that it was a prescient warning of a political gulf that would soon extend to the emotional and cultural realm.

The signs of mounting anger against the North were noticeable everywhere. One of Kim's leftist colleagues who had decided to stay in the South observed, "I sense that the toehold that we [leftists] once had has slipped and that the feelings that citizens have against the Reds have deepened."[91] This sentiment was particularly pronounced among those who had fled Seoul and now returned. For example, when Dr. Cho, Kim's rightist neighbor who had had friendly debates with his leftist neighbors about politics, returned to Seoul on October 22, he now had no tolerance for leftists: "For the time being, there should be a merciless purge and suppression [of leftists], even if it means shoving the principles of democracy aside."[92] While under the North the political binary had been patriotic democrats versus reactionaries, the new binary under the South became patriots versus collaborators. In much the same way that the North had scrutinized every institution to ensure that it reflected the new order, the South now demanded that every public and social institution purge itself of collaborators. Collaborators included those who had been employed by the North, those who had collaborated with North Korean institutions, and those who had served in the Volunteer Army.[93]

The neighborhood associations that had been co-opted by the North were subject to intense political scrutiny. The police announced that they were "investigating all heads of NAs and villages" as potential collaborators. NAs were told to provide a list of collaborators as well as a list of all property left by the enemy and to return any looted goods to their original owners.[94] Kim T'ae-sŏn, the security director of the Interior Ministry, stressed, "In purging collaborators, Citizens' NAs should live up to the standard of fairness, as ultimately this concerns neighbors. The Joint Investigation Headquarters has planned to establish a screening committee, but I hope that villages and NAs will create their own screening committee."[95] NA members were warned that the entire NA would be held accountable if anyone made false accusations of collaboration or protected collaborators from prosecution.[96] In short, the South's actions mirrored those of the North from three months before, when North Korean authorities had referred all NA heads to the People's Courts as potential reactionaries. The only difference was that the charge of "reactionary" had been replaced with the charge of "collaborator" (puyŏkcha).

Kim was upset by the South's decision to view all residents of the formerly occupied territory as potential North Korean collaborators. He had not forgotten that South Korean officials had evacuated the city without notice, leaving residents trapped. Instead of apologizing for this betrayal, they accused South Korean residents in the occupied zone of being collaborators, while touting those who fled as patriots.[97] The absurdity of using physical location during the military confrontation as a criterion for evaluating loyalty to the South left Kim disillusioned with the political pettiness of the postrecovery government. In his journal, he described the senseless investigations of citizens that dragged on for months as "national suicide."[98]

Kim was not alone in questioning the binary standard by the Rhee administration to measure patriotism. On September 29, 1950, the National Assembly introduced a bill to protect NA heads and others who had resided in the occupied zone from unwarranted charges of collaboration. The bill—Special Decrees on the Handling of Acts of Collaboration Through the Decision of the National Assembly (*Puyŏk haeng'wi t'ŭkpyŏl ch'ŏribŏp*)—required all provinces, cities, and counties to establish special committees responsible for reviewing alleged cases of collaboration and mandated that the police refer all such cases to the committees. A verdict of not guilty, the committees were advised, should be handed down in cases where collaboration was the product of coercion by the enemy and in cases where the extent of collaboration was limited to joining a pro-North organization. The bill, however, did not immediately go into effect. On October 12, 1950, Rhee vetoed the measure. Rhee later changed his mind, and the bill became law on December 1, 1950.[99]

Once the approach to assessing collaboration changed from the behavior to the intent behind the behavior, the number of cases decreased significantly. The reduction in cases also helped normalize the former People's NAs. Rather than being disbanded, they returned to being Citizens' NAs, but the diversity of political voices that once peacefully coexisted within the neighborhood space had ceased to exist, muffled by an anticommunist patriotism supported by the South Korean state.

CONCLUSION

Killed near his hometown in October 1951, Kim did not live to see the direction that Citizens NAs would take after the 1953 armistice. During his thirty-eight years, he witnessed the political co-optation of the neighborhood space by three states. In each, the state had used NAs to penetrate the neighborhood and by extension the intimate family sphere. While the ideology and names given to NAs were different under each state, the functions that NAs fulfilled were largely the same: information gathering, labor mobilization, and the enforcement of political conformity.

In describing his experiences under each, Kim never included the prefix; he only used the word for "neighborhood association" (*pan*). Although we cannot know for certain if this omission was a deliberate form of protest, Kim's diary entries clearly indicated his discomfort with the parallels between the three Korean states. He had hoped that liberation from colonial rule would lead to an independent, united Korea. Instead, he had witnessed the division of the nation. Like most Koreans, he had not believed the division permanent and was saddened when the Korean War solidified the ideological differences between North and South. He had seen the North's arbitrary prosecution of "reactionaries," followed by the South's arbitrary prosecution of "collaborators." With reference to the latter, he worried that the government was committing "national suicide" by promoting a form of patriotism that made former friends into enemies and prioritized anti-Communism at the expense of democratic values. This prescient concern would be realized in subsequent years as anticommunist patriotism became a moral requirement in NAs, constricting individual voices and justifying collective demands by the South Korean government that overrode the guarantee of individual rights.

CHAPTER 6

The Demise of Local Autonomy during the Postwar Recovery

The government is proceeding with the program of strengthening the Kungminban [Citizens' NAs]. . . . Past experiences indicate, however, that the Kungminban system probably cannot be developed into an efficient totalitarian system, and that if the program is pressed hard in that direction it may be counter-productive, rousing popular antagonism.

—Donald Macdonald, first secretary of the US Embassy in South Korea.[1]

In the fourth quarter of 1951, President Rhee was on the political defensive. After the successful Inchon assault in September 1950 that drove the North Koreans back across the thirty-eighth parallel, the UN and South Korean armies, led by the United States, decided to reunite the two Koreas by force; this decision drew Chinese military forces into the fray, forcing UN and South Korean forces to withdraw from the North. The anticipated decisive victory became a war of attrition as from this point forward, neither side was able to gain a significant advantage. Failure on the battlefront did not help Rhee recover his unstable position in domestic politics. Rhee got disappointing results in the May 1950 general elections; the candidates for the National Assembly who supported Rhee suffered defeat. Since the National Assembly had the authority to elect the president, the absence of support made it unlikely for the National Assembly to reelect him for a second term in the August 1952 presidential election.

The high likelihood of losing office led Rhee to reverse his previous stance on the incompetence of political parties and the prematurity of holding local elections. He judged that his best chance of maintaining office was through direct election by the people. After announcing that the delayed local elections would be held, he submitted to the National Assembly in November 1951 a constitutional amendment bill allowing for direct presidential elections and in December 1951 established the Liberal Party. In January 1952, the assembly rejected Rhee's proposed amendment. This prompted Rhee to impose martial law. On July 4, 1952, the assembly, surrounded by police, passed in an open vote the constitutional amendment allowing for direct presidential elections.[2]

Koreans had won a Pyrrhic victory, gaining the right to vote for the president through the imposition of martial law and the mass arrest of the opposition. Rhee's position on party politics, however, had not in fact changed; the creation of the Liberal Party was a ploy to exert his influence over the National Assembly. He still believed that parties too often focused on immediate interests at the expense of the supreme goal of politics, that is, the prosperity of the state and the public welfare. To differentiate the Liberal Party from other political parties, Rhee advanced the One Nation Ideology (*Ilminjuŭi*), which included the belief that the government, the ruling party, and social organizations should function as one organism.[3] Among the social organizations that Rhee chose to be a part of this organic governing body was the National Society, the organization responsible for mobilizing Citizens' NAs for "apolitical," patriotic campaigns. Because the leadership of the National Society overlapped with the leadership of the Liberal Party and that of the national government, its inclusion meant that Citizens' NAs were connected to three bodies: the National Society, organizer of national campaigns carried out by NAs; the Interior Ministry, charged with supervising local government administration; and the Liberal Party—all of which were under Rhee's control. This tripartite power-sharing arrangement, I argue, was an essential component of moral authoritarianism in the 1950s, because it allowed Rhee to incorporate into Citizens' NAs local administration, mass campaigns, and party politics.

When the government moved to tighten control over Citizens' NAs, it also began taking steps to reverse the decentralization of government that had resulted from the delayed implementation of the 1949 Local Autonomy Act. These initially parallel efforts by the central government to tighten its grip on local government and on the neighborhood space collided in 1958, when for the first time the Local Autonomy Act gave Citizens' NAs legal status in the local administrative hierarchy. Yet the unprecedented control that this act gave the central government over local administration and Citizens' NAs ultimately contributed to the downfall of the Rhee regime, as it made it impossible for the government to hide from view the authoritarian nature of the changes it had introduced. Thus, when in the 1960 election, the ruling Liberal Party blatantly used its close relationship with the National Society to mobilize Citizens' NAs to maintain its hold on power, NA members vocalized their objections. They reached critical mass when it was discovered that the ruling party had also rigged ballots. People took to the streets to protest the election results, which ultimately forced Rhee's resignation and catalyzed political reform. This chapter traces the increasingly authoritarian nature of the Rhee administration, paying close attention to the entangled struggles over local autonomy and Citizens' NAs.

THE INTERIOR MINISTRY'S POWER PLAY FOR CONTROL OVER LOCAL GOVERNMENT

In February 1952, the provincial governor of North Kyŏngsang contacted the Bureau of Public Information and the Interior Ministry for their legal opinions on if village heads qualified as civil servants. The provincial governor's request for clarification was prompted by the inquiry of a town governor, who wanted to know if a local village head could also serve as the leader of the local chapter of the National Society. Because the National Society was affiliated with the Liberal Party, by law its leaders could not be civil servants, as that would violate the constitution's political neutrality rule for civil servants.

The confusion about the employment status of village heads stemmed from the fact that Article 146 of the Local Autonomy Act stipulated that village heads were required to assist town governors in the administration of local government and authorized town governors to assign administrative tasks to village heads. However, according to the State Public Officials Act and the Local Public Officials Act, only employees of a government institution who received a regular income from their duties qualified as civil servants. Village heads were responsible for some governmental administrative duties, but they did not have an official employment contract and received no regular payment for those duties.

Unaware that the provincial governor of North Kyŏngsang had reached out to more than one governmental department, neither the Bureau of Public Information nor the Interior Ministry consulted the other before issuing their legal opinions. However, before making its decision, the bureau did consult with the Justice Ministry. The Justice Ministry determined that since village heads had no employment contract with state or local government and the post did not exist in the civil service ranking system, they did not qualify as government employees. Village heads, therefore, were free to hold office in the National Society and to join political parties. On February 12, 1952, the bureau sent this judgment to all provincial governors.[4]

Ten days later, on February 22, 1952, the Interior Ministry reached a different conclusion, which it too sent to all provincial governors. It found that village heads did qualify as public officials since their responsibilities included many administrative tasks. Therefore, they should not have any affiliation with political movements, campaigns, or parties.[5]

Having received two conflicting legal assessments, the provincial governors demanded that the three departments involved reach a consensus judgment.[6] The Interior Ministry placed substantial pressure on the Justice Ministry to change its position, because to maintain its administrative control over local government, it needed village heads to have the status of public officials. The Justice Ministry acquiesced to the Interior Ministry's argument that given the nature of village heads' tasks, they should be considered public officials.[7] However, this decision created another issue: If village heads were public officers, then in accordance with the State Public Officials Act and Local Public Officials Act, they could not hold another job. The position of village head, however, was not a paid position. Therefore, most village heads had a paying job and fulfilled their administrative tasks as heads during their off hours. If the state wanted to classify village heads as public servants, it would need to provide financial compensation. However, it clearly could not afford to add the approximately 250,000 village heads to the government payroll.[8] To resolve this issue, the Justice Ministry introduced a new category of public official: the honorary public servant, who did not receive pay. Village heads were assigned to this new category and placed under the supervision of the Interior Ministry.[9]

Once a new category of public official had been established, the question became, Were honorary public officials also obligated to observe the rule about political neutrality? The Justice Ministry argued that although village heads were unpaid public officials, they were still public officials and thus the rule applied.[10] By contrast, the Interior Ministry argued that they should be allowed to belong to the National Society and to a political party as well. With reference to the National Society, it argued membership in this organization posed no conflict of interest since its national campaigns were "pure" and "apolitical." Moreover, the National Society's links to the ruling Liberal Party were minimal.[11] As for political party membership, the Interior Ministry reversed its previous position that village heads as public officials should observe political neutrality and now asserted that, given that they were honorary public officials who received no compensation and that their process of election was informal (that is, by Citizens' NAs), there was no reason that they should not be able to join political parties.[12] Once again, the Justice Ministry accommodated the Interior Ministry's position and officially allowed village heads to engage in political activities.[13] The Interior Ministry had reaffirmed its control over village heads while at the same time preserving the links among Citizens' NAs, the National Society, and the ruling Liberal Party.

The Interior Ministry's determination to tighten its grip on village heads stemmed from its concern about upcoming local assembly elections and their potential impact on the central government's ability to mobilize local resources for the war effort. The newly elected local legislators would have the authority to elect and to dismiss town governors. This local chain of authority, the ministry worried, might lead town governors to prioritize the demands of local assemblies over those of the central government in cases in which the two disagreed. To avoid the possibility that local political conflicts might impede wartime mobilization, it needed to safeguard its control over village heads, who oversaw Citizens' NAs, the entity responsible for compliance with wartime mobilization.[14]

To prevent any decline in administrative efficiency owing to the decentralization of authority ushered in by local elections, the Interior

Ministry established the Korean Local Administration Society (*Taehan chibanghaengjŏng hyŏphoe*, hereafter the Society) in May 1952. The Society, whose honorary president was the interior minister, served two functions. First, it allowed the ministry to keep a close eye on the actions of local assemblies. Second, through its monthly magazine, lecture series, and annual conferences, the Society educated and informed local officials, who typically had little or no previous governmental experience.[15] Although membership was not mandatory, most public officials took part, allowing the ministry to develop yet another forum through which it could influence local administrative matters.

In August 1952, three months after local elections, the Society held a roundtable talk in Kimhae, a city near Pusan, the temporary wartime capital. Han Hŭi-sŏk, director of the Local Administration Bureau and vice-chair of the Society, as well as four other bureau officials, two provincial officers, and ten town officers, attended. The discussion topic was local administrative inefficiency. In a series of presentations, local officials explained that the inefficiency was largely the product of inadequate funding and understaffing. The upsurge in war-related administrative work, such as military conscription, labor mobilization, and relief work, had not been accompanied by an increase in pay.[16] They often received no reimbursement for their business trip expenses, and in the poorest counties, some often went months without receiving wages.[17] In turn, this had contributed to a sharp decline in the number of public officers. For example, in 1944, North Ch'ungch'ŏng Province had 2,731 public officials; by 1955, that number had dropped to 1,279—a decrease of over 50 percent.[18] Beyond the issues of financing and understaffing, the local presenters claimed that the population often refused to cooperate with government policies, because they mistakenly had assumed that the introduction of local government would be accompanied by a decrease in their national obligations. When local governments largely failed to lower taxes and shorten military service, the populace began to ignore government policies.[19]

In November 1952, in need of improving local administration, Director Han Hŭi-sŏk was sent on a five-month mission to Great Britain, France, Switzerland, and the US to study models of local administration that might be applied to South Korea. Han's research led him to conclude that it was unlikely that any foreign model or combination of foreign models would work in Korea, since each model was the product of specific historical, political, and economic traditions and structures. Thus, upon his return in March 1953, Han recommended that South Korea create its own local system of administration based on its unique national characteristics.[20] These national characteristics, such as inexperience in democracy and political division, were what had led Han prior to the Korean War to support delaying the enactment of the 1949 Local Autonomy Act.[21] Tasked with creating a "Korean-style" local government, he quickly moved to reestablish a stronger centralized hierarchy by amending the 1949 act.

THE MISCELLANEOUS TAX SCANDAL AND THE 1955 LOCAL AUTONOMY ACT

At roughly the same time that the Local Administration Bureau was reviewing the Local Autonomy Act with an eye to amending it, a tax scandal erupted. In June 1953, the Agriculture Ministry conducted a nationwide survey, "Realities of Farming Families." As part of this survey, it discovered that unknown to the central government, local governments were levying 56 types of miscellaneous taxes to cover local costs, including those associated with operating police stations, maintaining roads, providing compensation to war victims, and financing various semiofficial institutions. The amount of these taxes varied widely by county. For example, a family in Wanju County in North Chŏlla Province paid five hundred times more in miscellaneous taxes than a family in Sanch'ŏng County in South Kyŏngsang Province.[22] When the ministry published these findings on September 7, 1953, the report sparked widespread outrage within central government circles.

In particular, the Police Bureau under the Interior Ministry was incensed by the report, as it implicated local police departments in the tax scandal. The director of the Police Bureau released a statement that the bureau had launched an investigation of the allegations found in the report. If the allegations proved false, the director demanded that the Agriculture Minister apologize to local policemen.[23] The investigation, however, showed that the situation was far worse than that identified by the Agriculture Ministry. Rather than 56 unapproved taxes, the Police

Bureau discovered that there were roughly 280 types of taxes being lev-ied without the central government's knowledge.[24] Interior Minister Chin Hŏn-sik resigned in disgrace. Agriculture Minister Sin Chung-mok was also forced to resign for having failed to address the issue at the min-isterial meeting prior to making the findings public.[25]

Following the scandal, President Rhee made a series of personnel changes to the Interior Ministry. He appointed Paek Han-sŏng as the new minister and promoted Director Han Hŭi-sŏk to the position of vice minister. Both men had supported the colonial government. Paek had served as a judge under colonial rule and had been involved in the trials of independence activists. Han had worked as chief of the League of Con-certed National Power in South P'yŏng'an Province until liberation.[26]

The selection marked a significant departure in the types of persons Rhee appointed to ministerial offices. During the Korean War, Rhee had chosen individuals with ties to the US. For example, Rhee's sixth and seventh interior ministers, Yi Sun-yong and Chang Sŏk-yun respectively, had worked for the Office of Strategic Services, the CIA's predecessor, during World War II.[27] But as Rhee moved to create a stronger centralized government, he began consistently appointing former colonial officials as interior ministers. Rhee's twelfth minister, Kim Hyŏng-kŭn (April 1955–May 1956), had been a colonial police officer; the thirteenth, Yi Ik-hŭng (May 1956–February 1957), a prosecutor; the fourteenth, Chang Kyŏng-kŭn (February 1957–September 1957), a judge; and the fifteenth, Yi Kŭn-jik (September 1957–June 1958), a provincial leader of the Korean League for the General Mobilization of the National Spirit. Although they had switched allegiance from the colonial state to the South Korean state, they remained committed to a statist view in which the people were expected to sacrifice individual rights and freedoms for the good of the state. Thus, although Rhee had been forced to advance local autonomy to shore up his 1952 reelection prospects, he put in place a ministerial team intent on reversing the gains the populace had made under the 1949 Local Autonomy Act.

With Han's promotion to vice–interior minister, Sin Yong-u, the chief of the Administrative Section of the Local Administration Bureau, became the new director of the bureau. On his first day as director, he gave a speech in which he extolled local autonomy as the defining feature of the current government; it distinguished the current state from its colonial predecessor, from the US occupation government, and from the North Korean order. However, he railed against the administrative inefficiency that resulted from clashes between the local governments and the central government. Local institutions, he opined, must recognize the Interior Ministry's authority over them and comply with national policies.[28]

To develop a rationale for subordinating local government to national authority, Sin turned to Cho Chae-sŭng, a high-ranking official in the Local Administration Bureau. Cho theorized that in the modern world, local communities did not exist in isolation; the interests of one community intersected with those of another, inevitably leading to conflicts. Unable to see beyond localized interests, one community would advance its interests at the expense of another. Only through the central government's intervention, Cho asserted, could the autonomy of all local communities and the general welfare of society be preserved.[29]

The new team's first effort at centralization focused on resolving the issue of local governments imposing various miscellaneous taxes without the central government's knowledge or approval. The ministry understood that since the outbreak of the Korean War, local governments had been hard-pressed to make up budgetary shortfalls resulting from the decision to redirect local tax revenues to the national government. The land and household tax, which had accounted for 80 percent of local governments' income, had been merged into the Temporary Land Income Tax (*Imsi t'oji sudŭkse*), a national tax.[30] To cover this loss of funding, local governments levied miscellaneous taxes. Although the national government had been unaware of the practice, it was not illegal. Under Article 124 of the Local Autonomy Act, local administrations, with the approval of local assemblies, were authorized to impose additional taxes on residents.[31] However, as shown by the investigations of the Agriculture Ministry and the Police Bureau, the number of such taxes had become excessive. Tighter regulations, the Interior Ministry asserted, were needed until tax reform was introduced that eliminated local governments' need for such taxes as a funding source.[32] To this end, it required local administrations to obtain the ministry's approval before imposing any tax of more than 200,000 *hwan* and established detailed procedures for documenting miscellaneous taxes, which it defined as any tax other than a national, provincial, educational, or county tax.[33]

Under the new regulations, responsibility for collecting miscellaneous taxes fell to the heads of Citizens' NAs rather than public officials, whom the public viewed with distrust because of their repeated failure to use collected taxes for projects, such as new schools, as promised.[34] Under the new system, the collection rate increased, because this system bypassed unpopular town officials and reestablished the connection between payment obligations and the neighborhood space. Each household received an account book for recording the miscellaneous taxes that it paid. The book included a notation that if the head of the NA refused to record the amount paid, the household was within its rights to refuse to pay the tax.[35]

The Interior Ministry also utilized the miscellaneous tax scandal to argue that the 1949 Local Autonomy Act needed to be revised. It contended that the law had created the structural conditions that had made the tax scandal possible. Because local legislators were elected directly by the populace, who resented being taxed, they tended to support tax reductions, even though they knew that the government needed income to function. Lowered taxes increased budget deficits, which led to more miscellaneous taxes and fueled public disgust with the local administrations for demanding more money without producing any results. This vicious circle, the ministry maintained, was aggravated by the fact that town governors lacked the fortitude to stand up to local assemblies when they reduced taxes, since they were elected by the assemblies.[36]

Based on the above analysis, in December 1955, the Interior Ministry submitted to the National Assembly a revised Local Autonomy Act; the revised version, it claimed, would provide "a balance between democratic checks and administrative efficiency."[37] Under the new version, local assemblies were no longer charged with electing local governors (county, city, and town); town governors were elected directly by the people. The new version eliminated the no-confidence vote of local assemblies and the right of governors to dissolve local assemblies. It also gave local governors the authority to veto bills passed by local assemblies.[38] With these revisions, the act divorced local assemblies from the administration of local government, as governors no longer had to answer to them.

DEBATE IN THE NATIONAL ASSEMBLY OVER CITIZENS' NAs AND THE 1958 LOCAL AUTONOMY ACT

Just one month after his appointment, Interior Minister Chang Kyŏng-kŭn announced on March 25, 1957, at a conference attended by provincial governors, mayors, and heads of counties, his plans to alter the relationship between Citizens' NAs and local government. The plan, which included the following provisions, was billed by Chang as a groundbreaking action to promote democracy:

1. Citizens' NAs are requested to have a monthly gathering on the first day of every month.
2. Citizens' NAs should create a meeting attendance book and a notebook for recording residents' suggestions and comments on government.
3. Action lists from the government should be limited to five points.
4. Since the aim of monthly gatherings is to build a friendly neighborhood milieu, efforts to collect money for expenses, including taxes, and to mobilize labor are prohibited.
5. The monthly gathering should be held at a location where residents feel free to talk and express their wishes. Local institutions should address the requests of residents as soon as possible. If they are unable to act on requests, they are required to report them to higher institutions.
6. Heads should be accorded special treatment, such as doorplates for their residence and awards for exemplary heads.
7. The Committee of Citizens' NAs will be established under the jurisdiction of the Interior Ministry and answering to local governments.
8. Local governments should secure budgets for the expenses of Citizens' NAs.[39]

Chang's announcement provoked an intense reaction from national legislators belonging to the opposition parties. Already uneasy about the steps to enhance its authority at the national and local level, sixteen national legislators requested to interpellate Chang at the twenty-fourth

provisional session of the assembly on April 18, 1957. Over the course
of the next four days, a contentious debate unfolded in which Chang insisted on the democratic nature of his plan and his opponents charged
that it was authoritarian and ominously reminiscent of the policies that
had shaped Patriotic NAs under the colonial rule.

Citizens' NAs: A National Public Sphere?

Chang defined Citizens' NAs as a public sphere that was suitable for
South Korea's "underdeveloped" civil society. He explained that advanced
countries, such as the US, did not need NAs to act as a public sphere,
because they had a well-developed media that served as an arena for
information exchange and political debate. In contrast, in South Korea,
46.3 percent of the populace said that their primary source of news
was their neighbors, whereas newspapers were merely 19.9 percent or
radios 16.2 percent.[40] According to a government survey, in 1957 only
3.85 percent of households in the South, which was 137,031 out of
3,351,338 households, had a radio and it showed a huge difference between urban and rural areas.[41] The lack of access to information, he
claimed, explained why Koreans rarely sought redress for unfair public
policies, such as excessive miscellaneous taxes. It also made it difficult
for the central government to know if local public officials were implementing public policy as dictated. He envisioned Citizens' NAs functioning as a reliable channel through which the government could directly
communicate policy and receive feedback from residents. This improved
dialogic relationship, he claimed, would enhance the government's ability to respond to the populace's needs and eventually would allow Korean civil society to overcome its "backwardness."[42]

Assemblyman Pak Yŏng-jong challenged Chang's claims, stating that
the issue "was not a matter of an advanced society versus an underdeveloped one, but rather a matter of liberalism versus dictatorship (or totalitarianism)."[43] For Pak, a true liberal democracy required a public
sphere independent from the government. If a clear division was not
maintained between the public sphere and the power of the state, he
feared that censorship would take hold and South Korea's liberal democratic milieu would collapse. This fear was predicated upon his belief that
Citizens' NAs would be used to subordinate the people to government

authorities rather than to mediate between the government and the people. Moreover, he believed that through NAs, the Interior Ministry would be able to penetrate the private sphere and gain undue influence over community life and public opinion. For Pak, the ministry's plan was not a shortcut to establishing an advanced democracy in South Korea, but rather a ticket to dictatorship.

In a similar vein, Assemblyman Hyŏn Sŏk-ho took issue with the provision calling on public officials to attend monthly meetings. Linking the directive for public officials to provide instruction on public policy with Chang's remarks about police utilizing NA meetings to collect information, Hyŏn argued that the monthly meetings were for surveilling the populace rather than for encouraging open discussion. He went so far as to claim that the proposal "would turn all Koreans into policemen, leading to a totalitarian police state."[44]

In response to these harsh criticisms, Chang retreated slightly from his position on police attendance at Citizen's NAs. Noting first that NAs were already responsible for the system of Transitory Residence Registration, he claimed that in his earlier address he was simply encouraging officers to seek out assistance from Citizens' NAs in identifying ideological offenders. He also stated that the "instruction" provided by public officials would be limited to answering any questions that the people might have about government policies. Legislators' charges of foul play, he asserted, were unfounded.[45]

Rule by Law: The Constitutionality of Citizens' NAs

The constitutionality of Citizens' NAs was also called into question. Since membership in Citizen NAs was not optional and Chang's proposal included monitoring monthly meeting attendance, Assemblyman Hyŏn Sŏk-ho objected to Chang's proposal on grounds that it violated Article 13 of the South Korean constitution guaranteeing the right of association. According to Hyŏn, Article 13 protected the citizenry's right to associate as well as their right not to associate. Given that people were not free to quit Citizens' NAs, their involvement in NAs constituted a duty. However, the constitution specified only two duties: payment of taxes and military service. Based on this assessment, Hyŏn concluded that Chang's proposal was unlawful, since it would require the government to act beyond the scope of its delineated powers under the constitution.[46]

Chang answered this charge by asserting that his proposal involved administrative actions and, as such, did not require any legal foundation. He argued that his plan was no different from when local governments urged local associations and women's groups to work with them on civic projects, such as street cleaning. This administrative call for voluntary citizen cooperation only needed a legal foundation if penalties for noncooperation existed. Since his proposal included no punitive consequences for nonparticipation in projects or for failure to attend meetings, it required no legal justification.[47]

Chang entreated legislators to refrain from overinterpreting his plan. He acknowledged that under his proposal, the government would introduce action lists through Citizen NAs; however, these action lists were not the primary aim of the proposal. The primary aim, which he believed legislators failed to appreciate, was to provide a monthly forum through which the people could communicate their needs to the government. Thus, rather than infringing on the people's freedom of association, under his plan Citizens' NAs would become a vehicle through which Koreans could actively participate in public affairs and exercise their freedom of speech.[48]

The Specter of Colonial Patriotic NAs

Despite these reassurances, the opposition was not convinced that Chang's proposal would work as planned. One major reason for this skepticism was the numerous similarities between the current proposed structure and uses of Citizens' NAs and those of Patriotic NAs under Japanese colonial rule. Assemblyman So Sŏn-gyu enumerated several similarities, including that both the colonial government and the South Korean government utilized NAs to deliver action plans, to administer rationing programs, and to track the movements of the population. Assemblyman Chang T'aek-sang derisively noted that the structural organization of the two NAs was identical; the Interior Ministry had merely changed the name of the umbrella organization from the League for National Concerted Power to the National Society.[49]

This sentiment was echoed in newspaper coverage of the debate in the National Assembly. An editorial published in *Kyŏnghyang sinmun* disparagingly observed that despite papering the nation with flyers calling on citizens to eliminate all vestiges of Japanese colonial rule, the central government seemed intent on preserving the colonial legacy.[50] When the popular journal *Saebyŏk* invited its readers to comment on the issue; one citizen opined, "In recent days, a so-called campaign to strengthen Citizens' NAs has been underway. It is not only short of legal grounds but also a real drag. However hard the government embellishes it with patriotism or anticommunism, people are unlikely to be deceived. People have painful memories of the suffering that Patriotic NAs inflicted upon Koreans during the Japanese colonial period. I am fed up with the news that the government is transforming a colonial remnant into a Korean entity."[51] The public hostility made clear that few Koreans saw in Citizen's NAs a pathway to democracy. Instead, they feared that like Patriotic NAs, the government would use NAs as an instrument of control.

Although Chang admitted that the structures of Citizens' NAs and Patriotic NAs were identical, he warned against equating the two. He maintained that while Patriotic NAs had advanced a top-down approach to carrying out policy, as part of a democracy, Citizens' NAs would rely on a bottom-up approach in which the voices of local administrators and those impacted by policy would take precedence.[52] Chang expressed confidence that the differences in goals and in orientation would ensure that Citizens' NAs promoted democracy in Korea.

Concerns about Political Neutrality

The political neutrality obligation for public officials had been a source of confusion for most Koreans since the establishment of the national government in 1948. This was seen in the debate over the status of village heads in 1952 described in the first section of this chapter. The decision that village heads, as honorary public officials, could participate in party politics raised some thorny legal questions about other quasi-official entities, such as Citizens' NAs, that ostensibly were independent of the government but were charged with carrying out public administrative tasks. While village heads had been cleared to take part in political activities, Citizens' NAs had not been, since their assigned role in the administrative hierarchy was to lead "apolitical" national campaigns.

Chang's 1957 proposal for Citizens' NAs, the opposition parties feared, would place Citizens' NAs at the service of the political interests of the ruling Liberal Party. This concern was not without justification; in 1956, the Liberal Party and its allies had misused Citizens' NAs to advance Rhee's election for a third term as president. Following the 1954 constitutional amendment that opened the way for Rhee to run for a third term, the Liberal Party nominated Rhee for the presidency and Yi Ki-pung for the vice presidency. As chairs of the National Society and the Seoul Chapter of the National Society respectively, Rhee and Yi had mobilized Citizens' NAs for their reelection campaigns. On April 4, 1956, Yi sent a letter to city officials in Seoul, in which he asked for their cooperation in registering all heads of Citizens' NAs as special members of the National Society. Although it was charged with mobilizing Citizens' NAs for "independent" national campaigns, it did not have access to the contact information of NA heads; that information was in the hands of the Interior Ministry via its control over village heads. Yi claimed that the National Society needed this information so that it could contact NA heads directly to promote public education campaigns on participating in the election process. City officials forwarded the letter to district leaders, who in turn sent it to subdistrict leaders to actualize.[53] Once Yi gained access to the addresses of NA leaders, who like village heads could participate in political activities, he could use this information in his capacity as the Liberal Party's vice-presidential candidate to engage NAs in electioneering under the guise of promoting a public education campaign on election practices.

This was not the only instance in which the Liberal Party had used Citizens' NAs for political purposes. In July 1956, less than two months before scheduled local elections in August, the Liberal Party utilized a national campaign to update doorplates to prevent some opposition party candidates from registering to run. The doorplate campaign was an outgrowth of the effort to eradicate the colonial remnants. Under Japanese rule, as noted in chapter 3, Koreans had been required to adopt Japanese names. These Japanese names, along with their addresses, were to be displayed on residential doorplates in Japanese. Following liberation, a campaign titled "Let's Eliminate from Doorplates the Remnants of Japanese Rule" had been launched on October 23, 1946.[54] The success of this postliberation campaign had been undermined by the destruction and dislocation of the Korean War. While some residents removed doorplates to prevent enemy troops from knowing their identity, other doorplates had been made obsolete by the postwar migration to the cities. The absence of doorplates impeded the efficient delivery of mail and government notices.[55] The Communication Ministry urged South Koreans to create new doorplates that displayed the following information: address, name of the head of household, number of household members, and the Citizens' NA to which the household belonged.[56] The Communication Ministry also requested that the Interior Ministry mobilize Citizens' NAs to address the problem.[57] As a result, the heads of Citizens' NAs distributed leaflets and propaganda at the monthly meetings calling on members to help modernize the communication infrastructure by posting doorplates with the requested information.[58]

The NAs' doorplate campaign took a political turn when Kim Sŏyang was taken into custody by police. Kim, who previously had worked for the Pusan branch of the National Society, had switched his allegiance to the Democratic Party (*Minjudang*) and was planning to run as a Democratic Party candidate in the August 1956 elections. However, on July 6, 1956, he was greeted by three police officers at his front door at 5:00 a.m. Because his doorplate of eight years was missing, he was taken into police custody. Once at the police station, he was advised by police not to run in the upcoming election, to leave the Democratic Party, and to return to his job at the National Society affiliated with the Liberal Party. When Kim refused to comply, he was sentenced to a ten-day detention for the missing doorplate.[59] Thirteen other local Democratic Party candidates were also sentenced to five-to-ten-day detentions for various minor infractions under the Minor Offense Act.[60] The timing of their detention coincided with the candidate registration period. The Democratic Party charged that the detentions were a deliberate attempt by the police to interfere with elections. The police director dismissed the charge as untrue and asserted that the police would continue to hold households that did not display doorplates accountable.[61]

An anonymous political satirist, however, advised rather than post doorplates, those with political aspirations should "carve their information on the front door."[62]

These past abuses made members of the National Assembly extremely skeptical that the motivation behind Chang's 1957 proposal was a desire to promote democracy. For them, the timing of the proposal—one year prior to the 1958 general elections—was telling. The US Embassy shared this concern: "The strengthening of the Kungminban [Citizens' NAs] is part of a broad Liberal Party preparation for the 1958 elections. The party obviously fears that it may suffer a setback similar to that in the 1956 vice presidential race.... The Kungminban probably will prove useful to the Liberal Party and the administration only if they are used with moderation as targets for the propaganda and campaigning of the party."[63] As indicated in the US Embassy's despatch, although Rhee had won his presidential race in 1956, the Liberal Party's vice-presidential candidate had lost. Instead, Chang Myŏn, the Democratic Party candidate, had won the vice-presidential election. Consequently, the Democratic Party and other opposition groups were certain that Rhee and the Liberal Party would mobilize town officials to speak at the monthly NA meetings to sway public opinion in their favor for the 1958 elections.[64]

Chang rebuffed these concerns, reminding national legislators that the instruction provided by public officers was limited to explaining policy. Unless answering a question directly related to their duties as public officers, their attendance at monthly meetings was as private individuals. He also said that he was promoting this proposal in his role as interior minister, not in his role as chair of the policy board of the Liberal Party. Rather than anticipating abuse, he suggested that legislators should wait and see the results before acting against the proposal.[65]

The inquiry ended on April 21, 1957. Two days later, thirty-four legislators put forward a motion to strike down Chang's proposal to strengthen Citizens' NAs. However, on April 26, 1957, the Liberal Party, which held a majority of seats in the National Assembly, overruled the motion.[66] The opposition responded by organizing a committee in the National Assembly dedicated to blocking the implementation of the plan to strengthen NAs, which they denounced as "an attempt to establish a one-party dictatorship."[67] Their first action was to reject the 190-million-*hwan* budget for Citizens' NAs submitted by the Interior Ministry for the 1958 fiscal year.[68] They also threatened to withhold funding for the police. After a series of contentious disputes, the opposition struck a deal with the ruling party. They would approve funding for the police, if the ruling party agreed to withdraw its request for funding for Citizens' NAs.[69]

Against the backdrop of significant public opposition, Chang resigned as interior minister in September 1957. However, his resignation was strictly a symbolic gesture as the government did not abandon its plan to strengthen Citizens' NAs. Having failed to procure funding from the National Assembly, it diverted funds budgeted for the Local Administration Bureau and for general administration to Citizens' NAs.[70] The Interior Ministry also moved to amend the Local Autonomy Act so that NAs officially became part of the legal order. In introducing this amendment, which the Liberal Party successfully pushed through the National Assembly, the ministry used the suffix "*pang*" for NAs rather than the suffix "*pan*," which had been used for Patriotic NAs under Japanese rule. The "new" suffix, in fact, was a return to the one used in premodern Korea for a local administrative unit.[71] This orthographic sleight of hand represented an attempt to obfuscate the colonial origins of Citizens' NAs, so that the mobilization of the neighborhood space for national purposes would appear beyond reproach.

The 1958 version of the Local Autonomy Act drastically reduced Koreans' control over local government. In addition to legally recognizing Citizens' NAs, it took away the populace's right to elect local governors. The Interior Ministry reasoned that direct elections did not always result in the most qualified candidate gaining office; thus, they undermined administrative efficiency and increased budgetary waste. It also claimed that direct elections led to local governors focusing too much on immediate political interests in safeguarding their reelection.[72] Under the new version, the government directly or indirectly was responsible for the appointment of all local-level officials: the provincial governor was appointed by the president; county governors by the president via the Interior Ministry with the recommendation of a provincial governor; a town governor by a provincial governor; and village heads as well as the heads of Citizens' NAs by a town (city) governor.[73] After a decade-long struggle, Rhee and the ministry had finally achieved the centralized model of governance that they had first advanced in 1949.

Like the centralized model of governance ushered in by the 1958 act, the plan for strengthening Citizens' NAs restricted the agency of residents. Under the 1953 plan, Citizens' NAs were called upon to contribute to the development of local autonomy "by voluntarily conducting *administrative measures* and *national campaigns* under the supervision of the government and the local government, while concomitantly promoting *local patriotism* through mutual aid and moral amity."[74] In contrast, the new plan made no reference to promoting local autonomy, voluntarism, or communal bonds. Instead, NAs were to contribute "to the development of democratic administration and the national goals of anticommunism and unification by implementing government policies and reflecting popular opinions."[75] Thus, rather than a sphere of action, in which community values provided the foundation for voluntary national campaigns and patriotic displays, Citizens' NAs became a one-way channel for policy directives from the government that NAs were mandated to implement.

THE INTERIOR MINISTRY'S "DEMOCRATIC ADMINISTRATION" IN THE LATE 1950s

On July 10, 1957, Interior Minister Chang Kyŏng-gŭn sent a telegram to all ten vice-ministers in the government, titled "Regarding the Meeting of the Central Committee Administering Citizens' NAs." As the chair of the committee, he notified them of the date of the monthly meeting and asked them to study carefully the attached document before the meeting. It was the action list for August, which had five items: 1) In honor of the twelfth anniversary of independence, Koreans should work hard, be frugal, and resolve spiritually to strive for unification; 2) A warning about epidemic disease, especially encephalitis, was issued and Koreans were advised to kill mosquitoes and clean swamp-like areas; 3) Koreans were also asked to spray pesticides and weed; 4) The government asked for the populace's cooperation with summer grain collection and reminded them of its significance for the national rice plans and; 5) A crackdown on the outflow of military supplies to the black market was needed so that Korea would not be discredited.[76] The list was delivered to the roughly 210,000 Citizens' NAs for review at the August 1957 monthly meeting.

Under Chang's plan, the August NA meeting followed a set format, which the government deemed appropriate for an "underdeveloped" democratic country. Illustrative of the type of dialogic relationship that the government envisioned was the August meeting of the Fourth Citizens' NA in Sinch'on village, Kwangsan County in South Chŏlla Province. After the twelve men and three women representing the various households arrived, the NA head made opening remarks. He then read the August action list, which those in attendance discussed point by point. When this discussion concluded, the head reminded members of tax deadlines and best times for planting. These reminders were followed by the NA head notifying members of town officials' response to their request at the previous monthly meeting for more movie screening locations. Unfortunately, he explained, due to the financial crunch and the shortage of projectors, the town could not increase the number of movie screening sites. When one member continued to complain, another member explained that in addition to having to buy additional movie projectors, the town would also have to purchase a generator as many areas did not have electricity. The discussion then turned to suggestions that the NA would submit to the government for this month. One person proposed the distribution of tobacco through Citizens' NAs, because the price of tobacco on the free market was too high. The meeting ended after a female representative appealed for assistance with planting because her son was away on military service.[77]

The reintroduction of action lists, which were designed as a direct system of contact with the populace and a means by which the populace could provide limited feedback to the government, bore a striking similarity to colonial practice. Beyond their resemblance to colonial practice, this reversed the Interior Ministry's 1949 promise that it would allow the National Society to lead "independent" national movements, while it played only a secondary role. As seen in table 6.1, action lists, delivered in the form of campaign slogans, placed everyday Korean life at the service of instituting government policy. In effect, they created a

TABLE 6.1.   Action lists of Citizens' Neighborhood Associations

October 1957	Let's respect the national flag.
	Let's seek out North Korean spies.
	Let's repair roads.
	Let's put up doorplates.
	Let's protect forests.
December 1957	Let's establish adult education programs.
	Let's have secondary jobs.
	Let's enhance security to prevent crimes and fires.
	Let's finish the autumn grain collection.
January 1958	Let's reform everyday life.
	Let's increase the literacy rate.
	Let's drive out superstition.
	Let's prevent fire in the mountains.
	Let's mark prices on goods.
February 1958	Let's save rice.
	Let's have winter secondary jobs.
	Let's produce fertilizer for winter.
	Let's reduce illiteracy.
	Let's register children eligible for elementary school.
March 1958	Let's have anticommunism and anti-Japan spirits.
	Let's plant trees.
	Let's repair roads.
	Let's see the list of candidates of the national election.

South Korean National Archives, BA0085311and BA0085312, Ch'ongmuch'ŏ, ch'agwan hoeŭirok (Minutes of vice-ministers), 1957–1958.

state of constant mobilization in which the ministry became the center of state power. Its responsibility for the monthly action lists for Citizens' NAs gave it the authority to convene meetings of vice-ministers from all governmental departments. After receiving local requests for government action via NAs, it contacted and coordinated the response of the ministries under which the request fell. It produced statistical data based on its control of nationwide local information through NAs, commanded the police, and controlled local government.

But the power amassed by the Interior Ministry, and by extension the Liberal Party, over the course of the 1950s through its tightening grip over Citizens' NAs did not go unchallenged. A viable opposition party, the Democratic Party, had emerged in 1955 and defeated the Liberal Party's candidate for the vice presidency in 1956. Emboldened by this success and its success in the 1958 general elections, the Democratic Party stood poised to challenge Syngman Rhee's bid for a fourth presidential term in 1960.

THE 1960 LOCAL AUTONOMY ACT AND THE DEMISE OF DICTATORSHIP

The Democratic Party's remarkable success in the 1958 general elections did not bode well for the Rhee regime. Prior to its emergence in 1955, there had been no opposition party with sufficient support to challenge the ruling Liberal Party. While there had been a few mid-size political parties, independent politicians without party affiliation remained the second largest group in the National Assembly. The first indication that the Democratic Party was a viable contender came in 1956, when its candidate won the 1956 vice-presidential election. This success was followed by the Democratic Party gaining seventy-nine seats in the National Assembly in the 1958 general elections. While the ruling party maintained its majority (123 out of 233 seats), 1958 marked the first time that another political party controlled the second largest number of seats.[78] Against the backdrop of this unprecedented success, speculation grew that the ruling party might lose its hold on power in the 1960 elections. In 1959, Yi Ki-pung, the Liberal Party's 1958 nominee for vice president who had lost in 1956, recommended to Rhee that he appoint Ch'oe In-gyu, known for his fealty to Rhee, as interior minister. The timing of Ch'oe's appointment, just one year prior to the 1960 election, combined with Yi's past reputation for misusing Citizens' NAs in the 1956 election, did not go unnoticed by the opposition.[79]

As expected, the Democratic Party launched a presidential and vice-presidential campaign in 1960 under the slogan "No More Tolerance.

Let's Turn Over Control of the Government." The ruling party's counterslogan was "Better to have experienced leaders than novices."[80] The presidential election pitted Syngman Rhee against Cho Pyŏng-ok, while the vice-presidential election was a rematch between Yi Ki-pung and Chang Myŏn. However, Cho Pyŏng-ok passed away in mid-February, just one month before the March election. Since the Democratic Party could not advance another candidate, Rhee's reelection for a fourth term was guaranteed. The 1960 election now focused on the vice-presidential race.

Having lost in 1956 to Chang, Yi Ki-pung desperately wanted to win in 1960. As in 1956, Yi again turned to Citizens' NAs to advance his candidacy, but this time his misuse of NAs was more blatant. Citizens' NAs were encouraged to schedule special events to coincide with local rallies organized by the Democratic Party. For example, on February 29, 1960, the date that Chang was scheduled to speak in the city of Taegu, local NAs were instructed to show a film or arrange some other alternative event. Similarly, on March 1, 1960, one day prior to Chang's planned campaign rally in Chŏnju city, NA heads at the monthly meeting advised members not to attend Chang's rally. In some cases, to ensure that members did not attend, NA heads distributed rationing stamps for rubber shoes and soap during the scheduled rally time.[81]

The Liberal Party's manipulation of NA monthly meetings backfired, as it triggered widespread popular discontent with the party. Because the campaigns of Citizens' NAs were supposed to be apolitical, public officials chose their words carefully when calling on NAs to support Rhee. They described Rhee as someone who was above partisan politics and whose only ambition was advancing the nation's interests. However, officials were much less circumspect when it came to using anticommunist rhetoric to defame Democratic Party candidates. Public officials portrayed the Democratic Party as a threat to national security and accused Chang Myŏn of being a North Korean spy.[82] In March 1960, in Kangwŏn Province, this tactic triggered a confrontation between a public official and an NA member at the monthly meeting. After a public official gave a lengthy pro–Liberal Party speech in which he insinuated that a vote for the Democratic Party would result in national chaos, a member who was fed up with the Liberal Party's manipulations yelled, "It is illegal for a public official to promote an election campaign!" The public officer replied, "This is not an election campaign, but a save-the-nation movement."[83] While this response allowed the public official to reframe his actions as apolitical and patriotic, few NA members were convinced by the justification. Rather than advance its cause, the Liberal Party's misuse of NA meetings fueled public discontent.

This simmering discontent turned into spontaneous nationwide protests when it was revealed that Interior Minister Ch'oe In-gyu, in concert with the Police Bureau, had engaged in ballot rigging. In the National Assembly, the opposition called for Rhee's resignation, and at mass demonstrations across the nation, student groups, university professors, and ordinary citizens made the same demand. On April 26, 1960, after twelve years in office, Rhee announced that he would step down. With his resignation, the tripartite power-sharing arrangement between the Interior Ministry, the National Society (Citizen's NAs), and the Liberal Party collapsed. Following Rhee's resignation, Interior Minister Ch'oe In-gyu was arrested and sentenced to death for his role in rigging the 1960 elections. A warrant for the arrest of Chang Kyŏng-kŭn, the former interior minister who had advanced the 1957 plan for strengthening the ministry's control over NAs, was issued. However, he fled to Japan before he could be apprehended. His successors—Yi Kŭn-jik, Yi Ik-hŭng, and Kim Il-hwan—were arrested on various charges, including election fraud and conspiracy to assassinate Chang Myŏn.[84] The Liberal Party and the National Society, which under Rhee dominated national politics, now existed in name only.

The 1960 election scandal catalyzed a nationwide call for reform. Citing the presidential system as the cause for the nation's slide into authoritarianism, the National Assembly adopted a new constitution that provided for a parliamentary system with a bicameral legislature. In June 1960, voters approved the new constitution, thereby establishing the Second Republic. When elections were held the next month, the Democratic Party won 175 of 233 seats in the Lower House (*Minŭiwŏn*) of the National Assembly. Forty-nine seats went to independents, while the Liberal Party won only two seats. In the Upper House (*Ch'amŭiwŏn*), the Democratic Party won thirty-one out of fifty-eight seats, while independents won twenty and the Liberal Party won four.[85] Chang Myŏn, the leader of the Democratic Party, became prime minister and formed the first cabinet in August 1960.

Replacing the presidential system with a parliamentary system also required revising the 1958 Local Autonomy Act, as it was through this act that the Interior Ministry had gained control over local governments. It was in this context that the topic of the future of Citizens' NAs was first broached. On May 20, 1960, the Committee for Revising the Local Autonomy Act (*Kukhoe chibang chach'ibŏp kaejŏng wiwŏnhoe*) invited twenty-three representatives of provincial and city assemblies to discuss the provisional bill. While everyone in attendance supported the direct election of local governors, they were split over Citizens' NAs. Cho Pyŏng-bong, a member of the Kyŏnggi provincial assembly, insisted that NAs should be abolished to prevent their future abuse. In contrast, Kim Chu-hong, a member of Seoul's assembly, expressed reservations about abolishing NAs; he proposed allowing local governments to decide. The hearing ended with the matter of NAs still undecided.[86]

At first glance, the indecision of the National Assembly may seem surprising, given the strong objections to the 1957 plan for Citizens' NAs. But Citizens' NAs, despite their political abuses, had been the launch point for modernization campaigns. For example, NAs had played a critical role in the postwar recovery effort by providing a voluntary labor force for maintaining and repairing roads.[87] Despite the scandal described earlier in this chapter, the doorplate campaign had led to more efficient mail delivery, and the annual national competition to catch rats had improved public health.[88] In addition to their socio-economic functions, NAs were expected to play a substantial role in data collection; without the assistance of NA heads and their knowledge of members' households, the first National Census, scheduled for December 1960, was unlikely to go as planned.[89]

These practical benefits ultimately ensured NAs' survival. Rather than completely abolishing them, the National Assembly reached a compromise. While the 1958 Local Autonomy Act specified that villages were required to have "neighborhood associations" (*pang*), Article 145 of the 1960 Local Autonomy Act stated, "Villages may have suborganizations."[90] With the removal of the term "neighborhood associations", Citizens' NAs lost their legal status in the official administrative hierarchy. However, they could still exist, as Article 145 gave local governments the right to establish suborganizations, which typically took the form of NAs. Although Citizens' NAs as suborganizations were still linked to local governments, the likelihood of their being abused for political purposes under the 1960 act was low, because local governors—provincial, city, and town—were elected by residents. In addition, Article 146 provided for residents to elect village heads every other year. In the Second Republic, local communities controlled the destiny of Citizens' NAs.

CONCLUSION

In the 1950s, South Korea's first decade as an independent nation, its leaders sought to find a Korean way of balancing national and local authority. The delayed implementation of the 1949 Local Autonomy Act had given Koreans for the first time an active role in local governance. From the perspective of the Rhee administration, however, the decentralization introduced an unacceptable level of administrative inefficiency and contradicted Rhee's One Nation Ideology. Consequently, Rhee began appointing ministry heads and other officials who were intent on reversing the 1949 act. The Interior Ministry led the charge to reassert the central government's authority over local governments. Its crucial element entailed establishing a direct line of communication between the central government and Citizens' NAs. The ministry's 1957 plan for NAs reintroduced monthly action lists—a colonial vestige—for the purpose of mobilizing the populace to act on government policies presented to them in the form of slogans. At the same time, the plan established a process through which Koreans could submit requests to the government. This dialogic relationship, the ministry argued, would allow South Korea to transition quickly from an "underdeveloped" democratic polity into a mature one.

But the mobilization of Citizens' NAs was flawed from the outset. Following liberation, NAs had been defined as a volunteer, apolitical national movement of the populace. To separate them from partisan politics, they had been placed under the umbrella of the National Society, an organization ostensibly independent from the government. But their leadership overlapped with those of the ruling Liberal Party and of the government. The result was that the government had access to NAs through three entities: the National Society, the Interior Ministry, and the Liberal Party. On the one hand, this tripartite power-sharing arrangement allowed Rhee to bring together in one organization—Citizens' NAs—national campaigns, local administration, and party politics. On the other hand, it exposed and exacerbated inherent contradictions in governmental practices that ultimately contributed to the administration's downfall.

Citizen NAs were supposed to be apolitical voluntary associations, but membership in NAs was mandatory. At first, the government sidestepped this tension by imposing no penalties on members if they failed to participate in movement activities. But when police under the Interior Ministry detained an opposition politician in 1956, some critics openly expressed skepticism about the ministry's observance of constitutionally mandated impartiality. Criticism of the government mounted following the introduction of the 1957 plan for NAs and the 1958 Local Autonomy Act, which for the first time legally recognized NAs as part of the local administrative hierarchy. With the introduction of monthly action lists, the ministry replaced the National Society as the principal manager of Citizens' NAs. Against this backdrop, the voluntary aspect of Citizens' NAs receded, as increasingly public officers illegally used NA meetings and campaigns for electioneering. Once the veil of voluntarism and impartiality had been lifted, comparisons between the Rhee administration and Japanese colonial rule gained momentum, and popular discontent with the ruling party grew. This discontent boiled over when it was revealed that the government had manipulated the 1960 election results; the spontaneous mass protests led to Rhee's resignation and the creation of the Second Republic.

Citizens' NAs survived Rhee's downfall, but under the 1960 Local Autonomy Act, they no longer had legal status. In May 1961, however, General Park Chung-hee led a successful military coup, bringing an end to the Second Republic. On May 16, 1961, the new military government suspended the 1960 act, leaving the future of Citizen NAs to be determined.

PART III

People's Neighborhood Associations in North Korea

CHAPTER 7

Fatherland and People, 1945–1953

People's Neighborhood Associations are not an end organization of the government, but a mass organization built by the spontaneous will of people to carry out state policies voluntarily.
—O Hak-mo, chair of Chaenyŏng County People's Committee[1]

Following liberation in August 1945, the northern part of Korea was taken over by the Soviet army. Unlike the Americans in the South, they created the Soviet Civil Administration on October 3 and mostly consigned the administration to North Koreans.[2] Korean leaders established the North Korean Provisional People's Committee (*Pukchosŏn imsi-inminwiwŏnhoe*, NKPPC) in February 1946. Though led by socialists under the aegis of the Soviet Union, it included many nonsocialists and quickly introduced a series of reforms. In March 1946, it passed a land reform bill abolishing landlordism. In June, a new labor law guaranteed workers a minimum wage and an eight-hour workday and banned employers from hiring children under the age of thirteen. In July, the NKPPC passed the Gender Equality Law that freed women from the "triple subordination" of family, society, and politics. Under the new law, women gained equal political rights, equal access to education, and freedom of choice in marriage and divorce. The law also outlawed concubines and prohibited public and private prostitution. In August, the NKPPC nationalized the postal service as well as major industries, such as railways, mines, banks, and factories.[3]

The reform package did not seek to create a socialist society but to create the necessary conditions for the independence of fatherland and the liberation of people. The reformers understood that Japanese colonial policy, which combined features of feudalism and capitalism, had effectively denied the Koreans economic, political, and social agency. Landlordism had impoverished the Korean peasantry and the working class had to endure low wages and poor working conditions without labor laws. Japan's refusal to grant Koreans any political rights left Koreans politically inexperienced in self-rule, and inattention to the educational needs of the populace created widespread illiteracy. Reversing the colonial order that promoted dependency, the NKPPC believed, required conceptually foregrounding "people" (inmin)—people's sovereignty, people's economy, people's culture, and people's education.

Yet in foregrounding "people," the North did not eliminate all vestiges of colonialism. It retained neighborhood associations under the name People's NAs; the new prefix hid from view the continuity between the colonial past and the nascent people's democracy in the North. There is no evidence pointing to exactly when this transformation in name took place or who made the decision to change the name. However, the first known reference to People's NAs appears in a public document on urban administration dated November 20, 1945.[4] In March 1946, the words "People's NAs" appeared on rice ration cards, marking popular recognition and acceptance of the new nomenclature.[5]

In making the transition from Patriotic NAs to People's NAs, the North maintained its uncompromising stance on colonialism; however, it apparently did not assume that a person's past association with pro-Japanese social groups, especially Patriotic NAs, was tantamount to having collaborated willingly with the Japanese. Rather than associate collaboration with participation in mandatory Patriotic NA programs, such as the colonial rice rationing program, officials paid closer attention to an individual's involvement in voluntary groups and the scope of that involvement in assessing whether someone qualified as a collaborator.[6] This definition suggests a possible explanation for NAs' subsequent revival, despite their undeniable contribution to wartime colonialism, namely that North Korean leaders did not view NAs as collaborative bodies, since participation was mandatory.

Through NAs, which provided direct access to all Koreans, the North hoped to inculcate in the populace the patriotism that it believed would bind together Koreans of different classes and political affiliations. Led by the Workers' Party, this united national front would revitalize the economy, create a society free from foreign political influence, and re-store Korean culture. NAs would teach the masses that under people's democracy, personal interests and national interests existed in harmony; once the people understood this, they would voluntarily participate in state-building. Thus, People's NAs did not cultivate an apolitical moral patriotism, as had been the case under Patriotic NAs. The state created no quasi-independent agency to act as mediator between the state and People's NAs, as had both the colonial state and South Korea.

However, like Patriotic NAs and Citizen's NAs, an inherent contra-diction existed between NAs' status as voluntary organizations and their use by the state to implement policy. Prior to the war, the North had been able to maintain a precarious balance between the two. The early reform package generated widespread support for the NKPPC, and the people expressed their gratitude for the changes by answering the state's call for voluntarism. However, the onset of the Korean War disrupted this frag-ile balance. US air raids prompted People's NAs to reintroduce the air defense training that Patriotic NAs had previously provided. The gov-ernment also placed increased demands on People's NAs to participate in "voluntary" mass campaigns, such as building bomb shelters and re-pairing roads and bridges. As these campaigns grew in number, volun-tarism, already in decline, decreased dramatically, and local officials adapted more coercive approaches. As coercion replaced voluntarism, so too did the definition of the "masses of people" narrow.

WHO ARE THE PEOPLE AND WHAT ARE PEOPLE'S NAs?

The word "subject" (*sinmin*), indicating the subjugation of Koreans to the Japanese emperor, immediately disappeared from everyday parlance fol-lowing liberation. In its place, the word "people" (*inmin*) became the common designation for Koreans. But beyond being an alternative to "subject," the word did not yet have any political connotations or any as-sociation with the state; it simply referred to Koreans. That changed following Korea's occupation by US and Soviet forces. In the South, the word, because of its association with leftist people's committees (PCs) banned by the US in 1945, became shorthand for a leftist political bias. In contrast, in the North, the word became synonymous with the source of the state's sovereignty. Thus, the North needed to answer the question, who are the "people" that will participate in building the new state? The answer is also key to answering the question, what are People's NAs?

Beyond referring to a collective with responsibility for building the state in the North, "people" also encompassed patriotism. In an encyclopedia published by the North Korean government, the constitutive link between patriotism and people was explained as follows:

> More than anything else, the masses of people constitute a social group, based in the working people. The working people make up the majority of the masses of people and play positive roles in historical development. Also, the masses of people are a social group of persons with subjective demands and creative activities. It is misleading, however, to consider only working persons as belonging to the masses of people.... Neither social status nor class affiliation determines who belongs to the masses of people, rather it is their ideology. What transforms (or does not transform) persons of different classes into the mass people is not socialism or communism, it is patriotism. Anyone who is patriotic can serve the masses of people and be a part of the masses of people.[7]

Patriotism was the vehicle through which the North sought to embrace those of different classes and political beliefs as part of the "people."

The idea of patriotism as a constitutive element of the "people" can be traced back to Kim Il Sung. Born in Taedong County in South P'yŏng'an Province in 1912, he went to Jilin, China, in 1926. There, he joined an anti-Japanese guerilla force that was backed by the Chinese Communist Party. In the late 1930s, pursued by Japanese soldiers, Kim crossed into the Soviet Union to escape capture. Once there, he was trained as a special operation agent by Soviet forces. He returned to Korea in mid-September 1945 as part of his brigade. Shortly after returning, he took part in the Conference of Korean Communist Party Members and Enthusiasts in the Five Northwestern Provinces (*Chosŏn kongsandang sŏbugododang tang'wŏn mit yŏlsŏngja yŏnhaptaehoe*) held in Pyongyang from October 10 to 13, 1945, which resulted in the creation of the Korean Communist Party–North Korea Bureau

(*Chosŏn kongsandang-pukchosŏn pun'guk*). The day after the conference, Kim was introduced at a mass rally by Major General Nikolai Lebedev of the Soviet Union as a national hero and successful military man. The introduction made clear that Kim had eclipsed Cho Man-sik as Stalin's choice for leader of northern Korea.[8]

Prior to attending the conference, on October 3, 1945, Kim Il Sung outlined his political vision for Korea. In lieu of a return to monarchy, the establishment of a "bourgeois democracy," or the immediate creation of a socialist system, he proposed that Korea should "take the road to progressive democracy." A return to monarchy, Kim declared, was an attempt to "restore feudal autocracy." Similarly, he claimed that to establish a "bourgeois democracy" was to "betray the people." He contended that it was a "smokescreen for a handful of privileged classes to cover up their oppression and exploitation of the people," such as landlords and elites who had "worked hand in glove with the Japanese imperialists." However, he also opposed the immediate establishment of a socialist system, noting that the "considerable remnants of Japanese imperialism and feudal relations of exploitation" had to be eliminated first. Progressive democracy, he explained, must factor in Korea's "present level of historical development." It meant "nation-building which conforms to Korean reality, and correctly leads the masses to its attainment." An "independent and sovereign state based on progressive democracy," he explained, required organizing "as rapidly as we can in all localities" the people's committees that had been "set up on the initiative of the masses." Progressive democracy, he concluded, was the only viable path forward: "Correctly understanding the essence of progressive democracy and fully realizing it, we must establish a democratic people's republic, a genuine people's power and build a new flourishing and democratic Korea."[9]

Progressive democracy was people's democracy, and it served as the official ideology of the North until the end of the Korean War. In a people's democracy, diverse interests and classes were united in a coalition for the common good of the nation: "Our united front is a coalition of people of all sections of life based on the interests of the nation as a whole. . . . While firmly united under the single banner of democracy, all classes, political parties, and organizations retain their respective freedom to exist and develop independently with due regards to politics, ideology, organization, and information."[10] This "united national front," led by the Workers' Party, had its roots in the strategic coalition that had been formed to combat Japanese imperialism in the 1930s. Kim maintained it, because imperialism's demise was only the first step in building an independent state. By channeling the people's desire for independence into state-building, the national economy could be revitalized and Korean culture reclaimed. He also argued that unlike in a bourgeois democracy, which "guarantees the rights and freedoms to a handful of privileged classes and leaves the broad masses of people without any rights," people's democracy "pledges equal rights to all people in all spheres of politics."[11] In the economic sphere, it allowed for the parallel development of privately owned businesses and state-owned industries. It excluded from state-building only the landlord class and Japanese collaborators.[12] All other Koreans were welcome to participate.

Patriotism was the glue that allowed the North to bring together Koreans from diverse political and economic groups. But because patriotism was a concept also found in the colonial state and in the South, the North needed to distinguish its form of patriotism from these counterparts. The socialist theorist Kim Cho-hun did so by asserting that "they [Japanese imperialists and South Korean leaders] created a paradise for the ruling class and a deceptive trap for the poor and the dominated."[13] In both imperialist and bourgeois capitalist societies, he maintained, the masses' patriotism is placed at the service of the interests of the dominant class rather than the interests of all society. In such a scenario, patriotism devolves into ethnocentrism and becomes complicit with capitalist exploitation and annexation of peoples beyond national borders. However, popular patriotism in the North, he contended, would never lose sight of the people's interests, because in a people's democratic state the goal was creating a social order that promoted the freedom of all classes. In advancing this theory, he assumed that there was no conflict between personal and national interests in a people's democratic state. He believed that the people, recognizing that loyalty to the state was in their long-term best interests, would prioritize patriotism over their short-term interests.[14]

The political undertones given to the word "people" in the North had implications for the orientation of People's NAs. Posited as gatherings of voluntary patriots that freely served the collective interests of the people, NAs would advance the full independence of Korea by realizing the envisioned united national front at the neighborhood level. The neighborhood milieu in which People's NAs operated made possible the bringing together of people of diverse classes. Moreover, the various postliberation reforms such as land reform and gender equality had reduced tensions between neighbors. That said, utilizing People's NAs as the foundation for the national front was not without risks, as just like under their colonial predecessors, membership in these NAs was mandatory. Their alleged "voluntary" character did not mirror reality and the neighborhood was an unlikely locale for instilling patriotic fervor.

POLITICAL ENLIGHTENMENT IN CONCERT WITH THE DEMOCRATIC PROPAGANDA OFFICE

After introducing a host of social reform bills in 1946, the NKPPC called for people's committee elections to be held at all administrative levels, that is, provincial, county, town, and village. On September 5, 1946, it enacted a bill that established the election rules such that anyone over the age of twenty-one was eligible to vote by secret ballot.[15] Three elections were scheduled—elections for provincial and county PCs on November 3, 1946, village PCs on February 24–25, 1947, and town PCs on March 5, 1947. Kim Il Sung maintained that the democratic elections would "hasten the settlement of the Korean question" by awakening democracy-loving Koreans in the South to their exploitation under the US military government.[16]

In preparing for the elections, the NKPPC prioritized mass participation over competition between political parties. It made a voting system that allowed the roughly 2.3 million illiterate Koreans to participate, known as the black and white box system.[17] After hearing an election committee member read the name of the candidate on the paper ballot, the illiterate voter went into a booth and put the corresponding ballot into a white box, labeled "yes," or a black box, labeled "no." Literate voters were allowed to take the paper ballots for all candidates into the booth at the same time and place them in the box of their choosing.[18]

The NKPPC also understood that mass participation required educating Koreans on the voting process, including teaching them about key concepts, such as people's democracy, sovereignty, voting rights, and equality, that informed the process. Without such education, it recognized that Koreans would have difficulty grasping the importance of voting and thus would be unlikely to participate.[19] To rectify this situation, it ordered on September 21, 1945, that election propaganda offices (*Sŏn'gŏ sŏnjŏnsil*) be established in all election districts.[20] Propagandists affixed election posters to streetlamps and walls and delivered leaflets to every house. Radio announcements were made urging people to take part, and loudspeakers in public spaces were used to stress the importance of voting.[21] In addition, local lectures and roundtable talks on the elections were organized.[22] Heads of People's NAs also held frequent NA meetings to discuss the upcoming elections with members and went door to door to make sure everyone understood how critical the elections were for building an independent country.[23] A special effort was also made to speak one on one with seniors and those uninterrupted in politics to ensure that they too understood that every vote counted.[24]

The enlightenment campaign was a success. For the provincial and county PC elections on November 3, 1946, 99.6 percent of the eligible voting population turned out. In February 1947, the newly elected provincial and county PCs voted to turn the provisional national governing body into a permanent body; thus the NKPPC became the North Korean People's Committee (*Pukchosŏn inminwiwŏnhoe*, NKPC). Independent candidates won the most seats (50.1 percent); the Workers' Party came in second (31.8 percent), and the Democratic Party came in third (10 percent).[25] Voter turnout for the village PC elections and the town PC elections was also high—99.85 and 99.98 percent respectively.[26]

Tonghŭng village at Yŏnp'o town in South Hamgyŏng Province was one of the villages that elected a village PC in February 1947. Made up of fourteen People's NAs, it had about one thousand residents, who made their living by cultivating rice and potatoes, mining iron and copper, and fishing in the coastal area. On February 24–25, 1947, the 435 residents of the village who were eligible to vote (196 men and 239 women) elected five members to the village PC.[27] The five men chosen, whose ages ranged from the late twenties to the mid-thirties, all came from poor peasant families and belonged to the Workers' Party. As per the government's requirement, they created sixteen administrative departments, which they staffed with residents over the age of seventeen. They also established committees for campaigns, such as epidemic prevention, public hygiene, and eliminating illiteracy.[28]

On May 4, 1947, the chair of Tonghŭng village PC received a communication from the chair of Yŏnp'o town PC asking if a local democratic propaganda office (*Minju sŏnjŏnsil*), in accordance with the guidelines provided, had been established. On May 15, 1947, the village PC chair reported that the village had opened the "Democratic Propaganda Office of Tonghŭng Village in Yŏnp'o Town."[29] The office was a by-product of the election education campaign. Following the provincial and county PC election, the government interpreted the persistence of social practices inappropriate to the new political order, such as excessive pleasure-seeking, the squandering of money, complacency, and dislike of learning, as colonial remnants and indicative of the populace's insufficient political development.[30] In an effort to eradicate these outdated values, it decided to convert the election propaganda office into the democratic propaganda office in November 1946.[31] The new office was assigned to link the "masses of people" to the government, by convincing the people that the patriotic democracy was in the best interests of the people.

The democratic propaganda office organized mass campaigns and served as a venue for diverse local activities. Smaller villages were instructed to create one or two propaganda offices, while larger villages were advised to create more. In addition, local governments were advised to integrate all village facilities for reading and leisure activities into the propaganda office.[32] It utilized a standard layout; there were three rooms, one each for reading, leisure, and meetings. A national flag and a photograph of Kim Il Sung were prominently displayed on the walls, as were the latest political manifestos.[33] The reading room had books on political theory and major newspapers such as *Nongmin sinmun* (Peasant newspaper) and the Workers' Party Bulletin.[34] The walls of the conference room were covered with graphs showing the results of campaigns, including the campaign to eliminate illiteracy and the People's NA–led campaign to produce more straw-woven goods. The leisure room was equipped with a radio, musical instruments, a loudspeaker, and sports equipment that were made available for cultural performances and athletic tournaments.[35] By the end of 1948, there were 16,662 propaganda offices in the North.[36]

TABLE 7.1.   The staff of the democratic propaganda office in Tonghŭng village (September 1947)

Title	Name	Age	Information from other sources
Head of office	Mun, Chae-sŭng	30	Male, village PC member
Inspector	Kim, Yŏng-tŭk	37	Male, chair of village PC
Statistics	Pak, P'il-kŭn	30	Male, member of health committee
Chief propagandist	Kim, Hyo-yŏl	37	Male, vice-chair of village PC
Statistics on propaganda to People's NAs	Kim, Yun-ok	31	Female
Communication	Kim, Yŏng-tŭk	37	Male, chair of village PC
1st and 2nd People's NAs	Kim, 'To-in	25	Male, health committee
3rd and 4th People's NAs	Yi, Un-ho	27	Male
5th and 6th People's NAs	Mun, P'yo-do	34	Male
7th and 8th People's NAs	Shin, Ki-hyo	34	Male
9th–11th People's NAs	Han,??	52	Male
12th People's NAs	Ro, Pu-wŏn	38	Male
13th and 14th NAs	Maeng, Yŏng-jun	24	Male, headman of a people's NA

RG 242, SA2010, box 847, item 166, "Strengthening the Office and Reconstructing Communication" (1947), and box 862, item 97, *Staff List* (1949).

In Tonghŭng, the democratic propaganda office was closely connected with the fourteen People's NAs. To facilitate communication with the local populace, the Ministry of Cultural Propaganda (*Munhwa sŏnjŏnsŏng*) advised all offices to stay in regular contact with People's NAs.[37] Thus, the seven propagandists of the office in Tonghŭng village were each charged with contacting two People's NAs daily. Beyond these daily contacts, the office was also linked to People's NAs and to the village PC through the crossover of personnel. As shown in table 7.1, the office was managed by members of the village PC, and among the propagandists who provided the People's NAs with political materials was an NA head.

People's NA heads received political information from propagandists, who acquired their information from political enlightenment programs offered by the village or the town at least once a month.[38]

Workers' Party cells and various leagues for women, youths, peasants, and workers also offered beginner, intermediate, and advanced enlightenment courses to their members. Thus, a propagandist who belonged to one or more of these organizations most likely took additional political courses each month. After completing these political training courses, propagandists were expected to communicate what they learned to NA heads, who in turn were responsible for passing along the information to member households.[39]

Beyond relaying these political lessons, People's NAs were mobilized for mass political rallies. For example, on May 6, 1947, a mass rally was scheduled to take place at Tonghŭng school. The theme of the rally was the April 1947 letter exchange between US secretary of state George Marshall and the USSR's foreign minister, Vyacheslav Molotov. The letter garnered the attention of the NKPC, because it signaled the possible resumption of negotiations by the US–USSR Joint Commission. In preparation for the rally, the May 1947 edition of the monthly handbook for propagandists included a refresher course on the Moscow Agreement signed by the US, the USSR, and Great Britain in December 1945.[40] As noted in chapter 4, the agreement had placed Korea under a four-power trusteeship for a period of five years and established the US–USSR Joint Commission to make recommendations for creating a single Korean government. However, talks were indefinitely adjourned on May 6, 1946, because US authorities wanted to include in the consultation rightist groups that had objected to the trusteeship and Soviet authorities wanted to exclude groups that were against the Moscow Agreement. To express popular support for the resumption of negotiations, Yŏnp'o town planned mass rallies and ordered the villages to utilize People's NAs to mobilize at least a few hundred people to attend the rally.[41] Since the NKPC did not have official recognition under the US–USSR occupation, mobilizing People's NAs provided a means of demonstrating popular support for the resumption of talks and for the NKPC as the legitimate national governing body.

Despite popular support for the resumption of negotiations, the commission once again failed to reach an agreement, and on September 17, 1947, the United States brought the Korea issue before the United Nations, where the United States and the Soviet Union, as discussed in chapter 4, put forward two very different plans for creating a single

Korean government. Against the backdrop of this clash between US and Soviet officials, the propagandist handbook expressed support for the Soviet position, whereby US and Soviet troops would immediately withdraw, leaving the decision of how Korea would be governed to Koreans.[42] Soon, the propaganda office in Tonghŭng informed People's NAs that it would hold an emergency roundtable talk on the Korea issue. On September 26, seventy-one men, ninety-two women, and fourteen discussants attended the roundtable.[43] Although sources are silent on the roundtable's final resolution, given that the materials for the event were provided by NKPC, it is safe to assume that the roundtable declared its support for the Soviet position.

The People's NAs of Tonghŭng village held regular biweekly reading sessions (*tokbohoe*).[44] Based on the guidelines for these sessions, either a propaganda office staff member or an NA head led these meetings. If neither was available, the local cell of the Workers' Party would dispatch someone to lead the reading session.[45] Using *Rodong sinmun,* the newspaper of the Workers' Party, as the primary text for the meeting, a leader would read aloud news articles and editorials to People's NA members.[46] If an article was long or addressed complicated themes, the leader would summarize the article, rather than reading the full text. In general, the reading sessions lasted thirty to forty minutes, including the time budgeted for questions and answers.[47] Since the newspaper chosen represented the Workers' Party perspective, it was the perspective with which locals became most familiar; in turn, this increased the populace's receptivity to the Workers' Party in general. For this reason, the reading sessions were deemed a "militant weapon in agitating the masses of people," in that the sessions invoked patriotism, sparked popular support for the Workers' Party, and strengthened the political legitimacy of the NKPC vis-à-vis its competitor in southern Korea.[48]

While the regular reading sessions created the impression that the views of the Workers' Party were normative, the strong organizational ties between the party, People's NAs, and the propaganda office in Tonghŭng village also impacted the populace's favorable reception of the party. As of October 1947, 70 percent of NA heads in the village belonged to the party, and four out of five propagandists held party membership.[49] The high percentage of party members at the local level reflected the party's grassroots strategy to recruit the masses. In addition to sponsoring political enlightenment activities, its local branches were advised to assign one party member to every propaganda office and encourage the formation of party microcells within People's NAs.[50] NA heads should also be recruited to the party, so that they could serve as mediators between the party and locals. After each monthly NA meeting, the recruited NA heads were expected to provide the local party leader with a report.[51] These NA heads attended the regular local party meetings, along with party members who belonged to the village PCs, the Peasant Alliance, the Women's Alliance, the Occupation Alliance, and so on.[52]

The endless activities promoted by the propaganda alliance soon made clear that "voluntary" NAs were a de facto part of the government apparatus, as was apparent in the job list given the heads of NAs in Tonghŭng village:

1. Be prepared to do spring sowing, to make plans for the communal use of animal power, and to organize the labor network.
2. Discuss how to increase agricultural and fertilizer production.
3. Discuss how to achieve the people's economic plan advanced by the government.
4. Do daily cleaning to prevent contagious disease.
5. Raise a national flag on national holidays.
6. Encourage people to pay tax.
7. Drive out profiteers, gangs, and idle people.
8. Prevent fires and robberies, ban gambling, and take loving care of national assets.
9. Boost savings.
10. Cooperate always with other social organizations.
11. Hold biweekly reading sessions to promote mass enlightenment.
12. Conduct mass propaganda.
13. Collect tax-in-kind payments.[53]

The list clearly shows that People's NAs were deeply involved in carrying out government policy on farming, administration, mass enlightenment, propaganda, and local security. The broad range of jobs assigned NAs were orchestrated through the propaganda office and the village PC.

PARTICIPATORY ADMINISTRATION: MASS CAMPAIGNS FOR INCOME TAX COLLECTION

The patriotism cultivated in People's NAs became the vehicle through which the government inspired Koreans to participate in building a people's economy. The phrase "a people's economy" encapsulated the model of economic development advanced by the NKPC. Under this model, people could own land and develop private business enterprises. State intervention in the economy was directed toward preventing a resurgence of the structural inequalities that under Japanese imperialism had allowed a few to profit at the expense of the masses. To this end, in 1946, the NKPPC instituted land reform, nationalized the existing industries in the North, and abolished the colonial wartime policy that required Koreans wanting to start a business to obtain a permit from the Government-General. These policies, extremely popular among peasants and workers, went largely unchallenged, but they created a significant administrative challenge for the NKPPC with reference to collecting income taxes. The North's answer to this problem entailed launching voluntary patriotic mass campaigns to collect taxes.

Taxes-In-Kind in Rural Areas

The photograph below (see figure 7.1), captioned "The peasants of Kwan'u village in the Ch'ŏrwŏn County of Kang'wŏn celebrating tax-in-kind of rice," shows a festive milieu. In the photograph, taken in front of a train station on October 17, 1946, the people are seen waving flags and holding up giant posters with Kim Il Sung's image. A musical band is playing, and a cow is seen in the backdrop carrying a heavy load of rice. A note beneath the picture explains that despite having not yet received their tax-in-kind bill, the men and women are voluntarily bringing their payments of rice for transport to the warehouses of Ch'ŏrwŏn County PC. The message is clear: the villagers have organized a voluntary patriotic campaign to pay the taxes that they owe the state.

The move to taxes-in-kind began in July 1946 with the announcement "On the Enactment of Tax-in-Kind on Agricultural Produce." At the time, land reform was nearing completion. The new regulation

FIGURE 7.1. A mass rally for tax-in-kind. RG 242, SA 2010, box 863, photo album (Sajinch'ŏp 3jong). Courtesy of the NARA.

abolished colonial land taxes and introduced instead an agricultural tax-in-kind, set at 25 percent of all grain output. It also stipulated that there should be no quasi taxations, such as the requisition or forced purchase of grain that had been imposed on Korean farmers under Japanese rule. The new tax-in-kind was applied to spring crops harvested between July and August 1946 and to autumn crops harvested between November and December 1946. Towns and villages were told to make residents aware of the tax-in-kind, institute administrative measures for the immediate collection of taxes-in-kind for the spring harvest, and find warehouses for storing the collected crops.[54]

At first glance, the introduction of a tax-in-kind on agricultural produce seems like a return to an outdated practice, that is, to a pre-monetary system of taxation. As in the South, the NKPPC wanted to eliminate the remaining vestiges of the colonial economy. However, it worried that abruptly ending all colonial wartime regulations would lead to rampant inflation. Collection of taxes-in-kind allowed the government to redistribute collected grain to factory and office workers in urban areas, while at the same time allowing farmers to sell any surplus grain in a free market.[55] This strategy, in fact, allowed the North to avoid the inflationary crisis experienced in the South (see chapter 4).

The assessment and collection of a tax-in-kind were procedurally complex. Calculating the exact amount that each farming household should pay required extensive knowledge about the land each household owned. In particular, the government needed to know the size, location, crops, and average output of each farm. To obtain this information, the North needed a system that allowed government authorities to inspect the quantity and quality of agricultural output. It also needed secure warehouses for storing large stockpiles of grain and vehicles for transporting collected grain. To facilitate the harvesting of grains and the collection of taxes-in-kind, the North mobilized People's NAs, traditional communal networks of labor, and various youth and peasant leagues. It recommended pooling the community's draft animals for harvesting and delivering grain to collection points. Finally, it took advantage of People's NA meetings to hold community discussions about land size, crops, and agricultural output to ensure an equitable tax arrangement for households.[56]

The collection of taxes-in-kind was further complicated in some areas, such as Inje County, by the arbitrary division of Korea at the thirty-eighth parallel. Kangwŏn Province, to which Inje County belonged, was divided between the North and the South. Inje County belonged to the North, while the provincial capital fell within the borders of the South. This arrangement meant that the North lost access to administrative documents for Inje County and faced the daunting task of recreating them.[57] Its proximity to the South facilitated illegal cross-border trading as well as defections to the South. Such illicit movements of goods and people made it difficult for the North to assemble reliable statistical data on the county for taxing purposes.[58] Introducing the tax-in-kind in Inje County was also hampered by a flood of propaganda from the South criticizing the new tax; its geographic proximity to the South meant that officials from the North had difficulty blocking the distribution of such materials.[59] To tackle these obstacles, the county promoted collaboration between People's NA heads and local Workers' Party cells; working together, their job was to encourage voluntarism, that is, a willingness on the part of the people to comply with the tax-in-kind for the sake of building a people's economy.

The Sang'dap cell of the Workers' Party, associated with North village in Inje County, canvassed the Sixth, Seventh, and Eighth People's NAs of the village, which in total comprised sixty-six households.[60] Since all three People's NAs, heads—Yi Chun-gwŏn, Kim Sŏng-bong, and Wŏn Chong-su—were Workers' Party members, they attended the regular cell meeting held bimonthly at a member's house. At the cell meeting, representatives of the Peasant Alliance, the propaganda office, and the Self-Defense League were present. In early October, the cell organized the three NAs into four groups for the purposes of harvesting grain and collecting the tax-in-kind. One group was responsible for threshing, another for the postthreshing inspection, another for mobilizing NA members as well as other NAs, and a fourth group for transportation. Headman Wŏn was placed in charge of threshing, headmen Yi and Kim were assigned to inspections, and all NA heads were involved in transportation.[61] In addition to mobilizing the NA heads, the party cell allocated six straw bags for packaging grain to each household in every People's NA and asked each NA to organize its own collective work groups for barley seeding.[62]

Once harvesting commenced, the Campaign for Full Payment of Tax-in-Kind (*Hyŏnmulse wannap undong*) was launched; this was a competitive campaign in which People's NAs and villages competed against each other. After NA members threshed, winnowed, and dried grain, and packaged it in straw bags, the people in charge of transportation carried the bags to the designated collection points. In Sinwŏl village in Inje County, 125 peasants formed two lines to deliver approximately 5,280 kilograms of barley in one day alone; at the front of the line, a national flag was displayed.[63] Under a banner that read, "Peasants: Repay the Victory of Land Reform with the Full Payment of Tax-in-Kind," the Women's Alliance served tea and snacks, and elderly women ran a temporary nursery.[64] Once all grain had been transported, the propaganda office's staff compiled statistical data on the tax collection that was posted on the wall of the propaganda office for all to see.[65] Thus, each People's NA could see where it stood in relation to the other NAs in the village. The idea was to motivate and/or shame low-performing NAs so that they would try to improve their numbers.

In 1947, this competition-based campaign for collecting taxes-in-kind was repeated. Productivity was 200 percent higher than in the previous year, and the amount of grain collected for the tax-in-kind was 175 percent greater than that from spring 1946.[66] Although a flood in early August disrupted the harvest and delayed transport of agricultural products to collection centers, Inje County—with the exception of potatoes, which had been hard hit by the flood—met its quota for the tax-in-kind collection by the end of August.[67] In recognition of their contribution to the campaign, several of the NA heads received the title of "exemplary peasant."[68]

After paying the tax-in-kind, People's NAs urged peasants to donate their surplus rice to the Patriotic Rice Donation Campaign or sell it to consumers' cooperatives rather than to private wholesalers. Since it was prohibited to require any contribution beyond the tax-in-kind, NA heads encouraged voluntary participation by repeatedly reminding members of the debt they owed the state for introducing land reform.[69] They also promised that patriotic participation would be rewarded with preferential access to public stores where daily essentials were sold. Donated rice and grain were carried by a procession of peasants to the home of the NA head to be stored. As they walked there, the peasants chanted, "Save even a grain of rice and a scrap of thread, then donate them for state-building."[70] NA heads reported the amount of extra rice collected to town officials on the fifth day of each month.[71] Such patriotic donations in official reports were recorded with the phrase "The people have expressed their patriotic devotion for the task of building the state."[72]

Business Income Tax in Urban Areas

The North identified three types of income tax for urban areas: income tax paid by workers with permanent positions, business income tax, and income tax on day labor. On April 21, 1948, the chair of the North P'yŏng'an Provincial PC sent an official notice to Sŏnch'ŏn town requesting that People's NAs assist with tax assessment and collection. In the document, the chair expressed deep regret about the low rate of income tax collection for the first quarter in Sŏnch'ŏn. The town's collection rate for business income tax had been only 50 percent and 46.5 percent for income earned from day labor. The provincial government identified two reasons for the low collection rate. First, it blamed indiscriminate taxing—that is, the failure to consider residents' personal circumstances when assessing taxes owed. Second, it accused tax collectors of "rampant formalism." By this, the provincial government meant that rather than appealing to residents' patriotism and explaining how taxes contributed to building the people's economy, tax collectors relied on the same coercive techniques that had been used under Japanese imperialism. Involving People's NAs in the administration of taxes would allow the government to have more accurate information, thereby eliminating the problem of indiscriminate taxing. It would also allow the government to enlighten the people about why they should voluntarily pay taxes.[73]

In 1947, Sŏnch'ŏn town consisted of twenty-two villages and 27,317 residents. Its political loyalty was split between two parties: the Workers' Party with 1,966 members and the Democratic Party with 1,655 members. The divided political character of the town, which bordered China, was an outgrowth of its history. Under the colonial rule, the town had been a center of industrial and commercial development. As a result, workers accounted for roughly 33.5 percent of the population, while peasants accounted for only 9.1 percent. The strong presence of workers provided the Workers' Party with a strong foothold in the town. However, in the early twentieth century, the province in which Sŏnch'ŏn town was located was also the hub of a Presbyterian missionary group from the US. Thus, Christianity was the most popular religion in the town with 5,124 adherents. The second most popular religion, Cheondoism (Way of Heaven)—an indigenous Korean religion—had only 1,250 adherents, less than one-fourth those of Christianity. The town's large Christian community supported the Democratic Party led by the nationalist Cho Man-sik, as did the roughly 14.6 percent of the populace who made a living as merchants or craftsmen.[74] In the absence of an overwhelming majority, the Workers' Party struggled to meet the town's tax collection goals.

Once the use of People's NAs for tax collection was authorized, villages ordered NAs to have a regular meeting on the fifth day of each month.[75] At the meeting, NA heads gathered additional information on member households to ensure a fair tax assessment. They utilized the meetings to explain tax types, to confirm due dates, and to educate members on why paying taxes was important. NA heads were instructed to track the progress of tax collection and to encourage reluctant participants to voluntarily cooperate with tax collection. In 1948, just one year after involving People's NAs in the tax collection process, Sŏnch'ŏn town ranked number one nationally in tax collection.[76]

Despite its 1948 success, the following year the town designated the week of April 20–27 a special tax collection week. In November 1948, the NKPC replaced the colonial permit system with a business registration system. Under the new system, Koreans no longer needed to apply for a permit before starting a new business; instead, after establishing a new business, Koreans were supposed to register it with authorities. The North reasoned that since most large industries had been nationalized after liberation, allowing Koreans to start new small businesses was unlikely to reintroduce exploitive capitalist practices. It hoped that the resulting proliferation of small businesses would boost productivity levels. Sŏnch'ŏn town officials, however, feared that the upsurge in small business income would result in a comparable increase in tax evasion.[77]

To discourage tax evasion, Sŏnch'ŏn town launched a propaganda campaign to encourage businesses' voluntary cooperation with tax collection. At propaganda offices, in theaters, at train and bus stations, and in public squares, posters were hung encouraging business owners to pay their taxes. The guidelines for posters and other propaganda materials specified that every effort should be made to encourage voluntary compliance. Posters and leaflets should stress that the North, unlike colonial Korea, utilized tax monies to enrich culture and improve living conditions for the masses.

As previously, town officials also enlisted the help of NA heads. Appealing to members' patriotism and morality, NA heads encouraged business owners to provide the state with accurate information about income and to commit to paying their taxes by the due date. At the biweekly reading sessions, they devoted some time to answering questions about the new business registration law, as well as to explaining the town's concerns about tax evasion. As an example of immoral behavior, NA heads referenced merchants who started businesses but never registered them with the government to avoid paying taxes. Such unscrupulous business operators destroyed the reputation of virtuous merchants who provided the government with an accurate accounting of their profits and paid their taxes on time. People's NA heads warned members that businesses that failed to register would be forced to pay a penalty that was five times higher than the business registration fee.[78]

The propaganda campaign was followed by a competition-based tax campaign among People's NAs. At the local propaganda office, tax collection results were posted daily on the wall, and NA heads informed member households at the biweekly reading sessions of their current ranking in the competition. They visited households that had not yet made their tax payments. Following the final due date, a mass rally was held, in which NAs were arranged by their ranking in the tax collection. Town officials also bestowed praise upon nineteen People's NA heads for demonstrating their outstanding patriotism.[79]

THE KOREAN WAR: AIR RAIDS AND PSYCHOLOGICAL WARFARE

In 1950, the tension between NAs' official status as voluntary bodies engaged in mass campaigns and their de facto status as a state apparatus responsible for policy implementation was on display for all to see in Chaenyŏng County. The county in Hwanghae Province was home to 1,400 People's NAs. In February 1950, the county PC chair, O Hak-mo, concerned that some NAs responded with indifference to state projects, proposed a reform bill. Under the new bill, NAs' size would be reduced, and the position of vice head would be created so that NA heads would have a lighter workload. The chair believed that overworked NA heads were the primary reason that the spirit of voluntarism in some NAs was not as high as in others. To improve NAs' efficiency in implementing state policy, he also wanted to require People's NA heads to possess certain qualifications: credibility among residents, passion for local affairs, reading and writing skills, and experience in a political party or social group. Under his proposed reform, NA heads would need to attend village PC meetings regularly and hold NA gatherings on the fourteenth day and last day of each month. One day prior to these regular NA gatherings, village PCs should meet with NA heads to review assignments for People's NAs.[80]

This attempt to maintain the "voluntary" aspect of People's NAs while at the same time requiring them to collaborate with local PCs did not work well. By March, county officials noticed that village PCs were allocating administrative jobs to NAs and ordered them to stop. The county PC chair explained, "It is unfair to give an administrative command to People's NAs, because they are voluntary networks that assist with government actions; they are not part of the public administration."[81] However, such instructions did little to help People's NAs rekindle the spirit of voluntarism. Constant requests to participate in campaigns bred fatigue, and it became increasingly difficult for NAs to recapture the enthusiasm of earlier days. One campaign that pushed People's NAs to the limit was the county's construction project for May 1950. The county planned to stabilize riverbanks, build bridges, and dig wells. Since it lacked the financial resources to hire laborers, it needed volunteers to complete the projects and thus turned to People's NAs. The heads of People's NAs had to survey their available labor force and then contact individual households to notify them of the date and time they would be expected to work on the project. But these efforts were largely unsuccessful. In Sŏho town with the least cooperation, only 5.2 percent of those mobilized showed up for their work detail.[82]

The outbreak of the Korean War catalyzed this shift toward using People's NAs for administrative tasks. Although during the first months of the war, North Korean forces dominated on the ground, they quickly lost command of the air war once General Douglas MacArthur approved the proposal by George E. Stratemeyer, the commander of Far East Air Forces, to conduct strategic bombing campaigns against North Korea. Starting with the airstrike on the Pyongyang airfield by the Third Bombardment Group on June 29, US air forces launched a series of airstrikes on military targets, including harbors, major railways, oil refineries, supply centers, and steel mills in major cities, that devastated the North.[83]

Chaenyŏng County, located near the city of Sariwŏn—a major transport hub—was one of the targets of these airstrikes. Its railroads played a critical role in the transport of military supplies to cities in the west, such as Kaesŏng, Haeju, and Pyongyang. The county was also of strategic significance because of its iron mines and because it was a major food supplier for the North. But in early July 1950, US airstrikes damaged its railways and sparked fear among residents, as the bombing campaign brought home the reality of war.[84] In the wake of the airstrike, an immediate People's NA meeting was called to communicate new wartime regulations. Under the new regulations, private businesses, such as grocery stores, retail stores, restaurants, warehouses, bathhouses, laundries, and barbershops, were required to remain open; businesses wanting to close operations needed to receive permission from the government before doing so. In addition, residents were not allowed to travel outside the province unless they obtained a travel permit. Violators, the residents were warned, would be punished.[85] The new regulations also included mobilization orders for maintaining railways, bridges, highways, and factories.[86] An air defense brigade, consisting of five divisions—security, reconnaissance, firefighting, transportation, and hygiene—would need to be established immediately, the residents were informed, and People's NAs should comply with any orders issued by the brigade.[87]

As a result of US airstrikes, People's NAs reintroduced the air defense training that Patriotic NAs had provided the populace under wartime colonial rule. Part of this training included bomb shelter drills. However, when the NAs checked on the bomb shelters built during World War II, they discovered that many were severely damaged or flooded. Those shelters that had survived could only accommodate 60 to 70 percent of the population. Orders were issued to build new shelters, and the government distributed blueprints for several types of shelters or trenches. As shown in figure 7.2, the standard measurements for these shelters were 160 centimeters below ground and 70 centimeters wide, with two meters of stone or soil as cover. The county wanted People's NAs to build NA shelters as well as wanted families to build a simpler version of the shelter at their residences. Because many young men had been conscripted into the army, People's NAs were tasked with helping families that lacked sufficient labor force to build these residential shelters. Following airstrikes, NAs were also responsible for inspecting shelters to ensure their continued safety.[88] When bombings forced the closure of village markets in town centers, People's NAs relocated stored grain and military supplies to camouflaged warehouses or storage units in remote areas. Beyond building and maintaining bomb shelters, the populace was also reminded of the importance of adhering to blackout requirements. Smoking at night was prohibited and People's NAs teamed up with the Reconnaissance Division of the Air Defense Brigade to check that no lights from inside residences were detectable.[89]

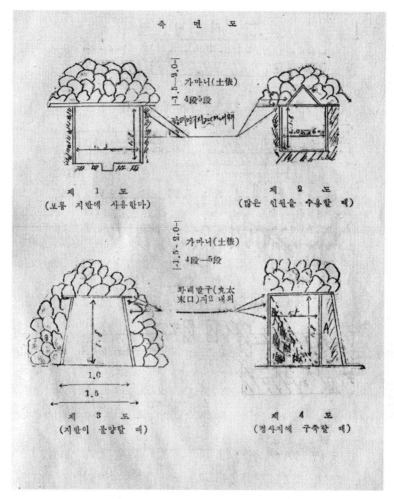

FIGURE 7.2.   Air raid shelters. RG 242, SA 2010, box 903, item no. 33, *A Booklet for Defense Training Leaders* (1950), 23. Courtesy of the NARA.

The North Korean government distributed to People's NAs pamphlets on air defense; these pamphlets provided information on identifying enemy aircraft, as well as on the different types of bombs used by the enemy and their destructive power. Armed with this information, NAs equipped themselves with water, sand, straw-woven bags, buckets, shovels, ladders, and first-aid supplies. They set up relief stations for the wounded and made sure that flammable materials were stored separately from other materials. Under the direction of the NA head, member households conducted firefighting drills. NAs were also encouraged to build relationships with neighboring NAs, so that if an NA was unable to extinguish a fire it could quickly contact the neighboring NA or the village's Air Defense Brigade for assistance.[90]

To enhance local security, on August 4, 1950, the county named a supervisor (*Inminban chidowŏnje*) for each People's NA. The Hwanghae provincial PC chair noted, "One of the most pressing tasks we must accomplish to strengthen our home front is to instill hostility toward the enemy and create an impregnable wall of patriotism."[91] The call to firm up the populace's patriotic resolve reflected the North's concern that the populace might succumb to the psychological warfare of South Korea and the US. Within twenty-four hours of President Truman announcing that US troops would come to the assistance of the South, a massive propaganda campaign had been launched. B-29 bombers dropped strategic propaganda deep behind enemy lines; frontline tactical propaganda was dropped by light bombers and spotter planes, or even fired from 105-millimeter howitzers. Each week, more than twenty million leaflets were being prepared and disseminated by UN forces. These propaganda leaflets varied in content: Some called on North Korean troops to surrender to UN forces. Others contrasted the political legitimacy of the South Korean government with the political illegitimacy of the North Korean government. Still others warned of the destruction that would be wrought by upcoming air raids.[92] It was the job of the new supervisors to stop the circulation of rumors in the neighborhood space that contributed to lowering public morale.

The introduction of supervisors tightened the relationship between People's NAs and the state apparatus. By the end of August 1950, 1,368 supervisors had been assigned to the 1,430 People's NAs of Chaenyŏng County. Of those, 942 were members of the Workers' Party and worked for the town or village PCs, the Peasant Alliance, the Women's Alliance, schools, or state-run companies.[93] Every other day, supervisors offered political lessons on the war's significance for international and Korean politics. They emphasized that the aim of the war was reuniting Korea and achieving the nation's independence from foreign occupiers. The

North Korean army, supervisors underscored, was well on its way to achieving victory. After these lessons and face-to-face meetings with residents, supervisors submitted reports detailing local morale and issues.[94]

PUBLIC IDENTIFICATION REGISTRATION: IN RETREAT AND POSTRECOVERY

Following the defeat at Inchon on September 15, 1950, the home front collapsed. On October 19, Pyongyang fell to the South, and the US–UN army forced North Korean troops to retreat toward the Chinese border. The South Korean government wanted immediately to impose its political order on the occupied territory—just as the North had done when it captured Seoul. However, the US–UN army argued that South Korean sovereignty should be confined to South Korea since the national election held in May 1948 had taken place only in the South. The South had no choice other than to comply, since US–UN forces had operational control over the war effort. The occupation proceeded according to stated UN objectives: maintain conditions of security throughout Korea and schedule national elections for the purposes of creating a united government. Until such time that a civil administrative plan could be put in place, the current governmental body was to remain in power.[95] However, the US–UN occupation lasted only fifty days. The Chinese Army entered the Korean War in mid-October and by December 4, 1950, US–UN forces had been forced to retreat from Pyongyang. Ten days later, they retreated from Hŭngnam, and by January 4, 1951, Seoul was back under North Korean control.

Once Hwanghae Province was back under North Korean control, it became apparent that Hunam town in Chang'yŏn County in Hwanghae had experienced a significant drop in population. Prior to occupation, approximately 8,300 people resided in Hunam; in January 1951, the number was 6,500. This 20 percent decline in population was accompanied by a reduction in the number of People's NAs from 136 to 110.[96] The population decline can be attributed to two causes. The first was political retaliation by the South; 30 percent of those killed during the occupation (266 out of 916) were members of the Workers' Party.[97] Their death seriously weakened the party's grip on the thirteen villages in Hunam town. In only two villages after the North regained control was the party able to maintain a cell.[98] In addition, only one PC chair belonged to the Workers' Party; seven had no party affiliation and five belonged to the Democratic Party.[99] The second reason was that middle-class peasants who supported the South had left the town, much as South Koreans who sympathized with the North had followed retreating North Korean troops.[100]

One of the first tasks pursued by town officials following the restoration of North Korean rule was investigating residents accused of collaborating with South Korea. Those "compelled by the enemy to join reactionary organizations" and those who had committed "minor errors" were not branded "collaborators."[101] Instead, the label "collaborator" was applied only to those found guilty of having willingly joined the pro–South Korean security forces or having worked for the occupiers in high-level positions. Individuals whose level of cooperation with the South met this standard forfeited their personal belongings, while the property of those who had defected was confiscated by the state.[102] In addition, Workers' Party members who destroyed their membership cards submitted statements of political conversion, or were subject to reeducation. The same held true for those who tried to shield from reprisal pro–South Korean residents who had protected them during the South Korean occupation of the North.[103]

People's NA heads were told to recreate the People's NA registry and the overnight-stay registry. The People's NA registry included information about the number of dwellings in the NA as well as information on member households, such as the age, gender, occupation, religion, and political affiliation of each person in the household.[104] The overnight-stay registry provided information on visitors, such as name, current address, occupation, and arrival and departure dates.[105] In addition to reporting this information to the local police as was the normal practice, NA heads tracked changes in population owing to the return of prisoners of war, completion of military service, and the influx of refugees from the South.[106] The reestablishment of the registries and their analysis was a necessary first step for restoring the public identification system (*kongminjŭng*) for those over eighteen years old and the birth certificate system for those under eighteen.

Rolled out on August 9, 1946, the system replaced the family registry that had been used to gather demographic information during
wartime colonial rule. For the North which viewed statistics are not
politically objective, the family registry was an instrument of colonial
oppression.[107] It had been used to allocate rations, coerce labor, and
forcibly conscript Koreans into the Japanese Army. Since the registry
discriminated against persons, such as orphans and illegitimate children,
who did not fall within the legal definition of family, it could not be rec-
onciled with the newly enacted Law regarding Equality between Men
and Women. The system had also proven inadequate for tracking the
movements of the populace resulting from urbanization and war. Thus,
to overcome these shortcomings, the North had abolished the registry
and issued public identification cards.

However, following the withdrawal of South Korean troops, officials
in Hunam town realized that almost half of residents over eighteen no
longer were in possession of their identification cards. The situation with
birth certificates was even worse; over half of those under eighteen did
not have a birth certificate.[108] Mismanagement and looting accounted
for roughly 90 percent of the missing cards. The other 10 percent of cards
had been deliberately destroyed by residents who feared that possession
of identification cards would make them more vulnerable to arrest by
the South Korean occupiers.[109] The missing identification cards disrupted the local administration, slowing the redistribution of farming
fields previously owned by those who had defected to the South, making it difficult to reassess productivity goals, and undermining the equitable rationing of fertilizer and consumer goods. Without accurate
information, the town could not process the claims submitted by
those whose lands had been damaged during air raids or reestablish the
communal networks responsible for seeding, tax-in-kind collection, air
raid training, and the local Self-Defense Force.

The town planned to issue temporary identification cards en bloc
from mid-July to mid-August 1951. On July 7, the town held an information session for People's NA heads, who would be responsible for
identifying those who needed temporary identification cards or birth
certificates.[110] Between July 10 and July 15, 1951, NA heads, in concert
with the propaganda office, posted notifications on streets, circulated
leaflets to member households, and held extra NA meetings to explain

the public identification policy. From July 15 to July 22, they double-checked the registries and inspected existing identification cards to ensure that all information was accurate and that the photos and town stamps on all identification cards met standards. Based on their findings, they created a final list of applicants for the temporary identification cards. NA heads made two copies of this list, one for archiving and the other for the local police. Applicants needed to get the signature of their People's NA head before submitting the required form to town officials. Those with identification cards were required to have the validity of their cards confirmed by the local police.[111] The rollout was a success; by August 1951, 95 percent of applicants had received their new temporary identification cards, and 1,880 existing identification cards had been inspected.[112] The temporary identification cards, which were valid for one year, were gradually replaced by permanent ones.

While People's NAs were promoting the public identification system, they were also preparing for US airstrikes. NAs were charged with repairing existing air raid shelters and building new ones. This task was urgent, given that Hunam town had only enough shelters to provide protection for 10 percent of the population, but the town was close to South Korea and near two cities that were major US targets, Sariwŏn and Haeju. Having learned, since the onset of war, the importance of shelters for preventing loss of life and preserving public documents, the town set aside a week in May 1951 to focus on the fortification of defense facilities. Two propagandists were dispatched to each NA to help mobilize member households for the task of building shelters and digging tunnels. NA heads held an extra meeting to allocate tasks to member households. However, the dislocation of war, combined with political conflicts during occupation, had undermined the social cohesion of People's NAs. The May fortification project failed to make substantial progress; the shelter capacity rose only to around 30 percent of the town's populace.[113]

By September 1951, however, the local government had restored order, and People's NAs were operating more efficiently. The number of air raid shelters built by People's NAs increased substantially, as did the number of underground warehouses. The grain that was collected as taxes-in-kind was secretly transported at night to these underground warehouses, which could each hold eight to sixteen tons.[114]

In February 1952, the Workers' Party held a conference to address problems of local administration, with local authorities in attendance. At the conference, party officials admonished town officers for assessing the tax-in-kind without factoring in a household's changed circumstances due to the war. They also criticized the town officers for pushing the populace too hard to meet the goals of economic campaigns and for excusing themselves from labor mobilizations. Such practices, party officials explained, were at odds with the socialist morality that the North sought to promote. Imbuing patriotic fervor required acknowledging the needs of the people so that they would willingly participate in the local administration. At the conference, it was concluded that the village was the ideal unit of local administration, rather than towns. The smaller size meant that village PCs were able to communicate directly with the people through People's NAs and to modify policies based on local circumstances.[115]

As the Workers' Party increasingly favored the village unit for local administration, the importance of the town unit, which had been strengthened under colonial rule, diminished until in November 1952, the town unit was removed from the administrative structure. Under the reformed local administrative system, the size of villages was enlarged, so that the number of villages dropped from 10,120 to 3,658. At the same time, the size of counties was reduced, which increased the number of counties from 89 to 168. To improve communication between county and village officials, each village was issued a motorcycle or horse to use for delivering official documents and newspapers in a timely fashion. Village PCs now came to have five to six full-time paid positions: village PC chair, general secretary, production manager, financial manager, tax collection manager, and propaganda office chair.[116] In the nongovernmental sector, People's NAs linked Village PCs to residents and assisted in tax collection, propaganda, production, and hygiene.

CONCLUSION

Following the liberation and division of Korea, leaders in the North wanted to convince Koreans that people's democracy provided a path forward that would benefit Koreans of all economic classes and political affiliations. They acted quickly to introduce a sweeping reform package aimed at constructing the political, economic, and social independence of Koreans that had been undermined and postponed by years of colonial rule. This reform package was augmented by a grassroots campaign to educate the people about people's democracy. Owing to their universal coverage, People's NAs offered a ready-made forum in which to explain people's democracy, cultivate familiarity with the Workers' Party, and implement government policy. Thus, rather than abolish Patriotic NAs, the North changed their name to People's NAs and introduced modifications to make them compatible with the new political order. People's NAs, unlike Patriotic NAs, recognized the political agency of the populace. Thus, rather than the apolitical moral patriotism of colonial rule, the patriotism promoted by NAs was directly linked to people's democracy. Only in a people's democracy, NA heads and propagandists explained, did patriotism serve the interests of the masses, rather than those of an exploitive elite class. Believing that the interests of the people and the interests of the state were in harmony in a people's democracy, North Korean leaders saw no need for a quasi-independent organization to mediate between the state and People's NAs. The people, once enlightened about how the state served their long-term interests, would voluntarily participate in state-building.

This strategy initially appeared successful; the people, appreciative of the reforms, embraced the early mass campaigns launched by the state. Both the voter education campaign and the 1946 tax-in-kind collection campaign achieved remarkable results. However, the spirit of voluntarism waned as increasingly it became apparent that People's NAs functioned as part of the state apparatus, rather than as a voluntary association of patriots. The decline in voluntarism accelerated with the onset of the Korean War; US airstrikes and wartime shortages of materials and labor prompted the government to rely more heavily on People's NAs to accomplish administrative tasks. Campaigns were launched that tasked People's NAs with building bomb shelters, repairing roads damaged by bombs, and fighting fires. Such campaigns exposed to the populace the continuity between People's NAs and Patriotic NAs, which had performed the same jobs under wartime colonial rule. As voluntary cooperation waned, local officials, like their colonial predecessors, increasingly relied on coercive techniques to meet campaign quotas. Although the government admonished local officials for failing to factor in local conditions when implementing state policies and introduced reforms intended to improve communication between the state and the people, the spirit of voluntarism, once lost, was difficult to rekindle.

CHAPTER 8

Into the Socialist Patriarchal Space

A People's NA head should be a mother to all members in a People's NA.[1]

In the 1960s, as indicated in the slogan above, female leadership of People's NAs had become the norm. While female leadership of NAs had been commonplace during Japanese imperial rule, following liberation, this trend was reversed in North Korea. Although there are no national statistics for the period from 1945 to 1953, there is anecdotal evidence suggesting the dominance of male NA leadership. In Tonghŭng village in Hamju County, all NA heads were male in 1948. When vice-heads were introduced in 1949, men continued to hold the vast majority of leadership positions; 90 percent of NA heads were men and 60 percent of vice heads were male.[2] Such resistance to female leadership in 1950 prompted O Hak-mo, chair of the Chaenyŏng County People's Committee, to advise all villages and towns in the county to start appointing qualified women as vice NA heads.[3] Yet after the Korean War, women reemerged as the primary leaders of People's NAs. This resurgence, I argue, was the result of two complementary ideologies introduced by the Workers' Party in the wake of the Korean War—Juche and the Great Red Family—aimed at mobilizing the population to transform North Korea from a people's democracy to a socialist state.

An estimated 8,700 factories, six hundred thousand houses, five thousand schools, one thousand medical facilities, 263 theaters, and thousands of cultural facilities had been damaged or destroyed during the Korean War by US airstrikes.[4] For Kim Il Sung, the tabula rasa created by war represented an opportunity to introduce a socialist order—that is, the collectivization of agriculture, national land planning, the relocation of production, and introduction of national housing. However, not all leaders in the party believed that North Korea was ready to make the transition to socialism. A power struggle ensued within the Workers' Party from which Kim Il Sung emerged victorious. Kim's opponents accused him of introducing a cult of personality in North Korea, whereas Kim accused them of slavish devotion to the Soviet model of socialism. As an alternative to the Soviet model, Kim put forward in 1955 Juche ideology—an indigenized form of socialism that emphasized revolutionary self-reliance. Juche provided the political rationale for his recovery program that emphasized the development of heavy industry, the introduction of agricultural cooperatives, and national land planning. However, Juche's strict focus on the political and economic sphere did not provide the ideological means to link the moral space of the neighborhood to the political sphere.

Needing to instill in North Koreans a socialist morality, the state turned to People's NAs. However, the war and the introduction of agricultural cooperatives had greatly weakened People's NAs. To revitalize People's NAs, the party needed a second ideology capable of restoring communal bonds and of enlisting every Korean in the effort to build communism. It was the Great Red Family, and in keeping with Juche's emphasis on incorporating Korean particularities, it drew on the image of the traditional Korean patriarchal family, including the gendered division of labor that made women responsible for the home and for children. The supreme patriarch of the Great Red Family that encompassed every Korean was Kim Il Sung, and women in their traditional role as educators and mothers became the primary leaders of the organized domestic sphere, that is, People's NAs. However, their educational responsibilities had changed; their new mission was to revolutionize families by eliminating idleness, frivolity, and outmoded ways of thinking. Socialist comradeship would replace individualism, thereby allowing the nation to achieve its economic and political goals.

Starting with the introduction of agricultural cooperatives, this chapter traces the economic and political transformations in postwar North Korean society that led NAs to become the central locus of moral authoritarianism and women its chief expounders. Unlike the colonial regime and the South Korean government, the North Korean government made no effort to maintain an artificial barrier between NAs and the political sphere. Instead, through the ideology of the Great Red Family, North Korean leaders seamlessly merged the political and moral realms.

AGRICULTURAL COOPERATIVES VERSUS PEOPLE'S NAs: A SHIFT IN THE BALANCE OF POWER

In 1958, when agricultural cooperativization was completed, local authorities in Ryongdong village in South Hwanghae Province observed a phenomenon that they found disturbing: People were no longer using the title "village people's committee (PC) chair." Instead, they referred to the village PC chair as the chair of the village agricultural cooperative management committee (*Hyŏptong nongjang kwalli wiwŏnjang*). Strictly speaking, the designation was valid since, as noted in figure 8.1, the same person held both positions. However, the two positions indicated two very different sets of responsibilities. This tendency to use one title to designate both positions, village officials worried, would create "the false impression that the cooperative's work brigades could take over [administrative] jobs performed by People's NAs."[5]

Village officials' concerns highlighted the growing tensions between People's NAs, which fell under the jurisdiction of village PC chairs, and work brigades, which answered to the village agricultural cooperative. Prior to the Korean War, People's NAs had exercised extensive authority in the neighborhood space. Owing to their association

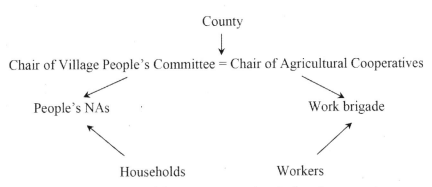

FIGURE 8.1. Village People's Committee and agricultural cooperatives

with village PCs and the propaganda office, they had played a leading role in launching mass enlightenment campaigns as well as been involved in tax and data collection. NA monthly gatherings had been used to educate people about the proper time for planting and to create collective planting schedules.[6] During the Korean War, they had built air raid shelters and provided labor for other wartime projects. But the introduction of cooperative agriculture after the war compromised the authority of People's NAs. Village agricultural cooperatives assumed responsibility for economic tasks, such as planting and harvesting, previously coordinated by NAs. As a result, work brigades now dominated rural life. As their power increased, they encroached on administrative jobs that remained the purview of People's NAs.

A primary cause for the debilitation of People's NAs was the introduction of agricultural cooperatives, the first step toward collectivized farming as part of post–Korean War recovery plans for the agricultural sector. While land reform in 1946 had eliminated the landlord class by confiscating and redistributing its lands to farmers, it had left untouched private ownership of the means of production. North Koreans could still own land and sell surplus grain on the free market after paying a 25 percent tax. The revised combination of land and labor inspired North Koreans to boost agricultural productivity. However, the Korean War had brought the peasant agricultural economy to the brink of collapse; total productivity dropped from 2,650,000 tons in 1949 to 2,260,000 tons in 1951.[7] Tensions between community members also developed, because some peasants took advantage of wartime devastation to advance their individual fortunes at the expense of their neighbors whose land had been damaged by airstrikes. While the war meant abject poverty for 40 percent of the peasantry, an estimated 0.4 percent of the peasantry amassed great wealth through usury and dishonest hiring practices that brought back bitter memories of landlordism under Japanese colonial rule.[8]

Reduced production rates, combined with increased poverty and usurious practices among the peasantry, alarmed leaders in the North. Worse yet, it was unlikely that the peasantry would rebound quickly from wartime devastation as the nation lacked the labor force, infrastructure, and agricultural equipment to rebuild. Five reservoirs had been hit by US airstrikes, flooding thousands of acres of farmland and laying waste to the essential food source for millions of people. Looming famine also had consequences for industrial production; it jeopardized the food supply for workers in urban areas, thus compromising their ability to do heavy labor. Faced with famine and economic ruin, support for introducing collective farming, which was believed to facilitate the concentration and rationalization of the labor force, as well as greater government control over industry, gained momentum among some political leaders.[9]

The transition to collective farming paralleled that taking place in China. In the wake of the establishment of the People's Republic of China in October 1949, Mao Zedong promoted land reform in 1950, to rectify the situation that an estimated 8–9 percent of landlords owned more than half of all land as of 1949. As it significantly boosted agricultural productivity, the Chinese government took a gradualist approach to collectivization. Between 1953 and 1956, peasants were encouraged to join one of three forms of cooperatives on a voluntary basis: "mutual-aid teams" made up of four or five neighboring households that pooled their labor, draft animals, and farm tools; "elementary cooperatives" in which twenty to thirty households combined their assets; or "advanced cooperatives," in which all means of production were collectivized. During this initial phase, most cooperatives were not "advanced cooperatives"; farmers retained ownership of land, livestock, and farming tools; and the cooperatives exercised only managerial authority. During the second phase (1956–1958), the Chinese government moved to transition all cooperatives to advanced cooperatives. Thus, while at the end of 1955, there were only 500 advanced cooperatives in China, by the end of 1957, there were 753,000 advanced cooperatives with 119 million member households.[10] This change in Chinese policy resulted from proponents of collectivization having won the intraparty debate on collectivization.

As in China, the proposal to introduce cooperative farming in North Korea triggered a contentious debate within the Workers' Party over the extent to which private ownership of land should be restricted. In 1953, some balked at the idea of rapid collectivization, arguing that the forces of production were not sufficiently mature to support full-scale socialism. A gradual phaseout of private property, rather than its complete elimination, was the appropriate next step for North Korea.[11] In the absence of consensus on rapid collectivization, a few experimental cooperatives were established in each county. However, no restrictions were placed on ownership of private property or on access to farming equipment for private farming.[12] Farming households impoverished by the war opted for the experimental program, which proved successful. In 1954, cooperatives outperformed private farms significantly, with productivity 10 to 50 percent higher and the income of participants two to seven times higher.[13]

The success of this pilot program was the tipping point; in fall 1954, the North promoted a mass campaign to establish agricultural cooperatives. Three types of agricultural cooperatives were proposed. The first type was defined as the most primitive form of rural socialism and consisted of roughly ten neighboring households. Work in this type of cooperative was to be done in common, but the land, draft animals, and farming implements remained under private ownership. In addition, each household retained control over what it produced. The second type was viewed as semisocialist. Farmers contributed their land and labor for common production; however, theoretically the land remained under their control. After the harvest, the cooperative deducted a certain proportion of the produce to cover production expenses and pay taxes-in-kind. The remainder of the harvest was then divided based on the amount of land and labor each household contributed to the collective endeavor. The third type was completely socialist in form, and distribution of the harvest after deductions was based solely on the number of days of labor each household contributed.[14]

To allay widespread fears that joining a cooperative would result in loss of private property, the government ordered the Agriculture Ministry to introduce a Rule of Agricultural Cooperatives no later than April 15, 1954. The rule guaranteed that peasants would retain ownership of their land if they chose to leave the cooperative. Propaganda leaflets explaining the different types of cooperatives as well as the Rule of Agricultural Cooperatives were distributed. To attract skeptical middle-class peasants whose cooperation was critical for the program's success, the North made clear that participants would receive preferential treatment when it came to receiving seed and livestock; they would also be allowed to rent irrigation pumps from the government and have preferential access to farming equipment and to consumer products at public stores.[15]

By the end of 1957, 18,032 cooperatives had been organized, and 95.8 percent of farming households belonged to the third type of cooperative. Production rates soared; North Korea reported a 112 percent increase in production over the previous year.[16] Motivated by these results, the government persuaded the remaining peasants to join, that is, wealthy peasants, peasants near cities who sold produce to urban people, and peasants in isolated areas. In August 1958, when the government declared that the mission to spread socialist cooperative farming had been completed, it changed the Rule of Agricultural Cooperatives so that those who left the cooperative could no longer withdraw their land from the cooperative.[17]

Cooperative ownership of land was an interim form of ownership between private and people's ownership (nationalization). Unlike industrial workers, employed in factories which had been nationalized shortly after liberation, cooperatives' members retained control over their management and dividends from the harvest belonged solely to cooperatives' members.[18] Still, this interim form of ownership sufficed to curb farmers' return to capitalist activities. After 1958, peasants who chose to leave the cooperative received only the wages owed them for labor; they forfeited any land, livestock, and equipment that they had contributed to the cooperative. The cooperative also had the power to expel members for engaging in prohibited profit-oriented activities.[19] Although members still could retain 100 to 165 square meters of land, a few pigs, some chickens, and small tools for private farming, these approved resources were insufficient to generate a viable income. In short, the cooperative system made each household dependent on the cooperative's success for its economic survival.

To increase the administrative efficiency of cooperatives and mobilize labor on a larger scale, the government made the rule One Cooperative for One Village in October 1958. Rather than each village having multiple small cooperatives consisting of ten to thirty households, each village now had only one cooperative made up of eighty to three hundred households from which local officials collected taxes and acquired census data. The rule drastically reduced the number of cooperatives from 18,032 in 1957 to 3,843 in 1958. The amount of arable land each cooperative farm controlled increased on average from 1,289,262 to 4,958,700 square meters.[20] Here too, North Korean policy closely paralleled policies being implemented in China, where 753,000 agricultural cooperatives were merged into 24,000 People's Communes as part of the Great Leap Forward movement from 1958 to 1962.[21] In both cases, the creation of larger cooperatives in line with government administrative units was intended to boost production by resolving the problem of mobilizing labor for large projects such as building irrigation canals and dams and maximizing the use of available farming equipment. Overcoming low productivity was a basic prerequisite for a socialist society.[22]

The North Korean government also took steps to streamline local economic networks. Local credit cooperatives and village consumer goods cooperatives were placed under the supervision of agricultural cooperatives. In October 1958, village PC chairs assumed responsibility for supervising the management committees of their agricultural cooperatives. Made up of fifteen to twenty-two members, the management committee was in charge of developing a plan for production, organizing work brigades, assigning tasks to work brigades, and coordinating the harvest.[23] After taking into consideration each member's skill sets, the size of fields, the types of work that needed to be done, and commuting distance for members, the management committee set up work brigades and appointed leaders. Each work brigade leader was required to report regularly to the management committee chair about the daily activities of the group and assumed full responsibility for ensuring that the group met the work quota.[24]

Since the village PC chair was also the chair of the management committee, the duties associated with each respective position became increasingly difficult to discern, especially in the context of mobilizing the populace for national campaigns. The village PC chair had authority over People's NAs; when a national campaign was announced, it was the PC chair's responsibility to coordinate the voluntary mobilization of People's NAs. However, because it was the responsibility of every institution, regardless of official function, to support the national government, the chair in his or her capacity as chair of the cooperative management committee also mobilized work brigades.[25]

The mobilization of both groups—People's NAs and work brigades—for campaigns fueled the populace's confusion about the role of People's NAs versus that of work brigades. The Rule of Agricultural Cooperatives obliged cooperatives to care for the cultural facilities of a village, including schools, nurseries, medical centers, communal restaurants, communal laundry places, public baths, and barbershops.[26] Although technically such caretaking activities had little bearing on the daily economic activities of work brigades, the stipulation did provide a legal basis for involving them in administrative tasks. From the perspective of the PC chair needing to get work done, it made sense to use his or her authority as chair of the cooperative management committee to mobilize disciplined work brigades for such administrative tasks, rather than volunteer groups from People's NAs. Although NAs previously had been the only group with nationwide coverage, this was no longer the case, as most households now belonged to disciplined work brigades through membership in agricultural cooperatives or through their work in state-owned industries.

The superior discipline of work brigades meant that village authorities increasingly contacted cooperatives, rather than People's NAs, when they needed a labor force for irrigation, land reclamation, and construction projects. As work brigades displaced People's NAs, some villages no longer saw a need for People's NAs and abolished them. In other villages, it became apparent that village PC chairs were using their authority as chair of the cooperative management committee to make work brigades coextensive with People's NAs. In such cases, the head of the work brigade was also made the People's NA head. Those who did not belong to work brigades were forced into separate NAs. It became clear that NAs were now used only to mobilize individuals who did not belong to work brigades.[27]

As the axis of power tilted toward work brigades, People's NAs became divorced from the economic sector. With the abolition of private property and peasant agriculture, the individual household ceased to be the primary unit of agricultural production. As a result, cooperatives, rather than individual households, became the primary unit on which taxes-in-kind were levied.[28] In addition to losing their role in tax collection, People's NAs also ceased to be the government's primary source for collecting data. Since agricultural cooperatives were now responsible for planning and managing planting and harvesting, the county began obtaining agricultural statistics directly from cooperatives, bypassing village officials.[29] Cooperatives had become the center of village life, which was hence why villagers, as noted at the beginning of this chapter, unconsciously switched to calling the village PC chair by his or her other title, chair of the cooperative management committee, no matter the nature of their business.

NATIONAL LAND PLANNING:
THE PHYSICAL AND CULTURAL
TRANSFORMATION OF NORTH KOREA

The postwar recovery of the North prioritized large cities and prewar industrial centers over the rehabilitation of nonindustrial areas.[30] The first postwar Three-Year Recovery Plan (1953–1956) made Pyongyang, the capital of North Korea, which had been devastated by US airstrikes, a showcase of its recovery efforts. The rebuilding plans for Pyongyang, designated a cultural and industrial center, included large-scale housing projects, museums, public parks, theaters, retail shops, schools, and medical facilities. All new facilities would have state-supplied electricity and gas, as well as state-of-the-art plumbing systems. The Three-Year Recovery Plan also highlighted rebuilding heavy industries such as steel and iron, chemicals, machinery and equipment, shipbuilding, construction, and energy.[31]

By 1957, the recovery plan prioritizing urban areas had made substantial progress. However, the gap between urban and rural areas became more pronounced. Only 17.1 percent of the population lived in urban centers in 1957, while most of the population lived in rural communities, which the plan had left largely untouched.[32] Most rural communities still lacked access to electricity and mechanized equipment as well as hygienic and educational facilities. Farmers could not learn about modern farming techniques, and so they continued to rely on traditional farming methods. The use of such labor-intensive techniques placed severe limits on agricultural productivity, which the North Korean leadership realized would soon stymie the nation's development of heavy and light industry.[33] In addition, they feared that a benighted peasantry would derail the goal of creating a modern socialist state. An ignorant peasantry, they believed, remained superstitious and too attached to old-fashioned social customs. Thus, it lacked a sufficiently developed political consciousness to participate in a modern socialist state. A more balanced recovery plan was needed.[34]

To address developmental gaps that had resulted from the Three-Year Recovery Plan, the government changed the orientation of the new recovery plan introduced in 1957. The new plan placed greater emphasis on developing light industry in rural communities and on investing in mechanized farming to boost agricultural productivity. It also sought to improve hygienic and educational levels in rural areas so that the peasantry would have the knowledge and skill sets required for modern farming, a living standard comparable to that of urban workers, and sufficient political awareness to participate in building socialism. By maximizing the efficiency of agricultural cooperatives and eliminating labor-intensive farming techniques, the North would create a larger labor pool from which the government could draw to turn smaller cities into industrial centers.[35]

Having reduced private ownership of land through the introduction of agricultural cooperatives, the government was free to advance its national plan for land development. The Korean War had made North Korean leaders painfully aware of the disadvantages of concentrating industry in any one region. While the industrial concentration in coastal areas during the colonial period had facilitated trade with Japan, it had made industry an easy target for US airstrikes during wartime. In addition, because raw materials, such as coal, on which industries relied were located inland close to industrial sites, supply chains had quickly broken down under war conditions.[36] Thus, rather than simply clearing debris and rebuilding preexisting structures, the government wanted to "relocate productive capacity," that is, rebuild so that even if factories in one area were decapacitated due to war or natural disaster, it would not wipe out the nation's industrial capacity. The land management plan called for the construction of small factories, especially light industry facilities, throughout the country. These facilities, which would produce consumer goods, required less expertise to build than heavy industry facilities and were much less expensive to construct. The government advised local officials to base the development of local industries on resources in the area. For example, if an area produces wheat, they should consider building a noodle factory; an area in which fishing is the primary source of income should develop fish canneries, and so on. Utilizing local materials and the volunteer labor of work brigades, light industrial facilities could be built without significant investment from the national government. The shortened supply chain would save money, and the dispersal of industry across North Korea would reduce recovery time in the event of airstrikes or natural disaster.[37]

The government chose the county as the local administrative unit best suited for economic self-sufficiency. In 1945, North Korea had eighty-nine counties, but their large size was viewed as an impediment to effective management. So, in 1952, the government rezoned to reduce the size of counties.[38] By the late 1950s, North Korea had 140 counties, and the government decided to make counties economic hubs for trade and cultural exchange. Because a county's size corresponded roughly to the distance that its inhabitants could travel in one day, agricultural goods from agricultural cooperatives could easily be transported to non-agricultural areas within the county and consumer products transported back to the cooperatives.[39] The minimal distance could also be used to encourage cultural exchanges between the urban working class and the peasantry. Through these interactions and through exposure to the city center, an exemplar of modern socialist culture, it was hoped that the peasantry would be inspired to embrace reforms directed at ending traditional rural practices.[40]

In October 1957, the government launched a national construction drive focused on building residential housing both in urban centers and in villages. The National Construction Commission, established in June 1953 to oversee rebuilding efforts and train architects and engineers, published blueprints for housing that were distributed to counties nationwide. By the end of 1957, the commission had provided ten basic blueprints for building public baths, libraries, residential buildings, and schools, as well as a manual on construction techniques.[41] For urban areas, the goal was to minimize the distance that workers had to commute to reach their place of employment. To achieve this goal, workers' districts were created in which workers would live and work. Each district would also have educational and medical facilities, as well as retail shops that would carry everyday essentials.[42] In the case of villages, village PC chairs were told to collaborate with village cooperatives; a map of the village and a plan for building housing and public facilities were to be submitted to the commission by October 1958. The provincial government was charged with securing building material as well as with arranging for building experts to visit villages to teach construction skills. Agricultural cooperatives were urged to invest their profits in the renovation effort as well as transport work brigades to construction sites so that they could participate in construction.[43]

The push to build housing was a major focus of local development. Between 1957 and 1960, 150,000 houses were built; that number increased to 800,000 between 1961 and 1967.[44] The vast majority of these houses were "culture houses" (*munhwa chut'aek*), small, prefabricated modern structures that could be quickly assembled.[45] By 1957, the North Korean leadership was confident that it had eliminated from all economic sectors the capitalist mode of production based on private ownership. However, as with ideology and technological know-how, it believed that additional efforts were needed in the realm of culture to complete the transition to socialism. For the leadership, cultural development required the introduction of modern, hygienic housing as well as supporting public facilities—such as libraries, nurseries, public laundries, and spaces for music, film, and sport—in residential areas.[46] The construction of culture houses was seen as a crucial step in narrowing the gap between the countryside and urban centers. The new homes would transform the worn-out appearance of the countryside, improve hygienic conditions, and eliminate backward modes of living and antiquated customs.[47]

Culture houses were not an invention of the socialist regime. They had been introduced in colonial Korea in the 1920s. Although stylistically these homes fused traditional Japanese and Korean architectural features with modern Western architectural elements, the primary emphasis was on breaking with tradition and embracing modernity. The homes typically were two-story structures equipped with amenities such as electricity, modern plumbing, and a heating apparatus. Because such homes were expensive, only the upper-middle class could afford them.[48]

Just like culture houses during the colonial period, the North Korean version of culture houses aimed at modernizing Korean society. Divorced from their previous association with so-called Western and upper-middle-class values, however, they were defined as the houses with "socialist content within a nationalist format."[49] The socialist content, as noted earlier, centered on being intended for the masses and reducing the distance between work and residences. While introducing more modern, hygienic features, the new structures incorporated many traditional features to which the populace remained attached. For example, for residential areas, the North chose south-facing sites that backed up to small mountains or hills. Each house had a traditional underfloor heating system called an *ondol* as well as used traditional rafters and roof tiling. To increase speed of building, a standard floor plan that allowed for some basic modifications, based on regional conditions such as climate and industries, was used.[50]

As the state-led drive to build residential housing progressed, the number of privately owned houses diminished, although in principle private home ownership was not impacted by the introduction of agricultural cooperatives or the people's ownership of industry. That said, an estimated 600,000 homes had been reduced to rubble, and another 140,000 homes had been irreparably damaged, during the Korean War. Against the backdrop of the postwar labor shortage and cash crunch, few households had the means to repair or reconstruct damaged homes. Thus, most North Koreans opted to sell their damaged homes to the government. The government repaired or rebuilt the homes, which were then allocated to workers or public officials for use.[51] In addition, once cooperatives were established, homes that were located on arable farmland, irrespective of their condition, were demolished to make way for cultivation, and their inhabitants relocated to culture house sites built at the base of mountains.[52] Finally, the North placed all privately owned houses on the government's management list; in making this move, North Korean leaders stressed the government's role as caretaker of the people and their property. In 1964, Kim Il Sung explained, "All houses belong to the socialist working class even if some of them are still privately owned."[53]

By the 1960s, the state-led housing construction drive and accompanying nationalization of housing had made substantial progress. As a result, the question of who was responsible for maintaining culture homes and public facilities became an important issue. Government officials often complained, "People are taking care of lands and resources, although these belong to the government, but no one takes responsibility for houses."[54] The government reminded the populace that culture houses and public buildings had greatly enhanced their daily lives, and so the people must develop a sense of pride in their common ownership of national property. The responsibility for maintaining the new facilities that the government had provided belonged to them.[55] The message was clear; if local inhabitants did not cultivate a socialist ethic—that is, a communal mentality of shared responsibility or local patriotism—the cultured (or civilized) life introduced by the government would collapse.

As voluntary associations of patriotic residents, People's NAs seemed the ideal organizations for advancing this moral approach to maintaining culture houses and public buildings. However, most People's NAs lacked the cohesiveness required to maintain them. The ties between members of People's NAs had been weakened by the introduction of co-operatives, which had taken over production-related activities previously performed by People's NAs. These neighborly bonds were further undermined by demographic shifts that began during the Korean War and continued after the war in the context of the postwar construction boom and the shift to cooperative farming. For example, the postwar migration from rural to urban areas meant that many Koreans did not yet know their neighbors very well and so did not feel a strong sense of attachment to the People's NAs with which they were affiliated. Moreover, because the balance of power had shifted to cooperatives, little attention had been paid to inculcating the socialist ethic in People's NAs. Given the novelty of meeting socialist standards, People's NAs faltered in the face of these new responsibilities.

In contrast, the work brigades, established by cooperatives, were well organized, disciplined, and had received extensive socialist indoctrination. However, giving workers' groups primary responsibility for maintaining buildings was not a viable solution, as time spent on building maintenance would distract from efforts to increase productivity. Moreover, placing work brigades in charge of building maintenance would exclude groups, such as housewives, students, and old people, who ostensibly had more time for such activities than already overburdened workers. For that reason, local officials were pressured to revitalize

People's NAs by creating the necessary communal milieu. They were also advised to reestablish People's NAs as a realm of action independent of work brigades.

The 199th and 200th People's NAs in Kilju town of North Hamgyŏng Province became a model of how the relationship between People's NAs and work brigades could be resolved to the benefit of both. Sim Sang-t'ae, a member of the 199th People's NA, worked for the Forestry Ministry. The members of his work brigade largely belonged to one of the two People's NAs named above. One day at work, a Workers' Party official informed him that his People's NA was no longer functioning properly; it had stagnated. This situation, the official opined, was particularly grievous, given that most members of his NA belonged to exemplary work brigades. Recognizing that his new apartment complex had dirt piles and mud puddles that no one bothered to clean and that quarrels sometimes erupted between housewives, he conceded the point and decided to act. Sim enlisted Kim Han-kyu, a member of his work brigade, to help him identify the causes of stagnation in the two NAs and to devise a solution.[56]

Sim and Kim attributed the stagnation of the two people's NAs to two interrelated factors: heads of household no longer showed interest in People's NAs, because they were so focused on their work brigade jobs, and too few residents were willing to take responsibility for building maintenance. To overcome the first cause of stagnation, Sim and Kim tried to get household heads to take a keener interest in People's NAs by reminding them of the link between work brigades and People's NAs. At the same time, to prevent residents from thinking that People's NAs answered to work brigades, they tried to discourage heads of household with leadership positions in work brigades from assuming comparable positions in People's NAs.[57]

Because within People's NAs there was an unspoken three-tier hierarchy, Sim and Kim arranged to meet with each group—male heads of household; adult women, including female NA leaders; and all remaining members, such as children, adolescents, and the elderly. At the meeting with male heads of household, they assigned jobs to each as members. To ensure that the male household heads remained committed to their jobs in the People's NAs, Sim and Kim decided to include these jobs in the work brigade's monthly assessment. This strategy ensured that household heads assumed a leading role in morning cleanings and in launching the campaign "Help out by doing more than one thing every week."[58]

After meeting with the male household heads, Sim and Kim met with female leaders in the NA, to teach them how to make detailed work schedules and create job-sharing networks within the NA. To reinforce the crucial role of People's NAs in the socialist order and the important role that women played in that order, they organized a reading group for housewives and introduced the housewives to Kim Il Sung's 1961 speech on the role of mothers in a socialist society. Then, Sim held the first general meeting of the People's NAs at which residents discussed neighborhood issues and allocated assignments to everyone from the children to the elderly. Afterward, they made it a rule to have a communal cleaning early every morning.[59]

Sim and Kim took steps to advance socialist enlightenment and national patriotism. They opened a reading room, where members could read Kim Il Sung's speeches and stories about anti-Japanese partisans and past patriots. Every fortnight, they held a two-hour reading group at which politics was discussed; a reading group was also established for the elderly, who found political discussions difficult to follow and boring. To encourage reading, they asked residents, whenever they traveled for business or to the county center, to secure new books. The various reading groups generated solidarity among neighbors, normalized regular gatherings, and created enthusiasm for the activities of People's NAs. Lastly, Sim organized outings for the two People's NAs. On film day, hosted by the planning office, the two People's NAs viewed films together and made small talk. The formation of strong community bonds led the two NAs to organize a singing and dance club that competed in a county competition.[60]

The 199th and 200th People's NAs were recognized by the province of North Hamgyŏng for their exceptional work in promoting socialist culture.[61] Their story of revitalization embodied the role that the North had envisioned People's NAs playing in the socialist order. While work brigades focused on improving economic productivity, People's NAs advanced the cultural values necessary to turn Patriotic NAs into happy red families, characterized by mutual trust, strong communal bonds, and a socialist work ethic.

COMPLEMENTARY IDEOLOGIES: JUCHE
AND THE GREAT RED FAMILY

In the 1960s, it was commonplace to liken People's NAs and village PCs to family relationships. A People's NA was a red family, and a village PC chair was its patriarch. Expressions such as "a village PC chair is a patriarch (*hoju*) taking care of people's lives" and "a village PC chair should be a true patriarch in a socialist society" were found in official parlance.[62] However, the use of the term "patriarch" marked a sharp departure from the North's previous policy. Prior to transitioning to full socialism, the North, as a people's democracy, had viewed traditional family structures as a vestige of feudalism and as a primary source of gender inequality. In 1946, a people's democratic North had replaced the family registry—a system of identification that reinforced traditional gender roles and patriarchal authority—with a new public identification system (*kongminjŭng*). In lieu of "patriarch" (*hoju*), the new identification system used the term "household head" (*sedaeju*) to designate a family representative. Now, though the North took steps to transition to a more advanced stage of socialism, it reintroduced the patriarchal family word, which according to Marxism was an integral part of capitalism.

Central to this blending of socialism with patriarchy was Juche (subjectivity) ideology—an indigenized form of socialism that became the official ideology of North Korea. Its introduction was an outgrowth of Kim Il Sung's crisis of authority in the mid-1950s. During the early stages of the Korean War, when North Korean troops were making substantial advances, the Workers' Party had granted him extensive authority. However, as the damages from US bombings mounted and war fatigue set in, some began questioning his leadership. This internal rift within the party was laid bare when in March 1953 key party figures, including Pak Hŏn-yŏng, Li Sŭng-yŏp, Rim Hwa, and Yi Kang-guk, were arrested on suspicion of being US spies. On July 2, 1953, Hŏ Ka-i, the leader of the Soviet faction—Soviet citizens of Korean ethnicity who had returned to Korea following liberation—was found dead shortly after defending the accused.

The cease-fire on July 27, 1953, did not ameliorate tensions within the Workers' Party. Party members remained divided on whether North Korea should advocate for transitioning from being a people's democracy to a socialist state. To stanch internal conflicts, at the plenary meeting in August 1953 the party advanced the slogan "Everything for the postwar recovery of the people's economy and its development."[63] The implicit message of the slogan was that North Korea would remain a people's democracy for at least three more years—the estimated time it would take for the nation to reach prewar productivity levels.

The calm did not last long; Kim Il Sung's insistence on prioritizing the development of heavy industry over light industry, his support for introducing agricultural cooperatives, and his demands that more restrictions be placed on private commercial enterprises rekindled the debate about whether North Korea was ready for socialism.[64] This placed Kim on a collision course with those within the party who wanted to use foreign aid to develop light industry and to introduce immediate improvements in North Koreans' standard of living. Against the backdrop of Stalin's death and Khrushchev's criticism of Stalin's "cult of personality" as alien to Marxism, Kim's opponents in the Workers' Party made similar allegations against Kim and his supporters at the August 1956 plenary meeting.[65]

Four months afterwards, Kim delivered a fiery concluding speech, "For a Great Revolutionary Upswing in Socialist Construction," at the December Plenary Meeting of the Central Committee. In his opening remarks, he declared that the party had reached an agreement on the tasks to be undertaken during the first year of the Five-Year Plan and spoke enthusiastically of members' "unanimous resolve to fulfill this plan without fail, valiantly getting over all hardships and trials." Yet, the body of the speech pointed to ongoing conflicts within the party. Repeatedly, Kim spoke of the need to guard against the influence of "class enemies and anti-Party, counter-revolutionary factionalists hiding in our ranks" and defended his decision to prioritize heavy industry, noting that if foreign aid had been used to raise living standards, North Korea would have only been "better off for a year or two." He reminded those in attendance that through securing "steel-like unity" and "displaying a spirit of revolutionary self-reliance," it could achieve economic, military, and political independence.[66]

This notion of "independent rebirth" (*charyŏk kaengsaeng*)—that is, being the master of the revolution and the reconstruction of one's own nation—became the overarching principle of Juche ideology. Independent rebirth, Kim Il Sung argued, must be pursued in all realms—that is, the nation must achieve domestic and foreign independence (*chaju*), military independence (*chawi*), and economic self-sufficiency (*charip*). On December 28, 1955, against the backdrop of mounting opposition within the Workers' Party, he articulated the importance of Juche for the first time in a speech to party propagandists and agitators. Denouncing dogmatism and formalism, he argued that the socialist revolution in Korea would fail unless a Korean subjectivity (*juche*) was developed: "The principal shortcomings in ideological work are the failure to delve deeply into all matters and the lack of Juche." It was not enough for propagandists and activists to "merely copy and memorize foreign things"; they must work "creatively" to apply socialist principles to actual conditions in Korea. This strategy, Kim asserted, required a deep knowledge of Korean history: "To make revolution in Korea, we must know Korean history and geography and know the customs of the Korean people. Only then is it possible to educate our people in a way that suits them and to inspire in them an ardent love for their native place and their motherland."[67]

Kim's emphasis on knowing the Korean context was a direct attack on the Soviet faction of the Workers' Party—his principal opposition within the Party. He lambasted them for paying more attention to Soviet developments than to the efforts of Korean workers, noting that at local offices they posted diagrams of the Soviet Union's Five-Year Plan, but no diagrams of North Korea's Three-Year Plan: "They do not even put any diagrams and pictures of our economic construction, let alone study the history of our country." In particular, he targeted Pak Ch'angok, Hŏ Ka-i's successor as leader of the Soviet faction: "Pak Ch'ang-ok was ideologically linked to the reactionary bourgeois writer Li Tae Jun in that he did not try to study the history of our country and our realities . . . he had the conceited idea that he knew everything without even studying the realities of our country." Rectifying this fallacy required rejecting a slavish commitment to the Soviet model of socialism: "There can be no set principle that we must follow the Soviet pattern. Some advocate the Soviet way and others the Chinese, but is it not high time to work out our own?" In attacking Pak Ch'ang-ok, Kim Il Sung also linked him to accused spy Pak Hŏn-yŏng: "Those who were influenced by Pak Hon Yong cannot all be his ilk or spies. But his ideological influence still remains in the minds of these people. We must fight against this." In demanding a creative, nationalist approach to Marxist-Leninist principles, Kim Il Sung had placed his critics on the defensive, setting the stage for their complete purge from the party by the end of the 1950s.[68]

In the wake of Kim's speech, the North turned its attention to creating a usable past, that is, writing a history of Korean culture that was compatible with socialism and inspired national pride. Under Japanese imperial rule, Korea's histories focused on the nation's failure to modernize and on dynastic succession. Japanese officials had invented traditions, such as the inherent backwardness of the Korean people, to claim that the Korean people were incapable of self-rule. In 1959, the Social Science History Research Center (*Sahoe kwa'hagwŏn ryŏksa yŏn'guso*) utilized a materialist concept of history to advance a new historical narrative that showcased the heroic struggles of the Koreans against dynastic and colonial rule. The narrative, designed to promote national fervor and class consciousness, was packaged for mass consumption; volumes such as *Hang'il ppalchi'san t'ujaenggi* (Stories of Anti-Japanese Partisans) used plain language to present socialism as the logical outcome of centuries of class conflict in Korea.[69] In short, this revisionist narrative of Korea's past related countless stories of the Koreans' resistance to domestic and foreign despots to demonstrate the particularities of Korean history that had prepared the people for socialism. Sovereignty, this narrative contended, rested with the people—the latent source of Juche—whose full potential had yet to be realized. Beyond history texts, this narrative was advanced through popular slogans such as "The Party divorced from the masses is like a fish without water" and "Without the people, how could the Party make the revolution? There would be no victory and the party would be endangered."[70] In contrast to the colonial state that imposed its will upon the people, the Workers' Party argued that it acted upon the will of the people.

But acting upon the will of the people did not mean that the Workers' Party believed that the political consciousness of the masses was sufficiently developed for them to lead the revolution. The Korean masses required the tutelage of the party leadership because they remained under the influence of nonsocialist values, such as individualism, liberalism, capitalism, and feudalism. These nonsocialist values, the party leadership contended, had survived the postliberation political upheaval, the people's democracy, the Korean War, and the socialist transition.[71] The populace's political immaturity became the mantra through which the party perpetuated its control over the masses.[72] Put simply, the new historical narrative established the people as the fount of revolutionary self-reliance, but it did not provide them a path to realizing political maturity. Any divergence from the party line became a harbinger of nonsocialist values, which in turn justified the party's ongoing tutelage and control over the people's will.

People's NAs were singled out in much discourse on Juche for failing to demonstrate revolutionary self-reliance.[73] As noted earlier, the introduction of cooperatives and work brigades had caused People's NAs to lose much of their cohesion. However, the party could ill afford for People's NAs to languish, as they gave the party unparalleled access to the neighborhood and residential space. Without People's NAs, it would be difficult for the party to inculcate socialist values in the domestic sphere or to advance the socialist mode of living in the home space. Party leaders expected People's NAs to manifest the beauty of Korea in the residential space by taking collective responsibility for the maintenance and management of residential buildings. In keeping with Juche ideology, they believed that employing foreign socialist catchphrases would not inspire the people to develop a communal sense of ownership and to abandon a private property orientation. They needed to find a different approach; appealing to the traditional communal unit of the family seemed a viable option to party leaders for two reasons. First, utilizing traditional familial language with which Koreans were familiar to encourage greater cohesion in People's NAs aligned well with Juche ideology's insistence on the need to indigenize socialism. Second, the hierarchical structure of the traditional Korean family meant that the North Korean leadership could easily position itself as supreme patriarch over the masses, who required supervision to reach their political potential.

But introducing familial rhetoric posed an ideological dilemma, as Marxist theory identified the patriarchal family with capitalism and with the oppression of women. Prior to the Korean War, North Korean leadership had echoed this position, but now party rhetoric began to shift. The patriarchal family was no longer viewed as coextensive with capitalism: "The authority of patriarchy in working-class families was not unconditional. They exercised authority under the social atmosphere, but something more than that was found; they loved and helped each other as they needed to overcome poverty together. . . . The unequal relation between patriarchs and family members disappeared after liberation, because the socioeconomic base which had introduced inequality into family life had been abolished."[74] By eliminating private ownership of property and introducing a socialist economic system, the party had removed the conditions that fostered oppressive patriarchal authority in the working-class family. Divorced from capitalism, the patriarchal family, party leadership claimed, could promote equal relations between family members. It also paved the way for the party to mobilize the family unit in the service of the socialist order.

The socialist family, as indicated earlier in this chapter, was more than a group of people related to one another by blood or marriage. According to the official North Korean encyclopedia, it was "the living unit of people who work for the Party, and its leader, society, and communities."[75] Kim Il Sung explained this concept in his speech "The Duty of Mothers in the Education of Children," given on November 16, 1961, at the National Meeting of Mothers: "Our ideal is to build a society where everyone is well fed, well clothed and lives a long life, a society where there is no laggard nor idler, and where everybody is progressive and works devotedly, a society where all people live united in harmony like *a big family.* Such a society, we can say, is precisely a communist society. . . . Further, in a communist society, people will have still closer relationships and the principle of 'one for all, and all for one' will be fully realized."[76] It was a harmonious community bound by the Juche ideology and committed to the common goal of building communism.

Juche ideology and Great Red Family ideology worked in tandem to combat the "obsolete ideas" that "persist in people's minds for a long time even after a change in a social system." But, as Kim Il Sung noted in his speech to mothers, the family was not immune to the insidious influence of outdated ideas. Mothers, he explained, must "play a really great role in combatting outmoded ideas." They must become communists, so that their children would embrace Juche ideology: "In order to educate your sons and daughters properly, you mothers must become excellent communists. You cannot simply ask your children to become good people, while you yourselves avoid work and study, and behave selfishly."

According to this formulation, even an untidy home called into question one's political commitment: "Only when children are reared to be tidy at home, will they keep everything spic-and-span at school and grow up into men of a new type who will live a cultured way in the future."[77] North Koreans had become part of one Great Red Family, in which the political and moral realms were indistinguishable.

At the apex of this family was Kim Il Sung, who was party leader and patriarch over the Great Red Family. As the political and moral leader, he was situated at the center of what historian Bruce Cumings described as "a hierarchy of ever widening concentric circles" that moved outward from the party apparatus down to People's NAs.[78] The People's NAs, the constituent element of the Great Red Family, were connected to the state patriarch Kim Il Sung through the local patriarchs, the village PC chairs.[79] However, unlike under colonialism, neither the People's NA heads nor the household heads were classified as patriarchs. As noted earlier in this chapter, the North changed the designation for family heads from *hoju* to *sedaeju* in 1946, because in keeping with socialist theory, it wanted to promote more equitable relations between family members. This change in title meant that in socialist North Korea, NA gatherings were not seen as assemblies of patriarchs; instead, they were considered an extension of the domestic sphere. Consequently, when women began taking over the NAs' leadership in the 1960s, it did not spark the controversy that it had under colonial rule.[80]

The North had done little to change the traditional gendered division of labor, despite official rhetoric proclaiming equality of the sexes. For example, during the Korean War, Kim Il Sung declared in a talk with workers of the Women's Alliance on August 15, 1951, "Just as husband and wife have their own duties in a family, so do men and women have their respective duties during war." As Kim Il Sung made clear, this division of duties made women the masters of the home front: "Today the women are the masters at home, and it is their duty to support the battle front. . . . The women, who are now in charge of affairs on the home front should repair damaged roads and bridges promptly to facilitate transport of war supplies."[81] This division of labor remained unchallenged after the war, as seen in Kim Il Sung's 1961 address at the National Meeting of Mothers, when he called on mothers to support the Seven-Year Plan (1961–1967) in their traditional roles as mothers and primary educators of children. He noted, "Through all ages, ancient and modern, there is scarcely a mother who is utterly indifferent to the education of children." However, prior to the introduction of socialism, "mothers' hopes of bringing up children with fine personalities could not be realized." Socialism, he explained, had eliminated the exploitive conditions that prevented success, but it had not changed women's greater role in the education of children than that of men: "A mother has to bear the primary responsibility for home education." Her burden was greater than the father's burden, as Kim Il Sung stated as follows: "Because it is she who gives birth to children and brings them up."[82] In short, he reaffirmed the traditional division of labor but redefined the end goal of children's education. The objective was no longer to guarantee the success of the individual but to advance the objectives of the socialist state. This reorientation also meant that women should concern themselves with the education of all children in the community: "I do not mean that there will be no family nor any distinction between one's own children and others in communist society. . . . But people in communist society will never love their sons and daughters exclusively. When communist society is achieved, the whole society will turn into a family and people will love and care for all children equally whether they are their own or not."[83] In assigning mothers, as individuals and as a collective, primary responsibility for the home education of children and for combating frivolity, selfishness, and obsolete ideas in the domestic sphere, Kim Il Sung set in motion women's replacement of men as the principal leaders of People's NAs.

The post–Korean War labor shortage appears also to have accelerated women's domination of NA leadership roles. The North believed it was critical to mobilize all able-bodied men for construction projects in rural and urban areas. Thus, when it became apparent that many men were opting for university study and for jobs that women could easily perform, Kim Il Sung expressed outrage in a speech delivered on January 7, 1963, at the Enlarged Meeting of the Political Committee of the Central Committee of the Workers' Party: "At county libraries, women can do the work perfectly well, but all librarians are men. What is worse, they are healthy young men. . . . It seems that male librarians have no sense of shame at all." He noted that the proportion of women in many economic sectors, such as light industry, commerce, administration, city

management, and bankingremained too low, despite earlier efforts to encourage the building of light industries near the home so that women
could contribute to the nation's productivity.[84] For example, in 1958, he
proclaimed, "Construction of local factories in county seats made it possible to make effective use of available labor potentials. In county seats
there are at present many housewives who spend most of their time at
home. You could build simple nurseries and employ anyone who wants
to work. . . . Then these women will get a job."[85] Thus, in his address on
January 7, 1963, he made clear that the party "should not hesitate to pluck
men out of such sectors" and "employ many housewives in their place."[86]
Maximizing labor efficiency required handing over all administrative
work to women, including People's NA leadership.

As People's NA leaders, women assumed primary responsibility for
the dissemination of Great Red Family ideology. Their leadership com-
plemented and completed Juche ideology, as it served as the vehicle
through which morality was placed at the service of the party's political
ends.

CONCLUSION

The reintroduction of female leadership of People's NAs was the product of two complementary ideologies—Juche and the Great Red Family—
to promote the building of a post–Korean War socialist state. While
Juche provided the political rationale for postwar political and economic reconstruction plans, Great Red Family ideology linked the
public and domestic spheres. People's NAs were reimagined as red
families, and women as NA leaders were charged with inculcating members in socialist values. At the apex of the Great Red Family was the supreme patriarch, Kim Il Sung. At first glance, this arrangement appears
to duplicate the patriarchal hierarchy that positioned the Japanese
emperor as supreme patriarch. However, because North Korea did not
define People's NAs as assemblies of male patriarchs (hoju), female
leadership did not create an internal contradiction in ideology as NAs
had under Japanese colonialism. Women were individually and collectively mobilized in their traditional roles as mothers, educators, and
home managers. Their educational mission in the organized domestic

sphere—People's NAs—was to revolutionize the family, that is, to prioritize the formation of communal bonds, mutual trust, and support for the party. Because it recreated the traditional division of labor in Korean society, the mobilization of women as the chief expounders of socialist morality did not spark widespread resistance among North Korean males. Thus, the merger of the political and moral realms into a single domain was accomplished with little fanfare at the local level.

CHAPTER 9

"People's Neighborhood Associational Life" in the 1960s

Our day-to-day life begins in the home and in People's NAs.[1]

In the 1960s, when the North was eager to indigenize socialism by in-fusing it with Juche and Great Red Family ideology, the new compound word "People's neighborhood associational life" (*Inminban saenghwal*, hereafter People's NA life) became commonplace in North Korea. *The Encyclopedia on North Korea* (*Pukhan taesajŏn*), published by a South Korean institution specializing in issues of communist countries, opined, "All people are obliged to participate in People's NA life as requested by a head, except when at work. . . . North Korea makes use of People's NAs to turn life outside of work into a collective network. People not only dislike People's NA life, but they also feel pestered as they are forced to participate in People's NA life even after coming home from work."[2] In contrast, the *North Korean Encyclopedia* (*Chosŏn taebaekkwasajŏn*), published by the North Korean government, quoted Kim Il Sung on People's NA life: "Since every person in our country belongs to and lives in a People's NA, taking care of families, revolutionizing families, and sorting out any inconveniences depend on People's NAs."[3]

The two Koreas agreed that People's NA life constituted a third realm in the daily life of North Koreans. A major difference, however, was that the South viewed this third realm as an intrusion by the state into the private sphere. In contrast, the North understood it as a bridge that al-lowed North Korean society to overcome the artificial divide between public and private life that had developed under capitalism, which, in its view, individualized and thus disempowered the people. By co-opting the language of the family, People's NAs, the North Korean government believed, would allow for a seamless merger of the two spheres. Within the space of People's NAs, as within a family, people would provide mutual support and communicate with other structures within the state from a position of empowerment.

Creating this socialist community also required transforming ordinary Koreans into revolutionary beings. As Kim Sŏng-bo explained, "Socialism entails devotion to revolution rather than personal interests. To maintain consistent political commitment, socialism needs 'revolutionary human beings,' and what makes that possible is culture."[4] People's NAs, I argue, became the cultural milieu through which the North Korean government endeavored to transform ordinary Koreans into revolutionary human beings. By having People's NAs assume substantial responsibility for both traditional familial tasks and economic activities, the government hoped to narrow the gap between the private and public spheres and to school the populace in communal life and collective decision making. Familial devotion to People's NAs, the government believed, would then radiate outward in concentric circles, inspiring allegiance to village and to country.

To foster familial bonds between persons linked only by geographic proximity, the government in the 1960s launched the Ch'ŏllima People's NA Campaign as part of a larger mass campaign to finish North Korea's transformation from a people's democracy into a socialist state. This campaign had four central features—the promotion of family-like bonds between neighbors, the creation of a socialist collective at the neighborhood level through experience with collective life and labor, the propagation of Juche (revolutionary self-reliance) by rewarding People's NAs that found solutions to communal problems without asking for government assistance, and the application of socialist values to all aspects of everyday life. These lessons were reinforced through stories of exemplary People's NAs published in *Minju chosŏn,* the official newspaper of the government. This chapter examines these stories—bearing in mind that the government and the press utilized such stories for purposes of propaganda—to understand how the state set out to create the Great Red Family and the ideal revolutionary subject, the problems it confronted, and the solutions it devised.

CH'ŎLLIMA PEOPLE'S NA CAMPAIGN

The Ch'ŏllima movement had its origins in a talk that Kim Il Sung gave at the Kangsŏn steel plant, located in South P'yong'an Province, in the winter of 1956. The plant, built by the Japanese company Mitsubishi, had been nationalized following liberation. In 1956, three years after the Korean War, the plant, which had been badly damaged by US aerial bombings, was moving to increase its productivity levels as part of the North Korean recovery plan that emphasized the expansion of heavy industries. Years later, Chin Ŭng-wŏn, a leader of a smelting work brigade at the factory, recalled how Kim had spoken casually with workers: "Have a seat. I came to see you. I always wanted to see workers smelting iron." During the visit, Kim also stressed to workers that in their labors they must exemplify endurance, speed, and consistency. They must model their work performance on the Ch'ŏllima, a legendary horse capable of running approximately four hundred kilometers every day. In making this comment, Kim signaled that the goal of building a socialist society appeared a distant possibility given current realities but could be realized quickly if the masses applied themselves consistently to realizing this goal.

Three years later, on February 17, 1959, Kim visited the same plant. He wanted the final mass campaign of the Five-Year Plan (1957–1960; ended a year early) to begin, as agricultural collectivization was completed; the last remaining private industries were nationalized; and his partisan faction attained control over the Workers' Party.[5] Kim repeated his earlier message that building socialism required the consistent commitment of the masses of people: "Building a communist society, which is a plan that greatly benefits all people, cannot be done by a few people. Unless the masses of people realize that this is their job, we are unlikely to succeed. Therefore, people must be firmly united around the Party and be enlightened." Inspired by these words, Chin created a Ch'ŏllima work brigade campaign on March 8, 1959, which used the slogan "Let's work, let's learn, and let's lead a communist life."[6] Pleased by Chin's efforts to organize a voluntary campaign, on March 17, 1959, the government bestowed upon Chin's work brigade the honorary title of "Ch'ŏllima."[7]

The bestowing of such honorary titles on sectors of the populace for conforming with state policy can be traced back to the Campaign for Improving Rural Areas, the first state-led mass movement by the colonial state in the early 1930s. Villages that enthusiastically embraced learning modern scientific farming techniques and adopted a modern way of life were given the title "model village." Likewise, Patriotic NAs and families that adhered to wartime assimilation policies were awarded plaques that read respectively "exemplary Patriotic NA" and "exemplary household." While continuing this practice, the North wanted to distinguish its use of such titles from that of its colonial predecessor. It stressed that its intent was radically different from the Japanese one; its goal was to mobilize the people to build a better life for everybody, rather than exploit them.[8] This difference meant that unlike the colonial government, it did not need to rely on coercion to ensure cooperation. To garner the public's enthusiasm, the government used the campaign slogan "Let's march forward as if we are riding on a Ch'ŏllima!" In November 1960, approximately 13,400 work brigades with 274,000 workers nationwide joined the movement, and 852 of them received the title of Ch'ŏllima.[9]

On August 22, 1960, in a speech delivered at the National Meeting of Vanguards of the Ch'ŏllima Work Brigade Movement (*Chŏn'guk ch'ŏllima chagŏppanundong sŏn'guja taehoe*), Kim Il Sung announced that the Ch'ŏllima campaign would be merged with another mass enlightenment project—"The Making of a New Human," initiated in 1958.[10] The Workers' Party was concerned that the consciousness of the masses had not caught up with recent radical social changes, such as the liberation from colonial rule, the introduction of people's democracy, the Korean War, and the transition to socialism. Party leaders feared that the remaining vestiges of feudalism and colonialism would disrupt the political and economic progress that North Korea had made to date. Thus, the North wanted to transform Koreans into exemplary communists who embraced communist morality and sought self-realization in the collectivity.[11] The Ch'ŏllima campaign, through which workers had rid themselves of "conservatism, mysticism, and all inactivity," must now extend to all the populace so that in "the realms of ideology and morality" North Korean society could make a clean break from "all depravity and backwardness inherited from the old society."[12]

Once the Ch'ŏllima campaign was extended to the spiritual and cultural sphere, it was divided into three branches: work brigades, schools, and People's NAs. The Ch'ŏllima Work Brigade Movement focused on acclimating the masses to the demands of collective work life. The Ch'ŏllima School Movement concentrated on teaching socialist principles to students; once these were learned, students were expected to apply these principles to their school life. The Ch'ŏllima People's NA Campaign would allow students and workers to apply socialist teachings to home life. For those, such as housewives, the elderly, and young children, who did not work or attend school, it created a venue within the neighborhood space where they too could learn and apply socialist teachings.[13]

Unlike the other two branches, the Ch'ŏllima People's NA Movement targeted the private sphere. Specifically, it sought to transfer tasks carried out by the family in capitalist societies to the collective domain by reconfiguring the neighborhood space as the smallest unit of the Great Red Family. However, this transformation first required creating communal bonds between persons whose only previous connection was geographic proximity. To achieve this end, the NA monthly gatherings were to be supplemented with daily activities that brought neighbors together to accomplish needed community projects. The extent to which neighborhoods embraced their new familial identity became the yardstick through which the state measured how deeply Great Red Family ideology had permeated the populace's psyche.

MY PEOPLE'S NA, MY VILLAGE, MY COUNTRY

By the 1960s, North Koreans could easily contact someone whom they did not know through the People's NA to which the person belonged. All they needed was the name of the village where the person lived. The village authority placed them in contact with the appropriate People's NA head, who maintained detailed records on member households as well as on those visiting from elsewhere.[14] But beyond being a repository of demographic information on member households, the government wanted People's NAs to become an object of affection—that is, it wanted members to experience People's NAs as a family unit that worked together for the collective good.

Thus, the task of the Ch'ŏllima People's NA campaign was not just managing the communal space of the neighborhood but creating among its residents a sense of belonging. Through active participation in NA activities, the state hoped, residents would develop a concentric sense of loyalty to their NA that would translate into loyalty to their village and to their country. Although the state defined the overarching mission of the Ch'ŏllima People's NA Campaign, its insistent rejection of formalism and emphasis on voluntarism meant that it gave People's NAs substantial autonomy in how they realized their assigned mission. However, large projects often required financial support and technical expertise that People's NAs did not have. Consequently, People's NAs submitted their plans to village PC authorities, who would remake the project as a village project involving multiple NAs. Successful projects received national accolades, thus ensuring a positive association between local creativity and the regime's supportiveness.

The Tong 2 District in Sariwŏn city of Hwanghae Province, consisting of fifty-four People's NAs, received the title of Ch'ŏllima for demonstrating exemplary city management. On January 16, 1966, *Minju chosŏn* praised the district's accomplishments: "Year by year, the district's streets and villages are being renovated. The noble efforts of residents who through their own efforts have rebuilt their hometown and managed their city well are inspiring visitors from across the nation who have traveled to the city."[15] Cho Un-ryong, Tong 2 District's general secretary, explained that their activities had been inspired by the visit to Ch'ŏllima Puksae in Pyongyang in spring 1965.

Puksae in Pyongyang had not been a model village in the 1950s; its roads were poorly maintained and there were few gardens, owing to the high sand content of the soil. The turning point came in March 1961, when local authorities attended a general rally of the Workers' Party of Pyongyang. The speaker was Chŏng Il-yong, vice prime minister of North Korea and Pyongyang's PC chair. In his speech, he proudly enumerated Pyongyang's post–Korean war achievements. He cited the numerous construction projects completed, such as culture houses, factories, hundreds of schools, hospitals, and modern sewage facilities. He declared that these projects had transformed Pyongyang into a productive socialist city and praised People's NAs for their effective management of state-built facilities.[16] In making this claim, Chŏng emphasized the idea of concentric circles of patriotism and thus the expected effect of Pyongyang's success on other locales: "Making Pyongyang a role model means that we should take good care of our family, our People's NA, our village, and own workplace." Through his repetitive use of the first-person possessive plural, Chŏng's aim was to translate the local patriotism of Pyongyang residents and of residents of other locations into patriotic allegiance to the state. By demonstrating revolutionary self-reliance, or Juche, exemplary People's NAs, he underscored, improved both their localities and the state.

Inspired by the speech, the People's NAs in Puksae developed collective projects to improve their community. Kwŏn Po-bi, headwoman of the Sixth People's NA, set up a weekly planting day for her NA. Soon, most of the houses had fruit and flower gardens, and the empty spaces around public laundries were filled with cucumbers and sponge gourds. The Seventh and Tenth People's NAs assembled a toolbox, which they used to repair homes. Community members could also borrow the toolbox to work on their own projects. Other projects included collecting recyclable materials to build a children's library, table tennis tables, and swimming pools. Kindergarten teacher Ri Hwa-sŏn persuaded other teachers to join her in creating an afterschool study group. In recognition of their communal efforts, the village received the title of Ch'ŏllima, and on July 6, 1966, Kim Il Sung honored the village by paying a visit.[17]

As noted earlier, Puksae's success prompted officials from Tong 2 District to visit the village in 1965. Upon his return, General Secretary Cho noted that he and his colleagues had realized that "the management of national properties could only be achieved through a mass campaign."[18] They planned to push ahead with a village development plan by People's NAs, in the expectation that it would strengthen NAs and promote the people's identification with the village. Cho and his colleagues requested that local People's NAs select members to inspect homes and public facilities, such as laundries, playgrounds, and warehouses, to determine what repairs were needed. Once inspections were completed and the problems identified, the forty-two inspectors divided the work according to category, and two to three inspectors were placed in charge of developing a plan of action for each category. To assist them in this task, they were allocated several People's NAs. After the groups developed their respective plans of action, they submitted them to the village PC, which turned the individual plans into a village-wide plan of action and created a work schedule. Each of the People's NAs then held a meeting to ensure that all members knew the plan and the role that they would be expected to play in carrying it out.[19]

Each People's NA in Tong 2 was then charged with producing a prototype of one or two elements of the plan. The Fifteenth People's NA built the prototype for a public laundry that other NAs could then copy; it also dug a model public well. The Twelfth People's NA built the prototype for an earthen wall; the Twenty-Third People's NA built a model flower garden. Under the general supervision of NA heads, six tractor drivers, eighteen truck drivers, and nineteen cart carriers in the village delivered pebbles and other materials that each People's NA needed. Those who worked outside the home were mobilized for two hours every morning, while the unemployed worked throughout the day. Thanks to these efforts, in summer 1965, major roads were paved, irrigation ditches constructed, and earthen walls reinforced. In addition to these improvements in infrastructure, five playgrounds were added, and the number of public laundries increased to eleven, significantly reducing waiting times.[20]

Once Tong 2 completed its development plan, it needed to create a system for managing the newly developed communal spaces. However, most NAs had difficulty finding one person with the time to manage the new facilities, since it was not uncommon for both men and women to work full time outside the home. For example, in the Sixteenth People's NA, made up of twenty-two households, the husband and wife in sixteen households both worked full time. Moreover, adult members of the NA who did not have paying jobs outside the home already worked for the People's NAs as part of the "home working team" (*kanae chagŏppan*)—a full-time job. Chŏn In-tŏk, a headwoman and full-time housewife with six children, left each morning at 8:00 a.m. to work for "the home working team." She did not return home from this assignment until 5:00 p.m. Thus, assigning one person responsibility for maintaining public facilities was unrealistic; a shared system of management, whereby everyone in the NA was responsible for maintaining and repairing public facilities, was the only viable solution. At the monthly gathering, NA members would discuss the various jobs that needed to be done and then divide those jobs among members. This communal approach to management was subsequently adopted by the entire village, which viewed it as a way of facilitating the development of strong bonds between neighbors, avoiding burnout, and ensuring consistency in job performance.

COMMUNAL PARENTING

An editorial that appeared in *Minju chosŏn* on January 25, 1967, noted, "Educating children who are the future of our country is one of the most crucial missions of People's NAs."[21] This indicates that People's NAs were expected to assume primary responsibility for the socialization of children—a role that traditionally belonged to the family. This shift from the family to People's NAs was seen as a solution to two pressing issues. First, owing to the upsurge in the number of women working outside the home in response to the government's call for women to participate in building the socialist state, the need for childcare facilities had increased dramatically. Utilizing People's NAs for childcare was a cost-effective and practical solution as it did not require the construction of new facilities; NAs were near the family's abode and using them allowed the state to take advantage of untapped labor in People's NAs. Second, it provided the state with an institution through which it could instill in children at an early age the moral, communal, and educational values it believed were necessary for making the transition from people's democracy to socialist society.[22]

The state placed a strong emphasis on communal parenting by People's NA, seeing it as critical for cultivating in the young the complementary ideologies of the Great Red Family and Juche, discussed in chapter 8. Under the leadership of a headwoman, who was viewed as the "mother" of the People's NA, women were expected to take a leading role in creating the Great Red Home, in which neighbors became family members and in which political and family life became one. Most importantly, women were to embrace Kim Il Sung's 1961 instruction to mothers to make no distinction between one's children and the children of one's neighbors. A communist society, Kim explained, was achievable only when women no longer "discriminate[d] between her children and others but loved them all alike."[23]

The envisioned harmonious relationship between families and People's NAs did not always work as planned, especially when it concerned children. An incident in the Ch'ŏllima Thirtieth People's NA of Kyŏngsang in Chung district in Pyongyang is illustrative. One day, a woman saw a boy from the neighborhood using a pencil to draw an airplane on a newly painted wall. The woman harshly scolded the child. Rather than apologizing, the boy lashed out at the woman and then broke into tears. Upon hearing her son crying, the boy's mother came out of the house to see what was going on. Rather than reinforce the woman's correction, she berated the woman for speaking so harshly to her son. The two women squabbled, and each went back inside her home angry with the other. The conflict between the two women escalated as neighbors took sides with either the mother or the woman. Those who took the mother's side exclaimed that the woman should have corrected the boy more gently. Those who sided with the woman criticized the mother for spoiling the child.[24]

The NA headwoman defused neighborhood tensions by transferring the blame for the incident from the two women to herself: "The two ladies are not at fault. Who does not scold a mischievous child? And who is happy to see one's child crying? The fault lies with me. As headwoman, I should have paid more attention to mothers in charge of parenting. If the woman scolding the child had been the child's mother, she would not have sworn. If the boy's mother knew of the parenting of great mothers, whose sons achieved greatness, she would not have taken her son's side."[25] The incident, the headwoman opined, was the product of her failure to cultivate an environment in which motherhood was a communal, rather than biological relationship. If the woman had perceived the child as hers, she would not have used harsh language, and if the mother had not clung to the idea of "my child," she would have been able to evaluate the boy's behavior objectively. The persistence of emotional walls between family units within the People's NA was a sign to the headwoman that she had failed at establishing the Great Red Home, in which parenthood was a collective responsibility.

To remedy this situation, the headwoman decided to organize mothers' meetings to discuss the challenges of communal parenting. At the meetings, they studied Kim Il Sung's 1961 speech "The Duty of Mothers in the Education of Children." They read stories about exemplary mothers, such as Kang Pan-sŏk—Kim Il Sung's mother and a well-known socialist. The headwoman also invited elderly women, whose children were now adults, to speak on the importance of childhood experiences in the formation of lifelong habits. The meetings led the women in the People's NAs to rethink how they treated children and neighbors. A decision was reached to address all neighbors, including children, with respect and to voluntarily extend help to others, such as those struggling to carry many bags into their homes. The goal was to model consistently the behaviors that they wanted children to emulate. The mothers also set up afterschool clubs, which the women took turns supervising. The women used old adages to help the children understand the importance of finishing today's homework today. Once homework was completed, the women on duty at the afterschool club would take the children to playgrounds and parks, where they would tell them stories about anti-Japanese partisans and exemplary boy scouts. Owing to the changes introduced, the headwoman proudly noted that most of the children in her People's NA were on the honor roll at school.[26]

Such success stories on communal parenting were often featured in *Minju chosŏn*. For example, the newspaper reported that in the Sixty-Fourth People's NA of Sŏn'gyo 1-dong in Sŏn'gyo District in Pyongyang, every student had received high academic honors, thanks to the efforts of Ch'oe Mun-ja, the NA's headwoman. Ch'oe had taken it upon herself to visit every school in which the children from her NA were enrolled. Based on these visits, she tried to provide the students with books that would help them in their studies. She personally tutored students who were behind in their studies or who were struggling with behavioral problems. She also arranged a tutoring system that matched older students with younger students. To encourage the children of her People's NA to develop a sense of community, she involved them in communal management, assigning them to tasks such as morning cleaning, weeding, and scrap iron collection. Every Sunday, as well as on national holidays and school vacations, she organized for the children in her People's NA trips to the cinema or visits to museums. Weather permitting, she also organized picnics in the mountains and trips to public parks and factories. The goal of these activities, which other People's NAs were encouraged to emulate, was to instill socialist values in children and to solidify bonds between neighbors, so that neighbors became family members, that is, "neighboring cousins."[27] Tighter communal bonds, North Korean authorities believed, would lead to the contraction of the private familial sphere over which it had less control.

ON-THE-SPOT SUPERVISION BY THE STATE PATRIARCH: EPICENTER FOR MOTIVATION

A common theme found in stories in *Minju chosŏn* on Ch'ŏllima People's NAs was the stunning improvements that followed on-the-spot supervisory visits (*Hyŏnji chido*) by the state patriarch, Kim Il Sung. The origins of such visits can be traced to the Korean War, when a public officer or local intellectual was charged with increasing voluntarism in People's NAs by providing the masses with political education and advising them on how they could adapt national policy to local circumstances. Beginning in winter 1956, to revive the populace's waning revolutionary fervor, Kim Il Sung and other party leaders restarted visiting various industrial sites.[28]

As noted in chapter 7, the constant nature of wartime campaigns had transformed public perception of People's NAs from voluntary groups of patriots to extensions of the state bureaucracy. Consequently, the members of People's NAs were no longer showing up for the mass campaigns that the state believed were critical for building a socialist state. To rekindle the popular enthusiasm that had characterized the postliberation period when the North Korean government had introduced wide-ranging social reforms, the North moved to reverse what it believed was the cause of diminished popular support, namely, that local authorities over the course of the war had reverted to coercive bureaucratic tactics to guarantee the populace's cooperation. As Kim Il Sung intoned on October 18, 1966, in a speech to the Central Committee of the Workers' Party, unless "formalism and bureaucracy" were eliminated from the party's organizational and ideological work, "the productive zeal of the producer masses" so vital for the revolution would be squandered.[29] On-the-spot supervisory visits, combined with encouraging the populace to incorporate local ideas into Ch'ŏllima People's NA campaigns, were seen as the way to restore the spirit of voluntarism.

On September 22, 1967, Paek Ch'an-bin wrote an article for *Minju chosŏn* in which he used Kim Il Sung's February 1959 visit to the Nineteenth People's NA in Ryongdang District in Haeju city to show how on-the-spot supervision had produced remarkable changes in the Ch'ŏllima People's NA campaign there. Paek claimed that because of the visit, the Nineteenth People's NA and other NAs in the district had built more reading rooms, where the people could study party policies and revolutionary traditions. He noted that from morning until dusk the streets were now bustling with NA members who were working on community improvement projects, such as expanding narrow roads, building fences, and cleaning community laundries. The renewal of the district's appearance, Paek observed, had been accompanied by a parallel rise in the people's commitment to communist virtues. Two banners were hoisted in the district to encourage people to maintain this level of commitment: "Let's continue the on-the-spot teaching of comrade Kim Il Sung!" and "Let's make our streets more hygienic and turn our villages into cultural centers so that they live up to the standard of the working class!"

Kim Il Sung's visit to the Nineteenth People's NA had not been planned. After touring a cement factory in Ryongdang, Kim decided that he wanted to see where factory workers lived. He went to the home of Kim Tae-suk, who belonged to the Nineteenth People's NA. Before leaving, he urged the People's NA to construct more culture houses and provided detailed information on building modern, hygienic workers' housing. According to Paek, residents and workers were "so deeply moved by his [Kim's] parental love that they made a firm resolution to be loyal to his teachings no matter how difficult their circumstances might be."[30] Their resolve and concrete actions to improve the neighborhood space resulted in the Nineteenth People's NA being awarded the title of Ch'ŏllima. Having achieved this title, Paek explained, the Nineteenth People's NA was now striving to earn a second Ch'ŏllima title for upholding the party's decisions and for revolutionizing families. The reporter ended the article by noting how the successes of the Nineteenth People's NA had inspired four other People's NAs in Ryongdang to launch comparable campaigns.

Articles in *Minju chosŏn* often described Kim Il Sung's relationship to the people as one of "parental love." For example, following Kim Il Sung's visit with the Thirty-Seventh People's NA in Ch'ŏnnae County of Kang'wŏn Province, the paper waxed eloquent about the familial bonds that existed between the party leader and the people:

> The people of the Thirty-Seventh People's NA in Ch'ŏnnae have had an unforgettably glorious day. It was May 18, 1956, when dearest father comrade Kim Il Sung visited the home of a working-class family belonging to a little-known People's NA. He asked about the family's circumstances and if the heating in their home was adequate. In his queries, he showed family-like warmth for the lives of the residents. . . . The people were so excited to experience his deep affection and father-like caring. . . . To repay his thoughtfulness, they launched with a united heart and will the ch'ŏllima People's NAs campaign to carry out his teachings.[31]

Given that *Minju chosŏn* represented the stance of the government, it is obvious that the repeated references in the newspaper's articles to Kim's parental love, the people's indebtedness to him, and familial loyalty tell us little about how the people felt. Rather, such articles can be reckoned as a window into the discourse promoted by the government and into the behaviors, attitudes, and actions that North Korea's leaders wanted from the people.

The Fifteenth Plenary Meeting of the Fourth Central Committee of the Workers' Party held in May 1967 was a decisive moment in the rise of the cult of Kim Il Sung. At the meeting, leading members of the Kapsan faction of the Workers' Party, including Pak Kŭm-ch'ŏl and Li Hyo-sun, were purged from the party for having taken a passive stance on promoting Juche as the only socialist ideology in North Korea in line with the Great Red Family and anti-Japanese revolutionary tradition. Moreover, in seeking to position Pak Kŭm-ch'ŏl as Kim Il Sung's successor, the faction had used the propaganda bureau to produce plays and films that equated Pak's revolutionary efforts with those of Kim Il Sung. In February 1967, Kim had warned faction members to stop activities of "individual heroism," but the group apparently failed to heed the warning and was expelled from the party. Once these last remnants of pluralism had been eliminated from the party, Kim's leadership went unchallenged, and the cult of Kim Il Sung intensified, much like the Red Guards' cult of Mao had intensified during China's Cultural Revolution that began in 1966.[32] People's NAs provided the means through which this cult of personality infiltrated the everyday lives of North Koreans.

READING THE REVOLUTIONARY NATIONAL PAST

Beyond appeals to familial loyalty, the North also painstakingly endeavored to advance a narrative of the past that would motivate the people to work toward an ideal socialist future. On the one hand, this narrative contrasted the harsh conditions of life under colonial rule with improved conditions under the North Korean order. On the other hand, it pointed to the harsh conditions that anti-Japanese partisans had endured in the 1920s and 1930s to encourage the populace's acceptance of Juche ideology, that is, revolutionary self-reliance. Under this ideology, austerity, personal sacrifice, and discipline would be rewarded in the future with the realization of an ideal communist society. As this narrative of the past permeated People's NAs, anti-Japanese partisans' lifestyle became an archetype of People's NA life.

On August 22, 1967, *Minju chosŏn* utilized this narrative to describe the positive effects that Kim Il Sung's on-the-spot supervision had had on the Thirty-Fourth People's NA in Hŭngnam. It noted how one resident was overcome with gratitude, as thanks to Comrade Kim Il Sung, she now lived comfortably in a modern culture home; this new life, she noted, was a radical departure from her life "before liberation" when she had lived in abject poverty. This appreciation, the paper highlighted, was accompanied by a new resolve by members to "study the lessons of Kim Il Sung and put them into practice, so that their actions and behaviors mirrored those of the anti-Japanese partisans who had loyally fought alongside comrade Kim Il Sung."[33]

This narrative, which advanced the socialist cause while also positing North Korea's unique history, was first used by Kim Il Sung, as noted in chapter 8, to counter the Soviet faction's challenge to his political authority during the Korean War. Once Kim emerged victorious over the Soviet faction, school textbooks began utilizing this narrative. In 1959, *Reminiscences of the Anti-Japanese Guerillas* (*Hang'il ppalch'isan hoesanggi*), a collection of memoirs of North Korean guerrillas who had fought against the Japanese in Manchuria during the 1930s and 1940s, was published and became a standard school textbook. In this book, the hardships experienced by guerrilla fighters and the national pride that came with independence were both emphasized to convince the people that their current hardships would be rewarded in the future.

This history was also standard fare at weekly reading sessions held in People's NAs. For example, *Minju chosŏn* reported that Kwangch'ŏn town in South Hamgyŏng Province held two types of reading sessions each week: one was for adults and the other was a study session that trained participants to present political information from newspaper stories and historical texts to individuals whose political consciousness was deemed insufficient. The newspaper described these reading sessions as follows: "Comrade Sŏ Kŭm-sun is faithfully administering revolutionary tasks in People's NAs. She attributes today's happiness to the bloody strife against Japanese under the leadership of comrade Kim Il Sung. Comrade Yang Kuk-cha is striving to revolutionize families. She swears unconditional loyalty to the leader and takes his indomitable spirit as a guideline by which to live her life."[34] The article's reflexive approval of the two local leaders' unconditional acceptance of the official narrative made clear that dissent or doubt would not be tolerated. Unconditional trust in the legitimacy of the party's policies was also reinforced by slogans, such as "There is nothing we cannot do. Our lives and our work shall embody the spirit of the anti-Japanese partisans," used by People's NAs.[35]

Minju chosŏn also published accounts showing how the ingenuity of Korean resistance fighters inspired members of People's NAs to overcome contemporary challenges. In July 1966, it reported that town officials in Pongsu town in Wŏnsan had decided to launch a campaign to improve roads and build parks and playgrounds. At the time of the decision, the town's People's NAs were not known for enthusiastically embracing such projects. Realizing that forcing participation would only generate more resentment, town officials provided on-the-spot supervision to the Twelfth People's NA, the lowest-performing NA, in the hopes of turning it into a role model. This supervision included instruction in the lives of anti-Japanese guerila fighters. According to the article, it worked. Members of the Twelfth People's NA immediately began designing a new village layout. When members discovered that they lacked sufficient workers and materials to complete the project, they did not seek help from town officials, but rather demonstrated revolutionary self-reliance. Having read the story of how in three days anti-Japanese partisans made hundreds of "Yŏn'gil bombs," a generic term for hand-made bombs that anti-Japanese partisans led by Kim Il Sung used against Japan in the 1930s, the members of the Twelfth People's NA were determined to prove that they could be equally resourceful. According to the newspaper account, members cut down trees from their own yards to build playgrounds and fences. Women planted sweet-brier and pine trees in the parks and streets; household heads graveled the roads and built stone walls. The result was that the Twelfth People's NA, once known as the town's worst NA, received the honorary title of Ch'ŏllima.[36]

The People's NAs in Sinjin-dong District in Ch'ŏngjin provided another exemplary case highlighted by *Minju chosŏn*. The People's NAs of the district had pledged to complete a community improvement project by October 10—the anniversary of the founding of the Workers' Party. When the NAs encountered technical difficulties, the paper reported that members discussed excerpts from three books dealing with anti-Japanese partisans: *United Force* (*Tanhaptoen him*), *Forty-Day Ordeal* (*Konanŭi sasibil*), and *Overcoming Hardship* (*Nan'gwanŭl ttulko*). Noting how the struggles of resistance fighters had brought the freedom that they now enjoyed, the members of the People's NA redoubled their efforts so that they could be like the resistance fighters who had been loyal to Kim Il Sung. The result, the paper exclaimed, was "miraculous" as the people united behind the slogan "One for all and all for one." The Twenty-Fifth People's NA, which had been honored with the double honorific title Ch'ŏllima–Ch'ŏllima, completed its part of the project and then volunteered to help other People's NAs that were behind schedule in completing their jobs.[37] In short, the life of anti-Japanese guerillas was rendered into the essential constituents of ideal People's NA lives.

PEOPLE'S NA HEADS AND THE CALL
FOR THE CH'ŎNGSANNI METHOD
OF COMMUNICATION

In February 1960, Kim Il Sung visited the Ch'ŏngsanni Agricultural Co-operative in Kangsŏ County to conduct an on-the-spot supervision. The rate of agricultural production, although increasing, had fallen behind that of industrial production, and he wanted to understand why. Over the course of two weeks of meetings with farmers and officials, Kim discovered that the farmers were not to blame. The problem was that the County PC had failed to provide them with appropriate guidance. Instead, he explained in a speech at a Plenary Meeting of the Kangsŏ County Party Committee on February 18, 1960, it had "conducted its work by sending down resolutions and written orders and urging them to submit statistics" without factoring in local circumstances or the ability of the people to understand such abstract instructions. Concrete guidance in simple language needed to replace political jargon, so that the rural populace would understand what was being asked of them. The same held true for urban areas; party cadres and local officials needed to have democratic discussions with the populace and incorporate local input in making economic plans. As Kim Il Sung admonished, economic plans should no longer be developed "for the sake of showing people who come down from above for inspection," but they should be developed in consultation with the people, who have practical knowledge of the land and of factory life.[38]

In the wake of Kim Il Sung's visit, the so-called ch'ŏngsanni method became the standard against which the communications of party and local officials with the masses were judged.[39] This method of communication, which emphasized tailoring the presentation of party policy to the audience, filtered down from local officials to NA heads.

On January 12, 1967, *Minju chosŏn* included a story about the Thirtieth People's NA of Kyŏngsang in Pyongyang, whose headwoman had learned the value of utilizing the ch'ŏngsanni method. Sim, the NA's headwoman, acknowledged that she had been guilty of merely reading government directives and policies verbatim at monthly meetings. Each month she had rattled off policy directives to which most members had responded with indifference. As a result, the success of various projects depended on the efforts of a few members who consistently displayed patriotic volunteerism. Sim did not understand why more members did not willingly participate in implementing policy. This changed when one day an elderly lady asked two questions: "What does it mean to implement the fiat on the plan for hygiene and culture?" and "What do you mean by 'supporting the rural area?'" After explaining to the woman using simple language that the former meant keeping streets clean and houses in good repair and the latter meant volunteering to help farmers with their work, the woman immediately volunteered to collect food scraps for feeding livestock. Based on this conversation, the headwoman realized the error of her previous method of presenting policy. She had not bothered to tailor lectures and discussions to the educational level of most of her members. Consequently, they had not understood what was expected of them and why their participation was important. She needed to tailor her presentation of information to her audience—that is, she needed to use one approach with children, another with the elderly, and so on.

The elderly in particular, Sim realized, had few opportunities to gain political enlightenment, since they did not work outside the home and there were no social groups that organized social and educational activities for the elderly. If she wanted the elderly to take a more active role in People's NA projects, she needed to develop communal activities for the elderly that considered their level of political awareness. To this end, she arranged trips to museums and to the cinema for elderly members; on these trips, she took the time to explain in simple language the political content of the exhibits and films that they saw. As a result of these activities, the elderly began to look for ways that they could contribute to the management and welfare of the NA. In addition to taking care of children whose parents worked full time, they volunteered to do small repairs and conduct regular checks on the underfloor heating systems. Some older women volunteered to take on many responsibilities of a doula, so that young mothers did not have to ask their mothers for help.[40]

By engaging at a more personal level with members, Sim learned much about the interests and talents of members and took steps to utilize these abilities for the benefit of the NA. For example, there were two household heads in her NA who were good at home repairs. Thus, she assigned them to building maintenance. One focused on repairing doors and windows utilizing the communal People's NA toolbox, while the other head conducted regular checkups on *ondol*s (the underfloor heating systems). Similarly, she asked a woman whose hobby was sewing to conduct demonstrations on how to make children's clothing, and a woman who was good at cooking was enlisted to offer cooking lessons to members.

Headwoman Sim also made use of the ch'ŏngsanni method to get ideas from neighbors about how they could improve projects, such as scrap metal collection. One day, when she met with the household head in charge of collecting recyclable materials for the People's NA, she brought with her a small piece of metal. Pointing to it, she explained how much work it took to extract the ore from the earth to make this piece of metal that was not even as big as her hand. Even more work, she elaborated, was needed to convert it into steel. "Our country now needs iron," she explained. "Is there any way to find it?" A few days later, the man came to her with a smile on his face, saying that he had found a wing of a US airplane that crashed into the Taedong River during the Korean War. From that point forward, he regularly went out on his small boat to search for scrap iron.[41]

From the perspective of *Minju chosŏn,* Sim's adoption of the ch'ŏngsanni method and its successes functioned much like a morality play, in that it was intended to model the appropriate conduct and actions that socialist leaders should display. The message was clear: NA heads should use bespoke languages to arouse patriotic voluntarism from people.

BUILDING ECONOMIC JUCHE

The Ch'ŏllima People's NA Campaign was aimed at realizing economic self-sufficiency. Kim Il Sung had first referenced economic self-sufficiency in 1955 when he discussed the implementation of the first Five-Year Plan.[42] After Khrushchev's 1956 denouncement of Stalin's "cult of personality," Kim's subsequent introduction of reforms aimed at de-Stalinization and Stalin's seemingly lower prioritization of North Korea had prompted Kim Il Sung to advance an ideology of national self-reliance specifically and to discredit members of the Soviet faction (see chapter 8). In March 1958, the deepening Sino-Soviet split led Kim to make economic self-sufficiency North Korea's official policy and to criticize the Soviet Union's proposed international socialist division of labor, because it required the subordination of North Korean interests and those of other socialist nations to the interests of the Soviet Union. If Korea was to realize revolutionary self-reliance—that is, becoming an independent socialist country—he argued, it must cultivate an economy based on the development of heavy industry and free from dependence on other countries, including the Soviet Union and China. However, two events in the early 1960s—the 1961 military coup of Park Chung Hee in South Korea and the Cuban Missile Crisis—led North Korea to shift its focus from economic development to a policy (*Kukpang-kyŏngje pyŏngjin nosŏn*) that emphasized the simultaneous development of the country's economic and military capacity.[43] Heavy investment in defense slowed economic development, which in the 1950s had progressed rapidly.[44] With the slowing of economic development, the government moved to mobilize People's NAs to help reduce the economic shortfall.

To ensure a fair distribution of scarce goods, the North utilized People's NAs to assess where the goods were most needed.[45] At People's NA gatherings, heads asked member households what consumer goods they needed. Based on their answers, the head assembled a list of needed items, which he or she then took to the local shop. A staff member at the shop reviewed the list to check which items local factories had in stock and then placed an order with local factories. When the goods arrived, the local store displayed them, at which point residents could come and purchase what they needed.[46]

However, even with this system in place, low productivity levels meant the state did not always have sufficient product on hand to fill orders. The insufficiency was more pronounced in rural areas because the peasantry tended to live farther from centers of production than the working class. To address the issue, People's NAs in rural areas were urged to produce basic consumer goods beyond the community management. People's NAs that succeeded in overcoming shortages without seeking government assistance were rewarded for their efforts with the title of Ch'ŏllima; urban People's NAs that helped rural NAs in reaching these goals also received the title.

Minju chosŏn glorified People's NAs that realized economic self-reliance. On February 14, 1967, it printed a letter by Kil Ung-gŏl, a reporter at the radio station in Kujang County in North P'yŏng'an Province—a major coal-producing area. Kil wrote that after airing the story of headwoman Sim's success, he and his colleagues had decided to visit some People's NAs to see their reaction. They found that only one NA—the 134th People's NA, which bore the honorary title of Ch'ŏllima—had decided to emulate Sim's example. Disconcerted by the seeming indifference of most NAs, Kil wrote, "We considered this matter seriously. Although every People's NAs listened to the same thing, why did NAs respond differently? What if every NA could think of things just as the Ch'ŏllima 134th People's NA had? . . . What came to us was that every household in a People's NA should raise pigs and cultivate napa cabbages and radishes."[47] The journalists hoped that by giving members an opportunity for personal economic gain, the stagnated People's NAs could be revived.

To test the viability of this idea, on February 2, 1967, Kil met with a group known as "Women of People's NAs in the Ryongdŭng Workers District." The meeting was attended by roughly three hundred participants, including People's NA headwomen, propagandists, women in charge of hygiene, the chair of the PC, mining managers, and the local Workers' Party secretary. After listening to the recorded broadcast on Sim's success, headwomen gave presentations on their plans. A key agenda item was to achieve self-sufficiency by having households produce meats and vegetables. Pak Hyŏn-suk, a People's NA propagandist, commented, "What a great thing it would be if all the women in the mining town raised pigs and cultivated vegetables, as the prime minister [Kim Il Sung] recommended. It would reduce the government's burden, while helping our lives." Identifying personal interests with national ones, she pledged that each household in her People's NA would produce over one hundred kilograms of meat and vegetables to achieve self-sufficiency.

Other People's NAs had similar ideas. Kim Ok-ja, the headwoman of the Seventy-Ninth People's NA, suggested planting home gardens with spinach, radishes, eggplants, and cucumbers, as well as building pigpens. The 126th People's NA wanted to raise goats to provide milk for children, and the 146th People's NA suggested growing fruit trees on both sides of roads. As the meeting came to an end, it was emphasized again that "all of these things are for us. . . . They are to improve our lives in our mining village." The tactic of combining the Ch'ŏllima People's NAs campaign with opportunities for increased personal income produced positive responses. Kil reported that People's NAs experienced a boost in the number of actively involved residents. Many members now joined local competitions to earn the honorary title of Ch'ŏllima.[48]

As People's NAs began to cultivate previously vacant areas, significant changes occurred in the neighborhood space. Vegetable gardens appeared on empty slopes; beans or wild sesame filled road shoulders, riverbanks, and outskirts of arable fields. Apple, chestnut, persimmon trees or peach trees were planted.[49] These efforts at self-sufficiency enhanced communal bonds, as seen at the case of the Thirteenth People's NA of Unbong village in Chasŏng County in North P'yŏng'an. Prior to the campaign, only one person in the Thirteenth People's NA, Ri Ki-hak, raised animals. Once the project started, his example became the standard; from 1965 onward, as part of the Ch'ŏllima People's NA campaign, every household in the NA built pigpens and henhouses. Every Sunday, the household heads went out in search of feed for the animals. Since raising animals allowed the People's NAs to produce more fertilizer, they could grow more vegetables, which in turn allowed them to have the fodder needed for raising animals. The households whose crops had the best output shared their seeds with neighbors. Thanks to the cycle of fodder from vegetables and fertilizer from animals, every household produced an average of sixty-five kilograms of meat and vegetables for the winter; by cultivating garlic, pepper, and green onions, People's NAs were well prepared for Kimjang, a major event in late autumn when communities collectively made and shared large quantities of kimchi, or fermented vegetables, to ensure that every household had enough to sustain it through the harsh winter. Thanks to collective efforts, they even had extra to sell to the government.[50]

In the same vein, People's NAs organized "home working teams" (*kanae chagŏppan*). The name chosen for these work brigades was intended to invoke the image of a traditional family working together on a manufacturing or business activity. However, rather than the traditional family, the new family to which neighbors owed their allegiance was the Great Red Family. These work brigades were made up of residents who did not work outside the homes, that is, full-time housewives and the elderly. When the government in 1958 began pushing for the development of local industries, the work brigades grew in popularity. Making use of faulty products or leftover pieces of materials from local factories, they began producing essential consumer goods, such as brushes, clothing, shoes, gloves, toys, needles, and tables. They also received from factories unfinished products whose completion did not require specialized equipment.[51]

An illustrative case is the home working teams of Sŏn'gyo 1-dong in Pyongyang, which included six Ch'ŏllima People's NAs. In May 1967, an estimated 380 residents of the district were employed in these work brigades. Seven local factories, including the Sŏngyo fabric plant, distributed unfinished products to them for completion. As headwoman of the Nineteenth People's NA and the leader of its home working team, Cho Mae-wŏl played a central role in this effort. Her home working team became well known for how quickly it finished its assignments. Thanks to its hard work, the Nineteenth People's NA was able to provide member households with extra income and accumulate communal savings, which the NA used to purchase winter coats for students and the elderly.[52]

Although the North closed most private markets when it nationalized the economy, the existing people's markets (*inmin sijang*) survived, adopting the new name of "farmers' markets" (*nongmin sijang*) in 1958. The decision to allow farmers' markets to continue to operate was not without controversy within the Workers' Party. Opponents argued that their survival would lead to the reintroduction of capitalism. Supporters countered that farmers' markets predated capitalism; thus, their continuation under socialism was unlikely to lead to capitalism. Moreover, so long as the state allowed farmers to till private plots, small as they were, and have other private sources of income, private exchange could not be eliminated entirely.[53] Proponents of farmers' markets believed that these markets would disappear naturally when the state supply of goods exceeded demand. Once these conditions were established, Koreans would naturally prefer state-run cooperative stores over farmers' free markets, since the former would guarantee that customers in urban and rural areas would be able to purchase goods of equal quality at fair prices.[54]

Even as the North Korean leaders gave their approval to People's NAs pursuing private economic activities, they also insisted that People's NAs contribute to the realization of national economic goals—as had been the case since liberation. An illustrative case from the 1960s involved the government's demand that People's NAs participate in the campaign to improve agricultural productivity. The campaign that operated under the slogan "Let's liberate our farmers from heavy work and increase harvest output!" had its origins in *Theses on the Socialist Rural Question in Our Country (Urinara sahoejuŭi nongch'on munje'e kwanhan t'eje)*.[55] The *Rural Theses,* adopted at the Eighth Plenary Meeting of the Workers' Party on February 25, 1964, aimed at eliminating the backwardness of the countryside. The goal was to reduce the gap between urban and rural areas and the corresponding class distinction between workers and farmers. The *Rural Theses* explained, "Only if agriculture is brought in step with the advancing industry, while industry is developed and its leading role steadily enhanced, can a rapid development of the national economy as a whole be expected, and systematic improvement of the people's livelihood assured."[56] It advanced three agendas for revolutionizing the countryside. First, technological innovations—such as the expansion of irrigation, the supply of electricity to enable mechanized farming, increased use of chemicals and fertilizers, and the reclamation of swamps—were to be achieved by having the industrial sector work with farming communities. Second, the living standards of the peasantry required improvement; to this end, modern housing, schools, and hospitals needed to be built. Finally, "through prolonged, persevering education and constant struggle," the ideological consciousness of peasants must be "remolded." The success of this project, the party explained, required working-class Koreans across the nation to lead: "The working class must not only lead the peasantry politically and ideologically, but also give it material, technical, cultural and financial assistance."[57]

The national call put People's NAs to the test. It was unclear the extent to which urban People's NAs would sympathize with rural problems and whether People's NAs tasked with maintaining the communal space would collaborate with work brigades from the productive sector of the economy. The ability to overcome these regional and sectional divisions, the state saw as a measure of the cohesiveness of the Great Red

Family socialist state. As with other campaigns, *Minju chosŏn* published stories intended to communicate to the populace how People's NAs should respond to the government's call for action. For example, on March 8, 1967, it featured a story on the People's NAs of Manwŏl in Kaesŏng city, which had teamed up with industrial work brigades to help agricultural communities. In 1966, Kaesŏng city had launched a campaign in support of agricultural cooperatives; factory workers took it upon themselves to build repair centers for agricultural machinery. Ch'ŏllima work brigades taught members of local agricultural cooperatives how to repair farm machinery and provided farms with extra manpower.[58] Inspired by the actions of these work brigades, People's NAs in Kaesŏng resolved to make fertilizer for agricultural cooperatives and build storage units for composting ash. By January 15, 1966, they had produced 450 tons of manure and, with the help of workers from the Ox Cart Transporting Office in Kaesŏng, delivered it to the Songdo Agricultural Cooperatives.[59] The next year, the city set a target goal of producing and delivering 30,000 tons of manure. Each People's NA was made responsible for producing 2,000 tons. NA heads then divided this quota among member households. To encourage participation, the city held competitions throughout the year to see which People's NAs could collect the most leaves and straws with which to make manure. *Minju chosŏn* reported that many People's NAs exceeded their quota.[60]

Such reports were designed to spur low-performing People's NAs into action. As Kim Il Sung proclaimed, the stakes were no less than the success of the revolution and failure was not an option: "This is a struggle to consolidate our revolutionary base as firmly as a rock, to give greater encouragement to the peasants and people in south Korea, and to hasten the accomplishment of the cause of national reunification."[61]

CONCLUSION

The 1960s witnessed a massive North Korean effort to transform the political consciousness of the people and consolidate the socialist mode of living, focusing on Juche ideology. Believing that institutional change had outpaced ideological and cultural change, the government launched the Ch'ŏllima People's NA campaign to narrow the gap. It employed multiple strategies to foster a sense of communal belonging and an unwavering commitment to socialist values. First, it encouraged People's NAs to take over many responsibilities that traditionally had been performed by families. In this way, it fostered a sense of family that embraced the entire neighborhood space. This narrowing of the private/public dichotomy that characterized capitalist society was also achieved by assigning economic tasks to People's NAs. They formed "home working teams" in which they carried out economic tasks designed to improve neighborhoods and to advance the nation's objectives. To hearten consistent commitment to this communal way of life, the government conducted on-the-spot supervisions, awarded high-performing People's NAs with honorary titles, and advanced a narrative of the past. Through stories of exemplary People's NA life, North Korea put forward a vision of the ideal communal life and the ideal revolutionary subject who overcame difficulties through ingenuity and self-reliance.

EPILOGUE

The Two Constitutional Amendments of December 1972

By shifting the focus from state policy to local society, this book has illustrated how each of the three Korean states utilized neighborhood associations to create moral relations between state and society that fostered authoritarianism. In the context of war and state-building, each state mobilized the discourse of Korean "backwardness" to advance state-led mass enlightenment campaigns aimed at modernizing and making the Korean masses support the causes of these states. Modernization was not understood by any of the three states as the wholesale adoption of a Western political system, economic model, or morality. Instead, through neighborhood associations, each state introduced an indigenized form of modernization in which the concepts of family and of familial morals took center stage. Koreans were encouraged to see their local village and their state as part of an extended, hierarchically organized familial unit at the apex of which was the state leader. The vehicle for this transformation of identity was the neighborhood association, which in each state was tasked with promoting a community-based morality and spirit of voluntarism that were juxtaposed with a selfish and amoral Western capitalism. In merging tradition with modernization, each state—despite claims by the colonial and South Korean governments that NA campaigns were apolitical—dissolved the lines between the political, economic, and moral realms to advance state objectives. These state-led campaigns, however, had no endpoint, as enlightenment always remained beyond the reach of ordinary Koreans. The discourse of Korean backwardness in its various manifestations retained at some level the idea that overcoming low civility and political immaturity would require permanent efforts to change Korean attributes. Consequently, the state could retain its supremacy over the populace at the most basic level of community organization, the neighborhood, idealizing the people's mass participation in the state and their unexhausted active response to state calls for action.

This epilogue extends that analysis to the constitutions introduced in South Korea and in North Korea on December 27, 1972, which respectively provided the legal foundation for two authoritarianisms, "Korean-style democracy" and "our own style of socialism." In each constitution, for the first time, the phrase "the peaceful unification of the country" appeared. The appearance of the word "unification" in both constitutions stemmed from the July Fourth North–South Joint Statement of 1972, the first official joint statement released by the two Koreas since the 1953 armistice. The consented three principles for unification in the statement, which were independence, peace, and national unity, encapsulated the unfulfilled goals of Koreans.[1] During the war decades, Koreans had experienced wartime colonial rule, military occupation, the Korean War, and division by political ideologies at variance with national unity.

However, this apparent progress at defusing Cold War tensions on the Korean Peninsula was not accompanied by a parallel liberalization of domestic policy in the two Koreas. Indeed, the 1972 constitutions of both states increased authoritarianism at home. The South Korean Yusin Constitution replaced the system of direct presidential election with an indirect one and allowed the president to serve a limitless number of six-year terms. President Park Chung Hee, who had been in power since 1961, remained in office until his assassination by the director of the Korean Central Intelligence Agency on October 26, 1979. Meanwhile, in North Korea, the 1972 constitution created the position of premier (*chusŏk*) and made this officeholder the head of state with no reelection limitations. Kim Il Sung, who had been in power since 1948, was inaugurated as the first premier—a position that he would hold until his death in 1994. In short, both 1972 constitutions created a formidable leader who had complete control over state affairs.

"KOREAN-STYLE" DEMOCRACY:
THE YUSIN CONSTITUTION AND
THE NEW VILLAGE MOVEMENT

While in power from 1961 to 1979, Park Chung Hee twice resurrected NAs for state-led mass movements. In the 1960s, he launched Reconstruction NAs for the Reconstruction Movement (*Chaegŏn kungmin undong*), and in the 1970s, he introduced New Village NAs for the New Village Movement (*Saemaŭl undong*). Each of these movements was coextensive with martial law. In May 1961, his military coup ushered in a period of martial law that lasted until a new constitution was approved by popular referendum on December 6, 1962. Under this document, the parliamentary system was replaced by a presidential system, and Park was elected president three times. On October 17, 1972, Park declared martial law for a second time. Once again, the National Assembly was dissolved, and all political activities were suspended. This state of affair remained in place until December 27, 1972, when the Yusin Constitution was adopted.

The Path to Authoritarianism: The Reconstruction Movement and Reconstruction NAs

Although the two neighborhood associations—Reconstruction NAs and New Village NAs—marked two distinct periods of Park's rule, the concept of "Korean particularities" was common to both. As discussed in Part I of this book, the concept of "Korean particularities" played a critical role in the reintroduction of neighborhood associations in the 1930s. Whereas in the 1920s the colonial authorities had associated the concept of "Korean particularities" with backwardness and used it as a justification for colonization, they now employed it also to signify Korean tradition and culture. The new signification, in combination with Japan's wartime assimilation policy, was intended to ensure the voluntary mobilization of Koreans for the Japanese war effort. The two emphases contained two inherent contradictions. First, whereas assimilation policy promoted the idea of "harmony between Japan and Korea," Patriotic NAs, as a manifestation of Korean particularity to which the notion of inferiority remained attached, implied that Koreans' level of civility would always remain subpar to that of the Japanese. Second, since Patriotic NAs were viewed as unique to Korea, the colonial government cited its superior knowledge of Korean culture to establish a certain degree of autonomy from the Japanese homeland in implementing imperial policy; but as this authority was based on knowledge of an allegedly inferior culture, greater autonomy for the colonial government did not translate into greater political agency for the Korean populace.

The concept of "Korean particularities" survived liberation and played a critical role in how Citizens' NAs were conceptualized in the South. While the colonial concept of "Korean particularities" implied Korea's inferiority to and differences from Japan, in South Korea, it meant that South Koreans were less politically mature than their Western counterparts who lived in liberal democracies. The alleged political immaturity of Koreans was used to discredit party politics, to downplay the ability of Koreans to participate in local governance, and to prop up the authority of the centralized political order. Under Syngman Rhee, this order was understood as an organic body, in which all sections of society, bonded by blood ties and history, worked in harmony toward a common goal. To realize this ideal organic state, state-led national movements, in which Citizens' NAs acted as the operative local unit, were promoted. NAs were the focal point of mass enlightenment campaigns whose goal was to raise South Koreans' level of civility to that of citizens in Western liberal democracies and to enhance national cohesiveness in preparation for national unification under the leadership of the South.

For Park Chung Hee, "Korean particularities" were the solution to Korea's woes. Rather than equating "Korean particularities" with backwardness or low civility, Park understood them as tradition and culture. It was the failure of the two previous administrations—the Rhee administration and the short-lived Chang administration—to restore Korean culture and tradition following liberation, Park argued, that had led to political corruption and economic stagnation. Both leaders, he claimed, had tried to introduce concepts and institutions that were foreign to Korean culture. The result was factionalism, political corruption, economic stagnation, and widespread poverty. Transforming Korea into a politically independent and economically prosperous nation required a return to so-called Korean values.[2]

The concept of reconstruction (*chaegŏn*) was central to Park's regime. Park and other leaders of the May 16 military coup described it as the "revolution for national reconstruction" (*chaegŏn hyŏngmyŏng*). Park argued that Korea should concentrate all its energy on eliminating old evils, thereby promoting "national morality" (*kungmin toŭi*) and national spirit, improving "national life" (*kungmin saenghwal*) in social, economic, and all other spheres. As indicated, political and economic reconstruction included a moral dimension. Fostering so-called traditional Korean values that had been forgotten, such as self-regulation, patriotism, public consciousness, work ethic, and self-sacrifice, Park believed, was an integral part of advancing economic development—a priority in state-building.[3]

Park's dual focus on economic and moral development was an outgrowth of his experiences under Japanese imperial rule. In the early 1940s, Park attended a Japanese military academy and subsequently served as a second lieutenant in the Japanese Army in Manchuria during World War II. As noted in chapter 1, the Japanese military viewed laissez-faire capitalism with moral contempt, believing that it encouraged the pursuit of personal interests at the expense of national interests. This view of capitalism as a destructive force imported from the West was particularly strong in Manchuria, where radical reformists in the Japanese Army steadfastly supported building a state-controlled economy.[4] Influenced by this negative assessment of capitalism, Park pursued a model of economic nationalism in which the state engaged in centralized planning of the economy, regulated the market-based economy, and subsidized private enterprises. Left unchecked, Park contended, capitalism would lead to gross economic inequalities, which in turn would make South Korea vulnerable to communism.[5]

The Reconstruction Movement was launched in June 1961. Koreans were urged to "follow the national cause [being united for building a completely independent society], by working with the government as one body."[6] The primary institution through which the masses demonstrated their commitment to working as one body was the neighborhood association. To distance them from their past use for colonial wartime mobilization and their association with political corruption during Rhee's rule, NAs were renamed Reconstruction NAs.[7] Under the Park regime, there were about 160,000 Reconstruction NAs; each NA was encouraged to have two persons in charge of delivering government policies and to hold both official and unofficial gatherings as needed.[8] The government defined the morally appropriate tasks for NAs as promoting anticommunism, frugality, a work ethic, productivity improvement, and national gymnastics to enhance public health.[9]

The strategy of utilizing the neighborhood moral space to advance the reconstruction movement resurrected the old issue of voluntarism. Both colonial Patriotic NAs and Citizens' NAs, as voluntary mass movements, were hampered by the fact that they were also part of the bureaucratic hierarchy. Wanting to keep both dimensions of NAs, the military government put forward a new justification for state involvement in the administration of NAs. The South Korean people, the military government claimed, were so accustomed to obeying orders from higher authorities that expecting them immediately to embrace self-determination was unrealistic. The government needed to provide them with gentle, implicit "guidance" (*chido*) so as to facilitate the populace's transition from being "passive and compliant" to embracing subjectivity (*juche*) and self-determination (*chayul*).[10]

Park and other military leaders realized that, at least ostensibly, they must create some distance between the government and NAs. The memory of how Rhee's administration had abused Citizens' NAs to advance its political fortunes remained fresh in the minds of South Koreans. If the military government pursued a similar tactic, it would undermine the rationale behind the coup, that is, to save the nation from the factionalism and corruption that it claimed had plagued its predecessors. Consequently, on June 19, 1961, Park appointed Yoo Chin-o, a well-respected civilian who had drafted the 1948 constitution, to lead the Reconstruction Movement.[11] However, Yoo's tenure was short lived due to differences with Park over the role that the state should play in the Reconstruction Movement. Yoo wanted the movement to be strictly civilian led, as he believed that this would prevent NAs from becoming entangled in political activities and would foster the people's ability to engage in self-rule.[12] Park, in contrast, believed that reconstruction required a state-centered approach. This difference resulted in Yoo's resignation just three months after his appointment. As Yoo's successor, on September 8, 1961, Park appointed Yu Tal-yŏng, a professor who taught in the Agricultural College of Seoul National University. Like his predecessor, Yu also endorsed a civilian-led model for the movement. This time, Park gave his promise that Yu would have complete control over the movement, and Yu agreed that the mass movement should focus on promoting anticommunism, principles of democracy, and reform of everyday life.[13]

Yu was determined that the Reconstruction Movement would not follow the pattern of previous mass campaigns—that is, the movement would not be closely tied to NAs and to the government. Yu's resolve was reflected in the amended version of the Reconstruction Movement Act, adopted in September 1961. Unlike the original version, which made NAs part of the organizational hierarchy of the movement, the amended version divorced NAs from the movement.[14] In lieu of NAs, local branches of the movement were encouraged to form youth groups and women's groups as the new driving force of the movement.[15] To ensure the movement's independence from the government, Yu established the National Reconstruction Movement Private Corporation in July 1964.[16]

Once Reconstruction NAs were divorced from the movement, NA was renamed to Citizens' NAs.[17] Voluntary participation in NA activities declined. Loss of interest in NAs was particularly pronounced in the cities.[18] Though NAs occasionally performed administrative tasks, such as notifying members of various government policies, their primary focus was on addressing localized concerns. The moral neighborhood space gradually ceased to operate as a national political space and returned to being part of the private and local sphere.

From Reconstruction to the Yusin Constitution and the New Village Movement

In February 1972, the Interior Ministry dispatched a formal notification instructing local officials to overhaul NAs. It ordered provincial governors to rezone NAs, to enforce regular monthly meetings, and to ensure that NA heads recorded attendance and meeting minutes. Town officials were told to prepare a bulletin for mass enlightenment programs, such as national security and the New Village Movement. It explained that the government needed an efficient communication system able to deliver policies to the Korean populace quickly and to listen to their voices under the current state of emergency.[19] In sum, the government moved to reassert control over NAs and renationalize their agenda.

Strengthening NAs in early 1972 presaged South Korea's transition to an authoritarian system at the end of the year, known as Yusin. Park Chung Hee, who had faced strong student protests since the 1969 constitutional amendment to allow for a third presidential term, sent military troops to universities in Seoul to suppress them in October 1971. In December 1971, he declared a state of emergency on the grounds that these protests made South Korea vulnerable to attack by the North. The argument was strengthened by President Richard Nixon's decision in 1971 to withdraw US troops from South Korea and by the prediction that Nixon would pursue rapprochement with China at the expense of Korea's interests.[20] Taking advantage of these international developments, Park proclaimed martial law on October 17, 1972, and introduced the Yusin Constitution in December 1972. He claimed that it was "fundamentally designed to reform the political structure," to address "the rapidly changing international situation," to further dialogue with the North on reunification, and to give legal backing to what he described as Korean-style democracy, which amounted to authoritarianism.[21]

Park equated "Yusin," meaning revitalization, with the restoration of the nation's prosperity (*minjok chunghŭng*)—the source of which he identified with spiritual values that were ingrained in tradition and culture: "We learned [from the 1960s] that traditional culture, seen as incompatible with modernization, was in fact instrumental to it."[22] Economic prosperity, thus, depended on pursuing an indigenous system rather than mimicking a Western economic model. He, then, extended this economic analysis to the political realm. Transplanting an American-style democracy to Korea, he argued, would not work, because "unlike the West which sees the individual as in confrontation with the state, Koreans see the two as part of a harmonious, holistic order."[23] Korea, therefore, must adopt a democratic system consistent with Korean values and the Korean situation.

Park focused on Korea's reunification in order to build a Korean-style harmonious, holistic order while deeming that the National Assembly would undermine it. This notion found legal expression in the preamble of the 1972 Yusin Constitution. The preamble showed two significant changes to the wording found in earlier constitutions. Unlike previous constitutions, it addressed the issue of reunification: "For the historical mission of peaceful *unification* [emphasis added] of our homeland, we, the people of Korea, aim at building a *new* [emphasis added] democratic republic capable of solidifying liberal democratic order." This addition was accompanied by an equally significant omission; it included no reference to the National Assembly in its closing lines, stating simply "do hereby amend, through national referendum, the Constitution, ordained and established on the twelfth day of July of 1948 and amended on the twenty-sixth day of December of 1962." It left out the words "following a resolution by the National Assembly." South Korea's legislative body, the National Assembly, had been excluded from the making of Korean-style democracy.

To promote reunification and to check the National Assembly, the 1972 constitution created a new national body, the National Conference for Unification (*T'ong'iljuch'e kungminhoeŭi,* hereafter NCU). Representatives to the NCU, like representatives to the National Assembly, were elected by the people. However, the new NCU dwarfed the National Assembly in size; whereas the National Assembly had between 200 and 220 representatives, the plan was for the NCU to have between 2,000 and 5,000 representatives. Since its focus would be Korean reunification—a topic seen as transcending partisan politics— Koreans who had served in the National Assembly or who belonged to a political party were disqualified from serving as a representative in the NCU. Political parties were banned from endorsing any candidate running for the NCU. To ensure that elections for this body did not become politicized, the use of political slogans on candidates' posters was banned. Posters could only include the candidate's name, picture, address, education, occupation, and election precinct. Instead of election campaigns by the candidates, one speaking event was scheduled, at which each candidate was given twenty minutes to make their case for office. The speech content was limited to the topic of unification. Once elected to serve a six-year term in the NCU, each representative remained obliged to abstain from party politics.[24]

The power balance between the two representative bodies was also heavily weighted in favor of the NCU. The Yusin Constitution characterized the NCU as the "depository of national sovereignty" that expressed the "collective will of the people for the peaceful unification of the homeland." Article 39, thus, gave it the power to elect the president, rather than the National Assembly. Moreover, Article 40 specified that the NCU had the power to choose from its ranks one-third of the National Assembly, which at that time equaled 73 out of 219 assembly members. Finally, Article 41 stipulated that although the National Assembly could propose constitutional amendments, the NCU, rather than a popular referendum, determined whether those amendments became law.

The massive power imbalance between the two representative bodies ended up reinforcing the presidential power. The right of the NCU to elect a president elevated the president to the status of an apolitical supreme leader, whose duty was unification—a national goal beyond partisan politics. Moreover, Article 36 made the president the chair of the NCU. As chair of the NCU, the president had the right to select the representatives from the NCU who would serve in the National Assembly. Once Park chose a list of representatives, the NCU could approve or disapprove those selected. Technically, this approval process meant that the NCU could act as a check on the presidential power. However, this seldom happened, because it lacked cohesion. Representatives in the NCU, whose positions were largely honorary, received no salary; they did not meet on a regular basis and had no specialized committees. The NCU had no institutional home in Seoul; when it did meet, it met at a stadium or other large facility. At the conclusion of the meeting, representatives collected their travel allowances and returned to their homes throughout Korea.[25]

The president's control over the NCU also critically undermined the ability of the National Assembly to act as a check on presidential powers. Although the Yusin Constitution endowed it with the power to impeach the president by a two-thirds majority, it was unlikely to happen, given that the president appointed one-third of the National Assembly and controlled the ruling party. It was also unlikely that the National Assembly could weaken presidential powers through a constitutional amendment, since the NCU, chaired by the president, had final approval rights over any amendment.

The "Korean-style democracy" built by the Yusin Constitution was a variation on previous moral authoritarian structures that had been utilized under colonial rule and under the Rhee regime. The Japanese governors general, Syngman Rhee, and Park Chung Hee each advanced a so-called apolitical national realm and created a nationwide organization to represent this realm. As discussed earlier, under colonial rule, it was the Korean League for the General Mobilization of the National Spirit (later renamed the League of Concerted National Power); under Rhee, it was the National Society; and under Park, it was the NCU.

However, there was a significant difference between the NCU and earlier "apolitical" national organizations. While earlier "apolitical" organizations had been linked to state-led mass movements in which NAs served as the basic unit of operation, the NCU had no such association. Most likely, this decision to disassociate the organization from mass campaigns was indicative of Park's inability to dominate the Reconstruction Movement in the 1960s. As noted earlier, its civilian leaders had insisted on civilian-led movements and organizational independence of Citizens' NAs to prevent a repeat of past abuses. Thus, rather than linking the NCU to neighborhood associations, the Yusin constitution made it a parallel representative body to the National Assembly and gave it significant control over the National Assembly.

NAs were linked to the state-led New Village Movement. Introduced at roughly the same time as the NCU, it was an economic modernization movement that sought to improve living conditions in rural areas by instilling the New Village spirit of diligence, self-reliance, and cooperation.[26] As it was expanded in 1973 to include urban areas, the name "New Village NAs" slowly replaced the old name, Reconstruction NAs.[27]

Beyond the economic goals, the New Village Movement, Park asserted, "is a *training school* to entrench Korean-style democracy, to foster patriotism, and to materialize the October Yusin ideology."[28] The remark summarized the ideal relationship that each Korean state since the 1930s had sought to develop with the masses through neighborhood associations. In likening the state-led movement to a training school, Park invoked the discourse of "Korean backwardness": that is, Koreans needed schooling in good citizenship and orderly behavior—a task that since the late 1930s the state had pursued through mass enlightenment programs. The New Village movement combined in one program elements from each of the previous state campaigns. Its focus on cultivating patriotism corresponded with that of both colonial Patriotic NAs and

North Korean People's NAs; its emphasis on democracy was in line with that of Rhee's Citizens' NAs; and its concentration on national restoration through economic revitalization mirrored that of Reconstruction NAs and that of People's NAs in the North. For Park, the three foci—patriotism, Korean-style democracy, and national restoration—were inseparable: "The New Village Movement is the October Yusin and the October Yusin is the New Village Movement . . . there should be no bystander or dropout in this nationwide movement in which everyone should participate voluntarily and of his own accord."[29]

The administrative structure of the New Village Movement was organized hierarchically, with the Interior Ministry serving as chair of the New Village Central Council. At the local level, villages were advised to choose a "New Village leader," who had a passion for rural community development; in addition, each village had a local planning committee that was encouraged to introduce innovations to the national plan, based on local conditions.[30] This emphasis on taking into consideration local conditions in implementing the campaign closely paralleled the ch'ongsanni method introduced by Kim Il Sung in the 1960s in the North. In fact, the New Village movement in the South and the Ch'ŏllima movement in the North had multiple similarities: voluntarism, self-reliance, community participation, competition, and modernization through the incorporation of tradition. Like the Ch'ŏllima movement, the imposition of a structured program of attitudinal training, referred to officially as "spiritual enlightenment" or "spiritual revolution" (*chŏngsin hyŏngmyŏng*), increasingly eliminated any space in which to embrace diversities and express political dissent. The moral authoritarianism of the Yusin Constitution and that of the New Village Movement reinforced one another, and at the center of both was Park Chung Hee.

"OUR OWN STYLE OF SOCIALISM": THE SOCIALIST CONSTITUTION AND THE CH'ŎLLIMA MOVEMENT

During the last ten days of 1972, the enactment of the Socialist Constitution had the full attention of all North Koreans, as it was first time that any major amendments to the 1948 constitution that created a people's democracy in the North had been proposed. On October 23, 1972, a committee to draft the Socialist Constitution (*Hŏnbŏp kich'owiwŏnhoe*) was established and a reading session was scheduled for the Plenary Meeting of the Central Committee of the Workers' Party. On December 25, 1972, the government submitted the Socialist Constitution to the Supreme People's Assembly (*Ch'oego inminhoeŭi*) for discussion.[31] On December 26, 1972, discussions were held, and the next day the Supreme People's Assembly approved the new constitution.[32]

A new constitution, the North Korean leader believed, was needed so that the law of the land reflected the state's expanding socialist policies. As Kim Il Sung explained to the Supreme People's Assembly: "Our situation today urgently demands the establishment of a new Socialist Constitution to give legal force to the tremendous achievements of our people in the socialist revolution and the building of socialism and to lay down the principles of the political, economic, and cultural features of socialist society."[33] The tremendous achievement to which Kim referred was the transition to a socialist economy. Since its adoption of the 1948 constitution, North Korea had introduced agricultural cooperatives and socialized commerce. Articles 5 and 7 of the 1948 constitution, which protected private ownership of the means of production, were at odds with North Korea's economic reality.[34] In deleting these outdated elements, the amended constitution also inserted new socialist contents. Article 18 specified that the means of production were owned by the state and cooperative organizations. However, Article 22 of the new constitution did recognize the right of cooperative farmers to have small private plots on which they could plant foodstuffs for personal use; it also acknowledged the rights of farmers to hand down these plots to family members.[35]

The new constitution also explicitly incorporated Juche as the guiding principle of the state. This ideology, introduced by Kim in a 1955 speech, centered on the particularities of Korean history and informed North Korea's indigenized approach to transitioning to a socialist economy in the 1960s. The opening articles of the 1972 constitution repeatedly referenced the key components of the ideology—political independence, economic self-reliance, a revolutionary tradition, a North Korean version of Marxism-Leninism, national unification, and self-defense:

Article 1. The Democratic People's Republic of Korea is an independent socialist state representing the interests of all the Korean people.

Article 2. The Democratic People's Republic of Korea rests on the politico-ideological unity of all the people based on the worker-peasant alliance led by the working class, on the socialist relations of production and the foundation of an independent national economy.

Article 3. The Democratic People's Republic of Korea is a revolutionary power which had inherited the brilliant traditions formed during the glorious revolutionary struggle against the imperialist aggressors and for the liberation of the homeland and for the freedom and well-being of the people.

Article 4. The Democratic People's Republic of Korea is guided in its activities by the Juche idea of the Workers' Party of Korea, a creative application of Marxism-Leninism to the conditions of our country.

Article 5. The Democratic People's Republic of Korea is working to achieve the complete victory of socialism in the northern half of Korea, drive out foreign forces on a national scale, reunify the country peacefully on a democratic basis and attain complete national independence.

Article 14. The Democratic People's Republic of Korea is based on an all-people, nationwide system of defense and follows a self-defensive military line.[36]

Beyond serving as an ideological guide, the Juche discourse found in the 1972 constitution reflected the changing postliberation concerns of the North. In the immediate aftermath of liberation, it had established a people's democracy (1945–1953) and concentrated its efforts on overcoming the remnants of Japanese imperialism and achieving independence from the US–USSR occupation of the Korean Peninsula. This dual focus, reflected in the 1948 constitution, was clearly articulated in the emphasis placed on the people (*inmin*) as the source of state sovereignty. While political independence remained central to the 1972 constitution, there were significant changes in how this theme was articulated.

The catalyst for this change was the Korean War. The entry of the United States reversed North Korea's early victories, and its aerial assault had reduced North Korea to rubble and threatened the nation with economic ruin. Moreover, in the wake of the 1953 cease-fire, US troops had remained on South Korean soil. Unsurprisingly, the United States replaced Japan as the object of North Korea's anti-imperialist rhetoric. The extensive damage inflicted by US bombs also accelerated the collectivization of agriculture and the socialization of commerce as the North Korean leader sought to hasten the postwar economic recovery.

The Korean War also affected North Korea's relations with the Soviet Union. When the war turned into a war of attrition, the Soviet faction of the North Korean Workers' Party, as noted earlier, challenged Kim's leadership. To counter his opponents within the party, Kim had criticized their slavish devotion to the Soviet model of socialism. This confluence of events led Kim Il Sung in a 1955 speech to first articulate the idea of Juche.[37] By December 16, 1967, when Kim gave his speech "Let Us Embody the Revolutionary Spirit of Independence, Self-Sustenance and Self-Defense More Thoroughly in All Branches of State Activity," Juche had been solidified into the "political program of the government of the Democratic People's Republic of Korea."[38]

Juche socialism under the 1972 constitution followed the classic socialist line, in that Article 10 professed that the North would "exercise the dictatorship of the proletariat" and "adhere to the class and mass lines." However, it also indigenized this line of argument by introducing a moral relationship between the state and the people in Article 12: "The State applies Ch'ŏngsanni spirit and Ch'ŏngsanni method in all its activities to guarantee that the higher bodies help the lower, the masses' opinions are respected and their conscious enthusiasm is roused by giving priority to political work, work with people." As noted in chapter 9, Kim Il Sung had created the Ch'ŏngsanni method during an on-the-spot supervision after realizing that during the Korean War local officials had fallen back on bureaucratic coercion to achieve mass campaign goals. In lieu of bureaucratism and dogmatism, he stressed the need for local officials to consider local circumstances and encourage local innovations when implementing state policy. By showing kindness, understanding, and affection for the people, Kim asserted, local officials could enhance the spirit of voluntarism and catalyze the masses to demonstrate a passionate commitment to the socialist cause.

This moral relationship, however, was not one between equals. As Article 13 made clear, the state had the right to guide and push the masses toward the realization of state goals: "The state hastens socialist construction to the maximum by constantly developing the Ch'ŏllima movement in depth and in scope." Beginning in the late 1950s, the Ch'ŏllima movement, which called upon Koreans to exemplify endurance, speed, and consistency in their work, had produced the collective enthusiasm from the masses that the North Korean leadership believed was essential for building the socialist economy. Its success in the economic sphere prompted it to extend the movement to the cultural sphere through mass campaigns that targeted the moral space of the neighborhood. This pattern of relying on mass campaigns, as we have seen, had its origins in the wartime mass campaigns launched under Japanese rule and mirrored in many respects the state-led campaigns launched by South Korea, its postwar ideological rival. The similarity between the three Koreas—colonial Korea, South Korea, and North Korea—also extended to the justification for these campaigns. Each of the three states utilized the invented tradition of "Korean backwardness" or "low civility" as a rationale for its actions. This so-called particularity of Korean history, according to North Korean officials, threatened to derail the state's economic progress; only by transforming ordinary North Koreans into revolutionary beings could future economic progress be guaranteed.

The implications of Juche ideology, of the Ch'ŏllima mass movement, and of the Ch'ŏngsanni method converged in People's NAs. Once the North reconfigured the moral space of the neighborhood as a voluntary gathering of patriots, who had political agency, People's NAs became the principal site for political enlightenment campaigns aimed at elevating the political consciousness of the masses; patriotic campaigns, such as rice donation, intended to ensure the nation's independence; and participatory administration to encourage people's agency. The Korean War was a turning point for People's NAs. Though People's NAs had worked in concert with village officials on wartime administrative tasks, they lost some administrative functions during the post-Korean War recovery period. Instead, People's NAs were tasked with communal management of residential areas. With the introduction of the two complementary ideologies of Juche and of the Great Red Family, the neighborhood space became coextensive with the familial and economic realms. NA leaders were encouraged to cultivate neighborly familial ties through assuming responsibility for tasks, such as childcare, that were traditionally reserved for the family. In addition, communal projects were designed to foster in Koreans a sense of belonging to one's NA that would radiate outward to the village and ultimately the country. Thus, in addition to representing female NA leaders as mothers of the community, the official North Korean newspaper portrayed Kim Il Sung as the supreme father of the Great Red Family. Once family became synonymous with the nation, it was natural to expect People's NAs also to function as an extension of the economic realm. The Ch'ŏllima movement enlisted the voluntary co-operation of People's NAs for building socialism using the Ch'ŏngsanni method. In short, so-called People's NA life did not simply link the public and private domains but also shrank the private domain, over which the state could exercise only limited control.

The 1972 constitution gave voice to the people's neighborhood associational life through its repeated use of the phrase "the socialist way of life." Article 38 declared that the state had eliminated the "the way of life inherited from the outmoded society" and replaced it with "a new socialist way of life in every sphere." Article 39 pointed to the new revolutionary persona being formed through People's NA life: "The state shall put the principles of socialist education into practice and raise the new generation to be steadfast revolutionaries who will fight for society and the people, to be people of a new communist type who are knowledgeable, morally sound, and physically healthy." This blending of the moral and political also found expression in the duties of the populace. Article 67 stipulated that the people "must observe the laws of the state, the socialist way of life, and the socialist code of conduct." In sum, the constitution gave official legal recognition to the merger of the moral and political realms.

This legal and political recognition was in fact what differentiated People's NAs from colonial Patriotic NAs and from South Korean NAs (Citizens' NAs, Reconstruction NAs, and New Village NAs), since neither Patriotic NAs nor South Korean NAs were recognized as political entities. The colonial state could not acknowledge the political character of Patriotic NAs, since Koreans had no political rights under colonial rule. The South Korean state, likewise, could not acknowledge NAs as political entities, since the mandatory nature of membership contradicted liberal democracy's concept of freedom of association. Thus, to maintain the illusion that NAs were apolitical, voluntary organizations, both the colonial state and the South Korean state created quasi-independent organizations through which the state could control NAs. But the North Korean government had no need to maintain this illusion and thus established no third entity to mediate between People's NAs and the state. It wanted North Koreans, through participation in People's NAs, to develop a political consciousness, as it associated an advanced political consciousness with loyalty to an independent Korea that under socialist rule would represent the interests of all Koreans.

Despite this difference, North Korean People's NAs had historical links to both colonial and South Korean NAs. On the one hand, People's NAs appropriated the patriarchal structure of colonial Patriotic NAs. In building the Greater East Asian Co-Prosperity Sphere, Japan had utilized family ideology to differentiate culturally East Asia from the West and to construct a hierarchical relationship in East Asia, in which the Japanese emperor as the supreme father maintained public morality and safeguarded economic and political interests in the region. After liberation, the North initially abandoned the patriarchal structure of Patriotic NAs, seeing it as at odds with the concepts of gender equality and popular sovereignty that were central to creating a people's democracy. Thus, in 1946, as noted in chapter 8, North Korea's new system of identification did not use the designation "patriarch" (*hoju*). Instead, it used "head of household" (*sedaeju*) to indicate the representative of the family. However, when in the context of the Korean War, Kim Il Sung moved to indigenize socialism, the concept of the state as an extended family was reintroduced in the form of the Great Red Family. The family-like People's NAs answered to the state patriarch and party leader, Kim Il Sung.

On the other hand, People's NAs, like their counterparts in the South, stressed the subjectivity of the Korean masses. Both Koreas believed it was critical to distinguish themselves from their colonial predecessor by highlighting the agency of the Korean people. Each also believed that the postliberation independence remained incomplete. Achieving full independence required developing the nation's economic, military, and cultural sectors, which in turn required overcoming the political immaturity of the populace that had resulted from years under colonial rule. This alleged political immaturity served as each state's rationale for utilizing the neighborhood space to provide moral guidance to the populace. This moral guidance, despite the two states' differences in political ideology, had multiple features in common: an understanding of patriotism that stressed obedience, an emphasis on the collective, and the promotion of a patriarchal morality. Thus, neighborhoods ultimately became makeshift schools in which each state's ideology—Yusin in the South and Juche socialism in the was put into practice.

In the wake of the 1972 constitutions, the two indigenized authoritarian orders became more ingrained. In South Korea, "Korean-style democracy" justified prioritizing the collective good over individual and human rights. With a focus on economic development, anticommunism, and a filial piety that extended to the state, Park Chung Hee argued that "the [economic] survival of 35 million Koreans is the highest form of human rights" and that filial piety and loyalty to the state represented "the basic forms of humanitarianism." As national rights were a precondition for human rights, South Koreans "should voluntarily restrain or reserve individual liberty" in the interest of the populace's collective economic welfare and national security.[39] Similarly, in North Korea, "our own style of socialism" became more entrenched. In the mid-1970s when the political influence of Kim Il Sung, was on the rise, he spearheaded a "revolutionary tradition" education program that included the development of revolutionary historical sites, museums, North Korean cinema, and theater.[40] In 1978, when Deng Xiaoping introduced market-oriented economic reforms in the People's Republic of China, Kim Jong Il moved to theorize Juche socialism, stating, "Let's live by our own way."[41]

"Korean-style democracy" and "our own style of socialism" competed to build a "true" Korea free from its colonial past and competent enough to achieve national unification by proving its superiority over the other. As seen in the use of neighborhood spaces for state-led mass movements, however, both inherited the wartime colonial structure: apolitical unity of the state in "Korean-style democracy" and patriarchal structure in "our own style of socialism." Although both still appealed to liberal democracy and socialism respectively, the collective culture of the democratic

South dominated individuality, while family diluted class consciousness in the North. Both postcolonial Koreas believed that states should enlighten the Korean masses and train them, which created authoritarianism, the nature of which forced participation rather than suppression. Consequently, colonialism, nationalism, democracy, and socialism were intermingled, all aiming to create a patriotic, patriarchal, and participatory mass in the moral space of local neighborhoods.

The 1987 constitutional amendment of South Korea began to decouple the neighborhood associations from state-led mass movements. It was the outcome of the continuing protests of South Korean civil society against the military regime that followed the assassination of Park Chung Hee in 1979. Under the 1987 constitution, a direct presidential election was held in December 1987, and local elections were held in 1991, thirty years after the previous ones in 1960. In 1995 the government handed over the authority of NA assemblies to local societies. In the twenty-first century, NA assemblies were either abolished or turned into spaces for discussing local issues. In contrast, People's NAs in the North, which kept "our own style of socialism," took responsibility for achieving a socialist mode of living.[42] The driving force that dissolved the wartime colonial legacy was not nationalism, but democratization.

NOTES

INTRODUCTION

1. Kim Sŏng-ch'il, *Yŏksa ap'esŏ- han sahakchaŭi 6.25 ilgi* (A historian's diary during the Korean War) (Seoul: Ch'angbi, 1993), 261; all translations of from Korean to English are mine unless otherwise noted.

2. Sŏ Hyŏn-ju, "Chosŏnmal iljeha Seourŭi habu haengjŏng chedo yŏn'gu" (Local administrations in Seoul from the late Chosŏn to colonial period) (PhD diss., Seoul National University, 2002): 78, 120–146.

3. For more on the antagonistic interdependence between the two Koreas, see Pak Myŏng-rim, "Pundan chilsŏŭi kujowa pyŏnhwa: chŏktaewa ŭijonŭi taessang kwan'gye tonghak, 1945–1995" (The structure of division and its change), *Kukka chŏllyŏk* 3, no. 1 (1997): 41–79.

4. On the evolution of the historiography of collaboration in South Korea, see Koen de Ceuster, "The Nation Exorcised: The Historiography of Collaboration in South Korea," *Korean Studies* 25, no. 2 (2001): 207–242.

5. Bruce Cumings, *The Origins of the Korean War: Liberation and the Emergence of Separate Regimes* (Seoul: Yŏksa pip'yŏngsa, 2002), 151–153; Chung Kŭn-sik, ed., *Singminji yusan, kukka hyŏngsŏng, han'guk minjujuŭi* (Colonial legacies, state formation, and Korean democracy) (Seoul: Ch'aeksesang, 2012).

6. Carter Eckert, *Offspring of Empire: The Koch'ang Kims and the Colonial Origins of Korean Capitalism, 1876–1945* (Seattle: University of Washington Press, 1991); An Pyŏng-jik and Nakamura Tetsu, ed., *Kŭndae Chosŏn kong'ŏphwa yŏn'gu, 1930–1945* (A study of modern Korean industrialization) (Seoul: Iljogak, 1993).

7. Kim Sŏng-hak, "Kundaesik hakkyo kyuyurŭi kiwŏn t'amsaek" (The origins of modern school discipline), *Kyoyuk pip'yŏng* 22 (2007): 107–127.

8. For colonial Korea, see Gi-Wook Shin and Do-Hyun Han, "Colonial Corporatism: The Rural Revitalization Campaign, 1932–1940," in *Colonial*

Modernity in Korea, ed. Gi-Wook Shin and Michael Robinson (Cambridge, MA: Harvard University Asia Center, 1999), 70–96. For North Korea see Bruce Cumings, "Corporatism in North Korea," *Journal of Korean Studies* 4 (1982–1983): 269–294.

9. On this antiliberal collective identity promoted by Japanese colonizers, see, for example, Mark Caprio, *Japanese Assimilation Policies, 1910–1945* (Seattle: University of Washington Press, 2011); on North Korean antiliberal collective identity, see, for example, Suzy Kim, *Everyday Life in the North Korean Revolution, 1945–1950* (Ithaca, NY: Cornell University Press, 2013).

10. See Kim Sŏng-bo, *Nambukhan kyŏngje kujoŭi chŏn'gae: Pukhan nong'ŏpch'ejeŭi hyŏngsŏng'ŭl chungsimŭro* (The economic structures of the two Koreas) (Seoul: Yŏksa pip'yŏngsa, 2013).

11. For more on the moral dimension of the neighborhood space in traditional and modern societies and on the dynamic boundaries of this space, see Dismas A. Masolo, "Community, Identity, and the Cultural Space," *Rue Descarte* 2, no. 36 (2002): 19–22.

12. Benjamin L. Read, *Roots of the State: Neighborhood Organization and Social Networks in Beijing and Taipei* (Palo Alto, CA: Stanford University Press, 2012), 40.

13. Sally Ann Hastings, *Neighborhood and Nation in Tokyo, 1905–1937* (Pittsburgh, PA: University of Pittsburgh Press, 1995); Robert Pekkanen, *Japan's Dual Civil Society: Members without Advocates* (Palo Alto, CA: Stanford University Press, 2006), 102–108; John W. Masland, "Neighborhood Associations in Japan," *Far Eastern Survey* 15, no. 23 (1946): 356.

14. See Theodore Friedgut, *Political Participation in the USSR* (Princeton, NJ: Princeton University Press, 1979); Richard Fagen, *The Transformation of Political Culture in Cuba* (Palo Alto, CA: Stanford University Press, 1969).

15. See Read, *Roots of the State.*

16. See Pekkanen, *Japan's Dual Civil Society.*

17. Ram A. Cnaan, "Neighborhood-Representing Organizations: How Democratic Are They?," *Social Service Review* 65, no. 4 (1991): 630.

18. For a brief overview of his understanding of the relationship between the history of concepts and social history, see Reinhart Koselleck, "Begriffsgeschichte and Social History," *Economy and Society* 11, no. 3 (1982): 409–427.

19. Michael D. Shin, *Korean National Identity under Japanese Colonial Rule: Yi Gwangsu and the March First Movement of 1919* (New York: Routledge, 2018), 116.

20. Shin, *Korean National Identity,* 114–143.

21. See Douglas R. Howland, *Translating the West: Language and Political Reason in Nineteenth-Century Japan* (Honolulu: University of Hawaii Press, 2001), 120–125; and Shen Guowei, "Translating Western Concepts by Creating New Characters: A Comparison of Japanese and Chinese Attempts," *Journal of Cultural Interaction in East Asia* 2 (2001): 51–61.

22. See Pak Myŏng-kyu, *Kungmin, inmin, simin* (*Kungmin,* people, and citizens) (Seoul: Sohwa, 2009).

23. Kim Sŏng-bo, "Nambuk kukka suripki inmin'gwa kungmin kaenyŏmŭi punhwa" (The conceptual divergence of people and citizens), *Han'guksa yŏn'gu* 144 (2009): 72–74.

24. Young Jak Kim, "Park Chung Hee's Governing Ideas: Impact on National Consciousness and Identity," in *Reassessing the Park Chung Hee Era 1961–1979: Development, Political Thought, Democracy, and Cultural Influence,* ed. Clark W. Sorensen and Hyung-A Kim (Seattle: University of Washington Press, 2011), 95–97.

25. Christopher Capozzola, *Uncle Sam Wants You: World War I and the Making of the Modern American Citizen* (Oxford: Oxford University Press, 2008), 85.

26. For examples of this approach, see Han Kŭng-hŭi, "Iljeha chŏnsich'ejegi chibang haengjŏng kanghwa chŏngch'aek" (The reinforcement of local administrations during the wartime colonial period), *Kuksagwan nonch'ong* 88 (2000): 205–242.

27. Melvin Gurtov, *Pacific Asia?: Prospects for Security and Cooperation in East Asia* (New York: Rowman and Littlefield, 2002), 5.

28. Ch'oe Chang-jip, *Han'guk minjujuŭiŭi iron* (A theory of Korean democracy) (Seoul: Han'gilsa, 1993); and Meredith Woo-Cumings, ed., *The Developmental State* (Ithaca, NY: Cornell University Press, 1999).

29. On the social construction of tradition, see Eric Hobsbawm and Terence Ranger, eds., *The Invention of Tradition* (Cambridge: Cambridge University Press, 1983).

30. Yi Yong-ki, "Singminjigi nongch'on chiyŏk sahoeŭi chungch'ŏptoen sigan" (Overlapped time in colonial rural areas), *Taedong munhwa yŏn'gu* 96 (2016): 111–144; Yun Hae-dong, *Chibaewa chach'i* (Domination and self-rule) (Seoul: Yŏksa pip'yŏngsa, 2006).

31. Joan Scott, *Gender and the Politics of History* (New York: Columbia University Press, 1999), 46.

32. Hyaeweol Choi, "'Wise Mother, Good Wife': A Transcultural Discursive Construct in Modern Korea," *Journal of Korean Studies* 14, no. 1 (2009):

56; Koyama Shizuko, "The "Good Wife and Wise Mother" Ideology in Post–World War I Japan," trans. Gabriel A. Sylvain, *U.S.–Japan Women's Journal*, no. 7 (1994): 31–52.

33. On the Japanese family system, see Toshitani Nobuyoshi, "The Reform of Japanese Family Law and Changes in the Family System," *U.S.–Japan Women's Journal*, no. 6 (1994): 66–82.

34. Vladimir Tikhonov, "Masculinizing the Nation: Gender Ideologies in Traditional Korea and in the 1890s–1900s Korean Enlightenment Discourse," *Journal of Asian Studies* 66, no. 4 (2007): 1029–1057.

35. Suzy Kim, "Revolutionary Mothers: Women in the North Korean Revolution, 1945–1950," *Comparative Studies in Society and History* 52, no. 4 (2010): 742–767.

36. See Im Chong-myŏng, "Che1konghwaguk ch'ogi taehanmin'gugŭi kajok kukkahwawa naep'i" (State families during the early First Republic), *Han'guksa yŏn'gu* 130 (2005): 291–330.

CHAPTER 1: THE BIRTH OF PATRIOTIC NEIGHBORHOOD ASSOCIATIONS

1. Shiobara Tokisaburō, "Kokuminseishinsōdōin Chōsenrenmei no soshiki to sono katsudō" (Organization of the Korean League for the General Mobilization of the National Spirit), *Monkyō no Chōsen* 176 (1940): 23.

2. Shiobara, "Kokuminseishinsōdōin Chōsenrenmei," 38.

3. Shin, *Korean National Identity*, 120.

4. Yoshimi Yoshiaki, *Grassroots Fascism: The War Experience of the Japanese People* (New York: Columbia University Press, 2015), 41.

5. "Kyŏnggyeŏmjungni'e Uwŏn ch'ongdok ch'agim" (Ugaki's inauguration), *Chosŏn ilbo*, July 16, 1931.

6. Louise Young, *Japan's Total Empire: Manchuria and the Culture of Wartime Imperialism* (Berkeley: University of California Press, 1998), 183–240; Yi Sŭng-nyŏl, "1930 nyŏndae chŏnban'gi ilbon kunbuŭi taeryuk ch'imnyakkwan'gwa 'Chosŏn kong'ŏphwa' chŏngch'aek" (The Japanese army's views on Japan's expansion in the early 1930s and Korean industrialization), *Kuksagwan nonch'ong* 67 (1996): 145–196.

7. Yi, "1930nyŏndae chŏnban'gi ilbon," 155–156.

8. Pang Ki-jung, "1930nyŏndae Chosŏn nonggongbyŏngjin chŏngch'aekkwa kyŏngje t'ongje" (Industrialization policies in the 1930s and economic regulation), *Tongbang hakchi* 120 (2003): 80–82.

9. Ugaki Kazushige, "Chōsen no shōrai" (Korea's future), *Chōsen no kyōikukenkyū* 73 (1934): 3–4.

10. Chōsensōtokufu (Government General in Korea), *Chōsenni okeru nōsangyoson shinkōundō* (Campaign for improving rural areas) (Keizō: Chōsensōtokufu, 1934): 8–9.

11. Ugaki, "Shōrai," 11–21.

12. Tanaka Ryuichi, "Chōsentōchini okeru zaiman Chōsenjin mondai" (The issue of Koreans in Manchuria during the colonial period), *Tōyō bunkakenkyu* 3 (Tokyo: Gakushūindaigaku tōyō bunkakenkyusho, 2001): 152–154.

13. See Carter Eckert, *Offspring of Empire: The Koch'ang Kims and the Colonial Origins of Korean Capitalism, 1876–1945* (Seattle: University of Washington Press, 1991), 154–187.

14. Pang, "1930nyŏndae Chosŏn nonggongbyŏngjin," 86.

15. Ugaki, "Shōrai," 4.

16. Sheldon Garon, *The State and Labor in Modern Japan* (Princeton, NJ: Princeton University Press, 1987), 157–228.

17. Kim In-ho, *Singminji Chosŏnkyŏngjeŭi chongmal* (The end of colonial Korea's economy) (Seoul: Sinsŏwŏn, 2000), 48; Chōsensōtokufu, *Chōsenni okeru nōsangyoson,* 4–5 and 10–11.

18. Ugaki, "Shōrai," 6–9.

19. Namae Takayuki, *Shakaikōkajigyō gaikan* (An outline of social education) (Tokyo: Tokiwashobō,1939), 1–3. For more on the social settlement movement, see Joyce E. Williams and Vicky M. MacLean, *Settlement Sociology in the Progressive Years: Faith, Science and Reform* (Boston: Brill, 2015); Asa Briggs and Anne Macartney, *Toynbee Hall: The First Hundred Years* (Boston: Routledge and Kegan Paul, 2013).

20. Chōsensōtokufu gakumukyoku, *Chōsen shakaikyōka yōran* (Korean social indoctrination) (Keizō: Chōsensōtokufu, 1938), 33.

21. O Sŏng-ch'ŏl, *Singminji ch'odŭng kyoyugŭi hyŏngsŏng* (The formation of colonial elementary education) (Seoul: Kyoyukkwahaksa, 2000), 36–57 and 125.

22. Ugaki, "Shōrai," 22.

23. Ugaki, "Shōrai," 6 and 22.

24. Chōsensōtokufu, *Chōsen shakaikyōka yōran* 1 (1923): 1–16.

25. Chōsensōtokufu, *Chōsen shakaijigyō yōran* (1933): 213.

26. For their personal resumes, see Integrated Korean History Information System. https://db.history.go.kr/item/level.do?levelId=im_215_12942 https://db.history.go.kr/item/level.do?levelId=im_215_00416 https://db.history.go.kr/item/level.do?levelId=im_215_00639

27. The book that Tominaga Fumikazu wrote in the 1920s is *Ōji no Chōsenni okeru jichi no hōga, kyōyaku no itpan* (The sprout of autonomy in old Korea) (Keizō: Chōsensōtokufu, 1923).

28. There were three Social Section chiefs under Ugaki: Yu Man-gyŏm from 1932 to 1934, Ŏm Ch'ang-sŏp from 1934 to 1936, and Kim Tae-u from 1936 to 1939. The choice of Koreans was noteworthy, given their marginalized position in the central government. See *Samch'ŏlli* 10, no. 5 (1939): 59.

29. Watanabe Yutahiro, "Chōsen no shakaijigyōni tsuite" (Korea's social work), *Chōsen shakaijigyō* 11, no. 9 (1933): 9. Emphasis added.

30. For local economic programs by Korean nationalists, see Albert Park, *Building a Heaven on Earth: Religion, Activism, and Protest in Japanese Occupied Korea* (Honolulu: University of Hawai'i Press, 2014), 150–190.

31. For socialist movement, see Chi Su-gŏl, *Iljeha nongminjohap undong yŏn'gu* (Peasant unions during the colonial period) (Seoul: Yŏksa pip'yŏngsa, 1993).

32. Chōsensōtokufu, *Chōsenni okeru nōsangyoson*, 48.

33. Yu Man-gyŏm, "Charyŏkkaengsaeng iran muŏdinga" (What is self-reliance?), *Chōsen* 17, no. 2 (1933): 9–11.

34. Hayashi Shigeki, "Minshinsakkōundō no honji" (The movement to awaken the mass spirit), *Shakaikyoka shiryō* (Keizō: Chōsensōtokufu gakumukyokushakaika, 1933), 126.

35. Yi Kak-chong, "Puragŭi sahoejŏk yŏn'gu" (A social study of villages), *Sinmin* 64 (1931): 71.

36. Ibid.; Yi Kak-chong, "Chōsen no nōson to shakaijigyō" (Social work in rural areas), *Chōsen shakaijigyō* 5, no. 3 (1927): 2–5.

37. Hayashi, "Minshinsakkōundō," 125–126.

38. Tominaga, *Ōji no Chōsen*, 1–5.

39. Tominaga, *Ōji no Chōsen*, 14–17.

40. Tominaga Fumikazu, "Hondōno tsuite nōson no shisetsu" (Rural areas in my province), *Jiryokukōsei kihō* (A bulletin of self-reliance) 1, no. 14 (1934): 6–9.

41. Chōsensōtokufu gakumukyoku, *Chōsen shakaikyōka yōran*, 51–54.

42. Chōsensōtokufu gakumukyoku, *Chōsen shakaikyōka yōran*, 91–92.

43. For example, Minami resolved the conflict between Ugaki and the Kwantung Army over Korean immigration. Tanaka, "Chōsentōchini," 152–154.

44. Chōsensōtokufu, *Atarashiki Chōsen* (New Korea) (Keizō: Chōsensōtokufu, 1944): 19–21.

45. For further information on Shiobara Tokisaburō, see Im Yi-rang, "Chŏnsich'ejegi Shiobara Tokisaburōŭi hwangminhwajŏngch'aekkwa ch'ujin,

1937–1941" (Shiobara Tokisaburo's wartime policies), *Yŏksamunje yŏn'gu* 29 (2013): 257–292.

46. Shiobara Tokisaburō, "Seidōundō no unyō" (Managing the movement for general mobilization of national spirit), *Sōdōin* 2, no. 7 (1940): 8–13.

47. Shiobara Tokisaburō, "Kokuminseishinsōdōin undōni tsuite" (The general mobilization movement), *Monkyō no Chōsen* (August 1939): 13.

48. "Jyukō hōkokukyōchōshūkan jitshigenkyō gaiyō" (A patriotic week), *Chōsen* 277 (June 1938): 23–30.

49. Shiobara, "Seidōundō no unyō," 11–12.

50. O, *Singminji ch'odŭng kyoyuk,* 411.

51. Chōsensōtokufu gakumukyoku, *Chōsen shakaikyōka yōran,* 49–50 and 97.

52. Shiobara, "Seidōundō no unyō," 13–14.

53. Shiobara, "Seidōundō no unyō," 11–12.

54. Shiobara, "Kokuminseishinsōdōin Chōsenrenmei," 24–25.

55. Son Chŏng-kyu, "Bisanjikyoku to hantono josē" (Korean women in emergency), *Sōdōin* 1, no. 2 (1939): 29.

56. Kawagishi Bunzarō, "Kojinshugitekina zētakushinwo sutete" (Giving up individualistic extravagance), *Sōdōin* 2, no. 9 (1940): 4–6.

57. Mizuda Naoshō, "Chochikushōrei no hitsuyōni tsuite" (Encouraging Saving), *Jiryokukōsei kihō* 59 (1939): 11.

58. Kim In-ho, "T'aep'yŏng'yang chŏnjaengsigi Seoul jiyŏgŭi saengp'ilp'um paegŭpt'ongje silt'ae" (The regulation of everyday essentials during the Pacific War), *Seoulhak yŏn'gu* 26 (2006): 75–76; Anjako Yuka, "*Chosŏn ch'ongdokpuŭi ch'ongdongwŏnch'eje hyŏngsŏng chŏngch'aek*" (General mobilization policies of the Government-General) (PhD diss., Korea University, 2006), 118.

59. Shiobara Tokisaburō, "Keizaisen no suikōwa seikatsuwo tsūjite" (Economic war and life), *Sōdōin* 1, no. 7 (1939): 6.

60. "Naisenittai," *Sōdōin* 1, no. 7 (1939):11.

61. Nakashima Shinichi, "Zentaishui to nihonseishin" (Totalitarianism and Japanese spirit), *Sōdōin* 2, no. 1 (1940): 14–18; Minami Jirō, "Watashi no kokuhū" (Our national spirit), *Kokuminsōryoku* (Concerted national power) 3, no. 4 (1941): 2–3.

62. Nakashima, "Zentaishui to nihonseishin," 14–18.

63. Kokuminseishinsōdōin Chōsenrenmei, "Senjikokumin seikatsutaisei" (People's wartime life), *Sōdōin* 2, no. 10 (1940): 23–24.

64. Shiobara, "Kokuminseishinsōdōin undōni tsuite," 2.

65. Shiobara, "Kokuminseishinsōdōin Chōsenrenmei," 19.

66. "Chōsenrenmeiwa imamade naniwo yatsutekitaka" (What the league has done), *Sōdōin* 1, no. 1 (1939): 49–52.

67. The board consisted of all bureau directors in the Government-General and leading figures from the Social Indoctrination Section, as well as some prominent Koreans who contributed to the league's launch. See "Chōsenrenmeiwa imamade," 54.

68. "Kungminjŏngsin ch'ongdongwŏn Chosŏn yŏnmaengbonbu pangmungi" (A visit to the league office), *Samch'ŏlli* 10, no. 10 (October 1938): 41–43.

69. In the case of South P'yŏng'an Province, the inaugural ceremony included two city (*pu*) associations, fourteen county (*kun*) associations, and twenty-one social groups; among these social groups were the Red Cross, Society for Social Work, the Youth Group of South P'yŏng'an, the Army Support Group, Financial Cooperatives, and the Association of Agriculture. Shiobara, "Kokuminseishinsōdōin Chōsenrenmei," 33–34.

70. Chōsensōtokufu, *Chōsenni okeru kokuminseishin sōdōin* (General mobilization of national spirit in Korea) (Keizō: Chōsensōtokufu, 1940), 79.

71. Chōsensōtokufu, *Chōsenni okeru kokuminseishin*, 49–50.

72. Chōsensōtokufu, *Chōsenni okeru kokuminseishin*, 79.

73. When the league published a monthly bulletin *Dawn* (J. *Akatsuki*) and distributed it to Patriotic NAs across the country, three weeks elapsed between the print date and the date of delivery to some remote Patriotic NAs. "Zensen aikokuhantchō no koe" (Voices from Patriotic NAs), *Sōdōin* 2, no. 2 (1940): 114–115.

74. "'Chōsenno shintaiseiwoiru' zadankai" (The Korean new order), *Kokuminsōryoku* 2, no. 12 (1940): 25.

75. Shiobara, "Keizaisen no suikō," 7; Shiobara, "Senjikokumin seikatsutaisei," 23–24; Shiobara, "Kokuminseishinsōdōin Chōsenrenmei," 18–19.

76. "Aikokuhan kyōka ikusei zadankai" (A talk about Patriotic NAs), *Kokuminsōyoku* 3, no. 6 (1941): 8–9.

77. "Seidō Ch'ungbukrenmei no katsudō" (The North Ch'ungch'ŏng League's activities), *Sōdōin* 2, no. 6 (1940): 45.

78. "Nongch'onŭl ponbadŭra. Tosi aegukpanŭl ilch'ŭng kanghwa" (Reinforcing urban Patriotic NAs), *Changnohoebo* 38 (1940): 3.

79. See Shin, *Korean National Identity*, 21–41.

80. "Kukkach'ongnyŏgŭi palwhiwa aegukpan" (Concerted national power and Patriotic NAs), *T'aeyang* 1–2 (1940): 27.

81. "Aikokuhan kyōka ikusei," 9.

82. "Aikokuhan kyōka ikusei," 11.

83. Nozaki Shinzo, "Matchi no aikokuhan" (Patriotic NAs in cities), *Kokuminsōryoku* 2, no. 12 (1940): 60.

84. Chōsensōtokufu gakumukyoku, *Chōsen shakaikyōka yōran*, 43; "*Nōsangyoson yagakukai kyū getsureikai shidōhōshin*," *Jiryokukōsei kihō* 71 (1939): 31–41.

85. "Chŏng'yŏnmaeng'ŭi aegukpanwŏn sanghoero ch'ongdong'wŏllyŏng" (Mobilizing all Patriotic NAs), *Tong'a ilbo* (hereafter *TI*), November 1, 1939.

86. "Aegugirenŭn hyuŏp" (No business on patriotic days), *TI*, November 1, 1939.

87. On the varying size of assemblies, see Tchūma Etsunosuke, "Watashinado no aikokuhan" (Our Patriotic NAs), *Kokuminsōryoku* 2, no. 12 (1940): 54.

88. "Ch'ongdokto ilbanwŏn sanghoe'e ch'ulsŏk" (The Governor General in assemblies), *TI*, November 2, 1939.

89. On creating the Imperial Subject Oath in October 1937, the Education Bureau sent it to all schools, public institutions, and companies, thereby ordering everyone to memorize it and recite it at all types of gatherings.

90. "Chŏng'yŏnmaeng'ŭi."

91. Kawagishi Bunzarō, "Hantotesu no danketsuhe," *Kokuminsōryoku* 3, no. 3 (1941): 45.

92. "Imokoji no hanashi" (A story about Imokoji), *Sōdōin* 2, no. 10 (1940): 83.

93. "Kokuminsōryokurenmei chihōsoshiki no sēbini kansuruken" (Realigning local organizations), *Kokuminsōryoku* 3, no.2 (1941): 134–136. Some local areas already had a similar practice. See "Seidō Ch'ungbukrenmei," 45.

94. Koezuka Shōtano, "Jōkai hayawakari tokuhon" (A guide to monthly assemblies), *Kokuminsōyoku* 3, no. 5 (1941): 122.

95. "Meiaikokuhanchō hōmonki" (Visiting happy Patriotic NAs), *Kokuminsōryokuu* 4, no. 1 (1942): 112.

96. "Jōkaiwo iru" (Talking about monthly assemblies), *Chōsen kōron* 338 (1941): 67.

97. Keizō renmei, "Jōkaino hirakikata" (Monthly assemblies), *Kokuminsōryoku* 2, no. 11 (1940): 68–69.

98. Kokuminsōyroku Chōsenrenmei, *Kokuminsōyroku tokuhon* (A reader of concerted national power) (Keizō: Kokuminsōryoku Chōsenrenmei, 1941), 93.

99. "Seisanryokukakujyūwa kyōdōsekinin," *Kokuminsōryoku* 3, no. 1 (1941): 23–24.

100. "Jōkaiwo iru," 63.
101. Koezuka, "Jōkai hayawakari tokuhon," 116.

CHAPTER 2: THE COLONIAL POLITICS OF NAMING

1. Okazaki Shigeki, *Jidai wo tsukuru otoko Shiobara Tokisaburō* (The man who made the times) (Tokyo: Ōsawatsukiji shoten,1942), 151.
2. "Aikokuhan to tonarigumi" (Patriotic NA and tonarigumi), *Kokuminsōryoku* 4, no. 10 (1942): 11.
3. For more on the US economic strangulation of Japan, see Edward S. Miller, *Bankrupting the Enemy: The U.S. Financial Siege of Japan Before Pearl Harbor* (Annapolis, MD: United States Naval Institute Press, 2007).
4. Andrew Gordon, *Labor and Imperial Democracy in Prewar Japan* (Berkeley: University of California Press, 1991), 237.
5. Gordon, *Labor and Imperial Democracy,* 279–280.
6. Gordon Mark Berger, *Parties out of Power in Japan, 1931–1941* (Princeton, NJ: Princeton University Press, 1977), 173.
7. Berger, *Parties out of Power,* 281–285 and 318–325.
8. Berger, *Parties out of Power,* 325–326.
9. Ikeda Taneo, "Kyūtaiseikara shintaiseimade" (From the old order to the new order), *Chōsengyōsei* 20, no.3 (1941): 32–33; Suzuki Masafumi, "Shintaiseioyobi keizaisaihensei" (The new order and economic restructuring), *Chōsengyōsei* 20, no.1 (1941): 7–9.
10. Minami Jirō, "Sōryoku no hakki" (Exercising concerted power), *Kokuminsōryoku* 2, no. 11 (1940): 9–13.
11. Minami, "Sōryoku no hakki," 14. Emphasis added.
12. Minami, "Sōryoku no hakki," 9–13.
13. 'Sinch'eje chwadamhoe" (A talk about the New Order), *Maeil sinbo* (hereafter *MS*), November 2, 1940.
14. Michael Robinson, *Cultural Nationalism in Korea, 1920–1925* (Seattle: University of Washington Press, 1988), 44.
15. Yi Ch'ŏl-u, "Iljejibaeŭi pŏpchŏkkujo" (Colonial legal structure) in *Ilje singminjisigiŭi t'ongch'ich'eje hyŏngsŏng,* ed. Kim Tong-no (Seoul: Hyean, 2006), 134–135.
16. Yi, "Iljejibaeŭi pŏpchŏkkujo," 128.
17. Chŏn Sang-suk, "Chosŏnch'ongdok chŏngch'ich'ejewa kwallyoje" (The politics of the Government-General and bureaucracy), *Han'guk chŏngch'i woegyosa nonch'ong* 31, no. 1 (2009):14.

18. Pak Ŭn-kyŏng, "Iljesidae Chosŏnch'ongdokpu Chosŏnin kwallyo'e kwan-han yŏn'gu" (Korean bureaucrats in the Government-General), *Han'guk chŏngch'ihak hoebo* 28, no. 2 (1995): 137–139.

19. Kim Tong-myŏng, "1931nyŏn Kyŏngsŏngbuhoe sŏn'gŏ yŏn'gu" (A study of the 1931 election in Kyŏngsŏng), *Han'guk chŏngch'iwoegyosa nonch'ong* 26, no. 2 (2005): 193–218.

20. Chŏn Sŏng-hyŏn, "Iljegangjŏmgi chibang ŭihoeŭi chŏngch'ijŏgin kŏtkwa han'gye" (The limits of local assemblies under colonial rule), *Yŏksa yŏn'gu* 39 (2020): 57–99.

21. Toshio Dōmoto, "Chōsengyōsei no tokushitsu" (The particularities of Korean administration), *Chōsengyōsei* 19, no. 4 (1940): 5–7 and 9–10.

22. Anjako, "Chosŏnch'ongdokpuŭi ch'ongdongwŏn ch'ejehyŏngsŏng," 74–75, 144–145.

23. To see the testimony of Cho Pyŏng-sang after liberation, go to https://db .history.go.kr/item/bookViewer.do?levelId=an_052_0090.

24. "'Chōsen no shintaisei wo iru' zadankai" (A talk about the "Korean new order"), *Kokuminsōryoku* 2, no. 12 (1940): 18 (hereafter "Zadankai").

25. "Zadankai," 19–20.

26. "Zadankai," 20.

27. "Zadankai," 20–21.

28. "Zadankai," 21.

29. "Zadankai," 21.

30. "Zadankai," 22.

31. "Zadankai," 20–21.

32. "Shiobara sēnenkyokutchōto Chōsensēnnendaihyō gaidan" (Talk between Shiobara and Korean youth representative), *Kokuminsōryoku* 3, no. 4 (1941): 21.

33. Kim Che-jŏng, "1930nyŏndae chŏnban Chosŏnch'ongdokpu kyŏngjeg-wallyoŭi chiyŏgŭrosŏŭi Chosŏninsik" (The regional consciousness of colonial bureaucrats in the early 1930s), *Yŏksamunje yŏn'gu* 22 (2009): 101.

34. "Taiseiyokusankaijibu Chōsenniwa setchisezu" (No IRAA branch in Korea), *Chōsenshinbun*, December 24, 1940.

35. "Pandoŭi ch'ongnyŏgundong" (Concerted movement in Korea), *Chang-nohoebo* 51 (1941): 3.

36. "Sōryokuundōwa sukozurukōhyō" (The concerted movement was praised), *Kokuminsōryoku* 3, no. 2 (1941): 27.

37. Kim Yŏng-hŭi, "Kungminch'ongnyŭk Chosŏnyŏn'maeng'ŭi samuguk kaep'yŏn'gwa kwanbyŏndanch'ee taehan t'ongje" (Reshuffling the league

of national concerted power), *Han'guk kŭnhyŭndaesa yŏn'gu* 37 (2006): 245–246.

38. Koezuka, "Jōkai hayawakari tokuhon," 111–114.

39. "Shōwa jūshichinenshigatsu tōjisahunshiyōshi P'yŏng'annamdo" (South P'yŏng'an provincial governor address, April, 1942), in *Chōsenshōtokufu no "gokugo" seisaku shiryō* (Collection of "National Language" policy of the government general, hereafter *Shiryō*), ed. Gumatani Akiyas (Osaka: Kansai University Press, 2004), 1.

40. Chōsensōtokufu, *Chōsen shakaikyōiku yōran* (Keizō: Chōsensōtokufu, 1941), 61.

41. Chōsensōtokufu, *Chōsen shakaikyōiku yōran*, 62–63.

42. "Zenkoku kyōwajigyō taikai" (National event of concord works), *Kyōwajigyō* 3, no. 1 (1941): 11–12.

43. Hirano Saiichi, "Kyōwakaiin to tonarigumi," *Kyōwajigyō* 3, no. 3 (1941): 14–17.

44. "Zenkoku kyōwajigyō taikai," 9–12.

45. "Kugŏbogŭp" (Japanese education), *MS*, May 17, 1942; "Kokugojōyōwo kyōchyō" (Emphasizing Japanese learning), *Asahishinbun Chōsenhan*, May 5, 1942.

46. "Kimiha jōyō shiteirukane" (Speaking Japanese all the time), *Keizōippō*, April 21, 1942.

47. "Gokugohukyū undōyōkō" (Movement for speaking Japanese), *Kokuminsōryoku* 4, no. 6 (1942): 85.

48. Chōsensōtokufu, *Chōsen shakaikyōiku yōran*, 62.

49. "Kokugojōyō no iehyōshō" (Speaking Japanese at home), *Asahishinbun Chōsenhan*, August 29, 1942.

50. "Naisenittaiwa kokugokara" (Japanese learning, the beginning of *naisenittai*), *Keizōippō*, May 29, 1942.

51. "Chōsenni okeru kokugokyōikuto 'Kokugono ichi' setteini tsuite" (Japanese education in Korea), *Mongyō no Chōsen* (February 1940): 41–42.

52. "Hwach'ŏn-gun tŏshinsho" (Replay of Hwach'ŏn County), *Shiryō*, 99.

53. "Sanbika no kokugoka" (Hymns in Japanese), *Keizōippō*, June 7, 1941.

54. "Gokugohukyū undōyōkō," 85.

55. "Shōwa jyūshichinengogatsu fuyungunshukai kyōgijikō: North P'yŏng'an Province" (Decisions in May,1942), *Shiryō*, 37–38.

56. "Yongsosŭm ch'inŭn kugŏ yŏl" (Passion for Japanese learning), *MS*, June 22, 1942.

57. "Shōwa jyūshichinengogatsu," 35–36; "Gokugohukyū undōyōkō," 85.

58. "Kugŏsang'yong'ŭn irŏke" (How to speak Japanese all the time), *MS*, June 29, 1942.

59. "Jogakusei to kokugo" (Female students and Japanese), *Keizōippō*, June 19, 1942.

60. "Tsuitachi ichigo" (One word every day), *Keizōippō*, May 17, 1942.

61. "Aikokuhanya matchirenmeide gokugono mōrenshū" (Practicing Japanese at Patriotic NAs), *Asahishinbun nishisenhan*, July 19, 1942.

62. "Hantōno chūten" (Korea's focus), *Asahishinbun nakasenhan*, May 8, 1942.

63. "Hwach'ŏn-gun," 98–99.

64. See, *Shiryō*, 5, 16, 21, and 33.

65. O, *Singminji ch'odŭng*, 36–57 and 125.

66. O, *Singminji ch'odŭng*, 112 and 133.

67. "Hwach'ŏn-gun," 98.

68. "P'ungsan-gun tōshinsho" (Reply of P'ungsan County), *Shiryō*, 120.

69. "Aikokuhan gokugokōshūkai" (Patriotic NA and Japanese learning), *Keizōippō*, August 2, 1941; "Shōwa jyūshichinengogatsu fuyungunshukai," 37.

70. "Hamgyŏngbuk-do Ŭnsŏng-gun tōshinsho" (Reply of Ŭnsŏng County), *Shiryō*, 158.

71. "Kangwŏn-do Yang'yang-gun tōshinsho" (Reply of Yang'yang County), *Shiryō*, 90.

72. "Kyŏnggi-do,Kap'yŏng-gun tōshinsho" (Reply of Kap'yŏng County), *Shiryō*, 16.

73. "Oragaaigokuhan" (Our Patriotic NA), *Keizōippō*, August 2, 1941.

74. "Hamgyŏngbuk-do, Chongsŏng-gun tōshinsho" (Reply of Chongsŏng County), *Shiryō*, 156–157.

75. "Jōkaiwa kokugo" (Assemblies and Japanese), *Keizōippō*, April 15, 1942.

76. "Aikokuhi jōkai" (Patriotic day assembly), *Keizōippō*, May 29, 1942.

77. "Gokugozenkaiundō natsunojin" (Summer for Japanese learning), *Kokuminsōryoku* 4, no. 7 (1942): 52.

78. "Kugŏhaedŭkchanŭn sahal" (Forty percent of people speak Japanese), *MS*, June 12, 1942.

79. "Han-kuchyō no kokugo kōshūkai" (Japanese lectures), *Keizōippō*, May 16, 1942.

80. "Ch'amdoen hwangguksinminŭn" (Genuine imperial subjects), *MS*, July 10, 1942.

81. "Han-ku chyō no kokugo kōshūkai"; "Hanchyōsanno kokugokōshūkai" (Japanese lectures for NA headpeople), *Keizōippō*, June 11, 1942.

82. "Hwach'ŏn-gun," 99.
83. "Shōwa jyūshichinengogatsu fuyungunshukai," 36–37.
84. "Kangwŏn-do, Kŭmhwa-gun tōshinsho" (Reply of Kŭmhwa County), *Shiryō*, 100.
85. "Kyŏnggi-do Changdan-gun tōshinsho" (Reply of Changdan County), *Shiryō*, 31.
86. "Kangwŏn-do, Kang'yuk-gun tōshinsho" (Reply of Kang'yuk County), *Shiryō*, 91.
87. "Hamgyŏngbuk-do, Chongsŏng-gun,"156–157.
88. "Kyŏngsangbuk-do, Ponghwa-gun tōshinsho" (Reply of Ponghwa County), *Shiryō*, 70–72.
89. "Kokugo aikokuhan" (Patriotic NAs learning Japanese), *MS*, June 8, 1942.
90. "Kangwŏn-do, Kosŏng-gun tōshinsho" (Reply of Kosŏng County), *Shiryō*, 88; "Kangwŏn-do, Kang'yuk-gun," 91; "Hamgyŏngbuk-do, Chongsŏng-gun," 158.
91. "Ch'ŏtchogŏni kugŏsang'yong" (Japanese; the first qualification to be a NA head), *MS*, August 22, 1942.
92. "Rinbojŏngsinŭi kkot" (Mutual aids), *MS*, March 10, 1942.
93. "Kyot'ong kigwansŏ solsŏnhaya" (Taking the lead in public transportation), *MS*, July 15, 1942.
94. Berger, *Parties out of Power*, 331–337.
95. Chŏn Sang-suk, *Chosŏn ch'ongdokchŏngch'i yŏn'gu* (Politics of the Governor-General in Korea) (Seoul: Chisiksanŏpsa, 2012), 253–257.
96. Takashi Fujitani, *Race for Empire: Koreans as Japanese and Japanese as Americans during World War II* (Berkeley: University of California Press, 2011), 66.
97. Frederick Cooper, *Colonialism in Question: Theory, Knowledge, History* (Berkeley: University of California Press, 2005), 153–242.

CHAPTER 3: AT THE INTERSECTION
OF FAMILY INDOCTRINATION AND
OPPORTUNITIES FOR WOMEN

1. "Aegukpanŭi kyŏlsŏngdanwi" (The Patriotic NAs' units), *Tong'a ilbo* (hereafter *TI*), June 28, 1939.
2. Minami Jirō, "Waga kokuhu" (National Spirit), *Kokuminsōryoku* 3, no. 4 (1941): 3.
3. It is kept in the Independence Hall of Korea, Item # 1–000977–000.

4. "Aegukpansanghoe'e radiohwaryong" (Using radios in assemblies), *Maeil sinbo* (hereafter MS), March 7, 1941.
5. "Chingbyŏngjedo unyong'ŭi kŭpsŏnmu hojŏk kiryu chŏngbihara" (Using family registries and residential registries for military conscription), *MS*, July 11, 1943.
6. Mizuno Naoki, "Chosŏnch'ongdokpunŭn wae 'ch'angssigaemyŏng'ŭl silsihaetsŭlkka" (Why did the Government-General implement the surname change policy?), *Naeirŭl yŏnŭn yŏksa* 15 (2004): 186–187.
7. Mizuno, "Chosŏnch'ongdokpunŭn," 150.
8. Ku Kwang-mo, "Ch'angssigaemyŏng chŏngch'aekkwa Chosŏninŭi taeŭng" (Koreans' response to the surname change policy), *Kukchejŏngch'i nonch'ong* 45, no. 4 (2005): 44–45.
9. Ku, "Ch'angssigaemyŏng chŏngch'aekkwa," 32.
10. Chŏng Chu-su, "Iljegangjŏmgi che1ch'a hojŏkkiryu ilje chosa paegyŏng ch'ŭngmyŏnŭi koch'al (9)" (Backgrounds of the first investigation of the family registry and residential registry), *Sabŏphaengjŏng* 59, no. 11 (2018): 69.
11. Chŏng, "Iljegangjŏmgi che1ch'a (9)," 69.
12. Chŏng, "Iljegangjŏmgi che1ch'a (9)," 60.
13. "Hojŏkkwa ch'ang'gue natanan insaengŭi hŭibigŭk" (At the Department of Family Registry), *Chogwang* 5, no. 2 (1939): 280.
14. Chŏng, "Iljegangjŏmgi che1ch'a (9)," 69–70.
15. Chōsensōtokufu, "Aigokuhanshinbunni kiji kēsai iraino ken" *Chōsen kiryureini kansuru shorui* (Residential registries in Korea) (September 15, 1942): 3–5.
16. See Yi Sŭng-il, "Chosŏnch'ongdokpuŭi Chosŏnin tŭngnokchedo" (Registration policy of the colonial government), *Sahoewa yŏksa* 67 (2005): 25–40.
17. "Chōsen kiryūrei kaisetsu" (Explaining residential registry), *Koseki* 2, no. 11 (1942): 3–13.
18. "Mōshiajitsenjikō" (What Patriotic NAs should practice this month), *Kokuminsōryoku* 4, no. 10 (1942): 5.
19. Yi Myŏng-jong, "Iljemalgi Chosŏnin chingbyŏng'ŭl wihan kiryujedoŭi sihaeng mit hojŏkchosa" (Residential registries and family registries for military conscription), *Sahoewa yŏksa* 74 (2007): 89.
20. Chōsen kosekikyōkai, *Chōsen koseki oyobi kiryū todoke shōkishū* (Family registries and residential registries in Korea) (Keizō: Chōsen kosekikyōkai, 1944): 275–294.
21. "Aikokuhankaihō" (The Patriotic NA newsletter), *Keizoihō* 261 (October 1943): 46.

22. South Korean National Archives, CJ0004278, Chōsensōtokufu hōmukyoku, *Chōsen kiryureini kansuru shorui* (Documents on residential registries),1942, "Kosekiseido oyobi kiryuseido no sendenni kansuru ken (Propagating family registries and residential registries), September, 1942.

23. "Danwashitsu" (Conversation rooms), *Koseki* 2, no. 11 (1942): 36.

24. The Independence Hall of Korea, Item 3–008681–000.

25. Chŏng Chu-su, "Iljegangjŏmgi che1ch'a hojŏkkiryu ilje chosa mit hojŏkchōngbi hojŏgyegyu ch'ŭngmyŏnŭi koch'al (1)" (Rules of the first investigation of the family registry and residential registry), *Sabŏphaengjŏng* 59, no. 3 (2018): 45.

26. Chŏng, "Iljegangjŏmgi che1ch'a hojŏkkiryu ilje chosa mit hojŏkchōngbi hojŏgyegyu," 42–48.

27. Chŏng, "Iljegangjŏmgi che1ch'a hojŏkkiryu ilje chosa mit hojŏkchōngbi hojŏgyegyu," 42–48.

28. Chŏng, "Iljegangjŏmgi che1ch'a (9)," 70.

29. Chŏng Chu-su, "Iljegangjŏmgi che1ch'a hojŏkkiryu iljejosa chedoch'ŭngmyŏng'e kwanhan koch'al (2)" (The first inspection of the family registries and the residential registries [2]), *Sabŏphaengjŏng* 59, no. 2 (2018): 55–56.

30. Hildi Kang, *Under the Black Umbrella: Voices from Colonial Korea, 1910–1945* (Ithaca, NY: Cornell University Press, 2001), 174.

31. Hŏ Yŏng-ran, "Chŏnsich'ejegi (1937–1945) saenghwalp'ilsup'um t'ongje yŏn'gu" (Wartime regulation of everyday essentials), *Kuksagwan nonch'ong* 88 (2000): 313–328.

32. "Senhuseikatsuto shokuryōjijyōwo kiku-zadankai" (Forum: The wartime food situation), *Kokuminsōryoku* 4, no. 9 (1942): 22–23,

33. "Shōhikippusei bunsho (2)" (Ration stamps [2]), *Keizōihō* 241 (1941): 12–16.

34. "Kateiyōhin haikyūni aikokuhanwo katsuyōsuru," (Patriotic NAs for rationing), *Kokuminsōryoku* 3, no. 5 (1941): 101.

35. "Senhu seikatsuto," 22.

36. "Shōhikippusei bunsho" (Ration stamps), *Keizōihō* 237 (1941): 28–29.

37. "Aegukpani yŏndaech'aegim" (Patriotic NAs' joint responsibility), *MS*, July 19, 1943.

38. Yūichi Higuchi, *Senjika Chōsen no nōminseikatsushi, 1939–1945* (Peasant life in Korea) (Tokyo: Shakaihihyōsha, 1998), 40–43.

39. "Kaizensareta Keizōfuno ryōshokukaikyūkikan," *Keizōihō* 259 (1943): 1–3.

40. "Kaizensareta Keizōfuno," 4–6.

41. "Iryong mulp'umdŭng paegŭbŭn panesŏ chach'ijero hamyŏnjot'a" (Everyday rationing by Patriotic NAs), *MS,* July 7, 1941.
42. "Shōhikippusei bunsho," 32–33.
43. "Shōhikippusei bunsho (2)," 13.
44. "Shōhi kippusei bunsho," 35–36.
45. Kim In-ho, "T'aep'yŏng'yang chŏnjaengsigi Seouljiyŏgŭi saengp'ilp'um paegŭp t'ongje siltae" (Control of everyday essentials in Seoul during the Pacific war), *Seoulhak yŏn'gu* 26 (2006): 87.
46. Chōsensōtokufu hōmukyoku, *Kēzai chian shūhō* (Economic security weekly) 60 (June 29, 1942): 441–442. During the five-day crackdown on economic crimes in North Kyŏngsang that began on May 25, 1942, 37 percent of those found guilty were either village or NA heads.
47. "Puin aegukpanjang pogo chwadamhoe" (Forum: Patriotic NAs' headwomen), *MS,* July 7, 1941.
48. "Aikokuhan kyōka ikusei zadankai" (Forum: Reinforcing Patriotic NAs), *Kokuminsōryoku* 3, no. 6 (1941): 16–17.
49. Araki Hideō, "Aikokuhanwa kakusenheri" (Powerful Patriotic NAs), *Kokuminsōryoku* 4, no. 11 (1942): 58; "Yongsanhōmen aikokuhanno katsudō" (Patriotic NAs in Yongsan), *Keizōihō* 256 (1943): 20–21.
50. On savings campaigns, see Young-Iob Chung, *Korea under Siege, 1876–1945: Capital Formation and Economic Transformation* (Oxford: Oxford University Press, 2006), 212–213.
51. "Tchochikuno eijokusei" (Everlasting saving), *Kokuminsōryoku* 3, no. 12 (1941): 36–39.
52. Mun Yŏng-ju, "Iljeha tosigŭmyung chohabŭi unyŏng ch'ejewa kŭmyung hwaldong, 1918–1945" (Finance cooperatives during the colonial period, 1918–1945) (PhD diss., Korea University, 2004), 134–135.
53. "Hantono sokojikarawo shimese" (Let's show the power of Patriotic NAs), *Kokuminsōryoku* 3, no. 6 (1941): 56–57.
54. "Aikokuhan tayori" (Convenient Patriotic NA), *Kokuminsōryoku* 3, no. 2 (1941): 73.
55. "Aikokuhan kyōka," 6.
56. "Aikokuhanihō" (A Patriotic NA's bulletin), *Keizōihō* 253 (1942): 48.
57. "Ch'aegwŏn haldang p'yojunŭl chŏnghaya," *MS,* June 16, 1943.
58. Ch'oe Chŏng-hŭi, "2wŏl 15irŭi pam" (The night of February 15) in *Singminjuŭiwa hyŏmnyŏk* (Colonialism and collaboration), ed. Kim Chae-yong (Seoul: Yŏkrak, 2003), 49–52.
59. Chŏng In-t'aek, "Ch'ŏngnyangni kyowoe" (Ch'ŏngnyangni, an outskirt of Kyŏngsŏng) in *Singminjuŭiwa hyŏmnyŏk,* 119–138.

60. See Hong Yang-hŭi, "Singminjisigi hojŏkchedowa kajokchedoŭi pyŏnyong" (Family registries and the family system during the colonial period), *Sahak yŏn'gu* 79 (2005): 167–205.

61. Chōsensōtokufu, *Chōsenni okeru kokuminseishin sōdōin*, 152; "Chōsen-reimei seitei no shuhu no seikatsu yoteihyō" (Housewives' daily schedules), *Chōsen kōron* 345 (1941): 119.

62. "Seikatsu satshinwa kateikara" (The reform of everyday life from the home), *Sōdōin* 1, no. 3 (1939): 22–23.

63. "Puin aegukpanjang."

64. "Kajŏng panghojohap haeso" (Dissolving home airstrike defense cooperatives), *MS*, November 21, 1940.

65. Sinsidaesa, *Aegukpan kajŏng'yong ŏnmun panggongdokpon* (A guide to the Patriotic NAs' air defense training) (Kyŏngsŏng: Pangmunsŏgwan, 1941): 54; "Aikokuhanseishinno tokushusei" (Spirit of Patriotic NA), *Kokuminsōryoku* 4, no. 7 (1942): 20–21.

66. Watanabe Katsumi, "Aikokuhantchōwo sabaku" (Judging headpeople), *Kokuminsōryoku* 4, no. 8 (1942): 28.

67. Shōhara Yorokuzō, "Bōkūrenshūshiken" (On air-raid training), *Kokuminsōryoku* 4, no. 11 (1942): 62–63.

68. Higuchi, *Senjika Chōsen*, 187.

69. Iwamoto Shōni, "Meiaikokuhan hōmonki" (Visiting famous Patriotic NAs), *Kokuminsōryoku* 4, no. 4 (1942): 96.

70. "Sŭranch'ima pŏtkosŏ nŭmnŭmhan momppe-pok" (Wearing *momppe*), *MS*, July 4, 1942.

71. Sinsidaesa, *Aegukpan-kajŏng'yong*, 127.

72. "Kokudobōei kitsu" (Defending lands), *Kokuminsōryoku* 3, no. 9 (1941): 18; "Puinbanghwa pudae" (The female firefighting army), *MS*, August 7, 1941.

73. "Sanghoee hoju annagamyŏn mulja paegŭbŭljungji" (No family heads in assemblies, no rations), *MS*, March 12, 1942.

74. "Aikokuhan kyōka," 17–18.

75. "Handokyotsute kairōsensenhe" (Let's work), *Kokuminsōryoku* 3, no. 10 (1941): 29.

76. "Aikokuhanjyōkai no shushitetteihōwo unagasu" (Patriotic NAs' practice lists), *Kokuminsōryoku* 3, no. 7 (1941): 61.

77. "Puin aegukpanjang."

78. "Puin aegukpanjang."

79. "Puin aegukpanjang."

80. "Keizono aikokuhanni hujinno hukuhantchōni" (Vice headwomen in Patriotic NAs), *Kokuminsōryoku* 3, no. 9 (1941): 74–75; "Aegukpane pubanjangje" (Patriotic NAs' vice heads), *MS*, August 12, 1941.

81. See Hontarō, "Hogaraka aikokuhan" (Cheerful Patriotic NAs), *Kokuminsōryoku* 3, no. 10 (1941): 90–91; "Yongsan hōmen aikokuhan no hatsudō" (Patriotic NAs in Yongsan), *Keizōihō* 256 (1943); "Aigokuhan no jitsenhōkoku" (Our Patriotic NA), *Kokuminsōryoku* 3, no. 2 (1941): 67.

82. "Hantono senjiseikatsu saikentō" (Reinvestigating Korea's wartime everyday life) *Kokuminsōryoku* 3, no. 8 (1942): 15.

83. "Matchirenmei kinrōaikokuhan no genkyōni tsuite" (Mobilizing Patriotic NAs), *Keizōihō* 250 (1942): 16.

84. "Matchirenmei kinrōaikokuhan," 17–20.

85. "Keizōhu sēsanjinkaishori to aikokuhanno kyōryoku" (Trash collection and Patriotic NAs), *Keizōihō* 238 (1941): 38–39.

86. "Matchirenmei kinrōaikokuhan," 16–18.

87. Yi Song-sun, *Iljeha chŏnsinong'ŏp chŏngch'aekkwa nongch'on kyŏngje* (Wartime agricultural policies and the economy) (Seoul: Sŏnin, 2008), 78–82.

88. "Zenaikokuhaninni uttahu" (To all members of Patriotic NAs), *Kokuminsōryoku* 4, no. 9 (1942): 11.

89. "Isikjuŭiŭi silhaeng" (Two meals per day), *MS*, July 10, 1940; "Chŏlmi undong'ŭi pangbŏbŭro hyŭnmisigŭl ŏmhaenghaja" (Let's eat brown rice), *MS*, March 25, 1943.

90. "Chŏlmiundong pon'gyŏkhwa" (The rice saving campaign), *TI*, November 1, 1939; "Chŏngdong'yŏnmaeng singnyang kandam" (A forum about food), *TI*, February 7, 1940.

91. "Setsumainarabeni beikoku kyōshutsu undōni kansuru ken" (Saving rice and rice donation,) *Kokuminsōryoku* 2, no. 12 (1940): 116–117; "Kŭmch'ŏn ŭpnaeesŏ chŏlmiundong" (The rice saving campaign), *TI*, February 26, 1940.

92. Araki, "Aikokuhanwa kakusenheri," 56–59.

93. "Aikokuhanseishinno tokushusei," 18–22.

94. "Jyōkainiwa kanaraju shujinshutsekino koto" (Men should attend assembly), *Kokuminsōryoku* 4, no. 2 (1942): 7.

95. "Taesŏngjŏn manonyŏne Chosŏnnyŏsŏng'ŭi kyŏljŏnsaenghwal 8" (Korean women's wartime life), *MS*, July 9, 1942.

96. "Taesŏngjŏn manonyŏne Chosŏnnyŏsŏng'ŭi kyŏljŏnsaenghwal 6," *MS*, July 6, 1942.

97. "Sŭranch'ima."

CHAPTER 4: REBORN INTO CITIZENS' NEIGHBORHOOD ASSOCIATIONS

1. Editorial board, *Seoul sinmun,* November 28, 1945.
2. United States National Archives, RG 242, SA 2011, box 1060, *Kanbu riryŏksŏ* (Resumes), "O Ki-hyŏk."
3. Cumings, *Origins* I, 69–72.
4. Cumings, *Origins* I, 375.
5. Yi Hye-suk, *Migunjŏnggi chibaegujowa han'guksahoe* (Korean society under the US military government) (Seoul: Sŏnin, 2008), 316–319.
6. Cumings, *Origins* I, 293.
7. "Inmin'gonghwaguk chonjaenŭn" (The People's Republic disrupting Korean independence), *Tong'a ilbo* (hereafter *TI*), December 13, 1945.
8. Kim Tong-uk, "*1940–50nyŏndae han'gugŭi inp'ŭleisyŏn'gwa anjŏnghwajŏngch'aek*" (Inflation and economic policies in Korea, 1940s–1950s) (PhD diss., Yonsei University, 1994), 54.
9. Kim Chong-bŏm, *Chosŏn sing'nyangmunjewa kŭ taech'aek* (Food issues in Korea) (1946; reprint, Seoul: Tolbegae, 1984), 28.
10. Kim, *Chosŏn sing'nyangmunje,* 57–58.
11. Nongsusanbu, *Han'guk yangjŏngsa* (Korea's food policies) (Seoul: Nong'wŏn munhwasa, 1978), 37.
12. Chosŏnŭnhaeng chosabu, *Kyŏngjenyŏn'gam* IV (Economy yearbook IV) (1949), 238.
13. See Kim Tu-sŏp, "Migunjŏnggi namhaninguŭi chaegusŏng" (The Korean population during the US military occupation), in *Migunjŏnggi han'gugŭi sahoe pyŏndonggwa sahoesa* (Social changes and social history during the US military occupation), ed. Ch'oi Yŏng-hŭi (Ch'unch'ŏn: Hallimdaehak ch'ulp'ansa, 1999).
14. Yi Yun-sik, "Haebangjikhu haewoedongp'oŭi kwihwan'gwa migunjŏng'ŭi chŏngch'aek" (Return of overseas Koreans after liberation and the USAMGIK's policies) (MA thesis, Seoul City Collage, 1998), 25–39.
15. See Asano Toyomi, *Sarasŏ toraoda* (The return of Koreans) (Seoul: Sol, 2005), 3–4.
16. Nongsusanbu, *Han'guk yangjŏngsa,* 49.
17. USAMGIK Ordinance No. 90, Economic Control (May 28, 1946).
18. USAMGIK Ordinance No. 75, Nationalization of Korean Railways (May 7, 1946).
19. Kim, *Chosŏn sing'nyangmunje,* 72–73.
20. Yi, *Migunjŏnggi chibaegujowa,* 326–338.

21. "Inmin-dang, kunjŏngch'ŏng'e mulkaanjŏng kin'gŭptaech'aek kŏnŭi" (A suggestion for price stability), *Chung'angsinmun*, December 12, 1945.

22. Kim, *Chosŏn sing'nyangmunje*, 77.

23. Kim, *Chosŏn sing'nyangmunje*, 79.

24. "Paegŭpche kanghwarŭl" (Reinforcing rationing), *Seoul sinmun*, November 28, 1945.

25. "Sijung'ŭi ŭnnikmirŭl susaekpaegŭp" (Finding hoarded rice), *TI*, February 12, 1946.

26. "Kakpanŭl t'onghaya paegŭphara" (Rationing through NAs), *TI*, February 12, 1946.

27. "Yang'gogŭn itkŏnman paegŭpjiji" (Slow rice rationing), *TI*, January 6, 1946.

28. "Tasuŭi yuryŏng'in'gurŭl chŏkpal" (Finding "ghost populations"), *KS*, May 15, 1947.

29. "Yuryŏng'in'gu chosa" (Census), *KS*, December 10, 1948.

30. Cumings, *Origins* I, 351–379.

31. Mark Gayn, *Japan Diary*, quoted in Hugh Deane, *The Korean War 1945–1953* (San Francisco: China Books, 1999), 34.

32. Cumings, *Origins* 1, 351–379.

33. "Yuryŏng'in'gujŏkpal sagae tongsŏ 1,400 myŏng" (Finding 1,400 "ghost populations"), *Kyŏnghyang sinmun* (hereafter *KS*), June 3, 1947.

34. "Kungminsaenghwal kyundŭng'ŭl pojangkojŏ" (For equal living standards of Koreans), *TI*, April 10, 1949.

35. "Kongjŏnghage" (Fairly), *KS*, April 19, 1949.

36. "Chungjŏmbaegŭp (sang)" (Selected rations), *KS*, May 7, 1949.

37. "Paegŭbi ŏpsŏ sijangsŏ ssalguhanŭn segungmin" (The poor in short of rationing), *KS*, May 3, 1949.

38. "Chungjŏmbaegŭbŭn malppun" (Selected rationing only in words), *TI*, April 29, 1949.

39. "Chiha'e muthin chŏk" (Underground enemies), *KS*, August 30, 1949.

40. William Stueck, "The United States, the Soviet Union, and the Division of Korea: A Comparative Approach," *Journal of American–East Asian Relations* 4, no. 1 (Spring 1995): 1–27. See also Jongsoo James Lee, *The Partition of Korea after World War II: A Global History* (New York: Palgrave MacMillan, 2006).

41. Kim, *Everyday Life*, 95.

42. Kim Tae-hwan, "Namhan'gyŏngjeŭi chŏn'gaewa nambukhan kyŏngjet'onghabŭi kwaje" (The South Korean economy and the economic unification of the two Koreas), in *Pundan 50nyŏn'gwa t'ongilsidaeŭi kwaje*

(The fifty-year division and unification), ed. Yŏksamunje yŏn'guso (Seoul: Yŏksa pip'yŏngsa, 1995), 171.

43. Chu Ch'ŏl-hŭi, "Yŏsu·Sunch'ŏn 10·19sagŏn tŭkpyŏlbŏp chejŏng pŏbryurane taehan chinsulsŏ" (Testimony for making special law on Yŏsun incident), in *Yŏsu·Sunch'ŏn 10·19sagŏn chinsanggyumyŏng mit hŭisaengja myŏng'yehoeboge kwanhan ippŏpkongch'ŏnghoe* (Materials for public hearings on *Yŏsun Incident*) (Seoul: Kukhoe haengjŏng'anjŏn wiwŏnhoe, December 2020), 6.

44. Hong Yŏng-gi, ed., *Yŏsunsagŏn charyojip* 1 (Records of the Yŏsun Incident) (Seoul: Sŏnin, 2001), 71.

45. Hong, *Yŏsunsagŏn*, 77–79.

46. Quoted in Danielle L. Chubb, "Statist Nationalism and South Korea's National Security Law," in *Patriotism in East Asia*, ed. Jun-Hyeok Kwak and Koichiro Matsuda (New York: Routledge, 2014), 139.

47. Kang Sŏng-hyŏn, "Kungminbodoyŏnmaeng, chŏnhyang'esŏ kamsidong'wŏn, kŭrigo haksallo" (The National Guidance League: Conversion, mobilization, and massacre), in *Chugŏmŭrossŏ nararŭl chikija* (Be ready to die for country), ed. Kim Tŭk-jung (Seoul: Sŏnin, 2007), 127–131.

48. Kukhoesamuch'ŏ, *Chehŏn'gukhoe sokkirok* (Records of the first national assembly) (1948–1950; reprint, Seoul: Sŏninmunhwasa, 1999), 804–805.

49. "Aegukpanunyŏng sech'ik" (Rules of Patriotic NAs), *Seoul sinmun*, April 25, 1949; "Ch'ian, haengjŏng'ŭi manjŏnch'aegŭro yusukkyerŭl silsi" (The Registration for security and administration), *TI*, June 5, 1949.

50. "Naemubu yusukkyesilsibang'an" (The Registration plan of the Interior Ministry), *Chosŏn chung'ang ilbo*, April 30, 1949.

51. "Yusukkyejenŭn wihŏn" (The Registration is unlawful), *TI*, May 1, 1949.

52. "Todŏkchŏgŭro hyŏmnyŏkhara" (Show moral cooperation), *KS*, May 12, 1949.

53. "Ch'ian, haengjŏng'ŭi manjŏnch'aegŭro."

54. "Seoulsalimŭi manhwakyŏng yusukkye" (The Registration in Seoul), *KS*, July 27, 1949.

55. "Seoulsinae kakkyŏngch'alsŏ" (Police stations in Seoul), *Seoul sinmun*, September 3, 1949.

56. "Kungminhoe taep'yohoeŭi" (Closing the meeting of the NS), *TI*, August 26, 1949.

57. Cumings, *Origins* I, 189–190.

58. Kim Su-ja, "1948nyŏn Yi Sŭng-manŭi ch'odaenaegagŭi kusŏng" (The first cabinet of Syngman Rhee in 1948), *Ihwasahak yŏn'gu* 23–24 (1997): 197–198.

59. Kim Su-ja, "1948–1953nyŏn Yi Sŭng-manŭi kwŏllyŏkkanghwawa kung-minhoehwaryong" (The use of the National Association by Syngman Rhee, 1948–1953), *Yŏksawa hyŏnsil* 55 (2005): 347–348.

60. "Kukhoeŭiwŏn imgiyŏnjangron" (A suggestion to extend national assem-blymen's terms), *KS*, September 24, 1949. .

61. An Ho-sang, *Ilminjuŭi ponbat'ang* (The fundamentals of *Ilminjuŭi*) (Seoul: Ilminjuŭi yŏn'guwŏn, 1950), 2, 27, 30, 87.

62. Cumings, *Origins* I, 190–191.

63. "Ch'odangp'aŭi kungminundong" (National movements beyond parties), *TI*, June 11, 1946.

64. "Tongnipchŏnch'wie yong'wangdoljinhara" (Let's achieve independence), *TI*, February 7, 1947.

65. "Minjokpanyŏkcharŭl sukch'ŏnghaja" (Let's purge national traitors), *TI*, May 12, 1946.

66. Kim, "1948–1953 nyŏn Yi Sŭngman," 352.

67. "Namjosŏnmanirado sŏn'gŏsilsihara" (Let's hold an election in the South), *TI*, October 24, 1947.

68. https://www.assembly.go.kr/portal/main/contents.do?menuNo=600111

69. Hong Chŏng-wan, "Chŏngbusuripki taehandongnip ch'oksŏnggungmin-hoeŭi kungminundong yŏn'gu" (A study of movements by the NSRRKI) (MA Thesis, Yonsei University, 2005), 18–22.

70. Kim, "1948–1953nyŏn Yi Sŭng-manŭi," 356.

71. "Panggong t'aeseganghwa" (Strengthening anticommunism), *TI*, Novem-ber 19, 1948.

72. Kim, "1948nyŏn Yi Sŭng-manŭi ch'odae," 203–209.

73. Article 97 in the South Korean constitution (1948).

74. Naemubu, *Chibanghaengjŏng simnyŏnsa* (Ten-year history of local admin-istrations) (Seoul: Naemubu, 1958), 31–32.

75. "Kungminhaengbok chŭngjin" (Promoting national happiness), *TI*, Octo-ber 5, 1948.

76. Naemubu, *Chibanghaengjŏng simnyŏnsa*, 34–36.

77. "Chibangjach'ibŏphaesŏl (3)" (Explaining the local autonomy act), *TI*, July 13, 1949.

78. Articles 107–109 in the Local Autonomy Act.

79. "Chang naemuch'agwandam" (Chang vice-minister's remarks), *TI*, July 7, 1949.

80. "Kungminundong kanghwa" (Reinforcing national campaigns), *KS*, August 26, 1949.

81. "Chibangjang'gwanhoeŭi ch'ianhwakpo'e chuan" (The provincial gover-nors' meeting), *KS*, August 26, 1949.

CHAPTER 5: THE SUMMER OF 1950

1. Kim Sŏng-ch'il, *Yŏksa ap'esŏ-han sahakchaŭi 6.25 ilgi* (A historian's diary during the Korean War; hereafter Diary) (Seoul: Ch'angbi, 1993), 89.
2. US National Archives, RG 242, SA 2011, box 1059, item 2–76, *Chŏndanji* (Pamphlet).
3. RG 242, SA 2007 II, box 623, *Horang'i* (Tiger) 5 (Pyongyang: Rodongsin-munsa, 1947): 5.
4. Diary, December 5, 1945.
5. Diary, February 11, 1946.
6. Diary, September 16, 1950. (Hereafter the year is 1950 unless otherwise written.)
7. Diary, March 19 and 22, 1946.
8. Yi Nam-tŏk, "Cho'guksunanŭi tongbanja" (My partner during the war) in *Yŏksa ap'esŏ*, 350.
9. Diary, July 2.
10. Diary, June 25 and 27.
11. Diary, June 27.
12. Diary, June 28.
13. Diary, June 28.
14. Diary, June 27.
15. Diary, June 28.
16. Diary, September 14.
17. Diary, July 2.
18. Diary, June 28, and August 19.
19. Diary, August 16.
20. Kim Chae-jun, *Pŏmyonggi* (Ordinary records) (Seoul: P'ulbit, 1983), 198.
21. Diary, September 6 and 12.
22. RG 242, SA 2010, box 902, item 23, "1950nyŏn ch'uch'ŏnsŏch'ŏl Ch'ŏng'jusi inminwiwŏnhoe" (Recommendations), 1950.RG 242, SA 2009 II, box 826, item 125, "Tosumaebu mit sanhagigwan chigwŏnjŏng'wŏnp'yo chech'ure taehayŏ" (Staff list), August 28, 1950.
23. Diary, July 26 and September 12.
24. Yi Hyŏn-ju, "Han'gukchŏnjaenggi 'chosŏninmin'gun' chŏmnyŏnghaŭi Seoul" (Seoul under North Korean occupation), *Seoulhak yŏn'gu* 31 (2008): 203–235.
25. RG 242, SA 2009 II, box 796, item 91, "Konghwaguk nambanbu hae-bangjiyŏgŭi kun, myŏn, ri inminwiwŏnhoe sŏn'gŏ'e kwanhan kyujŏng" (Election rules in the South), 1950.
26. Diary, July 26.

27. RG 242, SA 2009 II, box 796, item 91, "Konghwaguk nambanbu haebangjiyŏgŭi".

28. Diary, September 12.

29. Diary, July 26.

30. Diary, July 27.

31. Diary, July 14.

32. RG 242, SA 2009 II, box 812, item 107, "Ŭiyonggun myŏngdan" (Volunteer Army lists), August 5, 1950.

33. RG 242, SA 2009 II, box 766, item 54, "Kangni hogu chosawa kŏnp'yŏng chosa" (Household surveys), July-August 1950; RG 242, SA 2010, box 856, item 47.12, "Ŭiyonggun chŏngnyŏnja myŏngdan" (Lists of those eligible for Volunteer Army), September 1950.

34. RG 242, SA 2010, box 856, item 47.12, "Ŭiyonggun'e chamgaja t'onggyebogo" (Statistics of volunteer army) and "Ŭiyonggun chŏngnyŏnja myŏngdan," September 13, 1950; RG 242, SA 2009 I, box 716, item 114, "1950nyŏn 7wŏl Tongmyŏnnae chawidaemyŏngdan" (Lists of self-defense armies), July 1950.

35. RG 242, SA 2009 I, box 716, item 114, "Chawidaemyŏngdan chech'ure kwanhan kŏn (Submission of the self-defense army list), July 17, 1950.

36. RG 242, SA 2009 II, box 821, item 52, "Kyŏngbiilji Tong'myŏnpunjuso" (Security journals), 1950.

37. RG 242, SA 2009 II, box 766, item 54, Sobang kwan'gyejip (Firefighting documents), 1950.

38. RG 242, SA 2009 II, box 812, item 109, Kigyŏl sŏryuch'ŏl, Kyŏnggi-do P'aju-gun Yadong-myŏn Kŭmch'on-ri (Documents of Kŭmch'on, P'aju, Kyŏnggi Province), September 1950.

39. RG 242, SA 2009 II, box 812, item 109, "Kamanisumaesaŏbe taehaya" (Purchasing straw bags), September 8, 1950.

40. RG 242, SA 2009 II, box 812, item 109, "Kunjungdaehoe t'ahap kŏn" (Mass rallies), September 15, 1950, and "Kungjungdaehoe t'onggyebogosŏ" (Mass rallies' statistics), September 16, 1950.

41. RG 242, SA 2009 I, box 713–2, item 81, "Pang'ŏjinji sŏlch'ie taehan roryŏktong'wŏnŭi kŏn" (Building shelters); "Roryŏktong'wŏne taehayŏ," (Labor mobilization), September 8, 1950; "Kaok (chŏksangaok) t'onggyebogo" (Enemy property), July 29, 1950; "Nong'gach'onghosu mit sedaesuwa nyŏllyŏngbyŏl namnyŏ ch'ong'in'gut'onggye" (Household surveys and censuses), August 8, 1950.

42. RG 242, SA 2009 I, box 713–2, item 81, "Sŏyaksŏ" (Oath), August 11, 1950; "Piryo sigyŏm unbanjagŏphaldang'e kwanhaya" (Fertilizer and salt transportation), August 10, 1950.

43. RG 242, SA 2009 II, box 825, item 114, "Hojŏk mit kiryu kwangye sŏryubojone kwanhayŏ (Keeping family registries), August 28, 1950.

44. Chu Yo-sŏp, "Kil (Roads) (124)," *TI,* June 23, 1953.

45. Chu, "Kil (110)," *TI,* June 9, 1953.

46. Chu, "Kil (60)," *TI,* April 20, 1953.

47. RG 242, SA 2009 II, box 770, item 111, "Nong'ŏmnoryŏk, ch'ungnyŏk, kigyeryŏkchosap'yo" (Survey of labor force, livestock, and machinery), 1950.

48. RG 242, SA 2009 II, box 812, item 109, "Kukka ŭimuroryŏktong'wŏnp'yo songbue taehaya" (Mandatory labor mobilization), September 1950.

49. RG 242, SA 2008, box 640, *Tang'yŏlsŏngjadŭrege chunŭn chuganbo* (Weekly for party members) 3 (1950): 41.

50. Diary, July 15.

51. Diary, July 1, 29, and 31.

52. Diary, August 9.

53. Diary, September 15.

54. RG 242, SA 2009 II, box 767, item 55.1, "Yŏksan mit chŏksan'gaok chosabuch'aek" (Enemy property surveys), July 1950.

55. RG 242 SA 2009 I, box 713–2, item 77, "Konghwaguk nambanbujiyŏge t'ojigaehyŏgŭl silsihame kwanhayŏ (Land reform in the South), July 4, 1950.

56. RG 242, SA 2009 I, box 713–2, item 81, Molsutoji chosasŏwoe chapch'ŏl (Confiscated land survey and other documents), 1950.

57. RG 242, SA 2009 I, box 713–2, item 81, "Umach'a riŏka chajŏnch'a son'gurumaŭi tŭngnoksilsie kwnhayŏ" (Vehicle registration); "Yugu mit kit'a kach'uk chayuch'ŏbun kŭmjie kwanhan kŏn" (Permission needed to kill livestock), July 22, 1950.

58. Diary, August 13.

59. Diary, July 25 and August 1.

60. Diary, August 16.

61. Diary, August 13.

62. Diary, August 17.

63. Yi, "Cho'guksunan," 358.

64. Diary, August 30 and September 9.

65. Yi, "Cho'guksunan," 364.

66. Diary, September 9.

67. "Yugiorŭl hoesanghamyŏ (5) and (6)" (Remembering the Korean War), *KS,* June 15 and 16, 1952.

68. Diary, August 31.

69. Diary, July 3.
70. Diary, July 3.
71. Diary, August 2.
72. RG 242, SA 2010, box 895, item 42, "Nambanbu kakto(Seoul) munhwa sŏnjŏnsaŏp kyujŏng" (Cultural propaganda in the South), August 1950.
73. RG 242, SA 2009 II, box 813, item 115, "1950 munhwasŏnjŏne kwanhan kŏn" (Cultural propaganda), 1950.
74. Diary, August 29.
75. RG 242, SA 2009 I, box 693–1, item 183, "Sŏndong'wŏn such'ŏp" (Handbook for propagandists) (1950), 13; Diary, July 3.
76. Diary, July 25.
77. Diary, August 29.
78. Diary, August 29.
79. Diary, July 6.
80. Diary, August 21.
81. Diary, August 25.
82. Diary, August 28.
83. Yi Sang-ch'ŏn, "Han'gukchŏnjaenggi McArthur saryŏngbuŭi ppira sŏnjŏnjŏngch'aek" (McArthur's propaganda during the Korean War), *Journal of Korean Modern and Contemporary History* 58 (2011): 191.
84. Diary, August 4.
85. Diary, September 3.
86. Diary, September 16 and 22.
87. Diary September 23–24.
88. Diary, September 26.
89. RG 242, SA 2011, box 1078, item 9–25.5, *Chogukchŏnsŏn chosawiwŏnhoe podo* (Surveys by investigation committees) (Pyongyang: Chosŏn Rodongdang ch'ulp'ansa, 1951), 110.
90. Diary, October 10.
91. Diary, November 10.
92. Diary, October 22.
93. Pak Wŏn-sun, "Chŏnjaeng puyŏkcha 5manyŏmyŏng ŏttŏtke ch'ŏridoeŏttna" (What happened to approximately 50,000 collaborators during the Korean War), *Yŏksa pip'yŏng* (May 1990): 175–176.
94. Pak, "Chŏnjaeng puyŏkcha," 173, 179, and 180.
95. See Chŏn Kap-saeng, "Kungminbŏrigo yabandojuhan Yi Sŭngmanjŏngbu Seoul subokhu pobokhaksal chahaeng" (The revenge of the Rhee administration after recovering Seoul), *Minjok* 21 (2010): 102.

96. "Puyŏkchanŭn uri sonŭro" (Finding collaborators), *TI,* October 12, 1950.
97. Diary, October 16.
98. Diary, December 11.
99. Special Decree on the Handling of Acts of Collaboration, December 1, 1950.

CHAPTER 6: THE DEMISE OF LOCAL AUTONOMY DURING THE POSTWAR RECOVERY

1. "Foreign Service Despatch," *U.S. Embassy Despatch* 527 (June 18, 1957): 1.
2. Kim Pyŏng-ch'an and Chŏng Chŏng-gil, ed., *50nyŏndae chibangjach'i* (Local autonomy in the 1950s) (Seoul: Seoul National University Press, 1995), 4–6.
3. Kongbosil, *Taet'ongnyŏng Yi Sŭngmanbaksa tamhwajip* (Speech collection of Syngman Rhee) (Seoul: Kongbosil: 1959), 107–109.
4. South Korean National Archives, BA0607387, *Pŏmnyŏng chirŭich'ŏl* (Legal questions), 1952–1953, "Tong-rijang chŏngdangch'amyŏyŏbu chirŭiŭi kŏn" (The participation of village heads in political parties), February 24, 1952, 41–44.
5. BA0607387, "Tong-rijang," February 22, 1952, 29–30.
6. BA0607387, "Tong-rijang," February 22, 1952, 27–28.
7. BA0607387, "Tong-rijang," March 20, 1952, 36.
8. Naemubu (Interior Ministry), *Chibanghaengjŏng kaeyo* (An outline of local administrations) (Seoul: Naemubu, 1957), 32.
9. BA0607387, "Tong-rijang," December 31, 1952, 3–9.
10. BA0607389, *Pŏmnyŏng chirŭich'ŏl,* "Tong-rijang chŏngdangch'amyŏŭi kabuŭi kŏn," October 6, 1954.
11. BA0099165, "Kungminundong'e kwanhan kŏn" (National movements), June 13, 1952.
12. BA0607389, "Tong-rijang chŏngdangch'amyŏŭi kabuŭi kŏn," October 26, 1954.
13. BA0607389, "Tong-rijang chŏngdangch'amyŏŭi kabuŭi kŏn," November 1, 1954.
14. Provincial Law 86. Citizens' NAs rule in South Kyŏngsang (1953).
15. "Taehan chibanghaengjŏng hyŏphoeŭi paljok" (Launching the society of local administration), *Chibanghaengjŏng* (Local administrations, hereafter *CH*) 1 (1952): 83–87.

16. Chang Pyŏng-yŏn, "Chibang ŭihoenŭn muŏsŭl hanŭn'ga" (What do local assemblies do?), *CH* 1, no. 1 (1952): 61–62.
17. "Ilsŏnhaengjŏng'ŭl malhanŭn chwadamhoe" (The local officials' forum), *CH* 1, no. 8 (1952): 64–66.
18. Chang, "Chibang ŭihoenŭn," 61–62.
19. "Chwadamhoe," 62–63.
20. Han Hŭi-sŏk, *Unsang simmanni* (Traveling on the cloud) (Seoul: Taehanjibanghaengjŏng hyŭphoe, 1953), 128–131.
21. "Chibangjach'ibŏp haesŏl 3" (An explanation of the local autonomy act), *TI*, July 13, 1949.
22. "Iraesŏ nongch'onŭn kungp'ibilo" (The reason for rural poverty), *KS*, September 9, 1953.
23. "Kyŏngch'alsŏ chaejosahaltŏ" (Reinvestigations by police), *TI*, September 9, 1953.
24. "Chappugŭmjingsu muryŏ 280jong" (280 types of miscellaneous taxes), *KS*, October 30, 1953.
25. Kongbosil, *Tamhwajip*, 131–132.
26. See Chŏn Pyŏng-mu, *Chosŏnch'ongdokpu chosŏninsabŏpkwan* (Korean law specialists in the Government-General) (Seoul: Yŏksagonggan, 2012), 373–375; and Naemubu, *Kaeyo*, 249–250.
27. For their personal information, see *Han'gukminjokmunhwa taebaekkwasajŏn* (Encyclopedia of Korean Culture). https://encykorea.aks.ac.kr/Article/E0074805 https://encykorea.aks.ac.kr/Article/E0074807
28. Sin Yong-u, "Kangnyŏkhago t'ong'ildŏen chibanghaengjŏng" (Integrated local administrations), *CH* 3, no. 4 (1954), 4–6.
29. Cho Chae-sŭng, "Minjujuŭiwa chibangjach'i" (Democracy and local autonomy), *Pŏpchŏng* 11, no. 5 (1956): 29–31.
30. "Chibangsiljŏng tapsagi (ha)" (Observing local societies), *TI*, February 5, 1954.
31. Kuksa p'yŏnch'anwiwŏnhoe (National Historical Compilation Committee), DKI012–10–01C0026, "Chapchonggŭm kyŏngnigyuch'ik 1958" (Miscellaneous taxes), 1958, 68.
32. DKI012–10–01C0026, "Chapchonggŭm kyŏngnigyuch'ik 1958," 124–125.
33. Naemubu, *Kaeyo*, 61; DK012–10–01C0026, "Kyŏnggi-do Anyangsi 1961nyŏn sŏmuyegyuch'ŏl" (Administrative documents of Anyang), 1961, 67–89.
34. Pae Sang-ha, "Chŏnsi maltanhaengjŏng kanghwaron" (Reinforcing wartime local administrations), *CH* 2, no. 1 (1953): 76–77.

35. DK012–10–01C0026, "Chapchonggŭm t'ongjang" (Miscellaneous tax accounts),1958: 0139.
36. Kim Sang-yong and Yi Sŭng-jong, "Chibangjach'i chojigŭi pyŏnch'ŏn" (Changes in local administrative institutions) in *50nyŏndae chibangjach'i*, 223.
37. Naemubu, *Chibanghaengjŏng simnyŏnsa*, 52–53.
38. Naemubu, *Chibanghaengjŏng simnyŏnsa*, 54–57.
39. "Chibanghoeŭi kaemak" (The provincial governors' meeting), *Chosŏn ilbo*, March 26, 1957.
40. Yi Kon, "Chibang gongbosamuŭi kangwhach'aek" (Reinforcing public communication), *Naemuhaengjŏng*, no. 100 (1962): 20.
41. Ch'ae Ŭi-sik, "Kungminbanŭi hamnijŏgin unyŏngjidobangch'aek" (Citizens' NAs' management), *CH* 6, no. 11 (1957): 129.
42. "Kukhoe sokkirok palch'we" (National assembly stenographic records, hereafter "Palch'we"), *CH* 6, no. 9 (1957): 121, 129, 138.
43. "Palch'we," 124–126.
44. "Palch'we," 116–118.
45. "Palch'we," 121–123.
46. "Palch'we," 116.
47. "Palch'we," 122.
48. "Palch'we," 130–131.
49. "Palch'we": 132–134 and 140.
50. "Yŏjŏk" (Unfinished story), *KS*, April 15, 1957.
51. "Chigŭtchigŭthan aegukpanjanjae" (Tiresome remnants of the Patriotic NAs), *Saebyŏk* 5 (1957): 5.
52. "Kungminbanjojige kwanhan Changnaemu changgwan tapbyŏn" (Chang minister's answers on Citizens' NA), *CH* 6, no .9 (1957): 120.
53. "Sŏnŭl nŏmjianŭlga kunggŭm" (Crossing a line?), *TI,* April 8, 1956.
54. "Waesaekwaech'wirŭl sot'ang" (Cleansing Japanese remnants), *TI,* August 20, 1946.
55. Pak Sang-bong, "Ch'esinsaŏbe taehan ŭigyŏn" (Opinions on the postal service), *Ch'esin munwha* 27 (1955): 32.
56. "Cheilhoe chŏn'guk uryangjipbaewŏn chwadamhoerŭl mach'igo" (The first gathering of exemplary deliverymen), *Ch'esin munwha* 27 (1955): 58–63.
57. Pak, "Ch'esinsaŏbe taehan," 32.
58. "Chesamhoe up'yŏnjugan haengsabogo" (The postal service's special week), *Ch'esin munwha* 57 (1959): 40–41.
59. "Chibangsŏn'gŏ iphubo tŭngnok sunanja hyŏnjijwadamhoe (2)" (A talk about election registration), *TI,* August 1, 1956.

60. "Kwan'gwŏnŭi sŏn'gŏgansŏbŭn chinŭnghwahanŭn'ga" (Election intervention), *KS,* August 14, 1956.

61. "Sŏn'gŏbanghae sasilmugŭnida" (No election disruption), *KS,* July 21, 1956; "Munp'ae andalmyŏn ch'ŏdan" (Punishment for houses without a doorplate), *KS,* September 3, 1956.

62. "Kong'gich'ong," *TI,* September 4, 1956.

63. "Foreign Service Dispatch," *U.S. Embassy Despatch* 446 (May 2, 1957): 4–5.

64. "Kungminbanjundong" (The Citizens' NAs scandal), *Sasanggye* 5, no. 7 (1957): 91–92.

65. "Palch'we," 123 and 141–142.

66. Kukhoesamuchŏ, *Kukhoesa* (The history of the National Assembly) (Seoul: Kukhoesamuchŏ, 1957), 17.

67. "Foreign Service Despatch," 3–4.

68. "Naemubusŏ" (In the Interior Ministry), *Chosŏn ilbo,* July 5, 1957.

69. "Tansangdanha" (Ideas), *TI,* December 30, 1957.

70. "Yŏjŏnhi unyŏngdoenŭn kungminban" (NAs in operation), *KS,* April 9, 1958.

71. To distance NAs from the colonial era, the ministry emphasized *"pang,"* the term used in premodern Korea. Naemubu, *Chibanghaengjŏng simnyŏnsa,* 74.

72. Naemubu, *Chibanghaengjŏng* simnyŏnsa, 71–73.

73. Article 98 and Article 146 of the Local Autonomy Act (1958).

74. South Chŏlla kyuch'ik che35ho, "Kungminbanunyŏng kyuch'ik" (Citizens' NA' rules), October 5, 1953. Emphases added.

75. BA0181766, Kyuch'ik (Rules), *"Togaemyŏn pang'unyŏng kyuch'ik"* (Citizens' NA' Rules), 1959.

76. BA0085311, *Ch'agwan hoeŭirok* (Vice-ministers' minutes), "Kungminbanunyŏng chung'angwiwŏnhoe 27hoe" (27th meeting for Citizens' NAs), July 10, 1957.

77. "Chŏnnam Kwangsan-gun Songjŏng-ŭp Sinch'on-ri sanghoegwang'gyŏng" (Monthly assemblies in Sinch'on village), *CH* 6, no. 9 (1957): 147–160.

78. For the 1958 election results, see https://www.assembly.go.kr/portal/main /contents.do?menuNo=600111.

79. Sŏ Chung-sŏk, *Yi Sŭngman'gwa cheil konghwaguk* (Syngman Rhee and the First Republic) (Seoul: Yŏksa pip'yŏngsa, 2007), 188–190.

80. "Kane putko ssŭlgae'e putko" (Going to liver, going to gallbladder), *KS,* May 20, 1960.

81. "Komusinp'yo tŭngjang" (Buying votes), *TI,* March 3, 1960.

82. "Changbut'ongnyŏng moryakch'ugung" (Insulting Vice President Chang), *Chosŏn ilbo*, January 20, 1960; "Pangsanghoe t'onghae sŏn'gŏundong" (Election campaigns in assemblies), *Chosŏn ilbo*, February 7, 1960.
83. "3.15. sŏn'gŏ karŭt'e, Kangwŏn-do" (The March 15 election), *TI*, March 15, 1960.
84. "Susa'e chongjibu" (Investigation is over), *KS*, June 15, 1960.
85. See https://www.assembly.go.kr/portal/main/contents.do?menuNo =600111
86. "Chibangjach'iŭi ch'ŏljŏ" (Thorough local autonomy), *TI*, May 21, 1960.
87. "Kukto chibangdorobosu" (Repairing roads), *TI*, February 24, 1959.
88. "Ch'ong 1064manmari kusŏundong" (10,640,000 rats were caught), *TI*, December 19, 1954.
89. Naemubu t'onggyeguk, "Che3hoe t'ŭkbyŏlsido t'onggyesamujahoeŭi" (The third meeting of statisticians), *Taehanmin'guk t'ong'gyewŏlbo* (A monthly bulletin of Korean statistics) 2 (1960): 20.
90. Law No. 563, Local Autonomy Act, November 1, 1960.

CHAPTER 7: FATHERLAND AND PEOPLE, 1945–1953

1. RG 242, SA 2011, box 1076, item 9–2, "Inminban kanghwadaech'aege taehayŏ" (Reinforcing People's NAs), February 15, 1950.
2. Kim, *Everyday Life*, 45–49.
3. RG 242, SA 2009 II, box 763, item 22, "Haebanghu Chosŏn" (Postliberated Korea 1950), 79–99.
4. Ch'ae Kyŏng-hŭi, *Pukhan inminbane kwanhan yŏn'gu* (A study of People's NAs), (Seoul: Pukhan taehagwŏndae, 2008), 16.
5. RG 242, SA 2009 II, box 793, item 77, "Kakkŭp inminwiwŏnhoe yangjŏnggyet'ong samu ch'wigŭbyogang" (An outline of the food administration), 1948.
6. Ch'oe Yong-dal, "Sŏn'gŏ kyujŏng'ŭn ŏttŏtke ch'inilbunjarŭl kyujŏnghanŭn'ga" (Defining Japanese collaborators in election law), *Rodong sinmun*, October 3, 1946, in Kuksa p'yŏnch'anwiw'ŏnhoe (National Historical Compilation Compilation), ed., *Pukhan'gwangye saryojip* (North Korean sources, hereafter *Saryojip*) (Seoul: Kuksa p'yŏnch'anwiw'ŏnhoe, 1983-) 33: 241- 242.
7. *Chosŏn taebaekkwasajŏn* (The North Korean encyclopedia) (Pyongyang: Paekkwasajŏn ch'ulp'ansa, 2001), 646.

8. For further information, see Dae-sook Suh, *Kim Il Sung: The North Korean Leader* (New York: Columbia University Press, 1988).

9. Kim Il Sung, *Kim Il Sung Chŏjakchip* (Kim Il Sung Works, hereafter *Chŏjakchip*), 47 vols. (Pyongyang: Chosŏn rodongdang ch'ulp'ansa, 1979–1997) 1: 281–284.

10. Kim, *Chŏjakchip* 1: 285.

11. Kim, *Chŏjakchip* 1: 285–286.

12. *Chosŏn taebaekkwasajŏn,* 653.

13. Kim, Cho-hun, "Minjugukkaŭi aegukchuŭi" (Patriotism in democratic countries), 1947, *Saryojip* 42: 422.

14. "Minjugukkaŭi," *Saryojip* 42: 420–422.

15. "Pukchosŏn myŏn, kun, si mit to-wiwŏnhoe wiwŏnsŏn'gŏe kwanhan kyujŏng" (Election Rules of North Korea), (September 5, 1946), *Saryojip* 8: 67–68.

16. Kim, *Chŏjakchip* 2: 420–423.

17. Yi Il-u, "Munmaengt'oech'i mit sŏng'in kyoyuksaŏbŭi tangmyŏn'gwaje" (Eliminating illiteracy), *Inmin* 4, no. 8 (1948): 26.

18. "Pukchosŏn myŏn, kun, si," *Saryojip* 8: 73.

19. Kim, *Chŏjakchip* 2: 421.

20. RG 242, SA 2009 I, box 690, item 138, "Sŏn'gŏsŏnjŏn'gwa uriŭi immu" (Election propaganda and our mission), 1946, 40.

21. RG 242, SA 2007 I, box 411–1, item 1.59, "Inje-gun Nammyŏn kaktanch'e yŏnsŏkhoeŭirok" (Minutes of social organizations in Inje County), October 1946 and February 1947.

22. RG 242, SA 2007 I, box 417, item 13.5, "Myŏndangwiwŏnhoe hoeŭirok, Pukmyŏn" (Minutes of Workers' party committee, Puk Town) no. 14 and 15, February 1947. "

23. "Sŏn'gŏsŏnjŏnsaŏbŭl sŏn'gŏjaŭi kŏso'e chipchunghaja," *Rodong sinmun,* January 15, 1947; "Inje-gun Nammyŏn kaktanch'e yŏnsŏkhoeŭirok," February 14, 1947.

24. RG 242 SA 2005 4/2, box 83, "Yŏronjosa pogosŏ" (Survey), October 1946.

25. "Pukchosŏn myŏn mit ri(tong) inminwiwŏnhoe sŏn'jŏnŭn ŏttŏtke chinhaengdoel kŏsin'ga" (Elections in towns and villages), *Saryojip* 11: 575.

26. "Inminwiwŏnhoeŭi sŏn'gŏch'onggyŏlgwa kŭmhuŭi chungsimimmu" (Important missions after election), *Saryojip* 13: 290.

27. RG 242, SA 2010, box 847, item 167, "Tonghŭngni yugwŏnja chosap'yo" (Constituents in Tonghŭng), 1949; RG 242, SA 2009 I, box 687, item 50, "Materials of North Korean People's committees," 1947, 69–70.

28. RG 242, SA 2010, box 862, item 97, *Kanbumyŏngdan* (Staff list),1949.

29. RG 242, SA 2010, box 847, item 166, "Minjusŏnjŏnsil sŏlch'iwa changch'ie kwanhan kŏn" (Building democratic propaganda offices), 1947.

30. Kim, *Chŏjakchjp* 2: 552–554.

31. "Che107ho- sŏn'gŏ sŏnjŏnsirŭl minjusŏnjŏnsillo chonsoksikime kwanhan kyŏljŏngsŏ" (From election propaganda office to democratic propaganda office), November 8, 1946. *Saryojip* 5: 66.

32. RG 242, SA 2012, box 1163, "1950nyŏndo hoeŭirokch'ŏl" (Minutes), January 11, 1950.

33. RG 242, SA 2012, box 1220, 8/137, "Minjusŏnjŏnsil saŏpchidosŏ" (A guide for propaganda offices), July 1951.

34. RG 242, SA 2009 II, box 792, item 64, "1948nyŏn t'onggyech'ŏl (Togŏm sep'o)" (Statistics), 1948.

35. "Hyŏnjibogo hyangsangdoen maul" (Improved villages), *Chosŏn nyŏsŏng* (March 1950): 52.

36. Kim Sang-bŏm, "Han'guk chŏnjaenggi Pukhan minjusŏnjŏnsirŭi kyoyuk-kwa tongwŏn hwaldong'e kwanhan yŏn'gu" (Propaganda offices during the Korean war), *Kunsa*103 (2017), 78.

37. "Minjusŏnjŏnsil saŏpchidosŏ."

38. RG 242, SA 2012, box 1190, Sŏnjŏnwŏn such'aek che 9ho (Handbook for propagandists), "Kunjung sŏndongsaŏp kanghwarŭl wihayŏ" (Reinforcing propaganda), December 1948.

39. RG 242, SA 2010, box 847, item 166, "Kin'gŭp sŏnjŏnwŏn'gangsŭphoe kaech'oeŭi kŏn" (Urgent lectures for propagandists), October 28, 1947.

40. RG 242, SA 2007 I, box 432, item 75, Sŏnjŏnwŏn such'aek (Handbook for propagandists) 5, May 1947.

41. RG 242, SA 2010, box 847, item 166, "Migungmujanggwan Marshal ssiwa soryŏnwoesang Molotov ssiwaŭi Chosŏnmunje'e kwanhan sŏgan'gyoryu'e taehan pogo kunjungdaehoe sojibe kwanhan kŏn" (Mass rallies), May 5, 1947.

42. RG 242, SA 2007 I, box 432, item 75, Sŏnjŏnwŏn such'aek 8, August 1947.

43. RG 242, SA 2010, box 847, item 166, "9wŏl 26il Shtikovtaejang sŏng-myŏngsöe taehan sŏnjönsaŏp chŏn'gaeŭi kŏn" (Propaganda about the statement on September 26), October 9, 1947.

44. RG 242, SA 2010, box 847, item 166, "Inminban hoeŭiesö ch'wigŭphal munje" (Topics for People's NAs).

45. RG 242, SA 2009 II, box 792, item 64, Chapsŏryuch'ŏl (Miscellaneous documents), 1948.

46. RG 242, SA 2009 II, box 792, item 62, "1948 nyŏn t'onggyech'ŏl" (Statistics), 1948.

47. RG 242, SA 2009 II, box 793, item 78, "Haksŭpchegang" (Study materials), 1947.
48. RG 242, SA 2013, box 1252, item 2–271.9, "Sŏnjŏnwŏn such'aek (che 6ho)" (Handbook for propagandists), June 1948.
49. For NA heads' party affiliation, see "Kanbumyŏngdan." For propagandists' party affiliation, see RG 242, SA 2010, box 861–2, item 95, "Yŏnp'omyŏn Tonghŭngni inminwiwŏnhoe sŏndong'wŏn myŏngdan" (List of propagandists in Tonghŭng village PC).
50. "Sŏnjŏnwŏn such'aek (che 9ho)," 29. On microcells, see "Chosŏnrodongdang tangjojik chidosaŏbe taehan chisisŏhaesŏl" (How to organize Workers' party), 1949, *Saryojip* 17: 294–295.
51. RG 242, SA 2012, box 1163,1950nyŏndo hoeŭirokch'ŏl (Minutes, 1950), "January 11," and "June 19, 1950."
52. RG 242, SA 2012, box 1163, 1949nyŏndo hoeŭirokch'ŏl (Minutes, 1949), "August 24, 1949."
53. RG 242, SA 2010, box 847, item 166, "Tonghŭng-ri, Yŏnp'o-myŏn" (Tonghŭng village, Yŏnp'o town).
54. RG 242, SA 2007 I, box 416, item 12.7, "Nong'ŏp hyŏnmulse chejŏng'e kwanhan kŏn" (Tax-in-kind), July 18, 1946.
55. *Pukchosŏn pŏmryŏngjip* (North Korean laws), (Pyongyang: Pukchosŏn imsiwiwŏnhoe sabŏpguk, 1947), 94.
56. "Hyŏnmulsejingsu chidogyŏnghŏm" (Tax-in-kind collection), 1948, *Saryojip* 14: 326–327.
57. RG 242, SA 2009 I, box 689, item 103, "Kakto-inminwiwŏnhoe 2nyŏn'gan saŏpkaegwan" (Two-year works of provincial PCs') 1947, 51–52.
58. RG 242, SA 2012, box 1163, "1949 nyŏndo hoeŭirokch'ŏl" (1949 Minutes), July 18, 1949; RG 242, SA 2007 I, box 414, Chapch'ŏl, pimil (Documents, secret), "38inam tojunongho pogoŭi kŏn" (List of defectors to the South).
59. "Sangdapsep'o hoeŭirok" (Minutes of Sangdap Cell), July 24, 1949, *Saryojip* 15: 687.
60. "Sangdapsep'o," *Saryojip* 15: 675.
61. "Sangdapsep'o," *Saryojip* 15: 695–696.
62. "Sangdapsep'o," *Saryojip* 15: 695–696.
63. RG 242, SA 2007 I, box 414, "Aegungmaek hŏnnabe taehan pogo" (Records of donated patriotic barley).
64. RG 242, SA 2007 I, box 410–1, item 1.52, "Yosŏngdongmaeng tangjo hoeŭirok" (Minutes of Women's Alliance) 17, August 1948.
65. Ch'on Se-bong, "Nongbu" (Farmers) in RG 242, SA 2012, box 1112, item 1–91, Sosŏljip (Novels) (Pyongyang: Munhwa chŏnsŏnsa, 1949), 243.

66. RG 242, SA 2007 I, box 414, "Chogi changmure taehan 1946–1947nyŏnŭi suhwakko mit hyŏnmulseaek taebip'yo" (Tax-in-kind for 1946–1947 produces.)

67. RG 242, SA 2007 I, box 414, "Chogi hyŏnmulse'e taehan chŏnbomun" (Telegrams on tax-in-kind), August 6, 1947.; and "Kakchong chogihyŏnmulsejŭngsu sanghwang pogo" (Tax-in-kind collection reports), August 4, 1947.

68. RG 242, SA 2007 I, box 414, "Mobŏmnongmin ch'uch'ŏne taehaya" (Nominees for exemplary farmers), August 8, 1948.

69. RG 242, SA 2007 I, box 411–1, item 1.59, "Pukchosŏn rodongdang Kangwŏn-do Rinje-gun Nammyŏndang yŏlsŏngja hoeŭirok" (Minutes of Nam Town, Rinje County, Kangwŏn Province), 1947.

70. "Kŏnguksasang tongwŏn undonggwa aegungmihŏnnap undong" (Movement for mobilizing state-building spirit and rice donation movement), 1946, *Saryojip* 34: 275.

71. RG 242, SA 2007 I, box 417, item 13.12, "Che11ch'a myŏndangwiwŏnhoe hoeŭirok" (Minutes of town committee, no 11), January 3, 1947.

72. RG 242, SA 2007 I, box 414, "Aegungmihŏnnap pogogŏn" (Records of donated patriotic rice).

73. RG 242, SA 2006, box 279, item 36, Chech'amgosŏch'ŏl (Documents), "Chaejŏng saŏpch'ujin kanghwa'e taehan chisi" (Practicing financial policies), April 21, 1948.

74. RG 242, SA 2006, box 279, item 36, "Myŏnse ilban Sŏnch'ŏnmyŏn" (Sŏnch'ŏn Town information), 1947.

75. RG 242, SA 2006, box 279, item 36, "Sŏnch'ŏnmyŏn kaktong inwisaŏp ch'onggyŏl yogang" (1948 town administration), December 29, 1948.

76. RG 242, SA 2006, box 279, item 36, "Che5ch'a Sŏnch'ŏnmyŏn inwigyŏljŏng che10ho" (The PC's decision), March 23, 1949.

77. RG 242, SA 2006, box 279, item 36, "Saŏptŭngnok kyujŏngsilsie kwanhayŏ" (Business registration), November 12, 1948.

78. RG 242, SA 2006, box 279, item 36, "Napse'e taehan sŏnjŏnyogang" (Propaganda for tax payments), 1949 and "Sanggong'ŏpchadŭrege kang'ŭihal cheyogang" (Lectures for merchants).

79. RG 242, SA 2006, box 279, item 36, "Sŏnch'ŏnmyŏn inminwiwŏnhoe kyŏljŏng che10 ho" (Sŏnch'ŏn Town Decision no. 10), April 18, 1950.

80. Chaenyŏng County PC, "Inminban kanghwadaech'aege taehayŏ."

81. RG 242, SA 2011, box 1076, item 9–2, "Hagŭp inminwiwŏnhoe saŏp chidosang'e natanan myŏtkaji sigŭphi sijŏnghayŏyahal munje'e taehayŏ" (Urgent issues in lower PCs), March 15, 1950.

82. RG 242, SA 2011, box 1076, item 9–2, "Kŏn'guk ŭimuroryŏk tong'wŏne taehan myotkaji" (Labor mobilization for state-building), May 16, 1950.

83. Kim T'ae-u, *P'okkyŏk* (Air raids) (P'aju: Ch'angbi, 2013), 108–147.

84. RG 242, SA 2011, box 1076, item 9–2, "Chŏgŭi kongsŭbŭro inhan p'ihaejŏnghyŏng pogo'e taehayŏ" (Damages by air-raids), August 5, 1950; and "Sŏkt'an'gyo pokkugongsa" (Bridge repairing), July 6, 1950.

85. RG 242, SA 2011, box 1084, item 9–46, "Kakkŭp inminwiwŏnhoe saŏbŭl chŏnsich'ejero kaep'yŏnhalde taehan chisi" (Building wartime systems), July 13, 1950; "Inmin'gundae wŏnhosaŏp kanghwa'e taehayŏ" (Supporting the People's army), July 13, 1950; "Kunjŏngbu kyŏljŏng myŏngryŏng'ŭl ch'ŏljŏhi chiphaenghalde taehayŏ" (Keeping military orders thoroughly), July 1950.

86. RG 242, SA 2011, box 1084, item 9–46, "Province decision 1," June 30, 1950.

87. RG 242, SA 2011, box 1076, item 9–2, "Panggongdae chojige taehan kin'gŭpchisi" (Organizing defense forces), June 30, 1950; RG 242, SA 2011, box 1084, item 9–46, "Country order 19," July 9, 1950; and "Province order 23," July 10, 1950.

88. RG 242, SA 2011, box 1084, item 9–46, "Panggongsaŏp kanghwa'e taehayŏ", August 1, 1950; "Panggongdaebirŭl kanghwahalde taehayŏ," (Building bomb shelters), July 10, 1950.

89. RG 242, SA 2011, box 1084, item 9–46, "Kongsŭbe taehan pangbisisŏl saŏbŭl ilch'ŭng kangwhahalde taehayŏ" (Reinforcing defense facilities), July 17, 1950.

90. RG 242, SA 2010, box 903, item 33, Seoulsi min'gan panggongbu, *Min'gan panggong chidowŏn such'ŏp* (A booklet for defense training leaders) (1950), 15–16.

91. RG 242, SA 2011, box 1084, item 9–46, "Inminbanjidowŏnje silsi'e taehayŏ" (The introduction of People's NA supervisors), August 16, 1950.

92. Stephen E. Pease, *PSYWAR: Psychological Warfare in Korea, 1950–1953* (Washington, DC: Stackpole Books, 1992); Chŏng Yong-uk, "6.25 chŏnjaenggi ppira simrijŏn'gwa naengjŏn ideologi" (The psychological war and Cold War ideology during the Korean War), *Yŏksawa hyŏnsil* 51 (2004): 97–133.

93. RG 242, SA 2011, box 1084, item 9–46, "Inminbanjidowŏnje silsi'e taehan pogoŭi kŏne taehayŏ" (Supervising People's NAs), August 23, 1950.

94. "Inminbanjidowŏnje silsi'e taehayŏ."

95. Han Monika, "Han'guk chŏnjaenggi migugŭi pukhan chŏmryŏng-jŏngch'aekkwa t'ongch'igwon munje" (The US Army's occupation of

North Korea during the Korean War), *Yŏksawa hyŏnsil* 78 (2010): 61–193.

96. RG 242, SA 2011, box 1084, item 9–45, "In'gudongt'ae chosasŏ Hunammyŏn" (Censuses), August 31, 1950, and "Kongminjŭngsaŏp t'onggyejech'ure taehaya" (Public ID Statistics), March 20, 1951.

97. RG 242, SA 2011, box 1084, item 9–45, "Inmyŏngp'ihae chŏnghyŏngjosa pogoe taehayŏ" (Damage surveys), July 1951.

98. RG 242, SA 2011, box 1087, item 9–59, "Chŏngdangbyŏl t'onggye, Humanmyŏn" (Political party statistics), 1951.

99. RG 242, SA 2011, box 1086, item 9–56.3, "Kak ri-wiwŏnjang mit sŏgijang myŏngdan" (A list of village officers), March 16, 1951.

100. RG 242, SA 2011, box 1086, item 9–56.3, "Wŏllamjamyŏngdan pogo" (Those who went to the South), July 1951.

101. Kim, *Chŏjakchip* 6: 483.

102. RG 242, SA 2011, box 1085, item 9–53, "1951nyŏn pŏminsubae taejang" (Wanted), 1951; RG 242, SA 2011, box 1084, item 9–47, "Mulp'um molsudaejang" (Confiscation) and "38 inam tojuja singnyangmolsu'e taehayŏ" (Confiscating food kept by defectors to the South), July 16, 1951.

103. RG 242, SA 2012, box 1163, *1950nyŏndo hoeŭirokch'ŏl*, "Minute on February 2, 1951."

104. RG 242, SA 2011, box 1086, item 9–56.3, "Inminbanbyŏl chigŏppyŏl t'onggye" (Occupation statistics), July 1951.

105. RG 242, SA 2011, box 1084, item 9–45, "No. 18," January 4, 1951.

106. RG 242, SA 2011, box 1084, item 9–49, "In'gu yudong t'onggyep'yo" (Censuses), 1951.

107. Chŏng Il-yong, "Inminwiwŏnhoe chosat'onggye saŏp" (Surveys and statistics), 1947, *Saryojip* 13: 575–576.

108. RG 242, SA 2011, box 1084, item 9–45, "Kongminjŭng mit ch'ulsaengjŭng pojŏnjipkye t'onggye" (Statistics of public IDs and birth certificates), March 29, 1951.

109. "Kongminjŭng mit ch'ulsaengjŭng"; RG 242, SA 2011, box 1085, item 9–45, "Rimsi-chŭngmyŏngsŏ" (Temporary IDs), 1951.

110. RG 242, SA 2011, box 1084, item 9–49, "Rimsi-chŭngmyŏngsŏ kyobusaŏbŭl wihan kak ri-inminwiwŏnjang, sŏgijang, inminbandŭrege chunŭn chegang'yoji" (What village PCs and People's NAs should know in issuing temporary IDs), July 1951.

111. RG 242, SA 2011, box 1084, item 9–49, "Rimsi-chŭngmyŏngsŏ iljegyobu saŏbe taehayŏ" (Issuing temporary IDs), July 6, 1951.

112. RG 242, SA 2011, box 1084, item 9–49, "Rimsi-chŭngmyŏngsŏ kyobujŏn-ghyŏng t'onggye" (Statistics of newly-issued temporary IDs), August 19, 1951.

113. RG 242, SA 2011, box 1086, item 9–56.3, "Panggongjugan silsijŏnghyŏng pogo" (Air-raid training week), 1951.

114. RG 242, SA 2009 II, box 829, item 171, "Hoane taehaya t'oronyoji" (A talk about security), February 1951.

115. Kim, *Chŏjakchip* 7: 47–48.

116. Kim, *Chŏjakchip* 7: 380–381.

CHAPTER 8: INTO THE SOCIALIST PATRIARCHAL SPACE

1. "*Ch'ŏllima* inminban" (*Ch'ŏllima* People's NAs), *Minju chosŏn* (hereafter *MC*), January 12, 1967.

2. RG 242, SA 2010, box 862, item 97, *Kanbumyŏngdan* (Staff list), (Tonghŭng village PC, 1949).

3. RG 242, SA 2011 I, box 1076, item 9–2, "Inminban kanghwadaech'aege taehayŏ" (Reinforcing People's NAs), 1950.

4. (Charyo 79) *Chosŏnjung'ang nyŏn'gam* (North Korean yearbooks), 1954–1955, in Kim Chun-yŏp and Kim Ch'ang-sun, eds., *Pukhanyŏn'gu charyojip* (Research materials on North Korea) 2, (Seoul: Koryŏdaehakkyo aseamunje yŏn'guso, 2010) (Hereafter *Charyojip*).

5. "Ri-inminwiwŏnhoenŭn sahoejuŭinongch'onŭi ch'amdoen hojuga toeja" (Making a village head a genuine family head), *MC,* December 5, 1969, 2.

6. Kim Sŏng-bo, "Pukhanŭi t'ojigaehyŏkkwa nong'ŏphyŏptonghwa" (North Korean land reform and the collectivization of agriculture) (PhD diss., Yonsei University, 1996), 190–191.

7. Sŏ Tong-man, "50nyŏndae Pukhanŭi kongmulsaengsanryang t'ong'gye'e kwanhan yŏn'gu" (North Korean agricultural productivity in the 1950s), *T'ongil kyŏngje* 2 (1996): 69–70.

8. Kim, *Chŏjakchip* 9: 83.

9. Kim, *Chŏjakchip* 7: 371.

10. Dongzue Zhang, "Transition of governance mechanisms in China's agriculture: Land reform, the cooperatives, the People's Commune, HRS, and Agricultural Industrialization," *Kyoto Economic Review* 76, no. 2 (2007): 230–231; Justin Yifu Lin, "Collectivization and China's Agricultural Crisis in 1959–1961," *Journal of Political Economy* (December 1990): 1230–1234.

11. Kim, "Pukhanŭi t'ojigaehyŏk," 213–220.
12. Kim, *Chŏjakchip* 8: 30.
13. Sŏ Tong-man, *Pukchosŏn sahoejuŭich'eje sŏngnipsa 1945–1961* (The formation of North Korean socialism, 1945–1961) (Seoul: Sŏnin, 2005), 666–667.
14. (Charyo 3) "Urinaraesŏ sahoejuŭijŏk nong'ŏphyŏptonghwaŭi sŭngniwa nongch'on'gyŏngniŭi kŭmhubaljŏne taehayŏ" (Socialist agricultural cooperatives and agricultural development), *Rodong sinmun,* January 6, 1959, in *Charyojip* 4. See also Chong-Sik Lee, "The 'Socialist Revolution' in the North Korean Countryside," *Asian Survey* (October 1962): 9–22.
15. (Charyo 77) *Chosŏn chung'ang nyŏn'gam* (1954–1955) in *Charyojip* 2.
16. (Charyo 54) "Chosŏnrodongdang chung'angwiwŏnhoe 1956nyŏndo 12wŏl chŏnwŏnhoeŭi kyŏljŏngsilhaeng'e taehan nongch'on'gyŏngnibumunŭi saŏpch'onghwawa 1958nyŏndo kwaŏbe taehayŏ" (Decisions of Workers' Party in 1956 and development plan of 1958), *Rodong sinmun,* January 16, 1958, in *Charyojip* 3.
17. (Charyo 3) "Urinaraesŏ."
18. Kim, *Chŏjakchip* 16: 522–523.
19. See articles 6 and 7 in (Charyo 105) "Nongŏp hyŏptongjohap kijun'gyuyak (chamjŏng) ch'oan" ((Tentative) rule of agricultural cooperatives), *Rodong sinmun,* November 18, 1958, in *Charyojip* 3.
20. (Charyo 3) "Urinaraesŏ."
21. Lin, "Collectivization," 1234.
22. Pransenjit Duara, "The Great Leap Forward in China: An Analysis of the Nature of Socialist Transformation," *Economic and Political Weekly* 9, no. 32/34 (August 1974): 1365.
23. (Charyo 3) "Urinaraesŏ."
24. See articles 9, 16, 17, 22, 31, and 32 in (Charyo 105) "Nongŏp hyŏptongjohap."
25. Ibid., see articles 9 and 51.
26. Ibid., see articles 2, 10, and 12.
27. Yu In-jong, "Nong'ŏp hyŏptongjohabe taehan ri-inminwiwŏnhoeŭi chidosang myŏtkaji munje" (Problems with instructing agricultural cooperatives), *Inmin* (September 1955): 50 in Sŏ, *Pukjosŏn sahoejuŭich'eje,* 747–749.
28. (Charyo 21) "Nongŏp hyŏnmulse'e kwanhan pogo" (On tax-in-kind), *Rodong sinmun,* February 21, 1959, in *Charyojip* 4; (Charyo 5) "Nongŏp hyŏnmulserŭl wanjŏnhi p'yejihalde taehayŏ" (Abolishing tax-in-kind),

Rodong sinmun, April 29, 1966, in *Charyojip* 7. In 1966, all taxes-in-kind were abolished.

29. Kim, *Chŏjakchip* 11: 200–201.
30. Kim, *Chŏjakchip* 8: 18–25.
31. (Charyo 79) *Chosŏn chungang nyŏngam* (1954–1955) in *Charyojip* 2.
32. Kim Mun-jo and Cho Tae-yŏp, "Pukhanŭi tosihwawa tosimunje" (North Korean urbanization and urban problems), *Asea Yŏngu* 35, no. 1 (1992): 25.
33. Kim, *Chŏjakchip* 9: 38–39.
34. Kim, *Chŏjakchip* 9: 38–39.
35. Kim, "Pukhanŭi t'ojigaehyŏk," 250–51.
36. Kim, *Chŏjakchip* 8: 19.
37. Kim, *Chŏjakchip* 6: 269.
38. Kim Tu-sŏp, "Pukhanŭi tosihwawa ingubunp'o" (North Korean urbanization and its population), *Han'guk in'guhak* 18, no. 2 (December 1995): 72–73.
39. Kim, *Chŏjakchip* 12: 398.
40. (Charyo 64) *Chosŏn chungang nyŏngam* (1962) in *Charyojip* 5.
41. Chang Se-hun, "Chibang taedosiŭi konggan'gujorŭl t'onghae pon Pukhanŭi tosihwagwajŏng" (The urbanization of North Korea through spatial structure in local cities), *Han'guk sahoehakhoe sahoehaktaehoe nonmunjip* (June 2003): 95–121; Kim, *Chŏjakchip* 8: 35.
42. Kim and Cho, "Pukhanŭi tosihwa," 21.
43. (Charyo 40) *Chosŏn chungang nyŏngam* (1958), 58–69 in *Charyojip* 3.
44. Kim and Cho, "Pukkanŭi tosihwa," 40.
45. Chosŏnŭi minsokchŏnt'ong p'yŏnch'anwiwŏnhoe, *Chosŏnŭi minsokchŏnt'ong* (Korean folk traditions) (Pyongyang: Kwahak paekkwasajŏn chonghapch'ulp'ansa, 1994) 3: 122.
46. (Charyo 54) "Chosŏnnodongdang chung'angwiwŏnhoe."
47. See "Nongch'on munhwa hyŏngmyŏng" (The culture revolution in rural areas), *Chosŏn taebaekkwasajŏn* (North Korean encyclopedia) (Pyongyang: Paekkwasajŏn ch'ulp'ansa, 2001) 5: 339.
48. Yi Kyŏng-a and Chŏn Pong-hŭi, "1920–30nyŏndae Kyŏngsŏngbuŭi munhwajut'aekchi kaebare taehan yŏn'gu" (Culture houses in Kyŏngsŏng, 1920–1930), *Taehan kŏnch'ukhakhoe nonmunjip* 22, no. 3 (2006): 191–200.
49. *Chosŏnŭi minsokchŏnt'ong 3,* 124.
50. *Chosŏnŭi minsokchŏnt'ong 3,* 124–127.
51. Kim, *Chŏjakchip* 9: 89; *Chŏjakchip* 16: 328–329.
52. *Chosŏnŭi minsokchŏnt'ong 3,* 128.

53. Kim, *Chŏjakchip* 18: 176–177.
54. Kim, *Chŏjakchip* 18: 168.
55. Kim, *Chŏjakchip* 16: 325–326; (Charyo1) "Ch'ŏllimaŭi kisudŭrege saehaeŭi ch'ukkarŭl tŭrinda" (Happy new year to Ch'ŏllima workers), *Rodong sinmun*, January 1, 1959, in *Charyojip* 4.
56. Sim Sang-tae, "Tugae inminbanŭl mobŏminminbanŭro" (Making two People's NAs exemplary), *Ch'ŏllima chagŏppan* (Ch'ŏllima work brigades) (4) (Pyongyang: Chigŏptongmaeng ch'ulp'ansa, 1963), 282.
57. Sim, "Tugae," 283.
58. Sim, "Tugae," 284–286 and 290.
59. Sim, "Tugae," 286.
60. Sim, "Tugae," 293–294.
61. Sim, "Tugae," 295.
62. See "Suryŏng'ŭi kyosirŭl pattŭlgo sallimsarirŭl chal kkuryŏganŭn ri-inminwiwŏnhoe Chunghwa'gun Paegunriesŏ" (Following Kim's lectures, the Paegun village PC), *MC*, October 30, 1968.
63. Kim, *Chŏjakchip* 8: 17.
64. Kim, "Pukhanŭi t'ojigaehyŏk," chapter 4.
65. Kim Po-mi, "Pukhanŭi chŏnhubokkusi sahoejuŭijinyŏng'ŭi wŏnjowa 'juche'ŭi chegi, 1953–1955" (Foreign aids for Korean War recovery and the rise of Juche), *Asea yŏn'gu* 56, no. 4 (2013): 305–340; Yi Mi-kyŏng, "Pukhanŭi taewoegwan'gyewa juchesasang'ŭi hyŏngsŏng" (North Korea's foreign relations and the formation of Juche), *Kukchejŏngch'i nonch'ong* 41, no. 2 (2001): 73–94.
66. Kim, *Chŏjakchip* 10: 404–415.
67. Kim, *Chŏjakchip* 9: 467–468.
68. Kim, *Chŏjakchip* 9: 469–481.
69. For a socialist perspective on Korean development, see To Myŏn-hoe, "Pukkanŭi han'guksa sidaegubunron" (The periodization of North Korean history), in *Pukhan yŏksamandŭlgi* (Making North Korean history), ed. Han'gugyŏksa yŏn'guhoe (Seoul: P'urŭn yŏksa, 2003), 61.
70. Kim, *Chŏjakchip* 9: 478.
71. Kim, *Chŏjakchip* 9: 249–254.
72. Kim Sŏng-bo, "1960nyŏndae nambukhanjŏngbuŭi 'in'gan'gaejo' kyŏngjaeng" (The "human reconstruction" competition of the two Koreas in the 1960s), *Yŏksawa silhak* no.53 (2014), 161–165.
73. See "Inminbanŭl hwamokhago tanhaptoego saenggi pallarhan taegajŏng'ŭro!" (Making the People's NAs into a great family), *MC*, January 25, 1967.

74. See "kajŏng" in *Chosŏn taebaekkwasajŏn* 1: 150–151.

75. "Kajŏng," *Chosŏn taebaekkwasajŏn* 1.

76. Kim, *Chŏjakchip* 15: 329.

77. Kim, *Chŏjakchip* 15: 329.

78. On the North's concentric structure, see Bruce Cumings, *Korea's Place in the Sun* (W. W. Norton & Company, 1998), 419.

79. For more on the state patriarchal system, see Sonia Ryang, "Gender in Oblivion: Women in the Democratic People's Republic of Korea," *Journal of Asian and African Studies* 35, no. 3 (2000): 323–349 and Pak Kyŏng-suk, "Pukhansahoeŭi kukka, kabujangje, yŏsŏng'ŭi kwan'gye'e taehan siron" (The North Korean socialist state, patriarchy, and women), *Sahoewa iron* 21, no. 1 (November 2012): 327–375.

80. Although there are no national statistics on the number of women serving as People's NA heads in the 1960s, newspaper accounts from this decade overwhelmingly identified women as heads. See, for example, "Sahoejŏk kwallich'egyerŭl seugo modŭn tosiwa nongch'onŭl tŏ arŭmdapke kkurija" (Let's build a social management system), *MC*, January 16, 1966; "Ch'ŏllima inminban" (Ch'ŏllima People's NAs), *MC*, January 12, 1967. A North Korean defector whom I interviewed said likewise. Interview with Kim Ch'ol (pseudonym), January 30, 2014.

81. Kim, *Chŏjakchip* 6: 446.

82. Kim, *Chŏjakchip* 15: 340.

83. Kim, *Chŏjakchip* 15: 388.

84. Kim, *Chŏjakchip* 17: 53–54.

85. Kim, *Chŏjakchip* 12: 398.

86. Kim, *Chŏjakchip* 17: 53–54.

CHAPTER 9: "PEOPLE'S NEIGHBORHOOD ASSOCIATIONAL LIFE" IN THE 1960s

1. "Inminbanŭl hwamokhago tanhaptoego saenggi pallarhan taegajŏng'ŭro!" (Making People's NAs a unified family), *Minju chosŏn* (hereafter *MC*), January 25, 1967.

2. Pukhandaesajŏn p'yŏnch'anwiwŏnhoe, *Pukhandaesajŏn* (The North Korean encyclopedia) (Seoul: Kongsan'gwŏnmunje yŏn'guso, 1974), 879.

3. See "inminban" in *Chosŏn taebaekkwasajŏn* 28 (2001): 654.

4. Kim Sŏng-bo, *Pukhanŭi yŏksa* 1 (North Korean history 1) (Seoul: Yŏksa pip'yŏngsa, 2011), 113.

5. Cheehyung Harrison Kim, *Heroes and Toilers: Work as Life in Postwar North Korea, 1953–1961* (New York: Columbia University Press, 2018), 108–109.

6. "Inmindŭl sogesŏ 'yŏgiga ch'ŏllimaŭi kohyangimnida' Chin Ŭng'wŏn" (The Ch'ŏllima movement's hometown), *MC*, July 7, 1967.

7. "Inmindŭl sogesŏ."

8. Kang Tŏk-sŏ, *Saein'gan hyŏngsŏnggwa ch'ŏllima chagŏppanundong* (New human making and the Ch'ŏllima work brigade movement) (Pyongyang: Chosŏnrodongdang ch'ulp'ansa, 1961), 26.

9. (Charyo 78) *Rodong sinmun*, November 8, 1960, in *Charyojip* 4.

10. Kim, *Chŏjakchip* 14: 256.

11. Kang, *Saein'gan*, 49–85.

12. Kim, *Chŏjakchip* 14: 257–258.

13. "Charangsŭrŏun sutcha" (Numbers we are proud of), *MC*, August 22, 1967; "Ch'ŏllilma inminban ch'inghojaengch'wiundong" (The Ch'ŏllima People's NA Movement), *MC*, November 10, 1968.

14. Ri Myŏng-wŏn, *Kŏnsŏljagŏppanjang'ŭi sugi* (A construction brigade's leader) (Pyongyang: Minch'ŏngch'ulp'ansa, 1961), 109.

15. "Sahoejŏk kwallich'egyerŭl seugo modŭn tosiwa nongch'onŭl tŏ arŭmdapke kkurija" (Let's build a social management system), *MC*, January 16, 1966.

16. "Pyongyangsinŭn modŭn myŏnesŏ mobŏmi toeja" (Pyongyang, a role model city), *Rodong sinmun*, March 16, 1961.

17. "Modŭn inminbanŭl hanaŭi pulgŭn taegajŏng'ŭro!" (Making People's NAs into a red great family), *MC*, March 7, 1968.

18. "Sahoejŏk kwallich'egyerŭl."

19. "Sahoejŏk kwallich'egyerŭl."

20. "Sahoejŏk kwallich'egyerŭl."

21. "Inminbanŭl hwamokhago!"

22. "Inminbanŭl hwamokhago!"

23. Kim, *Chŏjakchip* 15: 338.

24. "Ch'ŏllima inminban" (Ch'ŏllima People's NAs), *MC*, January 12, 1967.

25. "Ch'ŏllima inminban."

26. "Ch'ŏllima inminban."

27. "Inminbanŭl hyŏngmyŏngjŏk saenghwalgip'ung'i ch'ungmandoen pulgŭn taegajŏngŭro!" (Building revolutionary lifestyle morale in People's NAs), *MC*, May 13, 1967.

28. Sŏ, *Pukchosŏn sahoejuŭich'eje*, 624–626.

29. *Kim Il Sung Works* 20: 416–452, quote at 449.

30. "Kajŏng'ŭl hyŏngmyŏnghwahamyŏ tonggwa inminbanŭl pulgŭn chiptanŭro!" (Revolutionizing families), *MC,* September 22, 1967.
31. "Ch'ungsŏng'ŭi maŭmŭro sŏro topko ikkŭrŏganŭn ch'ŏllima inminban" (Mutual help and Ch'ŏllima People's NAs), *MC,* January 18, 1969.
32. Yi Chong-sŏk, *Pukhanŭi yŏksa 2* (North Korean history 2) (Seoul: Yŏksa pip'yŏngsa, 2011), 45–48 and 64–71; Jae-Cheon Lim, *Kim Jong-Il's Leadership of North Korea* (New York: Routledge, 2011), 37–40.
33. "Ch'ŏllima inminbanundong'ŭi pulgiri sech'age t'abŏnjinŭn Hamhŭngsi" (The Ch'ŏllima People's NA Movement in Hamhŭng), *MC,* August 22, 1967.
34. "Hyŏngmyŏng chŏnt'ong haksŭbul saenghwalhago itnŭn inminbandŭl" (People's NAs learning revolutionary traditions), *MC,* September 22, 1967.
35. "Hyŏngmyŏng chŏnt'ong."
36. "Tong inminbanŭl hanmaŭm hanttŭsŭro" (Teaching People's NAs to have one heart), *MC,* July 7, 1966.
37. "Ch'ŏllimajin'gunŭi pulgillop'ŭn Ch'ŏngjinsi," (The Ch'ŏllima movement in Ch'ŏngjin), *MC,* September 22, 1967.
38. See *Kim Il Sung Works* 14: 82–108, quote at 92.
39. See "Ch'ŏngsanni Way" in *Chosŏn taebaekkwasajŏn* 21: 57.
40. "Inminbanŭl hyŏngmyŏngjŏk"; "Sahoejŏk kwallich'egyerŭl."
41. "Ch'ŏllima inminban."
42. Sŏ, *Pukchosŏn sahoejuŭich'eje,* 826.
43. Yi, *Pukhanŭi yŏksa 2,* 50–54.
44. Kim, *Pukhanŭi yŏksa 1,* 178–179. By 1956, the North Korean economy was already outperforming the pre–Korean War economy. In the industrial sector, economic growth was 1.8 times higher than that in 1949 and in the agricultural sector, it was 1.4 times higher.
45. "Sahoejuŭi sang'ŏpkwa konggŭpcheroŭi ihaeng" (Socialist commerce), *Rodong sinmun,* March 24, 1970.
46. "Chumindŭrŭi ch'amdoen chubang'ŭro" (Making people's kitchens), *MC,* March 7, 1967.
47. "T'an'gwangmaul inminbansaenghwaresŏ saeroun chŏnhwanŭl!" (People's NAs in mining areas), *MC,* February 14, 1967.
48. "T'an'gwang maul!"
49. "Hyŏptong nongjanggwa kajŏngdŭresŏ yŏksam, dŭlkkaerŭl mani simdorok" (Planting vegetables in agricultural cooperatives and homes), *MC,* March 26, 1967; "Inminban chidorŭl ri inminwiwŏnhoejŏgin saŏbŭro" (Focusing on supervising People's NAs), *MC,* January 23, 1966.

50. "Chimsŭngch'igiwa t'ŏtbatkakkugirŭl charhago itnŭn inminbanwŏndŭl" (People's NAs raising vegetables and livestock), *MC,* January 9, 1966.

51. See "kanaejagŏppan" in *Chosŏn taebaekkwasajŏn* 1: 61; Chang P'il-hwa, "Pukhansahoeŭi sŏngbyŏl punŏp" (Labor divisions in North Korea), in *T'ong'ilgwa yŏsŏng-pukhan yŏsŏng'ŭi sam* (Unification and women's lives in North Korea) (Seoul: Ehwa yŏjadaehakkyo ch'ulp'anbu, 2001), 88–90.

52. "Inminbanŭl hyŏngmyŏngjŏk!"

53. "Sahoejuŭigyŏngjeŭi myŏtkaji irone taehayŏ" (A theory on socialist economies), *Rodong sinmun,* March 4, 1969.

54. "Sahoejuŭi sangŏpkwa."

55. *MC,* January 22, 1966.

56. Kim, *Chŏjakchip* 18: 196–210.

57. Kim, *Chŏjakchip* 18: 196–210.

58. "Tosiga nongch'onŭl chiwŏnhago rodonggyegŭbi nongmindŭrŭl tomnŭnda" (Cities and working class helping rural areas and farmers), *MC,* March 8, 1967.

59. "Nongch'onŭl muljil, kisul, roryŏkchŏgŭro himkkŏt topcha" (Let's give rural areas materials, techniques, and labor), *MC,* January 21, 1966.

60. "Tosiga nongch'onŭl."

61. Kim, *Chŏjakchip* 18: 210.

EPILOGUE: THE TWO CONSTITUTIONAL AMENDMENTS OF DECEMBER 1972

1. South Korean National Archives, CEB0000211, "Nambukkongdongsŏng-myŏng palp'yo mit kijahoegyŏn" (The July Fourth North–South Joint Statement) July 4, 1972.

   "First, Korean unification must be achieved *independently* without any reliance on or intervention by foreign forces.

   Second, Korean unification must be achieved *peacefully* without the use of military forces against the other side.

   Third, both parties must promote *national unity* as a united people over any differences of our ideological and political systems." (Emphases added.)

2. Kukkajaegŏn ch'oegohoeŭi (The Supreme Committee for National Reconstruction), *Kungmindoŭijaegŏn mit kungmin kyŏngjejaegŏnŭl wihan chidoinyŏmgwa silch'ŏn yokang* (Reconstruction of national morals and economy) (Seoul: Kukkajaegŏn ch'oegohoeŭi, 1961, hereafter *Yokang*), 5–6.

3. Ibid., 5–7, 9–15, and 22–26.

4. Carter J. Eckert, *Park Chung Hee and Modern Korea: The Roots of Militarism, 1866–1945* (Cambridge, MA: The Belknap Press of Harvard University Press, 2016), 181–233.

5. Park Chung Hee, *Uri minjogŭi nagal kil* (Ways for our nation) (Seoul: Tong-a ch'ulp'ansa, 1962), 31–33 and 42–43.

6. Kukkajaegŏn ch'oegohoeŭi, *Yokang,* 34.

7. Seoulsisa p'yŏnch'anwiwŏnhoe, *Seoult'ŭkpyŏlsisa* (The history of Seoul) (Seoul: Seoul t'ŭkpyŏlsisa p'yŏnch'anwiwŏnhoe, 1965), 135.

8. "Kungminundong chojigŭl kanghwa" (Reinforcing national movement organizations), *KS*, September 1, 1961.

9. Chaegŏn kungminundong'e kwanhan pomryul (The Reconstruction Movement Act) at www.law.go.kr.

10. Kukkajaegŏn ch'oegohoeŭi, *Yokang,* 16–18.

11. Yoo Chin-o, "Chaegŏn kungminundong'ŭi sŏnggyŏk" (The Reconstruction Movement), *Ch'oegohoeŭibo* 1 (1961): 34–35.

12. "P'agoedoen minjujŏngch'ijaegŏn" (Reconstructing democracy), *TI*, June 29, 1961.

13. Hŏ Ŭn, "5.16. Kunjŏnggi chaegŏn'gungminundong'ŭi sŏnggyŏk" (The Reconstruction Movement under the 5.16 military government), *Yŏksamunje yŏn'gu* 11 (2003): 31.

14. For the full text of the two acts, see www.law.go.kr.

15. "Chaegŏn kungminundong kigugaep'yŏnŭi chich'im" (Reshuffling the Reconstruction Movement), *Chaegŏnt'ongsin* 6 (1962): 16–20.

16. "Chaegŏn'gungminundong paljok" (The Reconstruction movement's beginning), *KS*, July 21, 1964.

17. BA0172134, "Yangjugun kungminban sŏlch'ijorye kongp'o" (Citizen's NA's rule in Yangju County), March 1964.

18. For example, in Seoul, 26.4 percent of the city's NAs no longer held a monthly meeting and in 60 percent of the remaining NAs, attendance at monthly meetings had declined by over 50 percent. "Pansanghoe hanamana" (Stagnated NA gatherings), *Chosŏn ilbo*, November 18, 1965.

19. BA0038467, Pansanghoeunyŏng kanghwajisi (Reinforcing NA assembly), 1972.

20. Kwak Tae Yang, "The Nixon Doctrine and the Yusin Reforms: American Foreign Policy, the Vietnam War, and the Rise of Authoritarianism in Korea, 1968–1973," *Journal of East Asian Relations* 12, nos. 1–2 (2003): 33–57.

21. Park quoted in "South Korea Chief Orders Martial Law," *New York Times*, October 18, 1972.

22. Park, *Minjogŭi chŏryŏk* (National power) (Puch'ŏn: Kwangmyŏng ch'ulp'ansa, 1971), 271.

23. Park, *Minjogŭi chŏryŏk*, 74.

24. The full text of the 1972 Yusin Constitution is at www.law.go.kr. See articles 11, 30, 39, 41, and 50, Election Law of the NCU (November 25, 1972).

25. Appendix of the Law on the NCU (T'ong'iljuch'e kungminhoeŭibŏp sihaengryŏng, 1972).

26. Taet'ongnyŏng pisŏsil, *Saemaŭlundong chidoinyŏm* (The New Village Movement's ideology) (Seoul: Taet'ongnyŏng pisŏsil, 1975), 15–16.

27. BA0042321, "Koesan-gun saemaŭlban kyuch'ik" (Rule of New Village NA in Koesan County), June 30, 1975.

28. William W. Boyer and Byong Man Ahn, *Rural Development in South Korea: A Sociopolitical Analysis* (Newark: University of Delaware Press, 1991), 33–39. The address was at the first national rally of New Village Leaders in Kwangju on November 22, 1973.

29. Munhwagongbobu, *Minju, aeguk, yusinŭi silch'ŏndojang Saemaŭlundong* (The New Village Movement for democracy, patriotism, Yusin) (Seoul: Munhwagongbobu, 1973), 8–10.

30. Munhwagongbobu, *Saemaŭlundong: kŭ inyŏmgwa chŏn'gae* (The New Village Movement: Ideology and practice) (Seoul: Munhwagongbobu, 1973), 94–99.

31. "Urinara sahoejuŭijedorŭl tŏuk kanghwahaja" (Let's reinforce our socialism), *Rodong sinmun*, December 26, 1972.

32. "Ch'oegoinminhoeŭi che5ki che1ch'a hoeŭi che2il hoeŭijinhaeng" (The Supreme People's Committee meeting), *Rodong sinmun*, December 27 and 28, 1972.

33. "Urinara sahoejuŭijedorŭl."

34. RG 242, SA 2010, box 869, item 45, Chosŏnminjujuŭi inmin konghwaguk hŏnbŏp (The 1948 North Korean constitution), September 8, 1948.

35. For full text of the North Korean Socialist Constitution, see *Rodong sinmun*, December 28, 1972.

36. *Rodong sinmun*, December 28, 1972.

37. See Kim, *Chŏjakchip* 9: 467–495.

38. *Kim Il Sung Works* 21: 421–483.

39. "Pŏmmubusunsisŏ Park taet'ongnyŏng kangjo" (President Park in Ministry of Justice), *TI*, February 4, 1977.

40. Chŏng Yŏng-chŏl, "Kim Jung Il ch'ejehyŏngsŏng'ŭi sahoejŏngch'ijŏk kiwŏn, 1967–1982" (Political origins of Kim Jung Il regime, 1967–1982) (PhD diss., Seoul National University, 2001), 111–124.

41. Chŏng, "Kim Jung Il ch'eje," 219–236.

42. For People's NAs in the twenty-first century, see Yun Po-yŏng, "Ilsang'ŭi kwan'gyesŏng'gwa kongdongch'eŭi pyŏnju" (Everyday connection and community), in *Pukhan ilsangsaenghwal kongdongch'eŭi pyŏnhwa* (Everyday life community of North Korea), ed. Ch'oe Chi-yŏng (Seoul: T'ong'il yŏn'guwŏn, 2021), 217–267.

BIBLIOGRAPHY

OFFICIAL SOURCES

Colonial government in Korea (1931–1945)

Chōsensōtokufu. *Chōsenni okeru kokuminseishin sōdoin* (General mobilization of national spirit in Korea). Keizō: Chōsensōtokufu, 1940.

Chōsensōtokufu. *Chōsenni okeru nōsangyoson shinkōundō* (Campaign for improving rural areas). Keizō: Chōsensōtokufu, 1934.

Chōsensōtokufu. *Hantō no kokuminsōryoku undō* (Concerted national power movement in Korea). Keizō: Chōsensōtokufu, 1941.

Chōsensōtokufu gakumukyoku. *Chōsenno shakaijigyō* (Social works in Korea). Keizō: Chōsensōtokufu gakumukyoku, 1936.

Chōsensōtokufu gakumukyoku. *Chōsen shakaikyōka yōran* (Social indoctrination in Korea). Keizō: Chōsensōtokufu gakumukyoku, 1938.

Chōsensōtokufu gakumukyoku. *Chōsen shakaikyōiku yōran* (Social education in Korea). Keizō: Chōsensōtokufu gakumukyoku, 1941.

Chōsensōtokufu gakumukyoku. *Shakaikyōka shiryō* (Materials for social indoctrination). Keizō: Chōsensōtokufu gakumukyoku, 1933.

Chōsensōtokufu hōmukyoku. *Chōsenkoseki oyobi kiryū todoke shōkishū* (Family registry and residential registry in Korea). Keizō: Chōsen kosekikyōkai,1944.

Ch'ungch'ŏngnamdo. *Ch'ungch'ŏngnamdo dōzei itban* (South Ch'ungch'ŏng Province). Taejŏn: Ch'ungch'ŏngnamdo, 1936.

Kokuminseishinsōdoin Ch'ungch'ŏngnamdo renmei. *Kokuminseishinsōdoin renmeiyōran* (A booklet of general mobilization of national spirit). Taejŏn: Kokuminseishinsōdoin Ch'ungch'ŏngnamdo renmei, 1939.

Kokuminsōryoku Chōsenrenmei. *Chōsenni okeru kokuminsōryoku undōshi* (The concerted national power movement in Korea). Keizō: Kokuminsōryoku Chōsenrenmei, 1945.

Kokuminsōryoku Chōsenrenmei. *Kokuminsōryoku tokuhon* (A reader of concerted national power). Keizō: Kokuminsōryoku Chōsenrenmei, 1941.

South Korea (1945–1972)

National Archives

BA0034496. Ch'ungch'ŏngnam-do Nonsan-si Pujŏk-myŏn. Pangsanghoe t'ŭkpyŏl chujisahang (Citizens' NA assemblies). 1961.

BA0038467. Chŏllanam-do naemuguk. Pansanghoeunyŏng kanghwajisi (Reinforcing NA assembly). 1972.

BA0042321. Koesan-gun. Koesan-gun Saemaŭlban kyuch'ik (Rule of New Village NA). June 1975.

BA0084209. Ch'ongmuch'ŏ. Kungminban unyŏngyogang (Management of Citizens' NAs). 1957.

BA0085311. Ch'ongmuch'ŏ. Ch'agwan hoeŭirok (Vice-ministers' minutes). 1957.

BA0085313. Ch'ongmuch'ŏ. Ch'agwanhoeŭirok (Vice-ministers' minutes). 1958.

BA0085317. Ch'ongmuch'ŏ. Ch'agwanhoeŭirok (Vice-ministers' minutes). 1959.

BA0099165. Pŏmmubu pŏmmusil. Pŏmnyŏng chirŭich'ŏl (Legal questions). 1952.

BA0177481. Kyŏngsangnam-do kihoekkwallisil. Kyŏngsang-namdo kungminban unyŏnggyuch'ik (Citizens' NAs rule in South Kyŏngsang). 1963.

BA0181766. Kyŏngsangbuk-do Sŏnsan-gun naemugwa. Togae-myŏn panunyŏnggyuch'ik (Togae town's rule). 1952.

BA0607387. Pŏmmubu pŏmmusil. Pŏmnyŏng chirŭich'ŏl (Legal questions). 1953.

BA0607389. Pŏmmubu pŏmmusil. Pŏmnyŏng chirŭich'ŏl (Legal questions). 1954.

CEB0000211. Nambukkongdongsŏngmyŏng palp'yo mit kijahoegyŏn (The July Fourth North–South Joint Statement). July 4, 1972.

DKI012–10–01C0026. Kyŏnggi-do. Chapchonggŭm kyŏngni kyuch'ik 1958 (Miscellaneous taxes). 1958.

Kuksa p'yŏnch'anwiw'ŏnhoe (National Historical Compilation Committee)

Published Sources

Han'guk nongsusanbu (Ministry of Agriculture, Forestry, and Fisheries). *Han'guk yangjŏngsa* (Korea's food policy). Seoul: Han'guk nongsusanbu, 1978.

Kongbosil (Bureau of Public Information). *Taet'ongnyŏng Yi Sŭngmanbaksa tamhwajip* (Speech collection of Syngman Rhee). Seoul: Kongbosil, 1959.

Kukhoesamuch'ŏ (National Assembly Secretariat). *Chehŏn'gukhoe sokkirok* (Records of the First National Assembly), 1948–1950. Reprint, Seoul: Sŏninmunhwasa, 1999.

Kukhoesamuch'ŏ. *Kukhoesa* (The history of the National Assembly). Seoul: Kukhoesamuch'ŏ, 1957.

Kukkajaegŏn ch'oegohoeŭi (Supreme Committee for Reconstruction). *Ch'oegohoeŭibo* (Newsletter of the Supreme Committee for Reconstruction). Seoul: Kukkajaegŏn ch'oegohoeŭi ch'ongmuch'ŏ, 1961–1963.

———. *Kungmindoŭijaegŏn mit kungmin kyŏngjejaegŏnŭl wihan chidoinyŏmgwa silch'ŏn yogang* (Reconstruction of national morals and economy). Seoul: Kukkajaegŏn ch'oegohoeŭi, 1961.

Munhwagongbobu (Ministry of Culture and Public information). *Minju, aeguk, yusinŭi silch'ŏndojang saemaŭl undong* (New Village Movement for democracy, patriotism, and *yusin*). Seoul: Munhwagongbobu, 1973.

Munhwagongbobu. *Saemaŭl undong: kŭ inyŏmgwa chŏn'gae* (New Village Movement: Its goal and practice). Seoul: Munhwagongbobu, 1972.

Naemubu chibangguk (Interior Ministry, Bureau of local administration). *Chibanghaengjŏng Simnyŏnsa* (Ten-year history of local administration). Naemubu chibangguk, 1958.

Naemubu chibangguk. *Chibanghaengjŏng kaeyo* (An outline of local administration). Seoul: Naemubu chibangguk, 1957.

Taet'ongnyŏng pisŏsil (Office of the President). *Saemaŭlundong chidoinyŏm* (New Village Movement's ideology). Seoul: Taet'ongnyŏng pisŏsil, 1975.

North Korea (1945–1972)

United States National Archive and Record Administration. Record Group 242. Foreign Records Seized by US Military Forces in Korea, Shipping Advice (SA).

SA 2006

Box 279, item 36. Che ch'amgo sŏch'ŏl (Reference).

SA 2007 I

Box 411–1, item 1.59. Injegun Nam-myŏn kak tanch'e yŏnsŏkhoeŭirok (Meeting records in Inje County), 1947.

Box 416, item 12.7. Injegun inminwiwŏnhoebalsong munsŏch'ol (Documents of Inje County PC).

Box 417, item 13.5. Sŏhwari, Kajŏnni sep'odang'wŏn myŏngbu (List of cell members of the Workers' Party, Sŏhwa village).

Box 432, item 75. Sŏnjŏnwŏn such'aek che 5ho (Handbook for propagandists), May 1947.

SA 2007 II

Box 623, *Horang'i* (Tiger) 5 (Rodong sinmunsa), 1947.

SA 2009 I

Box 689, item 103. Kakdo inminwiwŏnhoe 2nyŏn'gan saŏpkaegwan (Two-year works of provincial PCs), 1947.

Box 690, item 138. Sŏn'gŏsŏnjŏn'gwa uriŭi immu (Election propaganda and our mission),1946.

Box 693–1, item 183. Sŏndong'wŏn such'ŏp (Handbook for propagandists), 1950.

Box 713–2, item 81. Molsutoji chosasŏwoe chapch'ŏl (Confiscated land survey and other documents), 1950.

Box 716, item 114. (Sihŭng-gun) Tongmyŏnnae chawidae myŏngdan (List of Self-Defence Force in Tong town), 1950.

Box 763, item 22. Haebanghu Chosŏn (Postliberated Korea), 1950.

SA 2009 II

Box 766, item 54. Sobang kwan'gyejip, Tongmyŏn punjuso, 1950nyŏndo (Materials regarding firefighting, Tong-town, 1950).

Box 767, item 55.1. Yŏksan mit chŏksan'gaok chosabuch'aek, Tongmyŏn punjuso (Enemy property surveys, Tong Town).

Box 792, item 62. 1948nyŏn t'onggyech'ŏl (Statistics, 1948).

Box 792, item 64. Chapsŏryuch'ŏl (Miscellaneous documents).

Box 796, item 91. Nambanbu t'oji kaehyŏge kwanhan chirŭiŭngdap (Nongrim-sŏng) (Q & A for land reform in South Korea).

Box 812, item 107. Ŭiyonggun myŏngdan (Volunteer Army Lists), August 5, 1950.

Box 812, item 109. Kigyŏl sŏryuch'ŏl Kyŏnggi-do P'aju-gun Adong-myŏn Kŭmch'on-ri (Matters settled).

Box 813, item 115. Kunsan-si Taeya-myŏn inminwiwŏnhoe sŏryuch'ŏl (Documents of Taeya town PC in Kunsan city).

Box 815, item 119. Kongjagilji (Daily records of works, 1950).

Box 822, item 58. Chawidaejojik unyŏng'e taehayŏ (Regarding Self-Defense Force).

Box 826, item 125. Migyŏlbu-Ch'ungbuk Ch'ŏng'wŏn-gun (Pending issues—Ch'ŏng'wŏn County).

Box 829, item 171. Kŏju mit sukpak tŭngrokpu (Residential registries).

SA 2010

Box 847, item 166. Tonghŭng-ri sŏnjŏnjip (Tonghŭng village propaganda file), (1949).

Box 856, item 47.12. Ŭiyonggun chŏngnyŏnja myŏngdan-Sillim-ri, Anyang-ri, Sihŭng-ri (Volunteer Army list).

Box 861–2, item 95. Yŏnp'omyŏn Tonghŭngni inminwiwŏnhoe sŏndong'wŏn myŏngdan (List of propagandists in Tonghŭng village PC).

Box 862, item 97. *Kanbumyŏngdan* (Staff list), (Tonghŭng village PC, 1949).

Box 863, Sajinch'ŏp 3jong (Photo album).

Box 895, item 42. Nambanbu kakto (Seoul) munhwa sŏnjŏnsaŏp kyujŏng (Cultural propaganda in the South), August 1950.

Box 913, item 121. Kŭkpi munsŏjip (Top secret documents), 1950.

Box 903, item no. 33. *Min'gan panggongjidowŏn such'ŏp* (A booklet for defense training leaders), 1950.

SA 2011

Box 1059, item 2–76. Chŏndanji (Pamphlet).

Box 1076, item 9–2. Myŏnhaengjŏng'e kwanhan sŏryu, Chaenyŏng-gun 1950 (Documents of town administration, Chaenyŏng County, 1950).

Box 1078, item 9–25.5. *Chogukchŏnsŏn chosawiwŏnhoe podo* (Surveys by investigation committees). Pyongyang: Chosŏn rodongdang ch'ulp'ansa, 1951.

Box 1084, item 9–45. (Kŭkpi) T'onggye kwan'gyejip Hunam punjuso (Top secret, statistical materials in Hunam) (1951).

Box 1084, item 9–46. (Pi) Kunjŏngbumyŏngryŏng, chisisabonch'ŏl (Secret, orders from county PC) (Sŏgijangsil, 1950).

Box 1084, item 9–49. Kongminjŭng samuyogangjip (Public ID) (Hunammyŏn punjuso).

Box 1086, item 9–56.3. (Kŭkpi) Ch'amgo charyojip (Top secret, references) (Humanmyŏn punjuso, 1951).

Box 1087, item 9–59. (Kŭkpi) Migyŏl (kiyo) (Top secrets, pending documents).

SA 2012

Box 1220, item 8/137. Minjusŏnjŏnsil saŏpchidosŏ (A guide for propaganda offices) (July 1951).

Box 1163. 1949nyŏndo hoeŭirokch'ŏl (Meeting records, 1949).

Box 1252, item 2–271.9. Sŏnjŏnwŏn such'aek che 6ho (Handbook for propagandists 6) (June 1948).

Published Sources

Chosŏnŭi minsokchŏnt'ong p'yŏnch'anwiwŏnhoe, *Chosŏnŭi minsokchŏnt'ong 3* (Korean folk traditions 3). Pyongyang: Kwahak paekkwasajŏn chonghapch'ulp'ansa, 1994.

Kim, Chun-yŏp, ed. *Pukhanyŏn'gu charyojip* (Research materials on North Korea). Seoul: Koryŏdaehakkyo aseamunje yŏn'guso, 2010.

Kim Il Sung, *Kim Il Sung chŏjakchip* (*Kim Il Sung Works*), 47 vols. Pyongyang: Chosŏn rodongdang ch'ulp'ansa, 1980.

Kuksa p'yŏnch'anwiwŏnhoe. *Pukhan'gwan'gye saryojip* (North Korean sources). Seoul: Kuksa p'yŏnch'an wiwŏnhoe, 1983.

Paekkwasajŏn ch'ulp'ansa. *Chosŏn taebaekkwasajŏn* (North Korean encyclopedia). Pyongyang: Paekkwasajŏn ch'ulp'ansa, 2001.

JOURNALS, NEWSPAPERS, AND WEBSITES

Chaegŏnt'ongsin (Reconstruction). 1961–1962.
Changnohoebo (The Presbyterian Weekly). 1939–1941.
Ch'esinmunwha (Communication culture). 1948–1960.
Chibanghaengjŏng (Local administration). 1952–.
Jiryokukōsei kihō (A bulletin of self-reliance). 1937–1939.
Kēzaichian shūhō (Weekly economic security). 1941–1943.
Keizōihō (Kyŏngsŏng bulletin). 1938–1942.
Kokuminsōryoku (Concerted national power). 1941–1945.
Koseki (Family registration). 1940–1942.
Mongyō no Chōsen (Education in Korea). 1935–1941.
Sōdōin (General mobilization). 1938–1940.
Taehanmin'guk t'onggyewŏlbo (A monthly bulletin of Korean statistics). 1958–1961.

Chosŏn ilbo
Kyŏnghyang sinmun
Maeil sinbo
Minju chosŏn
Rodong sinmun
Tong'a ilbo

"Han'gugyŏksa chŏngbot'onghap sisŭt'em" (Integrated Korean History Information System), http://koreanhistory.or.kr.

Korean laws. http://www.law.go.kr.

National Assembly. http://www.assembly.go.kr.

BOOKS AND ARTICLES

Asano, Toyomi. *Sarasŏ toraoda* (The return of Koreans). Seoul: Sol, 2005.

Berger, Gordon Mark. *Parties out of Power in Japan, 1931–1941.* Princeton, NJ: Princeton University Press, 1977.

Boyer, William W., and Byong Man Ahn. *Rural Development in South Korea: A Sociopolitical Analysis.* Newark: University of Delaware Press, 1991.

Capozzola, Christopher. *Uncle Sam Wants You: World War I and the Making of the Modern American Citizen.* Oxford: Oxford University Press, 2008.

Ceuster, de Koen. "When History is Made: History, Memory, and the Politics of Remembrance in Contemporary Korea." *Korean Histories* 2, no. 1 (2010): 13–33.

Chang, Se-hun. "Han'guk chŏnjaenggwa nambukkanŭi tosihwa" (The Korean War and urbanization in North and South Korea). *Sahoewa yŏksa* 67 (2005): 207–259.

Chi, Su-gŏl. *Iljeha nongminjohap undong yŏn'gu* (Peasant unions during the colonial period). Seoul: Yŏksa pip'yŏngsa, 1993.

Choi, Hyaeweol. "'Wise Mother, Good Wife': A Transcultural Discursive Construct in Modern Korea." *Journal of Korean Studies* 14, no. 1 (2009): 1–33.

Chŏn, Sang-suk. *Chosŏn ch'ongdokjŏngch'i yŏn'gu* (Politics of the Governor-General in Korea). Seoul: Chisik sanŏpsa, 2012.

Chŏng, Ch'ong-hwa, and Ri Hyŏng-u, eds. *Ch'ŏllima chagŏppan* (4) (Ch'ŏllima work brigades). Pyongyang: Chigŏp tongmaeng ch'ulp'ansa, 1963.

Chŏng, Chu-su. "Iljegangjŏmgi che1ch'a hojŏkkiryu iljejosa chedoch'ŭngmyŏne kwanhan koch'al (2)" (The First inspection of the family registry and the residential registries). *Sabŏphaengjŏng* 59, no. 2 (2018): 40–56.

Chŏng, Yŏng-ch'ŏl. "Kim Jung Il ch'ejehyŏngsŏng'ŭi sahoejŏngch'ijŏk kiwŏn, 1967–1982" (Political origins of Kim Jung Il regime, 1967–1982). PhD diss., Seoul National University, 2001.

Chŏng, Yong-uk. "6.25 chŏnjaenggi ppira simrijŏn'gwa naengjŏn ideologi" (Psychological wars and Cold War ideologies during the Korean War). *Yŏksawa hyŏnsil* 51 (2004): 97–133.

Chung, Kŭn-sik, ed. *Singminji yusan, kukka hyŏngsŏng, han'guk minjujuŭi* (Colonial legacies, state formation, and Korean democracy). Seoul: Ch'aeksesang, 2012.

Clare, George. *Last Waltz in Vienna: The Rise and Destruction of a Family 1842–1942.* New York: Holt, Rinehart, and Winston, 1982.

Clark, Donald. *Living Dangerously in Korea: The Western Experience 1900–1950.* Norwalk, CT: EastBridge, 2003.

Cnaan, Ram A. "Neighborhood-Representing Organizations: How Democratic Are They?" *Social Service Review* 65, no. 4 (1991): 614–634.

Cooper, Frederick. *Colonialism in Question: Theory, Knowledge, History.* Berkeley: University of California, 2005.

Crowley, James. *Japan's Quest for Autonomy: National Security and Foreign Policy.* Princeton, NJ: Princeton University Press, 1966.

Cumings, Bruce. *Korea's Place in the Sun.* New York: W. W. Norton & Company, 1997.

Cumings, Bruce. *The Origins of the Korean War: Liberation and the Emergence of the Separate Regimes, 1945–1947.* Seoul: Yŏksa pip'yŏngsa, 2002.

Duara, Pransenjit. "The Great Leap Forward in China: An Analysis of the Nature of Socialist Transformation." *Economic and Political Weekly* 9, no. 32/34 (August 1974): 1365–1390.

Eckert, Carter J. *Park Chung Hee and Modern Korea: The Roots of Militarism, 1866–1945.* Cambridge, MA: The Belknap Press of Harvard University Press, 2016.

Fagen, Richard. *The Transformation of Political Culture in Cuba.* Palo Alto, CA: Stanford University Press, 1969.

Friedgut, Theodore. *Political Participation in the USSR.* Princeton, NJ: Princeton University Press, 1979.

Fujitani, Takashi. *Race for Empire: Koreans as Japanese and Japanese as Americans during World War II.* Berkeley: University of California Press, 2011.

Garon, Sheldon. *The State and Labor in Modern Japan.* Princeton, NJ: Princeton University Press, 1987.

Grazia, Victoria de. *How Fascism Ruled Women: Italy, 1922–1945.* Berkeley: University of California, 1992.

Guowei, Shen. "Translating Western Concepts by Creating New Characters: A Comparison of Japanese and Chinese Attempts." *Journal of Cultural Interaction in East Asia* 2 (2001): 51–61.

Han'guk yŏksa yŏn'guhoe, ed. *Pukhan yŏksamandŭlgi* (Making North Korean history). Seoul: P'urŭn yŏksa, 2003.

Hastings, Sally Ann. *Neighborhood and Nation in Tokyo, 1905–1937.* Pittsburgh, PA: University of Pittsburgh Press. 1995.

Higuchi, Yūichi. *Senjika Chōsen no nōmin seikatsushi, 1939–1945* (Peasant life in Korea). Tokyo: Shakaihihyōsha, 1998.

Hŏ, Ŭn. "5.16. Kungjŏnggi chaegŏn kungminundong'ŭi sŏng'gyŏk" (Reconstruction national movement). *Yŏksamunje yŏn'gu* 11 (2003): 11–51.

Hŏ, Yŏng-ran. "Chŏnsich'ejegi (1937–1945) saenghwalp'ilsup'umt'ongje yŏn'gu" (Wartime regulation of everyday essentials). *Kuksagwan nonch'ong* 88 (2000): 289–332.

Hobsbawm, Eric, and Terence Ranger, eds. *The Invention of Tradition.* Cambridge: Cambridge University Press, 1983.

Hong, Yang-hŭi. "Singminjisigi hojŏkchedowa kajokchedoŭi pyŏnyong" (Family registries and family system during the colonial period). *Sahak yŏn'gu* 79 (2005): 167–205.

Hong, Yŏng-gi, ed. *Yŏsunsagŏn charyojip* (Collection of documents on the Yŏsun Incident). Seoul: Sŏnin, 2001.

Hori, Gazuo. *Han'guk kŭndaeŭi kongŏphwa* (Modern Korean industrialization). Translated by Ik-chong Chu. Seoul: Chŏnt'onggwa hyŭndae. 2003.

Howland, Douglas R. *Translating the West: Language and Political Reason in Nineteenth-Century Japan.* Honolulu: University of Hawai'i Press, 2001.

Kang, Hildi. *Under the Black Umbrella: Voices from Colonial Korea, 1910–1945.* Ithaca, NY: Cornell University Press, 2001.

Kang, In-ch'ŏl, ed. *Migunjŏnggi han'gugŭi sahoe pyŏndonggwa sahoesa* (Social history of Korea under the USAMGIK). Ch'unch'ŏn: Hallimdaehak ch'ulp'ansa, 1997.

Kang, Tŏk-sŏ. *Saein'gan hyŏngsŏnggwa ch'ŏllima chagŏppan undong* (New human making and the Ch'ŏllima work brigade movement). Pyongyang: Chosŏnrodongdang ch'ulp'ansa, 1961.

Kim, Che-jŏng. "1930nyŏndae chŏnban Chosŏnch'ongdokpu kyŏngjegwallyoŭi chiyŏgŭrosŏŭi Chosŏninsik" (The regional consciousness of colonial bureaucrats in the early 1930s). *Yŏksamunje yŏn'gu* 22 (2009): 73–107.

Kim, Chi-hyŏng. "Yusinch'ejegi Park Chung-Heeŭi nambuk kwan'gye kusanggwa silje" (Park Chung Hee's North-South Korean relations in the *yusin* period). *Yŏksawa hyŏnsil* 88 (2013): 69–100.

Kim, Chong-bŏm. *Chosŏn singnyangmunjewa kŭ taech'aek* (Food issues in Korea). 1946. Reprint, Seoul: Tolbegae, 1984.

Kim, In-ho. *Singminji Chosŏn kyŏngjeŭi chongmal* (The end of the colonial Korean economy). Seoul: Shinsŏwŏn, 2000.

Kim, Mun-jo and Cho Tae-yŏp. "Pukhanŭi tosihwawa tosimunje" (North Korean urbanization and urban problems). *Asea yŏn'gu* 35, no.1 (1992): 1–42.

Kim, Po-mi. "Pukhanŭi chŏnhu pokkusi sahoejuŭijinyŏng'ŭi wŏnjowa 'juche'ŭi chegi, 1953–1955" (Foreign aids for Korean War recovery and the rise of Juche). *Asea yŏn'gu* 56, no. 4 (2013): 305–340.

Kim, Pyŏng-ch'an and Chŏng Chŏng-gil. *50nyŏngdae chibangjach'i* (Local autonomy in the 1950s). Seoul: Seoul National University Press, 1995.

Kim, Sŏng-bo. "Nambuk kukkasuripki inmin'gwa kungmin kaenyŏmŭi punhwa" (The conceptual divergence of people and citizens). *Han'guksa yŏn'gu* 144 (2009): 69–95.

Kim, Sŏng-bo. "Pukhanŭi t'ojigaehyŏkkwa nong'ŏphyŏptonghwa" (North Korean land reform and the collectivization of agriculture). PhD diss., Yonsei University, 1996.

Kim, Sŏng-bo. *Pukhanŭi yŏksa 1* (North Korean history 1). Seoul: Yŏksa pip'yŏngsa, 2011.

Kim, Sŏng-ch'il. *Yŏksa ap'esŏ-han sahakchaŭi 6.25 ilgi* (A historian's diary during the Korean War). Seoul: Ch'angbi, 1993.

Kim, Su-ja. "1948–1953nyŏn Yi Sŭng-manŭi kwollyŏkkanghwawa kungminhoehwaryong" (The use of the National Association by Syngman Rhee, 1948–1953). *Yŏksawa hyŏnsil* 55 (2005): 347–379.

Kim, Su-ja. "1948-yŏn Yi Sŭng-manŭi ch'odaenaegagŭi kusŏng" (The first cabinet of Syngman Rhee in 1948). *Ihwasahak yŏn'gu* 23 (1997): 193–217.

Kim, Suzy. *Everyday Life in the North Korean Revolution, 1945–1950.* Ithaca, NY: Cornell University Press, 2013.

Kim, Suzy. "Revolutionary Mothers: Women in the North Korean Revolution, 1945–1950." *Comparative Studies in Society and History* 52, no. 4 (2010): 742–767.

Kim, T'ae-u. *P'okkyŏk: Migonggunŭi kongjung p'okkyŏk kirogŭro ingnŭn han'guk chŏnjaeng* (Air raids: Korean War in the US Air Force records). P'aju: Ch'angbi, 2013.

Kim, Tu-sŏp. "Pukhanŭi tosihwawa in'gubunp'o" (North Korean urbanization and its population). *Han'guk in'guhak* 18, no. 2 (December 1995): 70–97.

Kim, Yŏng-gŭn. "Iljeha Kyŏngsŏngjiyŏgŭi sahoe konggan'gujoŭi pyŏnhwawa tosi kyŏnghŏm" (Spatial changes in Seoul and urban experience during the colonial period). *Seoulhak yŏn'gu* 20 (2003): 139–180.

Kim, Yŏng-gŭn. "Migunjŏnggi kong'ŏpkiban'gwa saengsansilt'ae" (Industrial infrastructure and productivity during the US military occupation period). *Yŏksawa hyŏnsil* 22 (1996): 17–54.

Kim, Yŏng-hŭi. "Kungminch'ongnyŏk Chosŏnyŏnmaeng'ŭi samuguk kaep'yŏn'gwa kwanbyŏn tanch'ee taehan t'ongje" (Reshuffling the League of Concerted National Power). *Han'guk kŭnhyŭndaesa yŏn'gu* 37 (2006): 233–269.

Koselleck, Reinhart. "Begriffsgeschichte and Social History." *Economy and Society* 11, no. 3 (1982): 409–427.

Kumatani, Akiyasu, ed., *Chōsensōtokufu no"kokugo" seisaku shiryō* (Policy of the Government-General on Japanese language). Suita-Shi: Kansai University Press, 2004.

Kwak, Tae Yang. "The Nixon Doctrine and the Yusin Reforms: American Foreign Policy, the Vietnam War, and the Rise of Authoritarianism in Korea, 1968–1973." *Journal of East Asian Relations* 12, no. 1–2 (2003): 33–57.

Kwon, T'ae-hwan. *Korean Demographics.* Seoul: Seoul National University Press, 1977.

Masolo, Dismas A. "Community, Identity, and the Cultural Space." *Rue Descarte* 2, no. 36 (2002): 21–51.

Matsumoto, Takenori. *Shokuminchi Kenryoku to Chōsen Nōmin* (Colonial power and Korean farmers). Tokyo: Shakai hyōronsha, 1998.

Matsusaka, Yoshihisa Tak. *The Making of Japanese Manchuria, 1904–1932.* Cambridge, MA: Harvard University Press, 2001.

Minichiello, Sharon A, ed. *Japan's Competing Modernities: Issues in Culture and Democracy, 1900–1930.* Honolulu: University of Hawai'i Press, 1998.

Miller, Edward S. *Bankrupting the Enemy: The U.S. Financial Siege of Japan Before Pearl Harbor.* Annapolis, MD: United States Naval Institute Press, 2007.

Nobuyoshi, Toshitani. "The Reform of Japanese Family Law and Changes in the Family System." *US-Japan Women's Journal,* no. 6 (1994): 66–82.

O, Sŏng-ch'ŏl. *Singminji ch'odŭng kyoyugŭi hyŏngsŏng* (The formation of colonial elementary education). Seoul: Kyoyukkwahaksa, 2000.

Okazaki, Shigeki. *Jidaiwo tsukuru otoko Shiobara Tokisaburo* (The man who made the times, Shiobara Tokisaburo). Tokyo: Ōsawatsukiji shoten, 1942.

Pai, Hyung Il. *Constructing "Korean" Origins: A Critical Review of Archaeology, Historiography, and Racial Myth in Korean State Formation.* Cambridge, MA: Harvard East Asian Monographs, 2010.

Pak, Myŏng-kyu. *Kungmin, inmin, simin (Kungmin,* people, and citizens). Seoul: Sohwa, 2009.

Pak, Ŭn-gyŏng. "Iljesidae Chosŏnch'ongdokpu chosŏnin kwallyo'e kwanhan yŏn'gu" (Korean bureaucrats in the Government-General). *Han'guk chŏngch'ihak hoebo* 28, no. 2 (1995): 133–163.

Pak, Yun-jin. "Taeilbonbuinhoe Chosŏn ponbuŭi kyŏlsŏnggwa hwaldong (1942–1945)" (The great Japan wives' group in Korea). *Han'gukmunhwa yŏn'gu* 13 (2007): 185–221.

Pang, Ki-jung. "1930nyŏndae Chosŏn nonggongbyŏngjin chŏngch'aekkwa kyŏngje t'ongje" (Industrialization policies in the 1930s and economic regulation). *Tongbang hakchi* 120 (2003): 75–123.

Pang, Sŏn-ju, ed. *Han'gukchŏnjaenggi ppira* (Bills during the Korean War). Ch'unch'ŏn: Hallymdaehak asiamunhwa yŏn'guso, 2000.

Park, Albert. "Visions of the Nation: Religion and Ideology in 1920s and 1930s Rural Korea." PhD diss., University of Chicago, 2007.

Park, Chung Hee. *Minjogŭi chŏryŏk* (National power). Puch'ŏn: Kwangmyŏng ch'ulp'ansa, 1971.

———. *Uri minjogŭi nagal kil* (Ways for our nation). Seoul: Tong-A ch'ulp'ansa, 1962.

Park, Kyŏng-suk. "Pukhansahoeŭi kukka, kabujangje, yŏsŏng'ŭi kwan'gyee taehan siron" (A study of state, patriarchy, and women in North Korea). *Sahoewa iron* 21, no. 1 (November 2012): 327–375.

Pease, Stephen E. *PSYWAR: Psychological Warfare in Korea, 1950–1953.* Washington, DC: Stackpole Books, 1992.

Pekkanen, Robert. *Japan's Dual Civil Society: Members without Advocates.* Stanford, CA: Stanford University Press, 2006.

Read, Benjamin. *Roots of the State: Neighborhood Organization and Social Networks in Beijing and Taipei.* Stanford, CA: University of Stanford Press, 2012.

Reed, Benjamin, and Robert Pekkanen, eds. *Local Organizations and Urban Governance in East and Southeast Asia: Straddling State and Society.* Abingdon, UK: Routledge, 2009.

Ri, Myŏng-wŏn. *Kŏnsŏljagŏppanjang'ŭi sugi.* (A construction brigade's leader). Pyongyang: Minch'ŏng ch'ulp'ansa, 1961.

Robinson, Michael, and Gi-wook Shin, eds. *Colonial Modernity in Korea.* Cambridge, MA: Harvard University Press, 1999.

Ryang, Sonia. "Gender in Oblivion: Women in the Democratic People's Republic of Korea." *Journal of Asian and African Studies* 35, no. 3 (2000): 323–349.

Scott, Joan. *Gender and the Politics of History.* New York: Columbia University Press, 1999.

Seoulsisa p'yŏnch'anwiwŏnhoe. *Seoul t'ŭkpyŏlsisa: haebanghu sijŏng* (The history of Seoul). Seoul: Seoul t'ŭkpyŏlsisa p'yŏnch'anwiwŏnhoe, 1965.

Shizuko, Koyama. "The 'Good Wife and Wise Mother' Ideology in Post–World War I Japan." Translated by Gabriel A. Sylvain. *U.S-Japan Women's Journal,* no. 7 (1994): 31–52.

Shin, Michael D. *Korean National Identity under Japanese Colonial Rule: Yi Gwangsu and the March First Movement of 1919.* New York: Routledge, 2018.

Sinsidaesa. *Aegukpan kajŏng'yong ŏnmun panggongdokpon* (A guide to the Patriotic NAs' air defense training). Kyŏngsŏng: Pangmunsŏgwan, 1941.

Smilde, David, ed. *Venezuela's Bolivarian Democracy.* Durham, NC: Duke University Press, 2011.

Sŏ, Chung-sŏk. *Yi Sŭngman'gwa cheilkonghwaguk* (Syngman Rhee and the First Republic). Seoul: Yŏksa pip'yŏngsa, 2007.

Sŏ, Hyŏn-ju, "Chosŏnmal iljeha Seourŭi habu haengjŏng chedo yŏn'gu" (Local administrations in Seoul from the late Chosŏn to colonial period). PhD diss., Seoul National University, 2002.

Sŏ, Tong-man. *Pukchosŏn sahoejuŭich'eje sŏngnipsa 1945–1961* (The formation of North Korean socialism, 1945–1961). Seoul: Sŏnin, 2005.

Sorensen, Clark W., and Kim Hyung-A, eds. *Reassessing the Park Chung Hee Era 1961–1979: Development, Political Thought, Democracy, and Cultural Influence.* Seattle: University of Washington Press, 2011.

Stueck, William. "The United States, the Soviet Union, and the Division of Korea: A Comparative Approach." *Journal of American–East Asian Relations* 4, no. 1 (Spring 1995): 1–27.

Suh, Dae-sook. *Kim Il Sung: The North Korean Leader.* New York: Columbia University Press, 1988.

Suh, Jae-Jung, ed. *Origins of North Korea's Juche: Colonialism, War, and Development.* Lanham, MD: Lexington Books, 2013.

Summerfield, Penny. *Women Workers in the Second World War: Production and Patriarchy in Conflict.* Dover, NH: Croom Helm, 1984.

Tanaka, Ryuichi, "Chōsen tōchi ni okeru zaiman Chōsenjin mondai" (Koreans in Manchuria during the colonial period). *Tōyō bunkakenkyu* 3 (Tokyo: Gakushūindaigaku tōyō bunkakenkyusho 2001): 129–161.

Tikhonov, Vladimir. "Masculinizing the Nation: Gender Ideologies in Traditional Korea and in the 1890s–1900s Korean Enlightenment Discourse." *Journal of Asian Studies* 66, no. 4 (2007): 1029–1065.

Tominaga, Fumikazu. *Ouji no Chōsenni okeru jichi no hōga, hyangyak no itban* (Local autonomy in Korea, compact community). Keizō: Chōsensōtokufu, 1923.

Vogel, Ezra, ed. *The Park Chung Hee Era: The Transformation of South Korea.* Cambridge, MA: Harvard University Press, 2011.

Wall, Richard, and Jay Winter, eds. *The Upheaval of War: Family, Work and Welfare in Europe, 1914–1918.* Cambridge: Cambridge University Press, 1988.

Woo, Jung-En. *Race to the Shift: State and Finance in Korean Industrialization.* New York: Columbia University Press, 1991.

Yasushi, Yamanouchi, J. Victor Koschmann, and Ryuichi Narita, eds. *Total War and "Modernization."* Ithaca, NY: East Asia Program, Cornell University, 1998.

Yi, Chong-min. "Chŏnsiha aegukpan chojikkwa tosiŭi ilsangt'ongje" (Patriotic NAs and everyday life in urban areas). *Tongbang hakchi* 124 (2004): 839–881.

Yi, Chong-sŏk. "Taet'ongnyŏng sŏn'gŏwa pukhan" (Presidential elections and North Korea). *Yŏksa pip'yŏng* 9 (2002): 101–113.

Yi, Hye-ŭn. "Kyŏngsŏngbuŭi minjokpyŏl kŏjuji pullie kwanhan yŏn'gu" (The residential separation by ethnicity in Kyŏngsŏng). *Taehan chiri hakhoeji* 19, no.1 (1984): 20–36.

Yi, Kang-su. *Panmint'ŭgwi yŏn'gu* (The committee investigating Japanese collaborators). Seoul: Nanam, 2003.

Yi, Kyŏng-a, and Chŏn Pong-hŭi. "1920–30nyŏndae kyŏngsŏngbuŭi munhwajut'aekchi kaebare taehan yŏn'gu" (Culture houses in Kyŏngsŏng, 1920s–1930s). *Taehan kŏnch'ukhakhoe nonmunjip* 22, no. 3 (2006). 191–200.

Yi, Myŏng-jong. "Iljemalgi Chosŏnin chingbyŏng'ŭl wihan kiryujedoŭi sihaeng mit hojŏk chosa" (Residential registries and family registries for military conscription). *Sahoewa yŏksa* 74 (2007): 75–106.

Yi, Song-sun. *Iljeha chŏnsinong'ŏp chŏngch'aekkwa nongch'on kyŏngje* (Wartime agricultural policies and the economy). Seoul: Sŏnin, 2008.

Yi, Sŭng-il. "Chosŏnch'ongdokpuŭi Chosŏnin tŭngnokchedo" (Registration policy of the colonial government). *Sahoewa yŏksa* 67 (2005): 6–40.

Yi, Sŭng-nyŏl. "1930nyŏndaechŏnban'giilbonkunbuŭitaeryukch'imnyakkwan'gwa 'Chosŏn kong'ŏphwa' chŏngch'aek" (The Japanese army's views on Japan's expansion in the early 1930s and Korean industrialization). *Kuksagwan nonch'ong* 67 (1996): 145–196.

Yi, Yong-gi. "19segi huban-20segi chungban tonggyewa maŭljach'i" (A Study of Tong-gye and Village Autonomy from the Late Nineteenth Century to the mid-Twentieth- century). PhD diss., Seoul National University, 2007.

Yi, Yun-sik. "*Haebang chikhu haewoedongp'oŭi kwihwan'gwa migunjŏng'ŭi chŏngch'aek*" (Return of overseas Koreans after liberation and the US-AMGIK's policies). MA thesis, Seoul City College, 1998.

Yoshiaki, Yoshimi. *Grassroots Fascism: The War Experience of the Japanese People.* New York: Columbia University Press, 2015.

Young, Louise. *Japan's Total Empire: Manchuria and the Culture of Wartime Imperialism.* Berkeley: University of California Press, 1999.

Yuka, Anjako. "Chosŏnch'ongdokpuŭi ch'ongdong'wŏn ch'ejehyŏngsŏng chŏngch'aek" (General mobilization policies of the Government-General). PhD diss., Korea University, 2006.

Yun, Hae-dong. *Chibaewa chach'i* (Domination and self-rule). Seoul: Yŏksa pip'yŏngsa, 2006.

Zhang, Dongzue. "Transition of Governance Mechanisms in China's Agriculture: Land Reform, the Cooperatives, the People's Commune, HRS, and Agricultural Industrialization." *Kyoto Economic Review* 76, no. 2 (2007): 205–240.

Zevin, Alexandre. "Sahoech'ejeŭi pyŏnhwadŏen chŏnt'ong'ŭrosŏŭi pukhanŭi inminban" (People's neighborhood associations as modified social traditions). *Asea yŏn'gu* 37 (1994): 141–159.

Zweiniger-Bargielowska, Ina. *Austerity in Britain: Rationing, Controls and Consumption, 1939–1955.* Oxford: Oxford University Press, 2000.

INDEX

ABOUT THE AUTHOR

Shinyoung Kwon received a PhD in history from the University of Chicago and did Korea Foundation postdoctoral research at the University of Cambridge in the UK. She is interested in colonialism, postcolonialism and the Cold War, war and gender, and social movements.

HAWAI'I STUDIES ON KOREA

VLADIMIR TIKHONOV
*The Red Decades: Communism as Movement and Culture in Korea,
1919–1945*

SHINYOUNG KWON
*Moral Authoritarianism: Neighborhood Associations in the Three
Koreas, 1931–1972*